7.5.79

The Illustrated History of
COUNTRY MUSIC

The Illustrated History of COUNTRY MUSIC

by the editors of
Country Music
magazine

---

edited by
Patrick Carr

A Country Music *Magazine* Press Book
Doubleday & Company, Inc.
Garden City, New York
1979

Acknowledgments

This book has been a group endeavor of a number of authors working both together and separately. Charles K. Wolfe is the author of Chapters 1, 2, and 12; Douglas B. Green wrote Chapters 3, 6, and 8, and collaborated with Bob Pinson on Chapter 4 and with William Ivey on Chapters 10 and 11; J. R. Young was responsible for Chapter 5, and Roger Williams wrote Chapter 7; Nick Tosches is the author of Chapter 9. Together they have produced an outstanding work.

All of the photographs not otherwise identified are from the *Country Music* magazine archives.

Library of Congress Cataloging in
    Publication Data
Main entry under title:
The Illustrated history of country music.
    1. Country music—United States—History and criticism. I. Country music
       magazine. II. Carr, Patrick.
ML3561.C69I4   784

ISBN: 0-385-11601-2
Library of Congress Catalog Card Number
    77-82936

To Sasha and Kristy

Contents

Chapter One

Across the Ocean, into the Hills

The evolution of country music—the folk music of America's white, mostly rural working class—began as soon as the first settlers set foot on American soil; the original roots, however, predate the New World in some cases by centuries, for the oldest elements of country music are descended directly from the folk music of Elizabethan and pre-Elizabethan England, Scotland, and Ireland.

After the Industrial Revolution arrived in America, with its rapid development of communications, America's folk music expanded and changed at an ever-accelerating rate. Before then, when the population was primarily rural and isolated, change was slow indeed; hence, for almost two hundred years, the folk songs available to Americans were still essentially British in origin (as, for that matter, was the "high" culture of the rich and the town dwellers). The core of these songs was

brought over by the first settlers, and the songs ranged in age from medieval times to the days immediately before the ships sailed for the New World. Since the Middle Ages there had been a thriving folk-song culture among the English peasants and urban poor, and since these people were illiterate, the songs had been passed on orally from generation to generation. This process continued to function with little interruption once the settlers had established themselves in America; the songs were stories of love, death, drama, and infamy, and in those days of slow change they lost none of their appeal from generation to generation. They enabled the singers and listeners to see the world in very personal terms.

One way to understand the archetypal elements of these "old" songs is to understand ways in which the American pioneers modified and customized them. In many cases, we have early printed song texts from England that tell us what songs were like before they crossed the ocean; folk song study had become stylish in England by the turn of the nineteenth century, and antiquarians wandered about the country collecting and later publishing these "reliques of ancient poetry." Such study did not become popular in America until the 1880s, and even then, Americans were more interested in English folk songs than in their own. By the time serious collection of American songs had begun in the early twentieth century, the American folk

had had over a hundred years to tinker with their borrowed songs, and some of their customizing was wonderous to behold.

An old Irish song about going to America, "Canaday-i-o," modified into a song about lumberjacks, and, as the frontier pushed even farther west, into a song about buffalo hunters. Such well-known songs as "Sweet Betsy from Pike" and "The State of Arkansas" are British survivals with only minimal changes. There is also the case of the cowboy song "The Streets of Laredo," about a cowboy dying of a gunshot wound. Though the song contains all

The Binkley Brothers Dixie Clodhoppers, a colorful "Opry" band from the 1920s. From left to right: Tom Andrews, Gale Binkley (holding a cigar-box fiddle), Jack Jackson, and Amos Brinkley. Courtesy Charles Wolfe.

manner of references to the Old West —spurs, six-shooters, saddles, rifles, cowboys—it contains the refrain:

> *Oh beat the drum slowly and play the fife lowly,*
> *Play the dead march as you carry me along,*
> *Take me to the green valley, and lay the sod o'er me,*
> *For I'm a young cowboy, and I know I've done wrong.*

If the reference to fife and drum seems out of place in a song about the wild West, one can understand it better by comparing the Americanized text with the British version, which features a soldier dying of venereal disease. Though the Americans changed the setting and the circumstances of death—violence in the American folk imagination has always been more acceptable than sex—the reference to the British military funeral, with drum and fife, somehow remained intact. Odd, unexplained retentions like this mark many British ballads transplanted into American rural culture; mountaineers continued to sing old songs describing "milk-white steeds" and "knights" and "London town," though they knew of London vaguely only as a city "across the water."

The ways in which Americans changed these old British ballads tell a lot about the character of the American people. One thing the people did was to shorten the songs; a song originally called "The Lass of Loch Royal," for instance, ran to thirty-five stanzas in its original form, but survived in America in only three stanzas—the basis for the lovely country lyric "Who's Gonna Shoe Your Pretty Little Foot?" The old ballads described tragic events with a cold, detached, impersonal air; the American versions allowed the singer more involvement and reflected more sentiment toward the sad events of the song. This movement from the ballad (objectivity) to the lyric (emotional subjectivity) song form was to continue into the country music of today, where the majority of songs are emotional and sentimental.

British songs were also full of the supernatural, especially avenging ghosts and ominous omens. In "The Gosport Tragedy" a young man murders his pregnant girlfriend because he does not want to marry her; the murderer tries to escape on a ship, but the ship cannot get wind to sail, and the ghosts of the girl and her baby then appear on board and tear "him all in three." Singers in Kentucky renamed the song "Pretty Polly," dropped the whole section on retribution, with its supernatural overtones, and reduced the song to a grim, no-nonsense description of the murder itself. The American version usually ends:

> *He threw a little dirt over her and started for home,*
> *Leaving no one behind but the wild birds to mourn.*

The old ballads are full of lovers' quarrels, but instead of getting a divorce, as in modern country music, the protagonists here usually settle their business with a knife or a club. Even with this level of violence, though, the American ballads were generally more genteel than their British counterparts; some of the blunt descriptions of physical love found in British originals are missing from American versions. This is understandable when we realize that most American versions were being adapted during the Victorian age, when the sight of a woman's ankle was enough to cause a man to grit his teeth.

Occasionally, when the words of an Old World song were almost totally unadaptable to American culture, they were stripped away entirely and a completely new set of words was put to the old melody. An Irish song describing a rebellion in 1798, "Hurrah for the Men of the West," was fitted with completely different words to become "The Old Settler's Song" (with its familiar refrain "surrounded by acres of clams"). From this point it was easy to take the next step and create entirely new songs, with fresh words and fresh music. Thus a native American balladry arose next to the imported British balladry, and Americans were soon singing their own songs about their favorite outlaws, cowboys, murders, or disaster. The first collectors of folk songs were so interested in British songs that had survived in North America that they almost completely ignored the native ballads; but hundreds of these songs existed and they were far more popular than the British survivals.

Naturally, the native American songs were based on the structure of the British songs, but again there were some interesting differences. American ballads were more journalistic, giving names, dates, and places more readily than their British counterparts. We learn the name of the bank Jesse James robbed, the town the murdered girl lived in, the date of the great train wreck. In many cases,

American singers also tacked a moral on the end of their song. At the end of "Pearl Bryan," a Kentucky song about two medical students who murder a girl and cut off her head, we hear:

Young ladies, now take warning; young men are so unjust;
It may be your best lover, but you know not whom to trust.
Pearl died away from home and friends, out on that lonely spot;
Take heed! Take heed! Believe me, girls; don't let this be your lot!

The American Puritan ethic, after all, held that art for art's sake was frivolous, and for years American writers felt a pressure to justify their fiction by showing its morality. The folk composer felt the same pressure, and morals were tacked onto songs in ways that at times seem ludicrous. The long story of the "Wreck of the Old 97" is supposedly designed to admonish girls to "never speak harsh words to your sweetheart/He may go and never return." Even when a natural disaster occurred and no person could possibly be blamed for it, singers drew morals about the power of God. At the end of a song about a Mississippi River flood, we are told simply: "Let us all get right with our Maker/as He doeth all things well." Such tags tended to make the songs into moralistic parables—for those who wanted moralistic parables. For most listeners, the tag was probably a formality and a way to justify enjoying a good song.

In an age before radio or phonograph records, most of these old songs were naturally transmitted via oral tradition. Much of this transmission apparently took place within the family; one modern study of folk singers in Tennessee revealed that over three quarters of the songs were learned from family members. Of course, the diffusion was horizontal as well as vertical; as various members of a family spread out around the country, especially on the frontier, they took their songs with them. Songs were carried up- and downriver by boatmen, and cross-country by railroad workers and section hands. Various itinerant minstrels roamed the land, often playing for nickels and dimes on courthouse lawns and in railroad stations. Many of the musicians were blind and

had turned to this style of performing as one of their few available means for making a living.

In one sense, these anonymous minstrels were the first professional country musicians. About the only thing many of them left behind was a handful of tattered "ballet cards"— postcard-sized sheets containing the words to a favorite song they had either composed or popularized. The minstrels would often sell these cards to help pay their way, and the cards are direct descendants of the broadside ballads about current events once sold

The Morrison family of Searcy County, Arkansas, at the turn of the century. Although two of the brothers later recorded for Victor in the 30's, most of the Morrison music-making, like much early string-band music, was a family affair. Courtesy the Morrison family.

in the streets of eighteenth-century England. Yet the cards also show that not all the folk songs were transmitted orally; many a text obviously started from these printed cards, and many of the old mountain singers had scrapbooks full of pasted-in ballet cards, or handwritten copies of such cards. Some early publishers even came out with books that were little more than bound reproductions of these early ballet cards; one such book was *The Forget-me-not Songster*, which dates from the early 1800s and which contained numerous old broadside ballets from the War of 1812 and the Revolutionary War. Later on in the nineteenth century, newspapers and magazines provided still other ways for folk songs to get printed.

But in order to understand the effect of a music on society, we have to also know something of the singer and his role in society. What of the singers of these old songs?

Though the minstrels were important in song transmission, they were a rather small percentage of the overall singers, most of whom were farmers, mountaineers, and wives and husbands who sung for their own enjoyment. Cecil Sharp, who visited dozens of traditional singers in the mountains about the time of World War I, reported that very few of them seemed to have any sense of audience in their performance; most were so interested in the message of the song that they were unaware of what effect they were having. Singing was very much a natural part of life; one singer told Sharp that he couldn't remember the words to one particular song and then exclaimed, "Oh if only I were driving the cows home I could sing it at once!" All kinds of people sung for Sharp: men, women, children. "In fact," he recalled, "I found myself for the first time in my life in a community in which singing was as common and almost as universal a practice as speaking."

It is noteworthy that Sharp, and later collectors as well, have found as many women singers as men; as we shall see, women seldom played instrumental music in the mountains. Perhaps the folk communities saw singing as less a specialized art than fiddling or banjo picking. The early collectors also noticed that most of the singers performed without any instrumental accompaniment; the image of the typical folk singer today, replete with guitar or dulcimer, has relatively little historical support. The old-time singers sang with the "high, lonesome sound" and sang free of the rigid meters of the guitar. Nor were they self-conscious about the age of the songs; they were not consciously preserving old songs because they were old, but keeping the songs alive because the songs appealed to them. Sharp found that many of his singers did not know the history referred to in many of their old ballads, and once when he told a woman the "facts" behind the song she had just sung, the woman was delighted. "I always knew the song must be true," she said, "because it is so beautiful."

By the early 1900s people were looking on the southern mountains as sort of a giant cultural deep freeze, where songs and music that had died out elsewhere were still preserved in their original state. As early as 1904, a writer

The cover for a 1889 paperback songster; such songbooks were often published by patent-medicine companies, and contained, amid numerous "testimonials" about the efficacy of the remedy, texts for popular minstrel and vaudeville songs of the day, in addition to a few genuine folk songs. Given away free as advertising, these songbooks helped spread countless songs across the South. Courtesy Charles Wolfe.

for *Harper's* was describing a people "hidden among the mountains of Kentucky, Tennessee, and the Carolinas" whose music was "peculiarly American"; these mountaineers sang "many ballads of old England and Scotland" and their taste in music had "no doubt been guided by these. . . ."

Cecil Sharp, the first collector to actually prove that the mountain songs included British survivals, assumed that the isolation of the mountain folk was responsible for the preservation, and assumed that such preservation was unique to the southern mountains. In fact, later collectors found as many "child ballads"—songs of demonstrably English origin—in New England as in the South, and such songs have also turned up in non-mountainous areas like Mississippi and Texas. The South, with its veneration of tradition and love of the old values that the folk songs represented, probably did preserve more of the music than other parts of the country, but as early as the turn of the century, the South acquired a popular image as the only source for old-time songs; it was this image that caused folk-song collectors, and later record companies, to go into the South after their material.

In truth, the South was not all that isolated from outside musical influences. The development of the railroad and logging industries brought outsiders into the mountains and gave natives a chance to travel; and the Spanish-American War and World War I allowed southern soldiers to bring back infusions of the popular culture of the day. By 1920 Sears was sending out into rural America over five million copies of their catalogues, offering cheap instruments, song books, and sheet music, and many of these catalogues were going into the South.

Sheet music was by no means unknown in the mountains, and many songs once thought old folk melodies have been traced to published, copyrighted songs by nineteenth-century Tin Pan Alley composers. A song from sheet music would somehow get into the mountains, it would be passed on through several generations by word of mouth, a few words would be changed or simplified, and the author and the original source eventually forgotten. The song would become just another "old song" like the more genuine folk ballads.

George D. Hay, the founder of the "Grand Ole Opry," recognized this phenomenon when he said: "The line of demarcation between old popular tunes and folk tunes is indeed slight." It is thus possible to find early sheet music "originals" for many well-known folk and old-time country songs, including "The Ship That Never Returned" (1865), "Maple on the Hill" (1880), "The Letter

An 1843 minstrel-music folio. Courtesy Charles Wolfe.

Edged in Black" (1897), "Please Mister Conductor, Don't Put Me Off the Train" ("Lightning Express") (1898), and "Kitty Wells" (1861). Even the Carter Family classic, "Wildwood Flower," has its original source in an 1860 published song. In fact, this is an excellent instance of how the oral-transmission process can change the words of a song. The Carters, who apparently learned the song orally from someone in the mountains, usually sang the first line, "Oh I'll twine with my mingles/and waving black hair." This line had never made very good sense, and more than a few people puzzled over the meaning of the word "mingles." The explanation may lie in the original sheet music, in which the first line reads, "I'll twine 'mid the Ringlets." Somewhere along the line someone misheard the term "ringlets," or decided that the line was too hard to sing, and during the sixty years between its original publication and when the Carters found it in the Virginia hills, the line was simplified. So is "Wildwood Flower" a folk song or a popular song? It has elements of both genres, and it shows how the two cultures could and did interact in the early history of country music.

Nineteenth-century popular culture influenced archaic country music directly as well as indirectly. Even when it was not absorbed into the folk tradition, early popular music reached into the South and into the hinterlands via the immense popularity of the minstrel shows, vaudeville, the medicine shows, and songs of composers like Dan Emmett and Stephen Foster. All too often we tend to see music in nineteenth-century America as nothing but old ballads and fiddle tunes; in fact, from the 1820s America had a form of Tin Pan Alley music. A hit song during this time was defined not through record sales or radio airplay, but through sheet-music sales. Many homes had pianos, and in an age before radio and television, most families made their own music, and if they wanted to hear the latest hit, they sang it themselves.

Of course, there was professional entertainment as well. The minstrel show was one of the most enduring forms of this. The minstrel show was a series of tunes, jokes, and skits performed by white men dressed in blackface; much of the appeal of the show stemmed from this caricature of black music and black culture. The classic minstrel show consisted of three parts: a section of songs and jokes, an "olio" of skits and specialty numbers, and a longer drama or dramatic parody. In the 1830s a performer named Thomas ("Daddy") Rice dressed in blackface and rags and created a character named Jim Crow; soon Rice was popular across the country, and the idea of blackface entertainment was established. In 1843 four noted blackface comedians banded together to form The Virginia Minstrels, and the minstrel show itself was established. The Virginia Minstrels traveled throughout the country, including the South, where they proved exceptionally popular. Along with the crude parodies of black life and black culture, the Virginia Minstrels and those who followed them also brought a number of songs and performing styles.

Surviving accounts of these early minstrel shows suggest that much of the music they played would not seem out of place on the "Grand Ole Opry" today. The Virginia Minstrels featured music of the fiddle and banjo, much like the southern folk-dance music of forty years later. The fiddler Dan Emmett is now credited with composing two songs commonly thought to be folk songs, "Old Dan Tucker" (1843) and "Blue Tail Fly" (1846). In fact, minstrel musicians either originated or popularized a number of well-known "folk" classics. Minstrel singer Cool White published the popular "Buffalo Gals, Won't You Come Out Tonight?" in 1844 under the title "Lubly Fan," and in 1834 a Baltimore publisher issued a song entitled "Zip Coon," which became a country-fiddle standard under its more common title, "Turkey in the Straw." The song might well have been a folk melody before it was published (there are similar tunes in both Irish and English folk music), but its publication and subsequent performance in hundreds of minstrel shows across the country certainly helped establish it as an anthem of rural America.

Instrumental tunes were also popularized by the minstrels; an 1830s folio called *Crow Quadrilles*, for instance, contained the music to several tunes, generally considered "traditional" southern fiddle tunes, including "Zip Coon" and "Gettin' Upstairs." The folio even contains appropriate dance calls for each tune, calls that resemble modern square-dance calls. We know that such folios were sold in the South and that minstrel shows toured widely in the South. Throughout the nineteenth century, minstrel troups with colorful names such as the Christy Minstrels, the Sable Harmonizers, Ordway's Aeolians, and the Nightingale Serenaders provided the South with a steady diet of minstrel fare—and pop music. As late as 1925, when Vernon Dalhart was recording the first big-selling country music records, there were still half a dozen minstrel shows touring the country, and even in the 1930s Nashville's radio station WSM was broadcasting a Friday-night minstrel show using several members of the cast of the Saturday-night "Grand Ole Opry."

Even when the large professional minstrel companies broke up, elements of them survived throughout the rural South in the form of the medicine show. The medicine show consisted of three or four people who would pull their wagon or truck into small towns, give a free "entertainment" to attract a crowd, and try to sell various medicines and elixirs of somewhat dubious quality. The shows usually contained all the elements of a larger minstrel show: songs, jokes, skits, and even the burlesque drama (now called the "afterpiece"); the cast included one or two musicians, the "doctor" who hustled the medicine, and often a blackface comedian or a "Toby" clown. (The "Toby" character—named because of the red wig he wore—was a stereotyped rube figure who survived into modern country music as the comedy act, such as the one Spec Rhodes performs with Porter Wagoner.) Roy Acuff got some of his first professional experience traveling with such a medicine show in eastern Tennessee, and recalls that he strengthened his voice by playing all the different roles in the afterpiece and skits. Clayton McMichen, a member of the famous Skillet Lickers and national champion fiddler, recalled even more recent experiences with such medicine shows:

I worked in medicine shows as late as 1936. I rebuilt me a Dodge Northeast generator of 1,000 watts. Bought a little motor for lights and loudspeaker. We called the medicine shows "the kerosene circuit" or "the physic operas." People had tired feet and you had to be funny. . . . I was raised on one password: "Sold Out, Doc." The medicine to fight neuralgia and rheumatism cost $1.00 a bottle and we really sold it. We took in $300 or $400, traveled in a Model T, carried a hammer and saw to build a platform. Before and after World War I, Tennessee was thicker with physic operas than Georgia. Georgia cracked down on 'em.

The type of medicine sold in the shows, of course, varied from doctor to doctor, from show to show. Many of today's country musicians did their stints in medicine shows, and they tell hair-raising tales of what went into the medicines. Some were made up of just colored water, and some mountain shows actually used complex concoctions of herbs as the elixir, but "Opry" pioneer Kirk McGee recalls getting tangled up with a dope-sniffing doctor who used plain old gasoline as the base for his cure-all. The grass-roots medicine shows lingered on into the 1950s; they may not have exposed the South to the kind of pop hits the larger minstrel shows did, but they did offer employment for musicians and they did foster commercialization of the music. After all, from one angle the purity of folk tradition is a trap; in the nineteenth century, rural musicians who wanted to make a living playing music full-time simply had no place to go; many were not "folk" musicians by choice. By the turn of the century, a few professional opportunities for country musicians were beginning to open up in the medicine shows and the circuses.

And then there was vaudeville, which emerged in the 1880s as the popular successor to the minstrel shows. Vaudeville apparently developed out of the "olio" section of the minstrel show, and consisted of a *potpourri* of unrelated acts: musicians, comics, acrobats, dancers. Unlike the minstrel and medicine shows, vaudeville acts generally followed a well-defined tour route, since most of the booking was done by companies owning theater chains. While most of these chain theaters were in the East and Midwest, a number were located in key southern cities like Nashville. While some forms of vaudeville existed in the South from the earliest days of the 1880s, it was not until 1917 that the solid, regular routes were established. By 1910 the chiefly southern circuit of Delmar-Keith had some twenty-two theaters doing healthy business, and vaudeville magnate Marcus Loew was mounting a deliberate and expensive campaign to establish his chain in the South. This paid off, and by 1919 vaudeville performers were touring the South from Texas to Virginia.

Vaudeville singers brought even more popular music into the South, and they did so in the important decade that immediately preceded the first commercialization of country music. Yet most of the vaudeville performers of the 1917–23 era were still northern entertainers; there were very few "hillbilly" performers on the early vaudeville stage. After some of the first-generation hillbilly performers began to record and broadcast in the mid-1920s, many of them joined vaudeville tours: Charlie Poole, Al Hopkins' Hill Billies, and Uncle Dave Macon all made successful vaudeville tours. Uncle Dave Macon was an exception to the rule: Apparently he toured even before he recorded or broadcast, and did so well for Loew's Theater chain that a rival chain tried to hire him away.

By the late 1920s vaudeville was acting as a two-way conductor of musical styles: It was bringing Tin Pan Alley music into the South, and it was taking southern performers into the North and Midwest. For a number of years after the development of the mass media of records and radio, vaudeville and personal appearances still remained the best source of income for the would-be professional country entertainer.

Thus the commercial and the folk traditions fed countless songs into the repertory of the rural southern singer. But many fine singers ignored both these traditions in favor of yet a third: the sacred tradition. For entire generations of rural singers, church music and gospel music provided the main outlets for singing; many singers first learned to sing sacred songs, and many others refused to sing anything but sacred songs.

Throughout the nineteenth century "singing conventions" were held annually or quarterly in courthouse squares and churches across the South; people would gather to sing the old songs, visit, and enjoy "dinner on the ground." Many singers received what formal music education they had from "singing schools," where a self-styled "singing master" would come into a community and organize a singing class that would run from two to three weeks. At first these schools were run on the subscription basis: Each pupil paid a certain fee to the singing master. Later, some of them were sponsored by local churches or even gospel song-book publishers. Singing-school pupils were taught the "rudiments" of music: how to read notes, how to mark time (some masters did this by having students slap their desks with their hands, with the resounding whacks echoing throughout the countryside, and how to sing parts.

The songs taught at the singing schools were not quite commercial and not quite folk, but an odd combination of both. As Americans in the early 1800s went about settling their new country and establishing a bewildering variety of new independent religious denominations, it soon became evident that many of the sedate Old World hymns did not fit the emotions and the temperament of the New World. New hymns were written, many of them fitted to old folk melodies. Many early hymnbooks were published with words only; one compiler in the late 1700s advised of his texts, "Many of the Scots and English song tunes answer a few of them well."

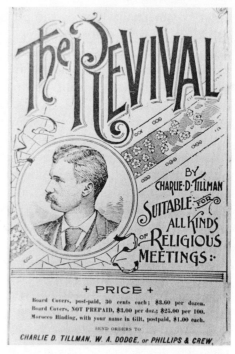

One of the many late nineteenth-century gospel songbooks. Much of this music was assimilated by the folk tradition. Courtesy Charles Wolfe.

The Great Revival—starting about 1801 and sweeping through Virginia, Kentucky, Tennessee, and much of the backwoods South—intensified this sense of grass-roots religion even more; one account from Kentucky describes a particular revival meeting with over two hundred thousand people singing. The frontier churches liked to sing; the Methodist Church, in fact, became known as "the singing Church."

Native American collections of sacred songs were not slow in coming. While many originated in the North, at least twenty major collections were published in the South between 1815 and 1855. One of the most successful song books was William Walker's *The Southern Harmony* (1835), a collection of over three hundred songs; the books was soon adopted by churches of all denominations across the South and was reprinted many times. (In fact, the book is still in print today and is still used at the annual "Big Singing" at Benton, Kentucky.) *The Southern Harmony* eventually sold over five hundred thousand copies, and its compiler, dubbed "Singin' Billy" by his fans, became one of the most influential figures in American church music. Walker got to where he would sign his name "William Walker, A. S. H." (Author of *Southern Harmony*).

By this time the more popular hymns and "white spirituals" had attached themselves to one particular melody, and the melodies were printed in many of the song books with an unusual notation system consisting of shaped notes. In shaped-note singing, pitch was indicated by the shape of the note (diamond, square, triangle, etc.) in addition to its position on the staff. In many churches using these books, it was customary to sing the first chorus of a song through by singing the name of the notes ("fa," "so," "la," etc.) instead of the words. This system of singing, which was designed to help semiliterate congregations cope with the printed page, originated in New England in the 1700s. It soon died out there, but it was kept alive in the South, where people saw it as a cultural tradition rather than an expediency. Rural singing masters from Georgia to Virginia continued to compile books using shaped-note music;

they composed some songs, "borrowed" others from earlier books, and "arranged" still others to reflect local singing patterns. Sometimes the authors got credit, sometimes not; many songs from books were committed to memory by congregations and thus entered folk tradition, just like many pop songs published in sheet music did. A Georgia collection, *The Sacred Harp* (1844), was so popular that it gave its name to an entire genre of shaped-note singing; the collection was constantly revised (at one point containing over six hundred tunes) and is still used widely in the South.

As the nineteenth century wore on, the evangelical religions tended to become more commercialized—or at least more organized. Though it was still possible for a local preacher or song leader to issue song books of regional appeal, people like singer Ira Sankey and evangelist Dwight L. Moody were combining their talents to conduct revival meetings on a national scale. The idea of a "revival hymn"—a sort of Tin Pan Alley hymn—became popular with the success of the Moody-Sankey revivals and the publication (starting in 1875) of a series of song books under their auspices. (The song books had reputedly sold nearly fifty million copies by the time of Sankey's death in 1908.) These new gospel songs (the term "gospel" was used in the title of Sankey's first collection) stressed individual salvation and the subjective religious experience more than the older songs of the Sacred Harp singers. The newer songs were considered more up-to-date and tended to describe the religious experience in rather striking metaphors.

Life is like a mountain railroad, ·
With an engineer that's brave,
We must make the run successful,
From the cradle to the grave.

According to authors Abby and Tillman, if you make it to the "Union Depot," with Christ as your "conductor," you'll meet "the Superintendent, God the Father, God the Son."

Sentiment was in vogue too, and the popular gospel song books of this era also contained numbers like "The Drunkard's Home," "The Drunkard's Lone Child," "The Dying Girl's Farewell," "The Mother's Good-bye," and "Mother Always Cares for You"— songs that made no specific references to Jesus or salvation, but translated the effusive sentiments of salvation songs into secular terms.

A sort of renaissance in gospel song-writing occurred at the end of the nineteenth century, and the period saw a number of well-known titles that later became country music standards. These titles include "When the Roll Is Called Up Yonder," "What a Friend We Have in Jesus," "Leaning on the Everlasting Arms," "Heavenly Sunlight," "Life's Railway to Heaven," and "Amazing Grace." (This last song, with words penned by John Newton in the eighteenth century, was popularized in America by "Singin' Billy" Walker; it is probably the best-known folk-country hymn today.)

Singing styles for the songs also changed during this period. Small group singing—usually done by a quartet—became popular, and music pub-

lishers began to sponsor professional quartets to tour the South. James D. Vaughan, a music publisher in Lawrenceburg, Tennessee, is thought to be the "inventor" of the gospel quartet; as early as 1910 Vaughan hired a male quartet of highly trained professional singers to travel to churches, revivals, and singing conventions, giving concerts and promoting the songs from Vaughan's songbooks. The idea caught on so fast that by the late 1920s Vaughan had some sixteen full-time quartets on his payroll. These quartets were the progenitors of what was to become a strapping cousin of country music, gospel music, and Vaughan's singers set the pace for later groups like the Chuck Wagon Gang, the Blackwood Brothers, and the Statesmen.

Much of the harmony so characteristic of modern country music can be traced to early gospel quartet harmony. Many early country artists, including A. P. Carter, the Delmore Brothers, and the McGee Brothers got their first singing experience in gospel quartets and old-time singing schools, and it is quite possible that country music's love of elaborate metaphor in song lyrics stems largely from the lyrics of nineteenth-century sacred music. In a sense, the gospel tradition acted as a sort of common denominator for most later professional country singers. Regardless of how far apart two singers are in their secular repertoires, they can always get together and harmonize on an "old gospel number."

Next to the human voice, the most important instrument in archaic country music was the fiddle. Fiddles were small and easy to transport, they could be repaired if damaged, and they could be constructed from scratch if necessary: They were ideal instruments for a society of pioneers moving into the wilderness.

For years, the fiddle was virtually the only folk instrument found on the frontier, and white settlers in the South were probably using the instrument as early as the seventeenth century.*

Many settlers brought fiddle tunes and traditions from Scotland and Ireland to the New World. Many jigs and reels, like their vocal counterparts, made their way across the water to find new homes and often new names. "Moneymusk," "Soldier's Joy," and "Fisher's Hornpipe" are eighteenth-century British tunes that entered American pioneer tradition and remained relatively unchanged throughout the years. Many titles were Americanized: "Miss MacLeod's Reel" was rechristened "Did You Ever See a Devil, Uncle Joe?" while a distinguished title like "Lord McDonald's Reel" was redubbed "Leather Breeches"—in tribute to green beans. Old tunes were preserved, new ones were created in similar molds, and frontier fiddlers added personal touches and new strains.

In a rural and semiliterate culture, instrumental tunes were more difficult to preserve than song lyrics; one had to write and read music, and few fid-

---

* Most folklorists now agree that there once existed a flourishing tradition of black old-time country music, a tradition that went into eclipse when blues became the dominant black folk-music form. W. C. Handy, famous author of "St. Louis Blues," recalled how this tradition touched his own life. Handy was born in 1873 into a family of freed slaves living in Florence, Alabama.

"With all their differences, most of my forebears had one thing in common: If they had any musical talent, it remained buried. . . . The one exception was Grandpa Brewer, who told me that before he got religion he used to play the fiddle for dances. That had been his way of making extra money back in slavery days. His master, the kindly man that I have mentioned, allowed him to keep what he had earned from playing.

"In his day, Grandpa Brewer explained, folks knew as well as we do when it was time for the music to get hot. They had their own way of bearing down. A boy would stand behind the fiddler with a pair of knitting needles in his hands. From this position the youngster would reach around the fiddler's left shoulder and beat on the strings in a manner of a snare drummer. Grandpa Brewer could describe vividly this old method of making rhythm, but for his own part he had forsaken such sinful doing, and I had to wait for Uncle Whit Walker, another old-time, to show me just how it was done.

"Uncle Whit, lively and unregenerate at eighty, selected his favorite breakdown, *Little Lady Goin' to the Country*," and would let me help him give the old tune the kind of treatment it needed. Uncle Whit fiddled and sang while I handled the knitting needles.

> *Sally got a meat skin laid away*
> *Sally got a meat skin laid away*
> *Sally got a meat skin laid away*
> *To grease her wooden leg every day.*

"Uncle Whit stomped his feet while singing. A less expert fiddler, I learned, would have stomped both heels simultaneously, but a fancy performer like Uncle Whit could stomp the left heel and right forefoot and alternate this with the right heel and left forefoot, making four beats to the bar. That was real stomping. Country gals and their mirthful suitors got so much enjoyment out of a fiddle at a breakdown or square dance as jitterbugs or rug-cutters get nowadays from a swing band." (W. C. Handy, *Father of the Blues* [1941], pp.5–6.)

An informal string band in Tennessee in 1890. The cello was not an uncommon sight in such bands. Courtesy Herb Peck.

dlers had that skill. Thus nobody really knows how many different fiddle tunes might have existed; a conservative guess by experts places the number at well over a thousand. Many of these tunes had dozens of different names in different parts of the country.

As the country grew, distinct regional fiddling styles developed in areas like New England, southern Appalachia, the Ozarks, northern Georgia, and the Southwest. These playing styles are similar to speech dialects, and modern fiddling devotees can play the same game as *My Fair Lady*'s Professor Higgins, placing a man by listening to his fiddling style rather than his accent.

Like American folk songs that retained Old World phrases, some fiddling styles retained Old World sounds. Many versions of "Sally Goodin" that feature the use of a drone string echo the Celtic bagpipe music that spawned so many old fiddle tunes. Even the pioneer fiddler's habit of holding his instrument against his chest instead of under the chin (as would a "violinist") seems to be a survival from early European fiddlers.

Fiddling had a number of important social functions in the frontier and farming communities of the nine-teenth century. While the individual often played to entertain only himself or his family, to while away long lonely nights, fiddlers were in demand for all types of rural social gatherings. People would often meet for "work gatherings" to do an especially big or arduous job, and then celebrate after-ward with a meal and perhaps a dance. Fiddling has been reported at log-roll-ings, log-raisings for barns and cabins, hog killings, "lassy makin'" (molasses making), husking bees, bean string-ings, and even quilting bees. In addi-tion to playing at such work parties, the fiddler might also be expected to show up at weddings, shivarees, wakes, the end of cattle drives or roundups, and "moonlights" (community pie-and-ice-cream suppers). Though it wasn't usually possible for a man to make a living playing his fiddle in those days, he could win a great deal of prestige and considerable local fame as an accomplished fiddler. The atti-tude of a frontier community toward its fiddler is reflected in this descrip-tion of a local fiddler in Sumner County, Tennessee, in 1793:

He and his fiddle (and they were in-separable) were always welcome, and everywhere. He had a sack of doeskin, in which he placed his "fiddle and his bow," when not in use or when travel-ing. . . . He could make his fiddle laugh and talk. There was such potency in its music that he often charmed away the pains of the body and silenced the groans of the sick. . . . Whenever there was to be much of an entertainment or considerable dance, the girls would say, "O get Gamble! Do get Gamble! We

know he will come." And Gamble was, indeed, always willing to come.

It was the country dance, or square dance, where the old-time country fid-dler really shone. In the South, such dances customarily lasted through the night; in Texas and the Southwest, where people were more scattered and gathering was more difficult, dances sometimes lasted for three days. Often a house was selected, the furniture moved out, a fiddler found, and the dance was on. Sometimes the fiddler was paid—one old custom was "ten cents on the corner," a complicated system relating to the number of sets the fiddler played. Sugar or meal was often spread on the rough wood floor to help the dancers, and prodigious quantities of food were cooked up ahead of time for a midnight supper. The fiddler was usually the whole band; he played by himself, did the dance calls, and lead the singing (if any). If the fiddler's endurance waned as the night wore on, and if his tech-nique slipped into little more than choppy sawing, the audience seldom complained. Ubiquitious stone jugs, pungent and stoppered with corn cobs, helped fuel the festivities, and many an old-time fiddler echoed the sentiments of "Grand Ole Opry" pi-oneer Uncle Jimmy Thompson: "I just naturally need a little of the white lightning to grease my arm."

Nobody is sure how the country square dance originated; it might have been derived from the French qua-drille (some old fiddlers occasionally still call their faster pieces "qua-drilles"), or it might have derived from English country dances. Whatever its origin, the country square dance soon developed a distinctly American quality; it lost much of its Old World dignity, courtesy, and formal movements and became an energetic, foot-stomping "frolic." The fiddle music that accompanied these dances reflected the good-times feeling; even the titles of the tunes reflect the wild, surrealistic humor of the American frontier: "Tramp the Devil's Eyes Out," "Shoot the Turkey Buzzard," "Jay Bird Died with the Whooping Cough," "Throw the Old Cow over the Fence," "How Many Biscuits Can You Eat?" and "There Ain't No Bugs on Me." Often the fiddler would sing a stanza or two as he gave the "calls" for the dance:

> Come along boys, don't be so lazy.
> Dip that hunk in a whole lot of gravy.
> Rope the bell, bell the calf,
> Swing your corner once and a half.
> Treat 'em all alike.

There were other stanzas that were interchangable and that floated back and forth between fiddle tunes, depending on the mood and memory of the fiddler.

> Fly around my pretty little miss,
> Fly around, my daisy,
> Fly around, my pretty little miss,
> You almost drive me crazy.

> My wife died Friday night, Saturday
>   she was buried,
> Sunday was my courtin' day, Monday
>   I got married.

Some of the titles and stanzas were pretty earthy, full of *double-entendre* for those familiar with folk speech; titles like "Forky Deer" or "Clabber Cod" are suggestive enough, but some fiddle-tune stanzas are even more explicit:

> Sally in the garden sifting, sifting,
> Sally in the garden, sifting sand,
> Sally in the garden sifting, sifting,
> Sally upstairs with a hog-eyed man.

Old-timers today won't tell a stranger what "hog-eyed" means, but they grin when somebody asks them.

It was partly because of such frolics and tunes that many righteous folk considered the fiddle "the devil's box." When settlers and mountaineers embraced religion, they did so with a zest that nourished intolerance, and fiddling—long associated even in the Old World with frivolity and indolence (cf. the fable of the grasshopper and the ant, or the legends of Nero fiddling while Rome burned)—soon had a very negative image in some quarters. "The man who 'fiddled' was hardly worth the damning," asserts a southern mountain man in the 1887 local-color novel *Behind the Blue Ridge*, and a folklorist writing at the turn of the century noted: "Particularly does the devil ride upon a fiddlestick. People who think it a little thing to take a human life will shudder at the thought of dancing."

Some fiddlers got converted and gave up fiddling, but, unable to bring themselves to destroy their beloved fiddle, they concealed it in the walls of their cabin. Others turned to church music; a Kentucky fiddler recalled, "Once I got the Spirit here I gave up frolic tunes and played only religious music."

In spite of all this, the fiddler endeared himself to the American folk, and fiddling has traditionally been associated with the classic American heroes. George Washington had his favorite tune ("Jaybird Sittin' on a Hickory Limb"), as did Thomas Jefferson ("Grey Eagle"). Davy Crockett was a fiddler, and Andrew Jackson's victory over the British in the War of 1812 is forever immortalized in fiddle standard, "The Eighth of January." Bob Taylor, one of the most popular politicians to be elected governor of Tennessee, played the fiddle on the campaign trail in the 1880s and asserted of the old fiddle tunes, "Every one of them breathes the spirit of liberty; every jig is an echo from flintlock rifles and shrill fifes of Bunker Hill. . . ." Henry Ford, the most popular folk hero of the early twentieth century, sponsored fiddling contests across the country and argued that old-time fiddling helped preserve American values. Politicians soon found that fiddling helped them win elections and helped mark them as true men of the people.

In truth, fiddling was a genuine folk art. While tunes were transmitted—and transmuted—a healthy folklore grew up about the fiddle itself. There was a lore about the proper way to make a fiddle, since many mountaineers and settlers had no other source; curly maple, poplar, and apple woods were popular in fiddle building, and horsehair was often strung for the bow. Many musicians also made it a point to know the history of their own fiddle if it had been passed down to them, and this lore became part of the fiddle culture. Rattlesnake rattles were said to improve the tone of the fiddle —especially if you had killed the snake

yourself. There was a lore about fiddle tunes, about where they were learned and what they meant, and even a lore about the great fiddlers: fiddlers who could play a thousand tunes, or who could play "triple stops" (sound three strings at once). A common tale even today tells of a "mystery fiddler" who shows up at a small local contest, speaks to no one, plays brilliantly, and vanishes into the night.

While dancing was the most common social event that featured fiddling, there soon developed another tradition that was to be of even more importance to the development of the music: the fiddling contest. Here groups of local fiddlers would meet together and compete with each other to determine who was the "best" fiddler. Often a prize was awarded, but many old-time fiddlers saw that as less important than the prestige attached to a contest. Fiddling was considered not so much a fine art as a manly skill, like shooting, boxing, or wrestling; many of the early fiddling contests were held in conjunction with shooting or wrestling contests at local fairs and celebrations. Well-known area "champion" fiddlers wore their reputations with the nervous aplomb of western gunfighters; there was always a brash youngster wanting to go up against the champion, and there was always the danger of the champion's age catching up with him. Some of the older contests were trials of endurance: One Texas contest at the turn of the century ran eight days. And both fiddlers and audience took the contests seriously; it was a matter of great local pride for a county to have a champion fiddler (even though

Late nineteenth-century fiddle contest in Knoxville, Tennessee. The left-handed performer is Governor Robert L. Taylor. Courtesy Mrs. Lucille Boyd.

the sobriquet "state champion" meant only that some promoter had decided to dignify his contest with the title). Researcher Dick Hulan has recently found that the first documented fiddling contest dates from November 30, 1736, and was held in Hanover County, Virginia. The Virginia *Gazette* of the time reported that "some merry-dispos'd Gentlemen" had decided to celebrate St. Andrews' Day by staging a horse race and by offering a "fine *Cremona* Fiddle to be plaid for, by any Number of Country Fiddlers." Other events of the celebration included "Dancing, Singing, Football-play, Jumping, Wrestling, &c." and the awarding of "a fine Pair of Silk Stockings to be given to the *handsomest Maid* upon the Green, to be

judg'd of by the Company." The winner of this contest is unknown, but the "merry-dispos'd Gentlemen" must have had a good time, for they were back the next year (1737) with an even bigger contest. This contest promised a horse race, wrestling, and a dancing contest, and the promoters announced "that a violin be played for by 20 Fiddlers, and to be given to him that shall be adjudged the best; No Person to have the Liberty of playing, unless he brings a Fiddle with him. After the Prize is won, they are all to play together, and each a different Tune; and to be treated by the Company." Singing got into the act this year with the announcement that "a Quire of Ballads" would be "sung for, by a Number of Songsters; the best Songster to have the Prize, and all of them to have Liquor sufficient to clear their Wind-Pipes." After the contest, the *Gazette* was able to report that "the whole was managed with as good Order, and gave as great Satisfaction, in general, as cou'd possible be expected."

Fiddling contests of various sorts continued throughout the nineteenth century, but did not become widely popular until after 1865 or so. Often they were held at one-room mountain schoolhouses or at the county seat when people came into town for the circuit-court meetings. The judges were often local prominent citizens, though on occasion other fiddlers judged. Most of the time a fiddler was expected to "whup it out by his-self," standing alone on the stage and playing solo, with no guitar or banjo backup man. In some early contests, every fiddler had to play the same tune, often a common one known by all, such as "Arkansas Traveler" or "Sally Goodin." In today's contests, fiddlers are expected to be creative as well as technically proficient, but in older contests, the prize often went to the person who played in the most authentic style. If a fiddler was suspected of having any formal training, he was disqualified.

Fiddling contests worked because the fiddle was the most common folk instrument of the nineteenth century and because many of the standard fiddle tunes were well known to audiences and musicians alike. A fiddler might learn an occasional new tune at a contest, but by and large the music he heard was as familiar and as comfortable as an old shoe, and it

served to reaffirm both his aesthetic and his social values.

In the smaller, local contests at the grass-roots level, the prizes did not always include much cash; it was common for local merchants to contribute goods as well. As late as 1931, a local Tennessee contest announced that prizes included "such handy and useful articles as fountain pens, flour, shirts, pocket knives, inner tubes,

Tennessee's famous Taylor brothers, Alf (Republican) and Bob (Democrat), ran against each other in 1886 in the famous "War of the Roses." Both were skilled fiddlers from eastern Tennessee, and though they probably didn't actually fiddle for votes from the platform, both used fiddling to endear themselves to a grass-roots audience—a practice to be followed by generations of later politicians in the South. Courtesy Tennessee State Archive.

rocking chairs, rubber heels, cigars, gasoline, shotgun shells, cigarettes, coffee . . . talking machine records, candy, cow feed, neckties, half soles, cakes, hair tonic, flashlights, pencils, and water glasses."

An important element of the fiddling contests—then as now—was nostalgia. Many Americans somehow associated fiddling with "the good old days," patriotism, and old-fashioned American values. A newspaper account of an 1891 contest mentioned that each fiddler "played the sweet old tunes of bygone time with charmed bow string." A 1909 account quotes a fiddler in a contest as bragging that he is playing his "great-grandfather's pieces." It was partially this element of nostalgia that was responsible for the growth and commercialization of these fiddling contests.

By the end of the nineteenth century, cities like Knoxville, Tennessee, and Atlanta, Georgia, were holding regular fiddling conventions that attracted scores of talented musicians from a radius of a hundred miles. The Atlanta Fiddlers' Convention—which was to play an important role in the development of the early country music recording industry in Atlanta—dates from 1913, while the country's most famous annual contest, that at Union Grove, North Carolina, dates from 1924. Though the contests often included other categories of musical competition such as singing, string-band playing, banjo picking, and "clog" or "buck" dancing, the fiddling remained at the center of the event: It always offered the most prize money, attracted the most contes-

tants, and was regarded the most seriously.

As fiddling developed throughout the nineteenth century, it was exposed to influences other than the Scots-Irish-English fiddling styles. In Texas and the Southwest, Spanish and Mexican styles were much in evidence, and in Louisiana Cajun fiddlers developed a distinctive use of high droning sounds. American Indian fiddlers brought a new sense of timing and harmonics to fiddling; Cherokee and Choctaw Indians living in the mountainous Southeast exchanged songs and ideas with white settlers in the area. Slave fiddling was rather common in some parts of the South, and there are numerous accounts of slaves fiddling for their masters' dancing parties. On their own time, black fiddlers experimented with sliding notes and unorthodox tunings, and devised their own instrumental styles, which were not exactly hillbilly and not exactly blues.

Fiddle music came out of the nineteenth century as the dominant instrumental music in the southern mountains and in rural America generally. It was gradually to be replaced by the guitar as the major symbol of country music, but for decades the fiddle carried the instrumental burden of American folk music. There is something archetypal about the fiddle, something that suggests not only the music it made but also the values of those who listened to the music.

The assault on the fiddle's supremacy in folk music actually began with the growing popularity of other stringed instruments in the late nine-

Burnett and Rutherford (fiddle), one of the first groups to record in the archaic banjo-fiddle style, which evolved in the mountains before the advent of the guitar. Courtesy Charles Wolfe.

teenth century. The first such instrument was the banjo, which has been called "the outstanding American contribution to the music of folklore." In reality, the banjo was of African origin and was almost certainly brought to the New World by slaves; throughout the first half of the nineteenth century the banjo, or *banza*, was associated almost exclusively with black musicians. Slave banjos were usually made from gourds and were reported in Maryland as early as 1774.

Thomas Jefferson, writing in 1781 about the blacks on his own plantation, remarked that "the instrument proper to them is the Banjar, which they brought hither from Africa." Another writer about the same time listened to a black singer accompany himself on the banjo, and a novel published in 1832 described a banjo player who could improvise songs on the spot or sing requested numbers, and who was as much at home playing for slave dancing as serenading the young ladies of his master's household. By 1847 we have accounts of a Negro dance that featured the music of banjos and fiddles being played together. In fact, the stereotype of the happy, fun-loving Negro playing the banjo was so established by midcentury that a foreign visitor would report, in all seriousness, that runaway slaves could be lured from their hiding place in a forest by the sound of banjo music.

The black folk tradition gradually transferred the banjo into white folk tradition, especially in the southern Appalachians, where musicians made banjos out of ground-hog skins and adapted their songs to the limitations of the instrument's harmonics, but at this time a parallel commercial tradition of banjo music that was to have even more effect on modern country music was also developing. This commercial tradition began with a "whitening" of black banjo songs. In the 1790s a Boston musician named Graupner heard a group of blacks in Charleston playing the banjo and singing to its accompaniment. He bought a banjo, learned to play it, wrote down some of the tunes, and in 1799 wrote the first "minstrel" song, "The Gay Negro Boy." The minstrel show developed as a major form of entertainment in the 1840s and established its basic format of white professional performers dressing as blacks and singing arranged songs that were supposedly derived from genuine "plantation melodies." The banjo became a central symbol of the minstrel show and of its stereotyped image of the black. The popular songs of Stephen Foster, songs like "Ring, Ring the Banjo," helped feed this stereotype. As the minstrel show gave way to vaudeville, the popularity of the banjo with white entertainers grew even more, but the racial connotations of the banjo were passed on also, and the 1880s saw a boom in lively banjo-thumping singers doing "coon" songs—songs composed in deliberate parody of black lifestyles. Many of these songs survived into the early commercial era of country music.

The person who perhaps best typifies the commercial banjo tradition was a Virginia man named Joe Sweeney, who supposedly "invented" the five-string banjo about 1830. This fifth string, a drone or thumb string higher in pitch than any of the others and fastened by a peg halfway up the neck, is what distinguished the country banjo from its city cousin. The latter has only four strings, and is used primarily as a rhythm instrument in jazz bands and dance bands; the five-string can be picked, and is often used as a solo instrument.

While Sweeney may have added the fifth string, the idea of a thumb string probably originated with black folk musicians, who sometimes used three strings with a fourth thumb string. Sweeney, however, did a lot to popularize the banjo and its music. He wrote many songs based on genuine black folk melodies he heard on his plantation. Billed as "The Banjo King," he toured through the South and made a hit on the New York stage (he even got to give a command performance for Queen Victoria in England). During all these performances he impressed many musicians both in the North and the South, with the potential of the banjo as a serious instrument, and by the 1850s, banjos were being manufactured and merchandised, a sure sign that the white lower-middle class was accepting the instrument.

Many of the performing styles of the nineteenth-century stage—from minstrel shows to vaudeville—were picked up by amateur musicians across the South and fed back into the folk tradition. Soon the solo fiddler at country dances was joined by a banjo player, and two thirds of the classic country string band was established.

The last third of the string band, the guitar, actually has a longer pedigree than the banjo, but it was accepted as an American folk instrument much later than was the banjo. It is perhaps fitting that the guitar, like the country music it has come to symbolize, was the product of two traditions: the popular commercial one and the folk-transmission process. Given the lack of informants to describe the folk processes of the nineteenth century, the commercial tradition is, naturally, better documented.

While the banjo was being played almost exclusively by blacks in the South, the guitar was recognized as a "proper" parlor instrument for the cultured upper classes of the North. An import from London drawing rooms, the guitar was seen as a link with Old World culture, and its early players included notables like Ben Franklin and Francis Hopkinson, one of the signers of the Declaration of Independence. Instruction books like *The American Guitarist* were appear-

ing by the 1830s, and a number of American "classical" guitarists made names for themselves on the concert stage.

By 1833, C. F. Martin had started making the guitars that would eventually have a legendary reputation among country pickers, but for much

An anonymous musician, Bristol, Tennessee, 1891. The relationship between the pistol and the home-made fretless banjo remains a mystery. Courtesy Herb Peck.

of the nineteenth century, the guitar tradition was confined to the cultured classes; it was only in the 1880s and 1890s that the parlor tradition began to filter down to the lower middle classes. By this time the light classical and semiclassical numbers of the earlier repertoire had given way to more popular compositions for guitar—numbers with titles like "Siege of Sebastopol," "Wild Rose Medley," and "Midnight Fire Alarm." These specific compositions for guitar had a pronounced influence on playing technique (such as thumb picking) and tuning patterns. Guitar historian Robert Fleder has pointed out, for instance, that the open D tuning of a piece like "Siege of Sebastopol" (1880) soon became popular even in folk tradition. Even today, black guitarists across the country call the D tuning "Vastopol."

By the turn of the century, the class diffusion of the guitar was well under way. In 1902, the Gibson Company —a name soon to be as revered as that of Martin by country pickers—began manufacturing mandolins and guitars, and shortly thereafter embarked on an orchestrated campaign to get its instruments, "The Musical Pals of the Nation," into every town. Gibson sponsored various mandolin and string orchestras everywhere, and printed pictures of them in their catalogues, proclaiming "Every one a 'Gibsonite.'" The mandolin and guitar societies, however, were still the provinces of the middle class; it took Sears to change that. As early as 1894 Sears was offering as many as seven guitar models in its annual catalogue, along with instruction books and even books

of popular vocal songs arranged for guitar accompaniment. By 1909 Sears' guitar line had grown to twelve models, indicating the success it was having with its cheap mass-market guitars. And cheap they were: The lowest-priced ("The Serenata") sold for about two dollars, while the cheapest Gibson cost well over one hundred. The guitar, unlike the banjo, was not easily homemade, and so a readily available source like Sears was important in making the guitar a folk instrument. The popular vogue for Hawaiian music in the era between 1890 and 1910 fueled added interest in the guitar, and especially in the use of the "steel" guitar.

Soon amateur string bands began to crop up in all sorts of rural settings, both north and south. Old photos show mandolin and guitar bands from Minnesota, Ohio, Indiana, North Dakota, and even upstate New York. Fiddlers, of course, were as ubiquitous as ever. The bands played rags, waltzes, polkas, schottisches, and even jazz, and for a time were a staple of rural lower middle class life. Sears catalogues went everywhere into rural America, and people who couldn't afford even a Sears model soon figured out how to build their own.

It was in the South, though, that this rural string tradition sank its deepest roots, and it was in the South where it was subjected to the commercial impetus that was to forge it into a popular art form called country music. The popular commercial guitar tradition especially had a substantial impact on the music of the South. After all, the first guitar manual in the country was printed in South Carolina in 1820, and though the various mandolin and guitar societies have been traditionally associated with large northern cities, the Gibson catalogues reveal that such orchestras existed across the South in cities like Knoxville, Macon (Georgia), Memphis, Houston, Jackson (Mississippi), and Atlanta. During the Spanish-American War and World War I, southern soldiers were exposed even more to the guitar. This double movement of the guitar into the working classes and into rural America reinforced the existing folk traditions and soon made the guitar immensely popular.

The folk (as opposed to classical) traditions of guitar music stemmed from two sources: the Mexican music of the Southwest and the black blues and ragtime music of the South. In Spanish America and Mexico the guitar was as ubiquitous as it was in the mother country, and as Anglo-Saxon settlers moved into Texas, New Mexico, and California, they found the Mexican settlers living there playing guitars. American cowboys learned from their Spanish and Mexican counterparts that the guitar was good company on the lonely prairies and long cattle drives, and by 1900 the guitar had established itself in the Southwest as an appropriate partner for the fiddle at local dances.

Though guitars were almost certainly known in rural areas of the South before World War I, many old-time musicians insist that they never saw a guitar before this time; furthermore, many of them recall that when they saw their first guitar, it was in the hands of a black musician. Folklorist

Alan Lomax, one of the first trained scholars to pay attention to folk instrumental styles, recalls: "Negroes introduced the guitar and the blues into the hills sometime after the turn of the century, so recently in fact that the most complex of hillbilly guitar styles is still called 'nigger pickin'.' "

Two anonymous black musicians in Spanish-American War uniforms. One theory on the popularization of the guitar in southern folk music suggests that the instrument was imported by returning veterans of the Cuban war. Courtesy Herb Peck and Charles Wolfe.

There are few written records to indicate how the guitar got into black
folk tradition, but it did, and black
singers soon adapted it to their blues
style. While at first the white country
guitarists played little more than
rhythm behind their singing, the black
country blues singers had devised ways
to punctuate their singing with melodies too. They used the index and
middle fingers to pick on the high
strings, while the thumb kept up a
steady rhythm on the bass strings. It
wasn't long, however, before white
country guitarists adopted this same
style, and the guitar became the third
instrument of the basic country band.

By the end of World War I, all the
diverse ingredients of modern country music were securely established in
rural southern life. The old ballad
singers had Americanized their British
models and developed a thriving native ballad tradition; semiprofessional
musicians in vaudeville shows, circuses, and medicine shows were ex-
posing rural and southern audiences
to popular music of the day, from the
sticky sentimental laments to the
rough-hewn minstrel parodies; gospel
publishing houses were encouraging
the performance and the writing of
new gospel songs, while singing
schools and conventions kept the older
church music alive; country fiddlers
were moving out of the exhausting
drudgery of night-long mountain
dances and into the limelight of the
fiddling contest where audiences were
listening with a new attentiveness; the
classic string band of fiddle, banjo,
and guitar was becoming the standard
instrumental combination, and amateur pickers across the South were
busy exploring the limitations and
possibilities of the string-band format.

These elements had already shown
a healthy tendency to overlap when
a song called "The Little Old Log
Cabin in the Lane" came upon the
scene. It had been written and published in 1871 by Will Hays, a Kentucky riverman who had a long and
successful career grinding out songs
for the vaudeville stage. It was one of
his biggest hits, and was sung widely
throughout the country as a pop song.
The tune and idea, however, had appealed to the folk imagination, for
soon settlers in the West were singing a version called "My Little Old
Sod Shanty on the Plains" and railroad men were singing another version called "The Little Red Caboose
Behind the Train." To complicate
matters more, a Salvation Army hymn-
writer named Charles W. Fry had
grafted a gospel lyric to the tune in
1881; this new hymn was popularized
widely in an 1887 edition of Ira
Sankey's *Gospel Hymns Number 5*
under the now-famous title, "Lily of
the Valley." Thus Hays's song had
started in the pop tradition, moved
into folk tradition, and even into gospel tradition.

And, perhaps symbolically, it became the first country song to be recorded. In 1923 the Okeh Phonograph
Corporation, as a favor to a client, recorded a fifty-five-year-old fiddler from
Fannin County, Georgia, named Fiddlin' John Carson. On his record, Carson combined two of the most important nineteenth-century performing
traditions: the solo fiddle and the

vocal. He sang in a rough, untutored voice, and played the fiddle simultaneously. And his two selections reflected two song traditions: "The Little Old Log Cabin in the Lane" was of course from the pop-vaudeville tradition, while the other side, "The Old Hen Cackled and the Rooster's Going to Crow," was probably an old minstrel song that had gone into folk tradition. The record, in short, was a perfect symbol of the diverse strains of nineteenth-century music merging under the pressure of the new mass media. But the executives of the Okeh Phonograph Corporation didn't see all this at the time; they thought Carson's singing was "pluperfect awful." They were sure that the record wouldn't amount to anything.

Chapter Two

The Birth of an Industry

To the men from New York, Bristol in the summer of 1927 must have seemed quaint, provincial, and remote. Located high in the Appalachians between the Cumberland Plateau and the Blue Ridge Mountains of Virginia, Bristol straddled the Tennessee-Virginia border; State Street, the town's main street, was literally the state line.

For years musicians from the nearby hills used the town as an informal gathering place. They would come down in wagons, on horseback, in model A Fords, even on foot; they would attend fiddling contests, have dances, gossip, and listen to the latest records played on the Victrolas local merchants would wheel out on the sidewalk in front of their stores. Not that there was much to interest the hill people on early Victrola records: most of the sides were dance-band music, the likes of Paul Whiteman's "Love Nest" or Zez Confrey's "Kitten on the Keys," or the Scots songs of Harry Lauder, or the vaudeville fare of Al Jolson. Some of the newfangled "blues" songs by Bessie Smith weren't so bad, but most of the hill people listened to the demonstration records out of simple fascination with the gimmickry of the thing; few of them toted any of the Paul Whitemans or Al Jolsons home with them.

Bristol had already enjoyed a reputation as a center for old-time folk music. Ten years earlier, in 1917, noted English folk-song collector Cecil Sharp had visited the region and had found that the mountains in the area were full of singers who knew old English folk ballads dating from the seventeenth and eighteenth centuries. Now, in late July of 1927, another folk-song collector of a slightly different type was arriving from New York. Where Sharp went about his work with notepad and good faith, this new collector was using a new electric recording machine and a file of contracts.

The "collector" was a young, moon-faced man named Ralph Peer, and his plan was not to collect material for some distinguished university archive but to make commercial phonograph records for the Victor Company. When he drove into Bristol he had with him his wife, two engineers, and half a carload of portable recording equipment. Peer rented an empty building on State Street—it was an old hat factory—and his engineers set out to fix it up as a temporary studio. Blankets were hung around the walls for sound baffles, and a six-foot platform was erected to hold the recording turntable. The crew worked for a couple of days getting the temporary

studio in shape and then took a break for the weekend to look over the town. They found a pleasant city of over eight thousand people, in a strange mixture of rural and urban culture. Some aspects of the city were right out of the recent best sellers by Sinclair Lewis: two newspapers full of wire-service reports, a super-active Kiwanis Club, a YMCA, an emerging upper middle class that dabbled in the bullish 1927 stock market, and a fancy new hotel—with a hot jazz band. Peer saw at once that his musicians would have to come out of the nearby hills, not out of the town. He also saw he had to justify his interest in "hill country" tunes to the newly sophisticated townsmen. Thus in the Sunday morning paper, Peer planted a news story that explained his mission:

Mountain singers and entertainers will be the talent used for record making in

Bristol. Several well-known native record makers will come to Bristol this week to record. Mr. Peer has spent some time selecting the best native talent. The mountain or "hillbilly" records of this type have become more popular and are in great demand all over the country at this time. They are practically all made in the South.

In no section of the South have the prewar melodies and old mountaineer songs been better preserved than in the mountains of East Tennessee and Southwest Virginia, experts declare, and it was primarily for this reason that the Victor Company chose Bristol as its operating base.

Peer had been through Bristol in the spring of 1927 and had auditioned several possible groups for recording; he lined these up to record during his first few days in town, and hoped that the publicity would attract other musicians from the surrounding hills. On Monday Peer began recording Ernest "Pop" Stoneman and his family, one of the "well-known native record makers" (and a family that was to endure into the present country-music era), and he deliberately let the word get out that Stoneman was not only making records, but also that he was getting paid for it—to the tune of a hundred dollars a day. The people of the town were astounded that people would pay to hear hillbilly music—but the aspiring musicians in the area were even more astounded, and they swarmed into Bristol looking for "the record man."

"I was deluged with long-distance telephone calls from the surrounding mountain region," Peer recalled. "Groups of singers who had not visited

Ralph Peer. Courtesy Charles Wolfe.

Bristol during their entire lifetime arrived by bus, horse and buggy, trains, or on foot." Relatives of informants who had sung freely and innocently for Cecil Sharp ten years earlier now had a burning desire to see their names on a Victrola disc. The commercialization of mountain folk music had come, and it had come with a bewildering suddenness.

At the center of the new hillbilly boom he had described for the local paper was Ralph Peer himself, and behind this watershed Bristol field trip was a fascinating four-year struggle to get early country music inserted into the channels of modern mass media. In a very real sense, Ralph Peer had grown up with the commercial recording industry. He was born in 1892 in Kansas City, where he spent his youth helping his father manage a store that sold sewing machines, pianos, and the then-new home phonograph machines. Before World War I Peer had gone to work for Columbia Records, working in a variety of positions and learning the ins and outs of the new record business. One early artist he worked with was W. C. Handy, famous composer of "St. Louis Blues." By the end of the war, Peer had joined the General Phonograph Corporation, a fairly new company that had just decided to start a record label called Okeh.

During this time the record industry was booming; major companies like Victor were reporting record sales of over one hundred million records in 1921. Most of these records, of course, were vaudeville songs, band music, light classics, and samples of a strange new instrumental cacophony called jazz. Compared to the major companies like Victor, Columbia, and Edison, Okeh was insignificant, with sales of only three million to four million records a year. Naturally, the company was looking for ways to increase sales. To make matters worse, a depression in 1921 crippled much of the entertainment industry; and worse still, by 1922 radio was becoming popular. Radio could offer sound reproduction comparable to that of many of the primitive acoustic records as played on windup Victrolas, and radio was much less expensive. Columbia's sales dropped off over 50 per cent just between 1921 and 1922; other companies had similar losses. The record

market seemed to be drying up, and any new ideas were welcomed.

One of these ideas was to create records that would appeal to a specialized, as opposed to a general, audience. For some time the record companies had produced ethnic records in various "foreign" series for sale overseas and to various ethnic immigrant groups in large northern U.S. cities. Peer was aware of this type of marketing, and so he was interested when he noticed that a recording he had helped supervise in 1920, Mamie Smith's "Crazy Blues," was having fantastic sales in the black sections of northern cities. Mamie Smith was one of the first black blues singers to record, and Peer sensed that such records could be marketed to the vast black population. Thus by mid-1921 the Okeh Company had initiated a special "race" series of records, a series designed to appeal to a black audience. Other companies soon followed, and blues became a lucrative part of the record business.

Peer decided to try a further appeal to specialized markets and determined to appeal to regional markets by doing a series of recordings "on location." Peer set out using some newly designed portable recording equipment and working with recording pioneer Charles Hibbard, a onetime associate of Thomas Edison himself. Peer asked his regional distributors to help round up local talent—jazz bands, church singers, amateur violinists, anybody popular on the local scene. June 1923 found him in Atlanta, where his local distributor, a furniture dealer named Polk C. Brockman, paraded his finds

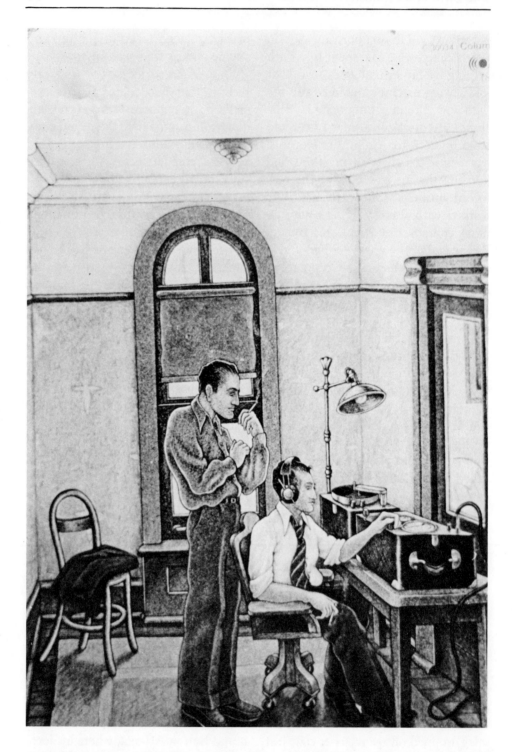

Artist Tom Wilson did this rendition of an early field-recording session for the Columbia LP Robert Johnson, Vol. II. *Courtesy CBS.*

before the microphones. Peer later recalled:

2052148

See, everything I recorded he agreed to buy, I don't know, two thousand records or something, just to make it worthwhile. Finally there was this deal where he wanted me to record a singer from a local church. . . . This fellow had quite a good reputation and occasionally worked on the radio. So, we set a date with this fellow . . . and he just couldn't make the date. So to take up that time, my distributor brought in Fiddlin' John Carson. He said, Fiddlin' John had been on the radio station and he's got quite a following, he's not really a good singer, but let's see what it is. So the beginning of the hillbilly was just this effort to take up some time. . . . I can't claim there was any genius connected with it . . . not on my part, not on his part.

Because Brockman had placed an advanced order for the Carson records, Peer went ahead and pressed them, though he thought John's archaic folk-styled singing was "pluperfect awful." Peer saw the job as a custom pressing, and didn't even give the record a catalogue number. Brockman received the records in Atlanta a month later, and took them with him to a local fiddling contest; there Fiddlin' John himself came onstage and played "Little Old Log Cabin in the Lane" and "The Old Hen Cackled and the Rooster's Going to Crow." Then Brockman put a windup phonograph machine onstage and played the same tunes as John had put them on record a month before. Brockman recalled, "We sold them just like hotcakes—right there in the hall. . . . That was the daddy of them. That was it."

Brockman reordered records from Peer in New York—and then reordered again. Finally the record was given a catalogue number, and Peer quickly made arrangements to record more of Carson. He sensed the presence of yet another vast, untapped record audience: the white, middle-class South. And, taking his cue from his experience with the "race" series, he set out to find the specialized music that appealed to this new audience.

Thus Fiddlin' John Carson's "Little Old Log Cabin in the Lane" became the first real "country" record and the first real "country" hit. To be sure, there had been earlier occasional attempts to record rural music. There had been occasional cylinder recordings of comedy-fiddle pieces like "Arkansas Traveler" and a few fiddle records such as John Taylor's "Devil's Dream Reel" for Victor as early as 1909. Charles Ross Taggart's "The Old Country Fiddler" pieces had been popular in the teens, and in 1922 Victor had recorded a couple of Texas fiddlers named Eck Robertson and Galliland. But the companies had seen these as novelty pieces and had not tried to market them to any specific audience. They certainly started no trend, as did Carson's (and, indeed, Victor didn't even release the 1922 Robertson sides until after the success of Carson's record). Carson's was the first conscious, deliberate attempt to program a music toward the traditional country-music audience. Carson, like many pioneer country-recording artists, had actually been performing for years at local fairs, carnivals, and political rallies, and he simply transferred this performing style

One of the first pieces of sheet music stimulated by a country-music recording. Courtesy Charles Wolfe.

to the new mass media of records and radio. In Carson's case, his reputation as a colorful entertainer had won him an invitation to broadcast on Atlanta radio in 1922, and his success on radio had a lot to do with his getting a chance to record. Much of the time, though, he used radio merely to publicize his personal appearances, and he looked on records in the same way: His touring car proudly bore the words, "Recording Artist." (In this respect he was like many of the early hillbilly performers who used mass media as a tool, a means to an end.)

Carson himself went on to have a long and successful career in music, recording dozens of times with his band, the Virginia Reelers, and with his daughter, an insouciant comedienne named Moonshine Kate. John's

songs were as colorful as his life: "If You Can't Get the Stopper Out Break the Neck," "You Can't Get Milk from a Cow Named Ben," "Who Bit the Wart Off Grandma's Nose?" "It's a Shame to Whip Your Wife on Sunday," and "What You Gonna Do When Your Licker Runs Out?" On a more serious side, John sung a number of very popular sentimental songs, like "You'll Never Miss Your Mother Till She's Gone," and even a few topical political songs such as "The Farmer Is the Man That Feeds Them All" and "Georgia's Three-dollar Tag" (about a license-tag controversy). Carson stopped recording in 1934, and spent his later years as the elevator operator at the Georgia State Capitol, a job given him by Governor Herman Talmadge, for whom he had campaigned. Carson died in 1949, a patriarch who had received at least some recognition for his role in transforming American popular music.

John's success inspired not only Peer but the other major record companies as well. Within a year several semiprofessional southern musicians gained status as recording stars. A millhand from Fries, Virginia, named Henry Whitter had the second country best seller in "The Wreck of the Old 97" and "Lonesome Road Blues." Whitter, who sang and accompanied himself with guitar and harmonica (using a wire rack), had actually recorded his songs before Carson's discovery, but the company had refused to release them. A fellow millworker of Whitter, Ernest Stoneman, heard Whitter's records, decided he could sing better, and soon found himself with a successful recording of a classic country ballad, "The Sinking of the *Titanic*." Also from Virginia came the Fiddlin' Powers Family to record fiddle tunes for Victor, while the northern Georgia team of Gid Tanner and Riley Puckett did the same for Columbia. Peer returned to Atlanta to find the Jenkins Family, the archetype of hundreds of modern country gospel groups, who were immensely successful on records and radio—and as songwriters. Samantha Bumgartner and Eva Davis, two young ladies from North Carolina who recorded with fiddle and banjo, became the first female country stars. Vocalion Records brought to New York from Tennessee three veteran minstrels—George Reneau, Charlie Oaks, and banjo-thumping Uncle Dave Macon—to record mountain ballads and old vaudeville songs. Though most of this first generation of country entertainers was from the Southeast, Okeh recorded a group called Chenoweth's Cornfield Symphony Orchestra from Dallas—the first Texas country band to be recorded—in 1924. By the end of 1924 the first country record catalogue had been issued by Columbia records: *Familiar Tunes on Fiddle, Guitar, Banjo, Harmonica, and Accordian,* designed to list the records of musicians whose "names are best known where the square dance has not been supplanted by the fox-trot."

Thus by early 1925—barely eighteen months after Carson's pioneering recording—most of the major record companies were so successful with this new type of record that they were establishing separate series of "hillbilly" recordings designed to feature rural southern artists and to be distributed and sold primarily in the South. Nobody, however, knew exactly what to call this music: some of it was genuine folk music, but a lot of it was comprised of old sentimental songs, old popular songs, and old vaudeville tunes. The different companies came up with an interesting variety of names. The Okeh Company called their product "Old-time Tunes;" Columbia chose "Familiar Tunes—Old and New"; other companies chose names like "Songs from Dixie," "Old Southern Tunes," and "Old Familiar Tunes and Novelties." When Sears got into the business and began to sell this music through their catalogues, they listed it as "Southern Fiddling and Song Records," "Mountain Ballads," and "Old-time Southern Songs."

In this early period, the term "country music" was never used, though Peer himself used the term "hill country music" as early as 1925, and Ward's catalogue listed the music as "Hill Country Melodies." Many Northerners persisted in using the term "hillbilly" to describe the music, though the term had very negative connotations for most rural Southerners. A 1926 writer for *Variety,* the show-business newspaper, discussed "hill-billy music" and explained that "the 'hill-billy' is a North Carolina or Tennessee and adjacent mountaineer type of illiterate white whose creed and allegiance are to the Bible, the chautauqua, and the phonograph." They had, according to *Variety,* "the intelligence of morons" and delighted in "sing-song, nasal-twanging vocalizing." However, partly because of the success of an early string band that appealed to vaudeville audiences by playing up their hayseed image and calling themselves The Hill-Billies, the adjective "hillbilly" gradually became attached to the music in the early 1930s. Today the term "hillbilly" is seldom used, and it is as offensive to a modern white country musician as the term "nigger" is to a modern black man. Its frequent use by northern recording executives in the early days reflects the fact that they looked down on the music and endured it only because it made money for them.

Many of this first generation of country performers were amateur or semiprofessional southern musicians, and many of them had been brought North to record in New York studios. Peer's occasional forays into the field were not emulated much by other companies; it was easier for them to record in permanent studios. But to do this, the companies had to locate genuine southern musicians, talk them into coming North, and take care of them as they wandered about the big city. Many of these musicians had rather limited repertoires, and some found it hard to learn new tunes. Ernest "Pop" Stoneman was very popular with the companies, for instance,

The Stoneman Family. Pop Stoneman is standing behind his fiddler wife. Courtesy Charles Wolfe.

because he could learn new songs easily and thus could produce "cover" versions of hit records.

An ideal solution to this problem was for the companies to find a way to combine the authentic elements of southern music with the professionalism of northern studio musicians. In one case, at least, these qualities were brought together in the person of country music's first superstar, Vernon Dalhart.

Dalhart—his real name was Marion Try Slaughter—was an East Texas native who had come to New York in 1912 to try to make it as a popular stage singer. He enjoyed moderate success at this, and was recording non-country songs as early as 1916, often specializing in "coon" songs in which he imitated black dialect. Because his pop career was on the decline, Dalhart decided to try to aim a record at the newly defined country market: He thus became the first pop singer to undergo the "Nashville treatment," whereby an artist tries to shore up a sagging pop career by "going country." Dalhart chose to cover Henry Whitter's hit "Wreck of the Old 97" and finally persuaded Victor to let him record it. For the B side, he chose a lonesome dirge called "The Prisoner's Song"; this tune, with its now-famous line, "Oh if I had the wings of an angel," was apparently written by Dalhart's cousin Guy Massey and Victor's sophisticated musical director, Nat Shilkret. It was hardly a folk song, but it sounded like one, and it soon went into folk tradition. And no wonder; the Victor pairing became country music's first million-selling record, and was so successful that it was rerecorded on as many as fifty different labels over the next two decades. Dalhart had succeeded in shoring up his career in spectacular fashion.

During the rest of the 1920s, Dalhart produced an amazing string of hits: there were old sentimental songs from the nineteenth century like "The Letter Edged in Black" and "Little Rosewood Casket"; there were genuine folk songs like "Golden Slippers" and "Barbara Allen"; there were new Tin Pan Alley rustic-flavored songs like "My Blue Ridge Mountain Home" and "The Convict and the Rose." But best of all, there were the event songs, topical songs about a tragedy, a murder case, or a famous criminal. Frank Walker, who supervised Dalhart's recording of dozens of such songs for Columbia Records, recalled:

An event song is something that had happened, not today, maybe years ago, but hadn't permeated through the South because of a lack of newspapers and no radio and no television in those days, but they had heard of it. For instance, some of the biggest sellers we were ever able to bring out was things like "The Sinking of the *Titanic*." Bring out a record after it happened and tell a story with a moral. "The Sinking of the *Titanic*" was a big seller, but there was a little bit of a moral that people shouldn't believe that they could build a ship that couldn't be sunk. That's the way they talked about it; of thinking God took it upon himself to show them that they couldn't build anything greater than He could. Everything had a moral in the event songs.

Dalhart sung event songs about everything from the Scopes "monkey" trial to Lindbergh's flying of the Atlantic, from the death of cave explorer Floyd Collins to the sinking of the submarine S-5, and from the exploits of Tennessee badman Kinnie Wagner to the California murder of Little Marian Parker. Though these event songs were all of contemporary composition, they were part of a long and noble folk-ballad tradition dating back to seventeenth-century England, when "broadsides" of recent events were sold in the streets. Oddly enough, some of the record companies sensed this connection and used it to add a certain dignity to their "hillbilly" event songs. A 1925 Victor catalogue supplement, describing Dalhart's "Death of Floyd Collins" disc, read:

> Popular songs of recent American tragedies. They belong with the old-fashioned penny-ballad, hobo-song, or "come-all-ye." The curious will note that they are even in the traditional "ballad" metre, the "common metre" of hymnodists. They are not productions of, or for, the cabaret or the vaudeville stage, but for the roundhouse, the watertank, the caboose, or the village fire-station. Both have splendid simple tunes, in which the guitar accompanies the voice, the violin occasionally adding pathos. These songs are more than things for passing amusement; they are chronicles of the time, by unlettered and never self-conscious chroniclers.

Perhaps the "unlettered and never self-conscious chroniclers" were not all *that* folksy: most of them had enough sense to copyright their event songs. There were some genuine folk composers in the lot—men like Peer's discovery, the Reverend Andrew Jenkins of Atlanta, a blind evangelist who wrote dozens of event songs, including "The Death of Floyd Collins," to order. Jenkins (or "Blind Andy," as he was billed on his own records) was able to synthesize older folk material with his own creative impulses to produce simple, moving songs that often were indistinguishable from American folk songs. Blind Andy was never much of a singer himself, but he found in Dalhart a superb interpreter of his work. This was yet another way in which Dalhart's music represented the ideal compromise between southern authenticity and New York professionalism. In one sense, Jenkins was the first successful country songwriter, but he was soon emulated by other writers who copied his style and technique, especially with event songs. Kansas-born Carson J. Robison worked closely with Dalhart in producing songs like "My Blue Ridge Mountain Home," and Robison had a number of his own records become popular; Memphis-born Bob Miller was an early A&R (Artist and Repertory) man for Columbia in the 1920s and wrote scores of popular songs, including "Eleven-cent Cotton and Forty-cent Meat" and "Twenty-one Years." Though both men became skilled Tin Pan Alley songwriters, both saw their early products popularized by country singers. The fact that all three of these men could make their living primarily by songwriting shows how quickly the music was becoming professionalized.

There were few singers as skilled as Dalhart in interpreting old-time songs, and though he recorded under dozens of pseudonyms, the companies soon realized they would have to find other ways to secure "authentic" material. The means for this came in 1925 when Western Electric engineers invented the new electrical recording process; this new "orthophonic" process yielded much sharper and louder sound reproduction and made it possible for a singer to be heard without bellowing his lungs out. More subtle singing and instrumental styles were possible, and for a music dominated by stringed instruments, like country music, the effect was considerable. Even more interesting, however, was the fact that the new electrical process meant that portable recording units were much more easily made, and once made they got much better sound in the field. Rather than have Dalhart try to imitate country singers, or try to transport authentic native singers to New York, it now became possible for the company to go to the singer and record him in his native South. By 1926, talent scouts were touring the South, driving across the dusty back roads in search of hill-country talent. Temporary recording studios were set up in towns and cities across the South, and the race was on.

Columbia and Victor soon emerged as the two dominant companies in the era of field recordings, probably due to their superb technology. Columbia had as its chief talent scout a man named Frank Walker. Walker's role in the development of early country music is almost as important as that of Peer; Walker pioneered recording techniques, invented ways to attract new talent, and found new ways to merchandise his product. Walker, who remained active in the recording industry until his death in the 1960s, later played a key role in the recording career of Hank Williams. In the 1920s it was Walker who was scouring the backwoods South looking for music. "I rode horses into the woods to find people who were individualistic in their singing and who could project the true country flavor," he recalled.

Walker, and the men who followed in his footsteps—men like Art Satherly, Dick Yoynow, W. R. Calloway, and Eli Oberstein—seldom went wandering aimlessly. They established a

Carson J. Robison and Vernon Dalhart.
Courtesy Doug Green.

(SONG)

Carson J. Robison.   Vernon Dalhart

network of local contacts, usually
men who were record dealers or radio-
station operators, and these people referred likely prospects to them. Then
a field unit would set up for a week
or two in a nearby city and all the
prospects from that area would be recorded. In an area especially rich in
musicians, such as eastern Tennessee,
advertisements for musicians to record were occasionally placed in local
papers. Working in this way, record
companies held field sessions at various southern cities, all the way from
Ashland, Kentucky, to Richmond,
Virginia, to Birmingham, Atlanta, and
Memphis from 1926 to 1933.* A by-
product of these early field sessions
was the preservation of many rare folk
songs and fiddle tunes, but few of the
recording companies were conscious
of this noble aspect of their work:
they recorded the songs for one reason and one reason only: to sell records and to make money.

Walker made Atlanta his base of
operations and began to visit the city
regularly twice a year. It wasn't long
before his visits proved to him that
one of the most popular and most authentic forms of old-time music was
string-band music. When John Carson had played the fiddle, he had
played it solo. The classic string-band
form, on the other hand, combined all
modes of old-time music: fiddle,
banjo, guitar, and singing. A group
called Henry Whitter's Virginia

* One of these field sessions was held in
Nashville in 1928 by Victor, thus becoming
the first recording session in Nashville.
Though several "Opry" artists were recorded, the expedition in general was a
failure; nearly half the sides were never
even released.

Breakdowners was probably the first
string band to record in the classic
style, but the records were hardly successful. Far more successful was an
offshoot of the Virginia Breakdowners, a four-piece band from North
Carolina and Virginia led by Al Hopkins, which recorded for Ralph Peer
in 1925. The band had no name, so
Peer dubbed them "The Hill-Billies."
The name stuck, both to the band
and to the music, and the group was
soon recording widely, touring, and
broadcasting over radio stations in
Washington, D.C. The band was a
highly commercial outfit, much given
to gimmicks and vaudeville routines,
yet it was home for a number of genuine folk musicians of considerable
talent, including Civil War fiddler
Uncle Am Stuart, early slide guitarist
Frank Wilson, and mountain fiddler
Charlie Bowman. The early string-
band recordings, however, were
marred somewhat by the limitations
of the acoustic recording technique,
and these early sides hardly captured
the hard-driving excitement of a
mountain string band. But by 1926,
when Walker and his crew descended
on Atlanta, the recording technology
could meet the challenge of string-
band music.

Atlanta had been an important
center for old-time music since 1913,
when the Georgia Old Time Fiddlers'
Association organized and began sponsoring an annual fiddling contest.
These contests quickly grew in prestige; in 1915 the Atlanta *Journal*
editorialized:

In these russet festivals, the melodies
of the Old South are awakened, and

the spirit of folklore comes back to flesh and blood. The life of mountain and meadow, of world-forgotten hamlets, of cabin firesides aglow with hickory logs, the life of a thousand elemental things grows vivid and tuneful. From every part of the State come the fiddlers, graybeards and striplings, some accompanied by their faithful "houn' " dogs, others bearing a week's rations strapped to their shoulders, and all asweat with ambition to play their best and win the championship. Unique in all things, Atlanta has nothing more distinctive than this.

A few years later poet Stephen Vincent Benét would immortalize one of these contests in the poem "The Mountain Whippoorwill." For many of the musicians in the area, these contests provided the first real forum for their music, the first hint that people would pay to hear such music, and the first vestiges of respectability for the music. John Carson had acquired his reputation at such contests prior to his radio and record work. In fact, when WSB radio started in Atlanta in 1922, it found an established pool of old-time music talent it could draw on. The climate established by the annual fiddling contest (which, incidentally, also included banjo picking, singing, flat-foot dancing, and string band categories), and the willingness of WSB to program old-time music, created a ready-made opportunity for the recording industry.

Two of the more popular musicians in town were a fiddling chicken farmer named Gid Tanner and a blind guitarist-singer named Riley Puckett. Tanner and Puckett had long been fixtures at the annual fiddling contest;

Riley Puckett. Courtesy Doug Green.

they had first teamed up at the 1916 contest, when they brought down the house with a version of "It's a Long Way to Tipperary." Tanner was a big, red-faced man who was as famous a clown as a fiddler; "he could turn his head around like an owl," a friend recalled. (It is noteworthy that Tanner and Carson, as well as Uncle Dave Macon, perhaps the three most famous country performers of their day, were regarded by their contemporaries as musicians *and* comedians, with equal weighting to the two professions.) In 1924, just after Fiddlin' John Carson's first record became a hit, Tanner and Puckett had gone north to record some of their old-time and vaudeville tunes.

Walker noticed that these two performers were immensely popular with Atlanta audiences, and he knew that their early records had been moderately successful. He also noticed that another local act, a band led by an automobile mechanic turned fiddler, Clayton McMichen, was a big hit on WSB. McMichen had recorded for Ralph Peer in 1925, but without much success. Though McMichen was a superb fiddler who could play the traditional fiddle tunes with ease and style, he was more interested in modern, jazz-tinged music. In this he was at odds with rough, rustic Gid Tanner, but Walker put his idea across anyway; he would combine Puckett, Tanner, and McMichen into a new sort of super string band, an outfit that would bring together Tanner's comedy and authentic folk music, Puckett's singing skill, and McMichen's fiddling virtuosity. One of the old groups that regularly played at the fiddling conventions during World War I had been called the Lickskillet Orchestra, and this name suggested the name for the new group: the Skillet Lickers. It was to become the most famous name in string band history and it was to sell more records than any other similar group of the time.

In a sense, the Skillet Lickers was a pick-up group, originally formed just for recording purposes. Its success marked one of the relatively few instances where the modern mass media actually affected the performing style and repertory of older folk musicians; usually traditional performers were able to make the transition from pre to post media music with minimum changes in their music or style.

The Skillet Lickers made their first recordings in early 1926, mostly of old traditional tunes like "Watermelon on the Vine," "Alabama Jubilee," and "Turkey in the Straw." Their biggest hit of that year, "Bully of the Town" backed with "Pass Around the Bottle and We'll All Take a Drink," ran up sales of over 200,000 copies. Soon the basic band (Tanner, McMichen, Puckett, and banjoist Fate Norris) was augmented with other musicians who dropped in and out of sessions with a confusing casualness. Frank Walker encouraged their use of as many as three fiddles on many sessions (an important innovation which anticipated by some years the multi-fiddle harmonies later popularized by western swing pioneer Bob Wills— even though Wills featured the harmonies on slower tunes, whereas the Skillet Lickers often had two fiddles playing fast breakdowns in near unison).

The Skillet Lickers' biggest record success arrived when Walker came up with the idea of mixing rustic comedy with the music. He wrote, with help from the boys, a skit called "A Corn Licker Still in Georgia," a playlet about a group of Georgia moonshiners who also happened to be musicians; between running off a batch of "sugar licker" (white lightning flavored with brown sugar) and getting in scrapes with the sheriff, the boys were always willing to "have a little tune." The original "Corn Licker Still" (1927) sold over 250,000 copies —an astounding figure for a regional audience—and inspired a series of sequels, which finally stopped during the Depression with "A Corn Licker Still in Georgia—Part 14."

The free-wheeling, hard-drinking

lifestyle of the northern Georgia musicians as portrayed on these skits was not too far from the private lives of the Skillet Lickers themselves; one of the band members had his fiddle hand shot off in a brawl in northern Georgia, and Atlanta bootleggers made regular stops at the Columbia studios down on Peachtree Street. A Skillet Lickers session was a party, and all kinds of bystanders got roped in; one old fiddler recalls recording on several Skillet Lickers sessions and "never getting anything but twenty-five dollars and drunk." Other old-timers recall a bathtub of moonshine, replete with a well water dipper. The 1929 Columbia catalogue reflected this high humor of the band:

> Here's a team indeed! It's a dance combination, and no high-stepping affair down their way draws the crowd like Gid and these pals of his, an all-star group.

The Skillet Lickers as a band made over eighty sides during the four years they stayed together, and individuals from the band made a good many more records under their own names; in fact, some of the members became regular studio musicians for Columbia's Atlanta studio. Yet the men of the band still made most of their money from personal appearances, not from records. Gid Tanner recalled those days: "Got to playing, making big hit records, and then we got on the road and made some money. Got tuxedo suits, y'know . . . they'd shine like silver. Said, 'We'll have to play a while for these, got to get up some money. . . .' " The Skillet Lickers did

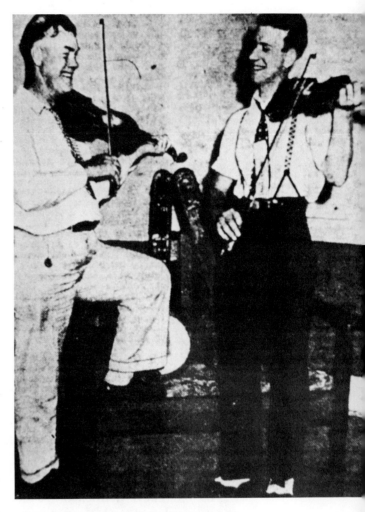

Gid Tanner (left) and his son Gordon, leaders of The Skillet Lickers, shortly after they recorded their hit version of "Down Yonder." Courtesy Charles Wolfe.

indeed make money for Columbia: They were responsible for making fiddle-band music the dominant form of country music in the late 1920s and for making Atlanta the Nashville of the 1920s. One of the Skillet Lickers' records, "Down Yonder," was still in print as late as the 1950s.

It was no wonder that Frank Walker bent over backward to keep

Hear these new southern fiddle and guitar records

NOT so long ago Gid Tanner with his violin, and Riley Puckett with his guitar came, fresh from the mountains of Georgia, to make records for Columbia.

Gid has walked away with the first prize at some of the Old Time Fiddlers' Conventions in Atlanta. Riley and his guitar are known to thousands in the South who have heard him perform at county fairs.

Hear these Tanner and Puckett records. No Southerner can hear them and go away without them. And it will take a pretty hard-shelled Yankee to

leave them. The fact is that these records have got that "something" that everybody wants. So listen to—

"Rock All Our Babies To Sleep"
"Little Old Log Cabin in the Lane"
Record 107 D

"Buckin' Mule"
"Hen Cackle"
Record 110 D

It will pay you to send in your orders at once for these two records. If ever there were a pair of double-barreled hits, these are.

COLUMBIA PHONOGRAPH CO. INC.
1819 Broadway   New York

Columbia
New Process **RECORDS**
Columbia has all the hits and usually first

A *1924 advertisement for a Tanner/ Puckett record.* Courtesy Archie Green.

the group together, but it was a hard job. The band was an unstable compound of brilliant, creative egos: Gid was too old-timey, McMichen was too pop-oriented, and Puckett was too experimental in his guitar runs. They bickered constantly and often toured separately, yet like the latter-day Beatles, they were less impressive as individuals than as a band. By coincidence, the Depression intervened and knocked the bottom out of the record business just as they were ready to dissolve anyway. Gid went back to chicken farming, while McMichen and Puckett tried to make it as professionals in the new musical world of the 1930s.

If one discounts citybilly singers like Vernon Dalhart, Riley Puckett was the first genuine country singing star. Puckett (1894–1946) was blinded shortly after birth, and as a teen-ager in Georgia he was playing and singing for dance parties and on street corners. He began broadcasting over Atlanta's station WSB in 1922, and had soon established a national reputation. He made numerous records with just himself and his guitar, and many approached hit status; he and Vernon Dalhart dominated Columbia's early country music charts.

After he left the Skillet Lickers, he began to record for Victor, but, unlike Jimmie Rodgers, he was never really able to attract a national audience. He tried to expand his repertoire, adding more traditional items like "Ragged but Right" and "Chain Gang Blues," and even going to straight pop material like "When I Grow Too Old to Dream." But he never really broke out; perhaps he lacked proper management, perhaps he lacked the kind of original material Rodgers had. Whatever the problem was, he ended his career playing radio stations across the South, making fiddling contests, and traveling with his own tent show. His two hundred-plus recorded songs remain as examples of fine, early straightforward country (as opposed to folk) singing, and his guitar backup style (featuring single-note bass runs) is still admired by guitar pickers today.

Following on the success of the Skillet Lickers, dozens of string bands with bizarre, surrealistic names paraded through the recording studios. There were Bird's Kentucky Corn Crackers, Dr. Smith's Champion Hoss Hair Pullers, Wilmer Watts and the

Lonely Eagles, The West Virginia Snake Hunters, Fisher Hendley and his Aristocratic Pigs, Gunboat Billy and the Sparrow, Seven Foot Dilly and his Dill Pickles, Joe Foss and his Hungry Sand-Lappers, Mumford Bean and his Itawambians (from Itawamba County, Mississippi), and Ephriam Woodie and his Henpecked Husbands. Many of them were family groups, and many were semi-professionals who played mainly for local dances. They would do a handful of recordings and then disappear back into the countryside; today researchers and fans of this vibrant and exciting string-band music are not even sure what part of the country some of the early recording artists came from. When such groups recorded at a field session, there was no discussion of royalties; they were usually paid a flat rate of fifty dollars per record, and that was the end of it. If the record did well, the band might expect another session the next time the field crew was in the area, but that was all. The musicians would resume their full-time jobs as mill hands, railroad men, farmers, sign painters, or whatever, unaware of where their records might have gone or whom they might have influenced.

A few country string bands did, however, make it big on records. A group from Mississippi called The Leake County Revelers sold nearly two hundred thousand copies of their "Wednesday Night Waltz" and helped win elections for Huey Long. A rural Texas dance band called The East Texas Serenaders made a string of successful recordings for Columbia; they featured a fiddle, guitar, banjo—

and a cello, played in both bowed and plucked style,† and their music helped pave the way for western swing. In the eastern mountains, the Carolina Tar Heels were popular; they used a harmonica instead of a fiddle and featured the strong mountain singing of Clarence Tom Ashley (later rediscovered and made a mainstay of the folk revival of the 1960's) and the whistling antics of a man who billed himself as "the human bird." Charlie Poole, a very influential singer whose career was cut short, and Kelly Harrell both pioneered the techniques of singing to string-band accompaniment, and functioned as transitional figures between the string-band style and the emergence of vocal stars in the early 1930s.

The main catalyst in this transition, however, was to be Ralph Peer, and the major event was to be his trip to Bristol in the summer of 1927. That trip has been called the starting point for modern commercial music, but Peer was hardly aware of that during his first week in Bristol. In one sense, he was trying to prove himself. After pioneering the recording of old-time music and the use of field recording sessions to collect authentic material, Peer had seen his ideas grow into the "hillbilly" boom of the late 1920s, but in 1926 he quit his job with Okeh and for a time decided to get out of the record business; he had an idea that he could get rich mass-producing apple pies in bakeries. It was an idea whose time had not quite come, and

---

† There are numerous reports of early rural string bands using the cello, though relatively few of them recorded with such combinations.

so he eventually went to work for Victor. Victor was certainly one of the leading companies of the time, but they had, partly because of their prestigious "Red Seal" image, not really gone after the "hillbilly" market. After a while, though, they could no longer resist the sales potential of this market, and so they hired Peer to go out into the hills after talent for them. They gave him sixty thousand dollars, two engineers, and a portable recording setup, and told him to head South.

Peer, for his part, wanted certain conditions. While working for Okeh (General Phonograph Corporation) Peer had sensed that the day would come when copyrighting these old-time southern songs would prove valuable. He had seen (in 1925–26) a complex series of copyright lawsuits follow in the wake of the success of "The Wreck of the Old 97," and had earlier suggested that the Okeh Company take over copyrights to the songs of their exclusive artists. So when he was negotiating with Victor, he brought this matter up. As he recalled later in life, "I sat down and wrote a three-paragraph letter and said that I had considered the matter very carefully and that essentially this was a business of recording new copyrights and I would be willing to go to work for them for nothing with the understanding that there would be no objection if I controlled these copyrights."

Not thinking there was much of a future in "hillbilly" copyrights, Victor had no objections, and in July 1927, shortly before he left for his field trip, Peer organized the United Publishing Company. Later it became The Southern Publishing Company, and Peer recalls he was looking at a three-month royalty check for a quarter of a million dollars.

Peer couldn't expect to make much money from actual sheet-music publication of the songs he recorded, but as publisher of the songs, he stood to make a good deal off record sales. (He later admitted that he made as much as 75 per cent of the royalties from record sales.) Thus it was to his advantage to find material in the field that was either original or traditional enough not to be in copyright, so that he could act as publisher for the songs. This had both good and bad effects. From a folklorist's point of view, it was good because it forced Peer to hunt out authentic folk performers of traditional material and to urge his musicians to emphasize original or traditional songs instead of pop material. (In this way, for instance, Peer recorded the first version of "Tom Dooley," in 1929, by blind Tennessee fiddler G. B. Grayson and singer Henry Whitter.) On the other hand, the method caused him to reject some fine musicians who didn't have original material. "That was the test," he recalled, and if artists didn't have original material, he threw them out. Later Peer became convinced that no country artist could really succeed unless he had original material, either written by himself or secured by his manager. He would also sign many of his field discoveries to personal management contracts if he thought they had potential.

He was testing these new methods of his for the first time in Bristol, and as he started his second week in the

Maybelle, A. P., and Sara Carter. Courtesy Doug Green.

town he found dozens of people eager to sign up and record. One of these new groups was a vocal trio from nearby Maces Springs, Virginia, consisting of farmer-carpenter-fruit tree salesman A. P. Carter; his wife, Sara; and his sister-in-law Maybelle Carter. Sara and A. P. Carter had been singing together for informal mountain gatherings for over ten years, and for the last year they had been joined by Maybelle. Sara played the autoharp (a zitherlike instrument fitted with a series of chording dampers, well known in the rural South) and usually sang lead, while Maybelle played guitar and sang harmony. A.P. seldom played an instrument and confined his singing to, in his own words, "basin' in" every once in a while. A.P.'s father had been a mountain banjo player who had gotten religion and turned to

old ballads and religious songs for his music; A.P.'s mother sang a number of old ballads like "The Wife of Usher's Well," "Sailor Boy," and "Brown Girl," and A.P. learned to appreciate them. The fondness for old ballads and religious songs was to mark the Carter Family repertoire throughout their career.

After reading the newspaper story about Peer's recording session, A.P. got his crew together, loaded them in his old model A Ford, and headed for Bristol. Peer was somewhat disarmed by the group that appeared at his recording studio: There were A.P. and Sara, their three children, and Maybelle, who was expecting a child in a couple of months. Peer recalled: "They wander in—they're a little ahead of time and they come about twenty-five miles and they've come through a lot of mud . . . and he's dressed in overalls and the women are country women from way back there—calico clothes on—the children are very poorly dressed."

Mrs. Peer took two of the children outside to feed them ice cream and keep them quiet, while the Carters began singing "Bury Me Under the Weeping Willow," "Little Old Log Cabin by the Sea," "Storms Are on the Ocean," "Single Girl, Married Girl." "As soon as I heard Sara's voice . . . that was it, you see," recalled Peer. "I began to build around it. . . . I knew that was going to be wonderful. And they had plenty of repertoire. . . . A.P. had been apparently quite a traveler—he'd gone around quite a bit—collecting songs." The Carters made six sides at this first session, with Sara singing lead on five of them.

When the first Carter Family record came out, A. P. Carter didn't even have a record player. He heard their first record on a floor-model Victrola at a store in Bristol; he didn't even know the record had been released. The local Victor dealer reported that he had sold two hundred copies of the disc in a few days and that Ralph Peer had reported that the release was doing well all over the South, having sold over two thousand copies within a month in Atlanta alone. The Carters soon got their first royalty check, which A.P. dutifully split up three ways; it was probably only .25 per cent of retail sales income, but it was enough to keep the family interested in making records.

Seven months later Peer called the group up in Camden, New Jersey, for their second session: twelve sides that were to include the family's most enduring songs. Recorded here were "Keep on the Sunny Side," an old 1906 pop song that became the group's theme song; "Anchored in Love," an old gospel hymn that became a Carter Family standard; "Little Darling Pal of Mine," later to become a folk-bluegrass warhorse; and "Wildwood Flower," an old pop song that the Carter Family had learned orally.

With the latter record, it became obvious that the family had another valuable asset in Maybelle's guitar style; she liked to pick the melody on the bass strings and keep rhythm on the treble strings. Her rhythm style and use of melodic lines, which served to sketch the tune in a deceptively simple outline, influenced generations of southern guitar players, all the way from blues singer Leadbelly to folksinger Woody Guthrie. "Wildwood Flower" became the test of accomplishment for all kinds of amateur guitar players, and remains so today. This style, along with the Carters' full, low-pitched mountain church harmonies and their easy, flowing tempo, made them unique among early country artists. They were the first successful country group vocal act; before them group singing had been pretty much a function of church or gospel music, and secular country music had been the province of solo singers or string bands. The Carters combined these two worlds in a beautiful and striking way.

But the Carters, in spite of their influence via records, could not become real professionals for a number of years. For instance, in 1929 A.P. had to leave Virginia to go to Detroit to find work as a carpenter—and this was during the height of the group's Victor recording career. In fact, the need to keep regular nonmusic jobs often kept the members of the family apart during the Depression years. Peer was publishing their songs on a fifty-fifty basis, and they were receiving Victor royalties, but this was not enough to allow them to make ends meet.

Peer was acting as unofficial manager for the band but felt that their appeal wasn't broad enough to get them booked into the big theater and vaudeville circuits, where the big money was. So while his other big country act, Jimmie Rodgers, was touring these circuits to the tune of six hundred dollars a week, A. P. Carter was nailing Carter Family posters to trees in backwater mountain communities: "Admission 15 and 25 Cents. The Program is Morally Good." Most of the Carter Family "personals" were the result of their own advertising and A.P.'s informal promotion; letters would come from people asking about concerts, and A.P. would casually arrange these—no formal booking, no contracts, no agents. They appeared throughout the mid-South, and as far north as Maryland and Indiana. The personnel of the concert shows would depend on which members of the family happened to be in the area, and this in turn depended on their full-time jobs and private lives.

Carter Family biographer Ed Kahn has sketched what a typical stage show in these days was like. Often the Carters would arrive at the hall or schoolhouse early, mingle with the crowd until showtime, and often sell tickets themselves. Shows would run from seven-thirty to nine or nine-thirty, and were usually opened by a little jingle that began, "How do you do, everybody?/How do you do?" A.P. would act as emcee for the show, introducing the members of the group, and perhaps telling a little about the songs —where they learned them, when they recorded them. The family never sold records from the stage, though they did sell little songbooks. Sara and Maybelle usually sat, while A.P. wandered around the stage; he was by nature very nervous, and this often gave his singing voice its distinctive quality. The group often took requests from the audience; if a request meant retuning the instruments, the audience waited; there was no comedy to cover it up. After the show, the Carters often stayed with a family in the neighborhood, and often they took these occasions to gather new material. A.P. was always interested in seeing old songbooks, handwritten ballets, or old sheet music. (Once the group was recording regularly, A.P. made regular song-hunting trips back into the hills, sometimes traveling with Leslie Riddles, a black guitar player, a friend of the family; while A.P. would copy the words of songs, Leslie acted as a sort of human tape recorder, remembering the melody line.)

The Carter Family continued to record until the eve of World War II, spreading some 270 sides over the labels of every major American record company. Their records were popular not only in America, but were released in Australia, Canada, England, India, Ireland, and South Africa as well, yet the Carters never really enriched themselves as much as they enriched the record companies, the publishing companies, and the radio stations. By the late 1930s, however, they were at least able to play full time professionally, and were broadcasting nationally over Mexican border station XERA. Beset by personality differences (Sara and A.P. had separated in the early 1930s) and changing musical tastes, the family broke up for good in 1943.

Various members of the Carter Family continued to make a mark in later country music. Mother Maybelle continued to perform with her daughters up until the 1960s, and A. P. Carter performed with his children until his death in 1960. June Carter later became a fixture of Nashville's "Grand Ole Opry" and eventually married singer Johnny Cash.

The Carter music has become a hallowed canon in both country and folk music. It was the Carters who arranged and popularized "Wabash Cannonball" in 1929, not dreaming that the song would become an anthem for the King of Country Music, Roy Acuff. "Worried Man Blues" ("It takes a worried man/To sing a worried song") and "Engine 143," old folk songs codified by the Carters, enriched the city-bred coffeehouse folksingers of the 1960s. "I Am Thinking Tonight of My Blue Eyes," "Foggy Mountain Top," "East Virginia Blues," and "Jimmie Brown the Newsboy," all performed by the Carters, became the bluegrass standards of Mack Wiseman, Flatt and Scruggs, and others. "Will the Circle Be Unbroken?" and "Gospel Ship" became gospel standards, and the former

gained new symbolic significance as the title of a 1971 folk-rock album by the Nitty Gritty Dirt Band. Not all the Carter songs were original compositions—many were recomposed or rearranged versions of older songs that Peer quickly stamped with a copyright —but no other early country music group preserved so many genuine folk items and injected them into commercial channels.

Peer, of course, could foresee little of this that hot afternoon in Bristol. After the Carters left, he continued to audition other acts: a gospel group, a family string band, a husband-and-wife vocal team. But then, on August 4, another singer with commercial potential showed up. His name was Jimmie Rodgers, and he had phoned Peer the week before from Asheville to say that he thought he had the kind of music Peer wanted, and asked for an audition. Peer granted it.

Rodgers arrived in Bristol the night before the session with a string band in tow, the Jimmie Rodgers Entertainers. They planned to audition together, but Rodgers and the band got into an argument over how they would bill themselves, and Rodgers went over to audition for himself. It was a historic audition, but few realized it at the time.

For Rodgers, it was another chance in his continuing scramble to make it as a professional entertainer. The annals of early country music are full of men who turned to music because of handicaps that prevented them from doing a "normal day's work"— many were blind, and a few (like Deford Bailey, the first black star of the "Grand Ole Opry") were physically handicapped. In these early days, there was little attractive about the life of a professional musician, and many turned to it only as a last resort. Jimmie Rodgers was probably one of these, at least at first. He was often in poor health, and by the time he was in his midtwenties he had contracted tuberculosis. Before then he had spent half his life working on railroads as a callboy, baggagemaster, flagman, and brakeman. This was nothing out of the ordinary, since he was the son of a section hand and since the time and place of his birth —Meridan, Mississippi, in 1897—gave him few other opportunities for a living.

Rodgers often carried a little banjo with him in his railroading days, and when he got sick in 1924, it was natural that he should join a medicine show and sing songs in blackface to rural audiences in Tennessee and Kentucky. He went through a series of such jobs, trying to make enough to support his family; for a time he even played in a dance band with his sister Elsie McWilliams, later to become co-author of many of his famous songs. Eventually he landed in Asheville, North Carolina, right in the middle of the southern Appalachians, and decided to form his own band; he told his wife that he wanted to get "boys who'll be willing to work whatever date I can get—schoolhouse, barn dance, roadhouse, beer joint, anything. . . . Folks everywhere are gettin' tired of all this Black Bottom—Charleston —jazz music junk. They tell me the radio stations keep gettin' more and more calls for old-fashioned songs: 'Yearning,' 'Forgotten,' things like

that, and even the old plantation melodies. Well, I'm ready with 'em." The band landed one job on Asheville radio, and it lasted barely a month; they were back to playing the sticks when they read the account of Peer's recording in Bristol.

When Peer first auditioned Rodgers, Peer had mixed feelings. He described them later for *Billboard*:

> . . . I was elated when I heard him perform. It seemed to me that he had his own personal and peculiar style, and I thought that his yodel alone might spell success. Very definitely he was worth a trial, We ran into a snag almost immediately because, in order to earn a living in Asheville, he was singing mostly songs originated by

The Jimmie Rodgers Entertainers, 1927. Jimmie is the one wearing glasses. Courtesy Bob Pinson.

New York publishers—the current hits. Actually, he had only one song of his own—"Soldier's Sweetheart"—written several years before. . . . In spite of his lack of repertoire, I considered Rodgers to be one of my best bets. Accordingly, I asked him to sign a managerial contract, explained to him the necessity to find new material, and talked to him about his future plans.

Rodgers' first record was "The Soldier's Sweetheart," his recomposition of an older folk song, and a yodeling song, "Rock All Our Babies to Sleep." Peer felt the choice was an accurate sample of Rodgers' skills. Rodgers wanted to record a song he had done on the radio with a lot of success, "T for Texas, T for Tennessee," but Peer felt he had enough for the time being. He paid Rodgers a token sum, and they parted.

Peer spent one more day recording in Bristol and then packed up his gear and headed for his next stop, Charlotte, North Carolina. In his two weeks in Bristol he had recorded over seventy tunes by twenty different groups; only a few of these groups would ever record again. Rodgers, for his part, moved his family to Washington, D.C., to play local clubs and theaters and await word from Peer.

Unlike those of the Carter Family, Rodgers' first record was not an immediate hit; it brought in a modest royalty check of twenty-seven dollars —and no call from Peer. Rodgers finally took it upon himself to go up to New York to ask for another session; Peer let him record four more numbers, one of which was "Blue Yodel," more commonly called "T for Texas." This song *was* an instant

hit, and within a month after its release Peer was hustling Rodgers back into the studios to record legendary songs like "In the Jailhouse Now," "Treasures Untold," and "Brakeman Blues." Within six months Rodgers' royalties jumped to over two thousand dollars a month. Peer took over as his manager, encouraged him to come up with more and more original material, and used it to establish his own Southern Music Publishing Company as a viable firm.

It is still unclear exactly what made Rodgers so immensely popular so fast. It might have been his singing style, it might have been his repertoire, or it might have been something nobody today can really understand. Rodgers was by no means the first successful country singer (as opposed to instrumentalist or string band); both Vernon Dalhart and Riley Puckett had preceded him by several years. Rodgers' stylistic innovations was to combine the imagery and stanza pattern of black country blues with the white tradition of yodeling. Rodgers' high falsetto wordless passages may have had more roots in old-time mountain "hollerin' " than in formal yodeling, but whatever the case there had been nothing like them in country music—or in pop music, for that matter. Unlike the Carters, Rodgers had few genuine folk songs in his repertoire; however, many of his "Blue Yodels" (there were eventually to be thirteen of them) contained stanzas borrowed from earlier blues singers.

Some argue, in fact, that much of Rodgers' success lay in his ability to popularize and "whiten" traditional Negro material, to make the ever-popular blues acceptable to a white audience. Carrie Rodgers, in her biography of her husband, describes how Rodgers as a boy would carry water to Negro section hands in Mississippi: "During the noon dinner-rests, they taught him to plunk melody from banjo and guitar. They taugh him darkey songs; moaning chants and crooning lullabies. . . . Perhaps that is where he learned that peculiar caressing slurring of such simples words as 'snow'—'go.' . . ." Songs like "In the Jailhouse Now" (recorded by blues singer Blind Blake before Rodgers recorded his version) gave Rodgers a black element in his repertoire. He recorded with a number of black sidemen, including, on one auspicious occasion, jazz great Louis Armstrong. The gulf that separates modern white country music from black music was not all that great in the 1920s, when white and black singers often shared stanzas and tunes. Rodgers simply took advantage of this lack of segregation.

Rodgers was undoubtedly the first country singing star to attract a national, as opposed to a regional audience. He was also the first country singer to get rich off of his music, and the techniques Peer used to build his success became lessons for later country singers striving for professional status. Peer co-ordinated incomes from record sales, publishing royalties, and personal appearances, and made Rodgers enough money so that in 1929, not quite two years after the first Bristol session, the singer could build his fifty-thousand-dollar "Blue Yodeler's Paradise" in his adopted hometown of Kerrville, Texas.

Peer did all this not by emphasizing Rodgers' country origins, as had Walker with the Skillet Lickers, but by minimizing them. Rodgers was always billed as "America's Blue Yodeler" and nothing more—nothing about old-time singing or hill-country roots. His publicity pictures showed him in a train brakeman's outfit, or in a white suit with broad-brimmed straw hat, or with a suit and a white Stetson hat, or even with a jaunty little beret and tie—but never in anything resembling hillbilly garb. Rodgers was able to get bookings on theater circuits and on tours that other country performers couldn't get, and his typical stage show was a Dutch mixture of different sorts of entertainment. In a 1929 stage show in Chattanooga, for instance, Rodgers used Clayton McMichen, the virtuoso fiddler who was trying to break out of his Skillet Lickers mold; Texas Tom, a blackface comedian; Billy Burke, of Fort Worth, "The Crooning Guitarist of WBAP"; Howard Campbell, a magician; and a backup band that included a clarinet player and a bass violinist. Such an assortment could indeed appeal to a southern audience—his Chattanooga concert filled the Municipal Auditorium and caused a mammoth traffic jam—but it could also appeal to a western or a midwestern audience.

Rodgers' wide appeal can also be measured by the fact that in 1929 he made a short ten-minute film called *The Singing Brakeman* and that the next year he did a screen test for a possible film with comedian Will Rogers. (Later, he also did a series of concerts with Will Rogers for the benefit of victims of the Dust Bowl in 1931.)

In his recordings, Rodgers soon abandoned his simple guitar accompaniment for backup units of various studio musicians: jazz bands, dance bands, Hawaiian music, trumpets, clarinets, jug bands, and even, on one occasion, a musical saw. These may be seen as concessions to commercialism, as Rodgers selling out his country roots, but they helped him attract the kind of "crossover" audience he needed at the time. People who say that modern country music started with Jimmie Rodgers often stress his folk-music background; it would, however, be more accurate to stress his (or Peer's) ability to package and merchandise the music.

Many of Rodgers' finest songs were co-authored by his sister-in-law Elsie McWilliams in 1928 and 1929; these included many of his sentimental favorites like "My Old Pal," "Daddy and Home," "The Sailor's Plea," "I'm Lonely and Blue," and "Mississippi Moon." Many of them were in the sentimental tradition of the nineteenth century, but others departed drastically from this genteel tradition. Such were the famous blues-based songs, like "T for Texas," "Blue Yodel No. 4 (California Blues)," "Blue Yodel No. 8 (Muleskinner Blues)," and "Blue Yodel No. 9 (Standin' on the Corner)," and the "rough and rowdy" songs like "Pistol Packin' Papa," "Waiting for a Train," and "In the Jailhouse Now." The persona —the speaker—of the heart songs of the 1890s was a prim, gushy, sentimental gentleman; the persona of these Jimmie Rodgers songs was a

tough gritty, realistic, and self-mocking workingman. He was, in short, the recognizable persona of the typical modern country song. This is one of the reasons why his songs have endured in the country repertoire more than those of any of his contemporaries.

Jimmy Rodgers died on May 26, 1933, two days after his last recording session; he was thirty-five, and his career had spanned only six years. How commercially successful was that career? Rodgers became such a legend so soon that it's difficult to get an accurate, meaningful picture. Sales of his records have been wildly exaggerated; by no means did he have a string of million sellers. The most recent evidence suggests that Rodgers, during his career, had only one genuine million-seller, the coupling of "Blue Yodel No. 1" ("T for Texas") with "Away Out on the Mountain." Only four of his releases reportedly sold more than 250,000 copies during his career, and his total sales on the Victor label (78 rpm only) were probably between three and four million; his last release, in the depths of the Depression in 1933, sold barely a thousand copies. Of course, in the 1920s a record sale of 100,000 was a giant hit, and Rodgers' records continued to remain in print throughout the years; sales today might well total over twenty million copies.

His influence was far greater than his sales would indicate. Singers like Gene Autry, Bill Cox, Cliff Carlisle, Daddy John Love, Ernest Tubb, and Hank Snow began by imitating Rodgers; probably three fourths of the country singers starting in the 1930s were in some way influenced by him. Rodgers himself became a culture hero, and a half dozen good songs (and a dozen bad ones) were written about his life and untimely death. The restless, rambling, hard-living, sentimental, family-loving Horatio Alger figure who dies before his time has become the archetype country singer hero; Rodgers' tragic fate has been re-enacted by later singers with almost ritualistic compulsion.

The tragedy of Jimmie Rodgers was not meaningless, for his music formed a new popular mass art form that became an integral part of the lives of millions of Americans suffering through the trauma of the Great Depression. He refined the music of these people, but more importantly, he devised ways to effectively communicate it in a world of mass media where the old channels of person-to-person folk transmission were being disrupted and the old values displaced. He made Ralph Peer and his publishing empire rich, to be sure, but he also made countless little people rich in another way. Roy Horton, later to be a key executive at Peer-Southern, was raised in the 1930s in a grim mining town in the Alleghenies, and he recalls an anecdote that illustrates this richness. "I recall that many times we went to the 'company store' to buy a loaf of bread, a pound of butter, and the latest Jimmie Rodgers record—he was that much a part of so many people's lives."

The development of the country recording industry was the first real step toward the commercialization of the music. Many old-time musicians first thought of going professional—

making money with their music, developing their music from a part-time hobby to a full-time vocation—when they had successful records. This pay, as we have seen, was meager enough—a $50 lump sum, or, for the lucky ones, royalties amounting to $.0015 per record on a release that retailed for $.75—but the business worked, and the companies never went lacking for singers and pickers to record.

In the 1920s the business was dominated by seven major companies, three of them located in Chicago. By 1926 Sears was selling country records, leasing masters from other companies, and issuing them on their own label; Ward's soon got into this business, too, and a number of southern department store chains followed suit. Thus while a wide variety of labels seemed to exist, many of the actual masters were drawn from common company archives. Furthermore, as Rodgers' case shows, record sales in the 1920s were often not commensurate with the musical influence of the records. The average old-time release in the 1920s sold around 5,000–10,000 thousand copies, and during the Depression 1,000 copies was a good sale. Frank Walker's important Columbia 15000 series, so much prized today by historians and folklorists, averaged sales of 15,000–20,000 copies per release in the pre-Depression years. In many years, just four or five big hit records would account for a third or even a half of a company's total old-time music sales. The total number of old-time titles issued by the seven major companies prior to 1930 number about 3,700. Yet it is unsettling to note how comparatively few recordings the major artists of this time made as compared to modern artists. Jimmie Rodgers' 110 recorded songs are the equivalent to only 9 modern albums—and a modern singer like George Jones, who is still in midflight, can claim at least 80 albums and over 700 songs to his credit. Early country records also had to get distributed without the most utilized tool of modern promotion, radio airplay. Ninety-five per cent of early southern radio was "live." Some record companies did start sponsoring shows to plug their latest records, but few of the companies felt that old-time music records were important enough to plug in this way.

There remains the matter of the authenticity of these early pioneer recordings: How accurately do they represent the voice of the people, and the music of the people? Some of the records were genuine folk music; some were mass-produced pop product. Only about 5 per cent of the pre-Depression old-time releases by major companies were old folk ballads in the strictest sense, but many older pop songs had gone into oral tradition and had been recorded by people who had little knowledge of the song's original publication and author. Many of the field recordings by men like Walker are probably fairly authentic reflections of rural folk culture, but there were many instances of the companies interfering with the musicians' repertoires, telling them to use some songs and forbidding them to use others (the Columbia field office in Atlanta had a well-stocked library of popular sheet music even during the heyday of the Skillet Lickers in the

late 1920s). The first generation of country-music recordings were not quite the simple, natural, folksy artifacts they are sometimes made out to be, but they were still a long way from the slick, rootless products of Tin Pan Alley.

If records were the music's prime medium in the 1920s, radio was to be the prime medium of the 1930s. Throughout the first decade of the music's development, radio was developing along with it. It is harder to understand the exact impact radio made on the country music fan of the 1920s, however, because none of the actual radio shows were preserved. They were all done live, of course, and there was no way to preserve them. We can go back today and actually listen to the first big country hits of Fiddlin' John Carson, but there is no way we can ever hear the actual sound of the early "Grand Ole Opry" or the "National Barn Dance." We can only rely on the memories of those who were there and measure the effect the shows had.

That effect was considerable. Unlike the record industry, which flourished for over twenty years before it discovered old-time music, the radio industry was interested in the music almost from the start. It is generally acknowledged that commercial radio began officially in 1920 when station KDKA in Pittsburgh broadcast the Harding-Cox election results to an audience of some 2,000. Sixteen months later, in March 1922, old-time music was on the air, courtesy of Atlanta station WSB, the South's first commercial broadcasting station. WSB had begun as a public-service station owned and operated (as were many

George D. Hay, "discoverer" of the "Grand Ole Opry." Courtesy Charles Wolfe.

early stations) by the local newspaper; finally the paper hired a station director, Lambdin Kay. Kay brought all kinds of rural talent into his broadcasting studios, including Fiddlin' John Carson, the Jenkins Family, and a group of Sacred Harp singers. He later explained his rationale by arguing that "hillbilly or country music talent appeared on the station, since this was a folk music of the region and was both popular and was available at little or no cost."

Most of the early artists were paid absolutely nothing for broadcasting, though they were allowed to announce where they were appearing, what fiddling contest they were a part of, or whatever. This sort of tradeoff continued on many rural stations well into the time of World War II. Early radio hardly encouraged country musicians to think they could make a living with their music, and it's noteworthy that the two biggest names of the time—the Carter Family and Jimmie Rodgers—seldom appeared on radio in the 1920s.

Radio grew with breathtaking speed. By the end of 1922, there were some 510 active stations broadcasting, and 89 of these were in the South. Some were tiny local stations with a radius of a few miles and a power of 10–20 watts; others were powerhouses like the 500-watt WSB, which easily commanded a nationwide audience. The formats of many of the smaller stations were extremely flexible, and anyone who wandered in with an instrument could probably get on the air.

Small-town newspapers seldom printed detailed broadcasting schedules, so today there is no way to determine the exact extent of local country programming, but researchers have determined that one of the first country "barn dance"-type programs originated over WBAP, Fort Worth, in January 1923. The "barn dance" format was to become one of the most common in country music broadcasting. It was usually an anthology program that featured a sort of repertory company of different types of musicians; it was informal and unstructured, and the company of musicians was presented as one big happy family. Audience feedback was important, and requests were often answered on the air. All sorts of old-time music was presented, from barbershop quartets to Hawaiian bands to comedians to singers of sentimental songs, but the key image of the barn-dance show was the fiddle band, and the fiddle-band music was often accompanied with square-dance calls so that those listening at home could dance along. (Nobody knows if anyone ever really danced to the music of these shows.) It was a warm, folksy show format, and it served to personalize the newfangled piece of technology, the radio, and to offer rural Americans an oasis of normalcy in a desert of strange accents and stodgy announcers.

The widespread popularity of Fort Worth's informal and irregular old-time show—it was heard as far away as New York, Canada, and Hawaii—attracted the attention of other program directors, who began to realize that there was a vast rural audience that was being ignored by the constant programming of semiclassical music, dance bands, and noodling piano players. During the early 1920s most Americans were living in towns of 8,000 or less population.

The two major barn-dance programs were soon born: the "National Barn Dance" of WLS, Chicago, and the "Grand Ole Opry" of Nashville. The "National Barn Dance" began in 1924 and was broadcast regularly until 1960; the "Opry" began in late 1925 and is still heard every week in the 1970s. The shows had a good deal in common: Both were started by companies that wanted to sell products to rural America, and both saw the means to sell this product turn into a product—the music—in its own right. The "Opry" tended to be a shade more authentic, a little bit funkier, perhaps because it drew from the vast pool of native southern talent in and around Nashville. There were few mountains around Chicago, though there were many Southerners attracted North by factory work, and a supply of vaudeville performers skilled at appealing to rural tastes.

WLS (the initials stood for "World's Largest Store," in deference to the station's owners, Sears, Roebuck & Co.) began the "National Barn Dance" on April 19, 1924, just a week after the station went on the air. They announced it as a program "planned to remind you folks of the good fun and fellowship of the barn warmings, the husking bees, and the

Studio A of WSM, first home of the "Opry." Courtesy Charles Wolfe.

square dances in our farm communities of yesteryear and even today."

The fiddle band of Tommy Dandurand (banjo, fiddle, guitar—and drums!) helped spark early shows. George C. Biggar, the director of the show, recalled other early successful acts: "When Chubby Parker picked his little old banjo and sang 'I'm a Stern Old Bachelor,' he struck responsive chords in countless hearts. Identified with earlier days of the "Barn Dance" also were Walter Peterson and his 'Double-barreled Shotgun' [Peterson played guitar, sang, and played harmonica on a neck rack]; Cecil and Esther Ward and the Hawaiian guitars; the good old Maple City Four;

and Bradley Kincaid, the 'Kentucky Mountain Boy.' Bradley was the first perhaps to popularize dozens of the unpublished mountain ballads."

Nearly all the early "Barn Dance" stars established their reputations solely by radio; few recorded very much, and what they did record was on Sears' own label and was sold because of their radio popularity (many of these record labels identified the performer as a WLS star). Bradley Kincaid, a rather self-conscious singer and collector of folk songs, reached a vast audience through his radio broadcasts and through his sale of song books over the air; his case proves that the history of country music is by no means the history of country music records.

The leading announcer for the "National Barn Dance" during its first year was former Memphis newspaper writer George D. Hay, who billed himself as "The Solemn Old Judge" and started each show off with an imitation train whistle. Hay was an Indiana native who had gotten into radio when the newspaper he worked on in Memphis started station WMC and Hay found himself appointed radio editor, which meant that he was also announcer on the station. WLS hired him away from WMC in 1924, and later that year he won the *Radio Digest* award as the country's most popular announcer. Hay was not at this time associated especially with the "Barn Dance": He was the leading announcer for all types of shows on WLS, so when the National Life and Accident Insurance Company of Nashville decided, in 1925, to build the fanciest radio station in the South, they went after the best talent. They asked Hay to come back to the South and become station director for WSM, "The Air Castle of the South."

Hay arrived in Nashville in November 1925 and began to cast about for ways to improve the rather anemic fare then being offered to the good citizens of Nashville: story ladies, brass bands, women's-club culture. He noted that some old-time musicians, including a lively string band led by a rural physician named Dr. Humphrey Bate, had already appeared informally on Nashville radio and had drawn a surprising audience response. He decided to experiment further, and on November 28, 1925, he invited a seventy-seven-year-old fiddler, the uncle of a staff musician, to play the fiddle on the air. The fiddler, a Tennessee native named Uncle Jimmy Thompson, had a repertoire that stretched back to the Civil War, and he was anxious, in his own words, "to throw my music out across the American."

Later, Hay himself described Thompson's first appearance:

Uncle Jimmy told us he had a thousand tunes. . . he was given a comfortable chair in front of an old carbon microphone. While his niece, Mrs. Eva Thompson Jones, played the piano accompaniment, your reporter presented Uncle Jimmy and announced that he would be glad to answer requests for old time tunes. Immediately telegrams started to pour into WSM.

One hour later at nine o'clock we asked Uncle Jimmy if he hadn't done enough fiddling to which he replied, 'Why shucks a man don't get warmed up in an hour. I just won an eight-day fiddling contest down in Dallas, Texas, and here's my blue ribbon to prove it.'

Other WSM executives were astounded at the response to Uncle Jimmy, but Hay was not really surprised; he had seen the same thing in Chicago when the "National Barn Dance" had begun to broadcast old-time music. Hay began to make plans; he told a friend that he planned to start a new show, "something like the 'National Barn Dance' in Chicago and expected to do better because the people were real and genuine and the people really were playing what they were raised on." Thus on December 27, 1925, about a month after Uncle

Jimmy first appeared on the air, the Nashville *Tennessean* announced: "Because of this recent revival in the popularity of old familiar tunes, WSM has arranged to have an hour or two every Saturday night. . . ." Thus a regularly scheduled barn dance show was born, and within a few months Hay had assembled about twenty-five regular acts for the show.

The people of Nashville were not too happy at the idea of having a hill-billy show originating from their city, which they liked to call "the Athens of the South." Some protested, but National Life was reaching a vast rural audience beyond the city of Nashville itself, and it was an audience to which they wanted to sell insurance. The show grew; soon it was running to over three hours on Saturday nights. WSM increased its power until it had the strongest clear-channel signal in the South, and soon, letters

The "*Opry*" cast, 1930. Courtesy WSM.

about the Saturday night "Barn Dance" were coming in from all over.

The NBC radio network was formed in 1927, and WSM signed on as an affiliate. Most nights the station carried slick, well-produced network shows originating out of New York, but on Saturday night, WSM refused the network fare and stuck to the "Opry"—except for one fifteen-minute segment when the "Opry" was interrupted by "Amos 'n' Andy." By this time other Nashville stations were trying to copy the WSM success by starting their own "Barn Dances," using the same local musicians who had made the "Barn Dance" a hit. Partly because of this, WSM started paying its performers. Usually it was only a token payment of something like one dollar a minute, and most performers seldom performed more than fifteen minutes.

Hay knew his audience, and he would often admonish his musicians, "Keep it down to earth, boys." He rejected innovations and new tunes. He wrote press releases that emphasized the rustic backgrounds of his performers; in 1929 he was arguing that "every one of the 'talent' is from the back country" and that the music represented "the unique entertainment that only Tennessee mountaineers can afford." He posed his musicians in overalls, in corn fields with coon dogs, even in pigpens; he gave the bands colorful names like the Gully Jumpers, the Possum Hunters, and the Fruit Jar Drinkers. This upset some of the musicians; many of them were not rustic at all, but were Nashville citizens working at occupations like garage mechanics, watch repair-

men, and cigar makers. For instance, Dr. Humphrey Bate, whose band Hay dubbed the Possum Hunters, was a well-educated physician who enjoyed classical music and wintered in Florida. Yet Hay, sensing the popularity of the hillbilly image that was enriching groups like the Skillet Lickers, continued to impose this image on his new show. The final touch came in December 1927 when Hay, in an off-the-cuff remark, dubbed the show "Grand Ole Opry." The name was a deliberate parody of "Grand Opera," the term used to describe a series of programs that had been coming to WSM over NBC. It stuck, and Hay used it to enhance the hayseed image of the show.

In spite of the fabricated nature of the hayseed image, the show was not lacking in colorful characters and authentic folk music. Uncle Jimmy Thompson, for instance, was wont to complain vociferously when his niece had his trousers pressed prior to his performance. "Hey thar," he would say, "who ironed them damned wrinkles in these britches? I like my britches smooth and round. Fit my kneecaps." Obed Pickard, the first vocal star of the show (much of the pre-1930 music was string-band fare), played for Henry Ford himself and parlayed his "Opry" success into a national network radio show of his own and the Pickard Family.

Dr. Humphrey Bate, whom Judge Hay called "the Dean of the Opry," was probably the first country musician to broadcast over Nashville radio. He was basically a harmonica player and he led a large band that often included as many as six or seven pieces;

Dr. Humphrey Bate and his Possum Hunters: the first string band on the "Opry."
Left to right: Oscar Stone (the fiddler who took over the band when Bate died in
1936), Walter Ligget, Staley Walton, Paris Pond, and Oscar Albright playing the
bowed string bass—a rare use of the bowed doghouse bass in country string-band
music. Note the business suits; a few years later George Hay, in an attempt to rusti-
cate the "Opry" image, would pose the same band in a cornfield. Courtesy Charles
Wolfe.

all the band members lived in a little hamlet northeast of Nashville and played together for years. In fact, Dr. Bate had led string bands in the area since the turn of the century, playing on riverboat excursions, picnics, and even for silent movies. Dr. Bate's band was the mainstay of the early "Opry" shows, and he appeared more than any other string band; for years, his band opened the "Opry" with "There'll Be a Hot Time in the Old Town Tonight." Dr. Bate learned a lot of his instrumental tunes from an old ex-slave he knew as a boy; Bate's repertoire was full of rare and unique folk melodies, as well as ragtime, pop music, and even Sousa marches. When Dr. Bate died in 1936 his band was taken over by his fiddler Oscar Stone and it continued to be a part of the "Opry" cast up until the 1950s. Dr. Bate's daughter, Alcyone Bate Beasley, started playing with the band at the tender age of thirteen and had a successful career in pop music at

WSM; she still appears on the "Opry" today. The band with which Alcyone plays, the Crook Brothers, is another early band from the first year of the Opry. Leader Herman Crook learned a lot from Dr. Bate, and carries on his tradition of the harmonica-led string band.

Deford Bailey was the Opry's sole black performer, a tiny, fiercely proud harmonica player and blues singer. Deford joined the Opry during its first year, and, though condescendingly labeled as the show's "mascot," he was immensely popular; in 1928, for instance, he appeared on the show twice as often as anyone else. Deford always worked alone, and specialized in harmonica virtuoso pieces like "Pan American Blues," "Fox Chase," and "John Henry"; in the days before amplification systems he used a large megaphone attached to his harmonica to make himself heard. Deford was almost certainly the only black man of his generation—or of several generations to come—to have a regular role in a major country radio show. Exactly what his presence on the early "Opry" implied for black-white music inter-change is still being debated by historians.

Deford apparently never really saw himself as a blues musician in a hillbilly setting. He grew up in rural Tennessee, not far from Nashville, in the early 1900s, and most of the music to which he was exposed during his formative years was what Deford himself called "black hillbilly music." As a boy Deford knew many black men who played old-time music; his father played the fiddle, and his uncle was the best black banjo player he knew. Deford's own picking had a delightful ragtime touch to it, and there were relatively few links between his music and that of other country blues artists of the time. He might well have been one of the last exemplars of the tradition of "black hillbilly music." It is a tradition hardly documented in the field recordings of the 1920s, since the commercial companies pigeonholed blues into special "race" series and country into the special "hillbilly" series. Black hillbilly music didn't really fit into either, and when the field scouts ran into it, they usually

Deford Bailey. Courtesy Charles Wolfe.

ignored it. It is interesting that Deford's own records were released in the "hillbilly" series by one company, and in the "race" series by another one.

Deford continued to play regularly on the "Opry" throughout the 1930s, traveling and touring with people like Uncle Dave Macon, Roy Acuff, and Bill Monroe. He left the "Opry" in 1941 amid a good deal of bitterness but still widely respected by thousands of white listeners as "the harmonica wizard," he opened a shoeshine stand in downtown Nashville.

The McGee Brothers, from Franklin, Tennessee, both served apprenticeships with Uncle Dave Macon (see below) and then went on to become mainstays of "Opry" string band music. The elder brother, Sam McGee, was one of the major purveyors of old-time mountain solo guitar style. Sam was one of the first country musicians to start playing the guitar in middle Tennessee; he soon developed a unique "flat top" style wherein he played the rhythm and melody simultaneously. By 1926 he was recording solo numbers like his famous "Buck Dancer's Choice," one of the most difficult of old-time guitar standards. Sam utilized a lot of blues and ragtime in his guitar stylings and came up with a creative mixture of folk and pop influences. Though he was not as well known as the other major old-time guitar stylist, Maybelle Carter, and though he spent much of his early career as a sideman, Sam's early records like "Franklin Blues," "Knoxville Blues," and "Railroad Blues" show that he was the first country musician to really exploit the guitar as a solo instrument. Up until his death in

Sam and Kirk McGee. Courtesy Charles Wolfe.

1975, at age eighty-one, he continued to play regularly on the "Opry." Discovered by the young northern musicians in the folk revival of the 1960s and given his due as the pioneer instrumentalist he was, Sam died with at least some idea of the influence his own music had had on the world. He was luckier than many old-time pioneers who died quietly in obscurity, never having any idea of the influence their old records had had on people.

Sam's younger brother Kirk McGee was a banjoist, a fiddler, and a singer who brought to the McGee Brothers act a repertoire of old fiddle tunes and a love of sentimental songs and even church songs. Kirk played with Sam most of the time and was the entrepreneur of the team—"I went out and got the business," he said later. In the 1930s the McGees teamed with a Dickson, Tennessee, fiddler named Arthur Smith to form one of the most influential string bands of the 1930s, the Dixieliners. Touring out of the WSM "Opry" bureau, the band traveled during the week and broadcast on Saturday nights; it was a no-nonsense, old-time string band that emphasized technical ability over showmanship, but the audiences ate it up. Kirk recalls, "Arthur was a very solemn fellow. But his fiddling impressed them. He just whipped it out and played and they sat up and listened." Smith popularized a long string of original fiddle numbers, many of which have gone into folk tradition and have become bluegrass standards. They include "Pig in the Pen," "Dickson County Blues," "More Pretty Girls Than One," and "Beautiful Brown Eyes." The Dixieliners never recorded in their prime, and they are another instance of how radio performers could and did influence the music without the benefit of hit recordings.

The mainstay of the "Grand Ole Opry" in its first decade was a man who has come to symbolize the spirit of old-time music, Uncle Dave Macon (1870–1952). Along with the Carter Family and Jimmie Rodgers, Macon was a prime influence in the music of the 1920s, and a major link between the folk and commercial traditions. However, unlike the Carters and Rodgers, who worked primarily on phonograph records, Macon was very active in both records and radio. A. P. Carter was thirty-six when he made his first record and launched his career, and Jimmie Rodgers was thirty, but Uncle Dave was fifty-four, and his musical heritage went a good deal farther back into the nineteenth century. In fact, Uncle Dave had a career that began with singing and playing the banjo on the vaudeville stage and at rural, lantern-lit schoolhouses, and extended all the way up to his appearance on television in the early 1950s. During this time he became one of the most beloved entertainers in the music's history; he is still enjoyed today, via his records, by millions who never saw him perform. People who know nothing else about the early generations of country music recognize his name. Folklorists have called Uncle Dave a cultural catalyst and a preserver of countless traditional songs; radio historians have called him "the first featured star of the 'Grand Ole Opry' "; the popular press of the time referred to him as "the king of the hillbillies" or "the Dixie Dewdrop." Uncle Dave was more modest; he described himself merely as "banjoist and songster, liking religion and meetings, farming, and thanking God for all his bountiful gifts in this beautiful world he has bestowed upon us."

Uncle Dave (born David Harrison Macon) came from the Cumberland plateau in middle Tennessee, near McMinnville. As a teen-ager he lived in Nashville, where his father, a for-

LOOK WHO'S COMING

UNCLE DAVE MACON

AND

SAM McGEE

BOTH FROM TENNESSEE

━━━ VOCALION RECORD ARTISTS ━━━

You are getting yourself TOLD about something entertaining and Worth While by seeing them in person. THEY DO DOUBLES AND SINGLES WITH BANJO AND GUITAR, INSTRUMENTAL AND VOCAL.

Uncle Dave Macon is the only man in captivity who plays and sings on two banjos at the same time. TRICK BANJO PLAYING IS HIS SPECIALTY.

Funny, Clean Jokes and Lots of Fun

BRING THE WHOLE FAMILY

━━━ WILL APPEAR HERE ━━━

ADMISSION

Courtesy Doug Green.

mer Confederate Army officer, operated an old hotel. This hotel catered to the many vaudeville and circus performers who came through Nashville in those days, and the young Macon learned to love their songs and music. By the time he was fifteen, he had his first banjo; in his own words, it was Joel Davidson, "a noted comedian and banjoist . . . that inspired Uncle Dave to make his wishes known to his dear aged mother and she gave him the money to purchase his first banjo." Soon he was learning many of the popular vaudeville songs of the day, and he began to play informally for friends and relatives. When he married, he moved back to the country and there continued to sing and learn old folk songs from people in the community. But he continued to play and sing only for his friends. He formed a

freight hauling company, the Macon Midway Mule and Transportation Company, and hauled freight with mule teams; many old-timers in the area today can recall him singing as he drove along, or stopping to rest under a shade tree and taking out his banjo.

In 1920 Uncle Dave became a victim of technological unemployment: A truck line started in competition with Macon Midway, and he chose not to compete. At the age of fifty, he began thinking seriously about a new career—one in music. His first public performance (about 1921) was a charity event in Morrison, Tennessee; as he recalled later: "The Methodist church there needed a new door. I gave a show, then passed the hat and collected the money, seventeen dollars." Soon a talent scout from the Loew's vaudeville theaters heard him and offered him a contract, and suddenly Uncle Dave found himself a stage star, playing his banjo and telling his jokes at Loew's theaters around the country. He was so popular that other theater chains tried to buy his contract. In 1923 he hired a young partner, a skinny Nashville fiddler and singer named Sid Harkreader. A little later he added a "buck dancer" to his cast. By 1924 Uncle Dave's name was famous across the South.

In the summer of 1924, a local furniture company sent Uncle Dave and Sid Harkreader to New York to make their first and most famous records: "Keep My Skillet Good and Greasy," "Hill Billie Blues," and his imitation of an old-time hunt, "Fox Chase." Uncle Dave also got his first look at the big city of New York, and took it in style. Once, after he had visited a barber shop and ordered "the works," he was presented a bill for $7.50 and was barely able to conceal a gasp. Finally recovering his poise, he muttered, "I thought it would be $10." Afterward he wrote in his expense book: "Robbed in barber shop . . . $7.50."

Uncle Dave's records were so successful that he was called back into the studios repeatedly in the 1920s; for a time he made regular trips to New York twice a year. The songs he recorded came from many sources. He learned some from oral tradition, many from the old vaudeville circuits, and a number from old sheet music via an aunt who played parlor piano. He owed—and acknowledged—a debt to black musicians; he was exposed to black music as a child on the farm and later as he listened to roustabouts working on the Cumberland River. Many of his songs were moralistic, such as "You Can't Do Wrong and Get By," an old gospel hymn; others had a rowdy, good-time flavor, such as "Bully of the Town" and "Keep My Skillet Good and Greasy." Some, like "Them Two Gals of Mine," can hardly be played on the radio even today. Apparently he saw no hypocrisy in singing a church song one minute and a gamey song the next. Once he took a string band into a recording studio and recorded one day as "The Fruit Jar Drinkers" and the next day as "The Dixie Sacred Singers." This sort of schizophrenia took its toll: Uncle Dave would often suffer from acute or chronic depression, and more than once was hospitalized for it.

Uncle Dave was also a skilled banjo player, and his style continues to in-fluence pickers like Pete Seeger today. His "rapping" style was a three-finger style probably derived from the minstrel techniques of the nineteenth century; his combination of thumb, index, and middle fingers yielded a bewildering variety of rolls and runs. He was also a trick banjoist; one of his early posters announced, "Uncle Dave Macon is the only man in captivity who plays and sings on two banjos at the same time." He would twirl the banjo, toss it in the air, and dance around it, never missing a beat. His *tour de force* was called "Uncle Dave Handles a Banjo the Way a Monkey Handles a Peanut."

Uncle Dave also pioneered country comedy. On many of his records he would introduce his songs with a story or a joke, or even a bit of doggerel poetry. On "Tennessee Jubilee" he starts by saying:

Well, well folks, I'm a-feeling fine, just ate a hearty dinner and now I'm going to play you something that's round here, an old Tennessee Jubilee. But before I sing you the piece, I have a cousin lives down in Rutherford County, Tennessee. She's a woman, and her brother was a-telling me about her swappin' a dry cow for an old Ford car last summer. And she learned to run it pretty well in the wheat fields after they got done thrashing. And she decided to go into the city on Saturday. But she went out to the highway, and the traffic was so thick that she backed out, and started to go in at night. First thing she done, she drove over the signal line and the traffic officer stopped her and there she was; she stuck her head out the window and says, "What's the matter?" The traffic gentleman says, "Why, you haven't got your dimmers on." She says, "Lord, Lord, I reckon I have—I put on everything Mam laid out for me to wear before I left home." And she says, "Who is you anyhow?" He says, "I'm the traffic-jam man, ma'am." "Well, I'm mighty glad to you told me. Mam told me to fetch her a quart—have it ready for me when I go out, will you, please?"

Uncle Dave wanted to make each record sound more personal, to get across with each song some of his own high spirits and good humor. He wanted each record to be a miniature performance, just like he was used to giving onstage. Whereas the barn-dance format functioned to personalize the machine of the radio, Uncle Dave's format tended to personalize the machine of the phonograph.

Though Uncle Dave recorded more than most other musicians of his day, he continued to tour on personal appearances for most of his income. His sometime partner Sam McGee recalled traveling hundreds of miles in an old touring car with side curtains on the windows. When Uncle Dave was not booked on the vaudeville circuit, he booked his own shows through voluminous personal correspondence. He was his own agent, booker, and advertising agency. He felt, however, that the best advertising was word of mouth. When he drove into a town where he wanted to do a show, he usually headed for the school. There he would offer to do a free show for the children. After the show, he would be sure to mention where he would perform that night (it was often the same schoolhouse) and let the kids carry the word home to their parents.

The grapevine would do the rest, and the evening show would be well attended—at twenty-five cents a head.

When Hay's "Barn Dance" started in 1925, Uncle Dave was one of the first performers; in fact, for some time he was about the only real professional on the show. He was not on every show—he could still make more money from touring than from Hay's one dollar a minute—but when he did appear, his audience was waiting for him. One local Tennessee resident recalls that his family had one of the first radios in the community, and when they learned that Uncle Dave would be on the "Barn Dance," they kept the news quiet; they were afraid the neighbors would find out and "swarm into the house to hear Uncle Dave and trample us." Since Uncle Dave was the Opry's first really big star, it was natural that in 1931 he headlined the first touring company sent out by the "Opry": Uncle Dave Macon and his Moonshiners.

By the early 1930s Uncle Dave was a regular fixture on the "Opry," and in 1939 he went to Hollywood to star with Roy Acuff in the film version of "Grand Ole Opry." He also toured with such legendary figures as the Delmore Brothers, Roy Acuff, and Bill Monroe. Until just a few months before his death, Uncle Dave was playing regularly on the "Opry"; by then he had become one of the "Opry's" most cherished links with its folk heritage, for his colorful personality and stubborn individuality made him a legend. Even today, veteran musicians still sit around the "Opry" dressing rooms and endlessly swap "Uncle Dave" stories; one can argue that

Uncle Dave has become one of the music's few occupational heroes.

Some people like to call the 1920s the "golden age" of country music, but for the musicians, it was far from that. Few enjoyed the success of a Rodgers or a Dalhart. Most struggled constantly to improve their lots and to try to make a decent living—or part of one—with their music.

The period was a bewildering transition era that saw the music attempting to define itself and to adapt itself to the new forces of mass media, yet it is not quite accurate to speak of the age in terms of crass commercialism finally winning out over a noble folk tradition. Since the late nineteenth century, commercialism had been an ever-present part of the folk tradition;

the term "old-time music" embraced all forms of older music, folk and pop alike. The impulse to professionalize was present throughout the 1920s, from the earliest recordings of Fiddlin' John Carson and Henry Whitter. However, it was only toward the end of the era, when Peer and others had established country music as a distinct genre of pop music, that this impulse bore real fruit.

For his part, Peer only realized the effect he was having on the music after the fact. He later recalled that he had intended to use the profits of his hillbilly business to establish himself as a publisher of mainstream popular songs—but before long, he was realizing that his means were overshadowing his end.

Chapter Three

Depression and Boom

The popular image of country music in the 1930s—the Depression years—is romantic. It features southern families filing into grocery stores, ordering up what meager supplies they could afford "and the latest Jimmie Rodgers record"; it is a Norman Rockwell portrait of a frail and feeble, threadbare but proud, slowly growing musical outcast isolated on Walton's Mountain. The facts of the matter are another story.

Country music in the 1930s was far from just a regional southeastern phenomenon; it was a genuine daily event all across rural America. More than that, though, it was also an era of experimentation and creativity that has yet to be matched in country music's history. It seemed that the whole country was bursting with excitement over the music. Radio had discovered a dedicated market, the American farmer, who warmly accepted country music into his home and listened to it with clockwork regularity, and no one group was more excited than the talented singers and musicians who suddenly found that by playing music (whether creating it or re-creating it) they could make a living. Young musicians from literally every part of the country began forging unique and individual sounds and styles, combining the music from whatever their ethnic background might be with the diverse new sounds brought to them by record, by radio, and, as time went by, by personal appearances. The era was tremendously creative and exciting musically. The panorama of musical styles developed was extremely diverse, and the entire decade, despite the hardships wrought by the Depression at one end and the threat of world war at the other, was for country music one of stretching and flexing young muscles, striving to grow and develop in innumerable ways all at once.

At the beginning of the decade, country music was made up of four basic styles: the fiddle bands, the solo singers, followers of the Carter Family, and followers of Jimmie Rodgers. Despite the grinding effects of the Depression, there were imitators and practitioners of all these styles trying to earn a living in music, most of them through the medium of radio.

Although radio had been around since the early 1920s, its popularity skyrocketed during the Depression for the simple reason that while a phonograph and a radio might have roughly the same initial price (which was rather high for the era), the continuing cost of buying new records (at $.75 each) made the phonograph a luxury fewer and fewer could afford. Roland Gellatt, in his *The Fabulous Phonograph*, first pointed out the astonishing statistic that record sales reached a peak of 104 million in 1927, but by 1932 the total sales for the year were but six million, an astonishing 5.8 per cent of the entire total of only five years earlier.

Records continued to sell, of course, but into this astounding sales gap stepped radio, with its one-time purchase price and free programming. Its boosters were quick to respond to rural America's desire for country music, filling the early morning and noontime hours with live local broadcasts, alternating homespun country music with ads for farm products or tools. It was a forum in which most of the country stars of the next decade got their start.

The Saturday nights were some-thing else again. The music that caught the interest of the farmer in the early morning and noontime hours seemed a natural for a full-fledged barn dance on Saturday night, a nostalgic harkening back to the real dances in barns and the apple peelings and corn shuckings that were a staple—romanticized with the passage of time—of life before World War I, "The War to End All Wars." No other single factor explodes the myth of country music-as-southeastern-phenomenon-in-the-1930s as much as the quick and widespread proliferation of these Saturday night radio barn dances on a nationwide basis throughout the decade.

One of the earliest was the "National Barn Dance," heard over WLS in Chicago. Contrary to the commonly held assumption that the "Opry" reigned supreme from its inception, the "National Barn Dance" was in fact far more popular in this era, serving an immense amount of midwestern, Great Plains, and southern territory with its homespun acts, many of whom—like big-voiced sentimental singer Henry Burr and organist Grace Wilson—were not really "country," but had a definite romantic and nostalgic appeal to a segment of rural listeners.

Among those we would call real country entertainers, longtime staples of the show were the immensely popular Lulu Belle and Scotty, the Hoosier Hot Shots, Arkie the Woodchopper, Mac and Bob, the Cumberland Ridge Runners, and Karl and Harty. A list of cast members who came and went on to other things is even more impressive: Gene Autry, Rex Allen, Ed-

Roy Acuff and the Smokey Mountain Boys. Courtesy Country Music Foundation.

die Dean, Patsy Montana, George Gobel, Louise Massey and the Westerners, Homer and Jethro, and Red Foley.

The importance of the WLS "National Barn Dance" is nearly impossible to underestimate, and is even more dramatic when some statistics are brought to bear on the subject: In 1930, 40.3 per cent of American homes had a radio, and more than three quarters of those were in the northeastern and north-central United States. In the South (including Texas and Oklahoma) only 16.2 per cent of families had radios at all; taken together, they amounted to a mere 11.9 per cent of the total number of radio owners in the nation. Thus the

audience to which the Chicago-based WLS was beaming at fifty thousand clear-channel watts was much larger than that of Nashville's WSM or any of the South's other radio barn dances. Also, the "National Barn Dance" from WLS went on the NBC Blue Network (sponsored by Alka-Seltzer) in 1933, a full six years before the "Grand Ole Opry's" famous "Prince Albert Hunt Show" was carried by a national network.

How the "National Barn Dance" lost such an overwhelming advantage, —so that by 1950 it was completely overshadowed by the "Opry," and by 1960 had disappeared from WLS—is an interesting and intricate story, and is inextricably entwined in the narrative of this history. For the moment, however, it is important to see it as the reigning barn dance of this era, influencing and catering to the tastes of millions of rural Americans on a nationwide basis.

The "National Barn Dance" was the first of the barn dances to form their own Artist Service Bureau, which booked touring casts and further whetted public appetite for country music. Their tours rarely took them too far South (although Tennessee and Kentucky were not at all out of reach), but they blanketed the Midwest and not infrequently reached the mining towns of northern Minnesota and the isolated Upper Peninsula of Michigan.

Although the show had decided pop elements and even pop leanings, it was the country singers—particularly Gene Autry, whose success on the station in the early 1930s was phenomenal—who were the stars, the focal points of the show.

Autry's full career will be described in Chapter Five, but his few years (1931–34) on WLS are of singular importance. His early professional career was spent in direct imitation of Jimmie Rodgers, a style with which Autry was moderately successful. After a short stint at KVOO in Tulsa, he came to WLS with an entirely new image: "Oklahoma's Yodeling Cowboy," replete with rope tricks (at which he was adept, having grown up on a ranch) and flashy outfits. No longer restricted to Rodgers-like blues, he scored with plain country songs like 1932's "Silver-Haired Daddy of Mine" (the first of his many megahits) and western numbers like "Yellow Rose of Texas" (1933) and "The

Last Roundup" (1934). His popularity rose explosively and before long Sears was selling thousands of Gene Autry Roundup guitars at $9.95 from its catalogue (since Sears owned WLS —World's Largest Store—for its first few years, such tieups were only logical). It was Autry's WLS-developed popularity that led him to be considered as a candidate for Mascot Films' singing cowboy experiment, which in turn led to his becoming the first truly national country music star.

The WLS "National Barn Dance" dominated both its era and its area, but there were other important shows of a similar nature, even in WLS' home territory, the great Midwest. The WHO "Iowa Barn Dance Frolic," for example, began in 1932, and by 1936 had boosted its signal to the legal maximum of fifty thousand watts. The WHO show was reminiscent of WLS, featuring heavy doses of barber-shop quartets, organists, and novelty acts. On the other hand, like WLS it had an artist service bureau to book tours of its cast members, and featured as headliners a host of country entertainers, most of whom (with the exception of Zeke Clements and Texas Ruby) have drifted into obscurity. Like the "National Barn Dance" and unlike the slowly changing "Grand Ole Opry," the "Iowa Barn Dance Frolic" laid heavy emphasis on singers and singing, featuring very little instrumental string-band music. The "Iowa Barn Dance Frolic" was never able to attract the major performers necessary to make it as important as WLS, but its central midwestern location and the clear-channel power of its signal spread country music over a broad segment of the Midwest.

Another big barn dance, launched when longtime fixture David Stone left the "Grand Ole Opry" to create and develop a barn dance in Minnesota's twin cities of Minneapolis and St. Paul, was the KSTP "Sunset Valley Barn Dance." The emphasis was on the solo singers and the cowboy—the show's stars were Billy Folger, Cactus Slim the Lonesome Serenader, Trapper Nash, Six-gun Mel, Chuck Mulkern the Flash of Rice Street, and Frank and Esther the Sweethearts of Radio—but the big fifty-thousand-watt station had goals typical of nearly every radio barn dance. As their 1943 song folio states: "Hundreds of thousands of people from all parts of the country have attended these shows and listened to the broadcasts and enjoyed to the fullest the songs of hearth and home, the breakdowns and fiddle tunes, ringing banjo melodies, harmonica blues, together with the fun and comedy of the big Saturday night jamboree."

Two other fifty-thousand-watt stations in America's heartland developed barn dances: KVOO in Tulsa, famous as the longtime home of Bob Wills and his Texas Playboys, developed a show under the direction of Herald Goodman (who had been a member of the Vagabonds on the "Grand Ole Opry") called "Saddle Mountain Roundup." "The Southwest's Greatest Barn Dance," in 1938. The stars were Goodman, singing cowboy Ray Whitley, and the fiddle team of Georgia Slim (Rutland) and Big Howdy (Forrester). Similarly, Pappy Cheshire led a gang called his

Gene Autry. Courtesy Country Music Foundation.

Hill-Billy Champions over a CBS network barn dance out of KMOX in St. Louis, Missouri. Again, the show was short on the major names that seemed ultimately to make or break a barn dance, but it did feature Decca artist Sally Foster and one of the finest yodelers to come out of the era, Skeets Yaney.

Roy Acuff (at left) and his Crazy Tennesseans. Courtesy Les Leverett Archives.

Country music and the radio barn dance, however, were not restricted to just the Southeast and the Midwest in the 1930s, for by the end of the decade there were barn dances on both the East and West coasts of the nation. In New York (where country music had been active since the days of Vernon Dalhart), Crazy Water Crystals—a company that sponsored country music nationwide all through the 1930s—had sponsored a series of shows on WMCA, starring Zeke Manners and Elton Britt, who had recently returned from California having split with the original Beverly Hillbillies. By 1935 the sponsor and the artists had moved to WHN, and two singing cowboys who had come to the Big Apple to seek their fortune were named co-hosts: Tex Ritter and Ray Whitley, both of whom soon left for Hollywood to pursue film careers. The WHN "Barn Dance" lasted several years in all, and Manners followed it in 1938 with the "Village Barn Dance," broadcast live from Greenwich Village. On the West Coast there was the "Hollywood Barn Dance," hosted by Peter Potter. Gene Autry had made western music (and musical Westerns) quite a fad, and so the emphasis here was heavily on sagebrush symphonies: The show's stars were the Sons of the Pioneers, Ray Whitley, and Smiley Burnette. This cast formed the first all-star radio cast to tour the West Coast.

There were other, smaller nonsouthern barn dances that seemed to threaten to nearly glut the era: the WOWO "Hoosier Hop" from Fort Wayne, Indiana; the KMBC "Brush Creek Follies" from Kansas City, Missouri; the WFIL "Sleepy Hollow Ranch" from Philadelphia, and even the CKNX "Barn Dance," which originated in Wingham, Ontario. The existence of all these institutions goes to prove that country music and the barn dance were not at all exclusively southeastern or even Midwestern phenomena, but constituted a form of entertainment that appealed to rural North America as a whole.

Still, the barn dances that lasted longest are those that began in the Southeast; it was these (with the exception of the once-mighty "National Barn Dance") that supplied the nation with its country stars. Yet they too have mostly faded; today, the "Wheeling Jamboree" over WWVA and the "Grand Ole Opry" in its new home at Opryland are the sole survivors of a once strong tradition.

The whole barn-dance concept actually began in the Southwest in 1923, when WBAP in Fort Worth began its short-lived barn dance. Perhaps the scarcity of radios in the region made for the demise of the program, but it was obviously an idea whose time had come. WSB in Atlanta began its barn dance the next year, featuring the area's newfound recording star, Fiddlin' John Carson, and this show was to survive well into the 1940s. Within a couple more years WLS and WSM had started their barn dances. It is interesting that the first recording, the first million-selling record, and the formation of the three major barn dances in country music history all happened in the years between 1922 and 1925.

WSB's "Barn Dance" originally featured Fiddlin' John Carson, the Skillet Lickers, and others, but later on shifted to more modern entertainment such as James and Martha Carson and Cotton Carrier. This kind of shift in emphasis was undertaken by all major barn dances, and the idea that it was the "Opry" that began the shift from string bands to singing stars with the coming of Roy Acuff is actually erroneous: the "Opry," in fact, was rather recalcitrant in moving to singing stars, and proved rather inept until the coming of Acuff, when it did make the effort.

For some time the general impression (not denied by Acuff himself) seems to have been that when Acuff joined the "Opry" in 1938, he brought the art of vocalizing with him, and his tremendous success marked an abrupt shift in country music tastes away from string bands toward singing stars. It is evident from a quick glance at the makeup of most of the other barn dances that by 1938 *all* of them were devoted to the singing-star format and that Acuff came extremely late to be considered a trend setter. In fact, historians like Charles K. Wolfe and Richard Peterson have, with a minimum of research, discovered that the "Opry" was well into the process of becoming a singing-star-oriented program when Acuff arrived. Acuff's role was that of the singing star with enough talent and charisma to bring it off.

The move actually began in the early 1930s, when groups like the Vagabonds, the Delmore Brothers, and Asher and Little Jimmy Sizemore —with not a fiddle among them—were hired. The Vagabonds (composed of Dean Upson, Curt Poulton, and Herald Goodman) were a smooth-singing semipop trio who specialized in sentimental songs and who wrote one of the "Opry's" early hits, "Lamp-lighting Time in the Valley." Sentimental songs (with the age-old appeal of a talented child singing them) were the stock-in-trade of Asher and Little Jimmy Sizemore, and the Delmore Brothers' careful, intricate harmony, guitar lead, and strong blues influence were far from the string-band sound. They too had an early "Opry" hit, "Brown's Ferry Blues," in 1933. Zeke Clements and his Broncho Busters

The Vagabonds. Courtesy Doug Green.

featuring Texas Ruby—hardly a mountain string band—joined the "Opry" in 1933, and then there were Ford Rush, a WLS alumnus, and Jack Shook and the Missouri Mountaineers, both acts joining before Acuff and featuring heavy reliance upon vocals. Following their incorporation into the "Opry" came the arrival of Pee Wee King and his Golden West Cowboys—a big, slick band featuring a cowboy image and a penchant for western songs, and, soon after joining the "Opry," a spectacularly voiced young man called Eddy Arnold—in 1937.

Acuff, in this light, is obviously far more a part of a trend than a trend-setter. He was simply the most successful of the "Opry" vocalists, his "Great Speckled Bird," "Wreck on the Highway," and "Wabash Cannon-ball" becoming some of the biggest hits of the era. He was followed—again as a part of this trend—by Zeke Clements ("The Alabama Cowboy") and Bill Monroe (who despite the strong instrumental tradition of bluegrass, was best known on the "Opry" for his rafter-reaching tenor voice and crackling yodels) in 1939, and they in turn were followed by a parade of vocalists who marched into the 1940s: the Williams Sisters, Clyde Moody, Ernest Tubb, Wally Fowler, Eddy Arnold, Paul Howard, Red Foley, and many more.

If the "Opry" was late in finding the singing star of national stature they sought, they were still very much in the mainstream of barn-dance practice in attempting such a move. This is not to denigrate Acuff's importance —he literally put the "Opry" on the map nationally, and it is a tribute to his tremendous popularity that after only two years on the program (a period that qualified him only as a relative rookie) he was chosen to host the "Opry's" first radio network tieup, the "Prince Albert Grand Ole Opry" in 1939, and to star in the first movie about the show, *Grand Ole Opry*, in 1940. It was not until the end of the 1940s, when Ralston Purina picked up an Opry show starring Eddy Arnold and featuring Bill Monroe, Curly Fox & Texas Ruby, Uncle Dave Macon, and Rod Brasfield for network broadcast, that the "Opry" began to challenge the "National Barn Dance" for the No. 1 national slot.

Other southeastern barn dances sprang up in the 1930s, and their histories are pretty much a repetition of the same formula: WWVA in Wheeling, West Virginia, for instance, began their well-known "Wheeling Jamboree" in 1933 as a string-band program, but quickly expanded in popularity with the addition of its first star vocalists, Cowboy Loye and Just Plain John the following year, who were joined by longtime favorite Doc Williams and the Border Riders in 1937.

The barn dances that began toward the end of the decade followed the then-standard formula: They featured singing stars hosting the shows, with little mention of string bands or "authentic" old-time music. WHAS in Louisville began broadcasting the "Renfro Valley Barn Dance" in 1937 with Red Foley and later Ernie Lee as hosts. (Cincinnati's "Boone County Jamboree" on WLW also had Foley as its headliner for a while, the star

obviously being as important as the format as the decade rolled along.) WRVA in Richmond, Virginia, began its "Old Dominion Barn Dance" at the close of the decade, with its longtime star Sunshine Sue at the helm. The only anachronism seemed to be the "Crazy Water Crystals Barn Dance" over WBT in Charlotte, North Carolina, which emphasized a fine string band, Mainer's Mountaineers—but even they proved most successful with Wade Mainer's vocalizing on songs like "Maple on the Hill" and "Sparkling Blue Eyes."

The 1930s, then, were marked by a tremendous proliferation of barn dances, particularly in the early part of the decade when the Depression laid low much of the record industry. In a way, the move to singing stars over string bands can be seen as a function of this very process: nostalgia-oriented string-band-heavy barn dances were valuable alternatives for the fans when recordings by Dalhart, Rodgers, the Carter Family, and others were still affordable. When the records became difficult to afford, it was more than logical that radio should step in to try to fill both needs. Barn-dance shows, still carefully maintaining that nostalgic image and flavor yet stocked with singing stars who sang the latest hits (and their own if they had them), became the order of the day.

While the barn dance is a handy reference factor, there was plenty of other national country music activity in the 1930s. In fact, the landscape of country music reflected in great measure the vast panorama that was the working America of the decade: farmers, dust bowl refugees, factory workers, the elderly, the young, those entranced by show business or the magic of Hollywood or radio or record, the small-businessman, the thousands who made up rural and small-town America, who heard in the country music of the time a nostalgic return to pioneer (or at least prejazz) America—either that or their own feelings and emotions expressed for them with an eloquence they could not achieve themselves.

Take California, for instance. When the Sons of the Pioneers formed in 1933, with their sole emphasis on songs of the range, the plains, and the cowboy, they were commonly assumed to be Texans. In fact, their makeup was extremely diverse, demonstrating the already wide spread of country music: Bob Nolan was a Canadian; Len Slye (Roy Rogers) was from Duck Run, Ohio; and Tim Spencer was a native of Missouri. Only the Farr Brothers (Hugh and Karl) were Texans, who had migrated to California to find work in the 1920s—and even they were hardly Texas cowboys, a major portion of their ancestry being American Indian.

The early 1930s in California found the Beverly Hillbillies, who had formed in the 1920s, still going strong, and Texan Stuart Hamblen, who had formed his Lucky Stars in California, scoring big hits with "Texas Plains" and "My Mary"—and Gene Autry's success on the screen as a singing cowboy proved so monumental that an entire chapter of this history is devoted to the subject. Suffice it to say here that, never slow to pick up on a

The Sons of the Pioneers. Courtesy Bob Pinson.

money-making idea, Hollywood began cranking out hordes of these "horse operas," and a stampede of singing cowboys rushed to Hollywood from all over the country to fill the demand: Tex Ritter and Ray Whitley from New York City, Bob Baker from Colorado, Art Davis and Bill Boyd from Texas, Johnny Bond and Jimmy Wakely from Oklahoma, and Eddie Dean from Chicago. Although occasionally caught in the Hollywood glitter, these men at one time or another made some exceptionally fine country music of the era on record, on transcription, on film, or in person.

Texas, too, has made such a mark on country music that it has been assigned an entire chapter of this history. We should note here, however, that the single most impressive characteristic of Texas music in the 1930s was its diversity. Within the era, the music of Bob Wills, the Light Crust Doughboys, and Milton Brown had come to be called western swing, one of the most popular sounds in the country. Texas, moreover, had sent its share of singing cowboys to Hollywood, and yet it was also the home of of two of the most popular of the gospel singing groups, the old-fashioned Stamps Quartet and the more modern Chuck Wagon Gang, who pioneered the bridging of the gap between country and gospel music.

In this era Texas produced Cajun music in the far eastern part of the state and fostered the unusual combination of western swing and Bohemian dance music in the person of San Antonio's Adolph Hofner. Honky-tonk got its start with Crisp's Ernest Tubb and Denton's Al Dexter.

Big (but not necessarily swing) bands reigned in Texas as well, Bill Boyd's Cowboy Ramblers providing two big instrumental hits ("Under the Double Eagle" and "Lone Star Rag"), while Ted Daffan's Texans became known nationwide for Daffan compositions like "Worried Mind," "No Letter Today," "Heading Down the Wrong Highway," and the country music classic "Born to Lose." Yet solo singers like Tex Owens ("Cattle Call") and old-fashioned duets like the Shelton Brothers ("Just Because") also thrived in this region and decade.

Texas' neighboring state, Louisiana, was also active musically. Famous for the Cajun music that continues to hallmark the state's sound, it also was the home of Jimmie Davis, who started his career as a Jimmie Rodgers imitator in 1929 but who had a stream of hits on Decca Records, including "Nobody's Darling," "Sweethearts or Strangers," "It Makes No Difference Now," and of course the ubiquitous "You Are My Sunshine," in the 1930s.

Texas' neighboring nation, Mexico, managed to provide some of the most interesting, bizarre, and influential music of the decade, thanks to the so-called X stations (Mexico's radio stations were assigned the initial letter X, like the United States' W and K and Canada's C), which boomed tremendous amounts of country music over North America during the decade.

The Mexican border station era was introduced by a shady and fascinating entrepreneur named Dr. J. R. Brinkley, who lost his radio license in Milford, Kansas, because of his more-than-questionable goat-gland op-

Bob Wills (at left) and his Texas Playboys. Courtesy Bob Pinson.

eration designed to restore sexual potency to men. Brinkley moved to Mexico in 1930, setting up station XER at Villa Acuña, stationed right across the border from Del Rio, Texas. The main features of XER and the many other X stations that followed were country music and innumerable ads for patent medicines, geegaws, baby chicks, and the like. Bill Malone, in *Country Music U.S.A.*, quotes one of the owners of such a station as saying "[this] programming . . . was giving listeners the unsophisticated material that the big networks neglected."

For whatever the reason, a number of important country entertainers were prominent on these border stations, either live or (more frequently) on transcriptions: The original Carter Family ended up their careers on XERA (1935–41); also featured on such stations at one time or another were the Delmore Brothers; the Pick-

ard Family; the Callahan Brothers; Mainer's Mountaineers; J. R. Hall ("the Utah Cowboy"), Roy Faulkner ("the Lonesome Cowboy"), who moved with Brinkley from Milford to Del Rio; and the king of the border stations, Cowboy Slim Rinehart.

The reason the border stations were so influential was their tremendous range. It seems that in the early days of radio, the governments of the United States and Canada divided up the long-range broadcast band between them, leaving neither Mexico nor Cuba with any clear channels at all. Understandably miffed, the Mexican Government did not apply the fifty-thousand-watt upper limit to a station's broadcast power stipulated by the United States and Canada, so even when WSM and WLS were at their peak, broadcasting at fifty thousand watts on a clear channel, they were no match for border stations blasting across the entire West at two, three, and as much as ten times their power. The old story that you could tune in one of the Mexican stations simply by sticking your head up against the nearest barbed-wire fence sounds too good to be true, but it does illustrate the immense power generated from across the border. The stations came in as clear as locals well into Canada, and for those who cared to listen (and put up with the relentless advertising), they provided a fine source of often excellent (and sadly underrecorded) country music.

Another rather unlikely locale for country music was Miami, where a handsome San Antonio cowboy named Red River Dave McEnery, who kept bouncing in and out of New York City all through the decade, was the chief radio attraction. Best known in the 1930s for his "Amelia Earhart's Last Flight," he achieved notoriety in the 1970s for "The Ballad of Patty Hearst." Other local favorites of the Miami area were the Rouse Brothers, best known for their instrumental classic "Orange Blossom Special."

As far—ethnically and regionally—from Miami was Milwaukee. Although heavily influenced by the "National Barn Dance" sound, the area retained its own ethnic flavor and in the 1930s gave country music one of its best-liked characters and best songwriters: an accordionist of Polish descent who became known as Pee Wee King. He began his career in Milwaukee dance bands (his father was a polka-band leader), but, always enamored of the western image, he formed his Golden West Cowboys after apprenticing with Frankie

More's Log Cabin Boys in Louisville. Similarly, Red Blanchard, longtime fixture of the last gasps of the "National Barn Dance," got his start on several Wisconsin radio stations.

The Great Lakes provided starts for a few more entertainers: Skeets Mac-Donald got his start on WEXL in Royal Oak, Michigan, and WFDF in Flint, the same place from which Little Jimmy Dickens was to launch his career a few years later. In fact, the Detroit area was to be a fruitful one for country music during the war years—Ernie Lee, Jerry Byrd, and others appeared there—but only after the influx of Southerners into the war plants. Rural Michigan listened to a good deal of WLS talent, but actually produced rather little of its own.

Yet another northern industrial city had a surprising amount of country music in the 1930s: Pittsburgh's KDKA (the station famous for pioneering radio by broadcasting returns of the 1920 presidential election) featured, at one time or another in the decade, ex-Skillet Lickers Clayton McMichen and Slim Bryant, Mac and Bob, and Bradley Kincaid.

Bradley Kincaid, a Kentuckian who pioneered country music on WLS while in college in 1922, deserves a great deal of credit for opening up the Northeast to country music, for although he was with barn dances on WLS, WLW, and WSM at different times in his long career, he spent the bulk of the 1930s on WBZ in Boston, WGY in Schenectady, New York, WTIC in Hartford, Connecticut, and WHAM in Rochester, New York. His taste ran to pure mountain folk music, and may well explain the Northeast's historic preference for that particular facet of country music, as opposed to more "modern" types. Other country music stars spent time in New England during this time as well: Grandpa Jones in Hartford, Otto Gray in Schenectady, and Yodelin' Slim Clarke in Maine.

Proceeding farther north, Canada was in those days—as it still is—a thriving country music area, although in the 1930s attention centered pretty much around three individuals: Wilf Carter, a yodeling cowboy who found fame in the United States after moving to New York City and billing himself as Montana Slim; a young Nova Scotian who first began recording in the 1930s as The Yodeling Ranger (in imitation of his idol Jimmie Rodgers, the Yodeling Brakeman), Hank Snow; and Don Messer, a fiddler who led a large semipop dance band he called his Islanders, because of their association with CFCY on Prince Edward Island.

Perhaps the most surprising of all, however, was the activity in New York City, where a considerable amount of country music was heard locally, on network and local radio and on records, during the 1930s. Those who were there at the time say it was definitely an uphill battle for acceptance, but there appeared to be at least enough interest for a country music "scene" to thrive throughout the decade. For one thing, New York City was left with the legacy of Vernon Dalhart and Carson J. Robison, both of whom were still quite influential as the decade opened. Early in the period, Frank Luther and Zora Layman,

Zeke Manners, Ray Whitley, Tex Ritter, and Elton Britt came to the Big Apple, many of them appearing on WMCA, which had a six-city hookup ranging as far north as Boston and as far south as Washington, D.C. Rex Cole's Mountaineers had a long-running show on a rival station, and when WHN began their "Barn Dance," they dipped deeply into this pool of talent, hiring as co-host the young Texan who was aspiring toward a career on the Broadway stage, Tex Ritter.

Wilf Carter (as Montana Slim) proved a success on network radio, and Denver Darling became a long-time fixture of the scene, introducing superyodeler Rosalie Allen (herself from Old Forge, Pennsylvania) late in the decade. Perhaps the most interesting of the New York City musicians, though, was a young Okie who apprenticed on radio in California, where he became increasingly sympathetic to the plight of his fellow migrants, drifting through the Depression as described in *The Grapes of Wrath*. Becoming increasingly political, Woody Guthrie left behind his country-singer aspirations (which his cousin Jack did not, becoming a popular country singer of the 1940s) and moved to New York, where he became the darling of the socially conscious set and the founder of a whole movement of American music quite on his own. More than any of the self-conscious folk singers to come out of the 1940s, Woody Guthrie's roots as a 1930s country singer were quite evident, nowhere more than in the many melodies taken directly from Carter Family songs to which he wrote his own words, for example, "Wild-wood Flower" becoming "Reuben James," and "Little Darling Pal of Mine" becoming "This Land Is Your Land."

The other area where country music was surprisingly strong—as surprising, in a way, as New York City—was the Great Plains. Eddie and Jimmie Dean, for instance, played stints in Yankton, South Dakota (WNAX), and Topeka, Kansas (WIBW), before heading to Hollywood, and Bill and Charlie Monroe worked Shenandoah, Iowa, and Grand Island, Nebraska, before heading to the area of their greatest fame, Charlotte, North Carolina. The Willis Brothers played in such far-flung outposts as Shawnee, Oklahoma, and Gallup, New Mexico, while Dr. Brinkley, as noted, pioneered country music in Milford, Kansas, using the talents of Fiddlin' Bob Larkin and Roy Faulkner ("the Lonesome Cowboy") between pitches for his goat-gland operation. The reason why there wasn't more local country music actually was twofold: the fifty-thousand-watt power of WLS beaming in from the Midwest and the fantastic coverage of the hundred-thousand-watt-plus border stations to the south. Given the small and widely scattered population and a half-dozen radio stations that could be picked up as well or better than local five-hundred- or five-thousand watters, there was little need for the local stations at all, and in fact they were scarce in the Great Plains in the 1930s.

Finally, regarding regional diversity in country music, it is interesting to look at the rise of country music parks—now a widespread phenomenon, and in a sense the precursor of the outdoor bluegrass festivals currently in vogue. Probably the first outdoor park was opened by Buck and Tex Ann Nation, a couple of New York City country music personalities, in 1934. This was the C-Bar-C Ranch in Pennsylvania, a state that has always been among the most active in its support of country music. Four other parks—Sleepy Hollow Ranch, Sunset Park, Himmelreich's Grove, and Ravine Park—opened up in the area shortly thereafter and, significantly enough, when the Nations decided to relocate the C-Bar-C Ranch in 1941, their move was not to the south, but north to Maine. It was not until 1948, in fact, that such parks began opening in the Southeast, perhaps the most famous being Roy Acuff's Dunbar Cave near Clarksville, Tennessee, and Bill Monroe's Bean Blossom near Nashville, Indiana.

In short, the point is that country music was a nationwide phenomenon in the Depression-to-World War II era, not something introduced to Northerners by southern soldiers or defense workers, as has been commonly assumed (although, of course, this kind of interaction took place as well).

Regional diversity, however, was not the most impressive or even the most important characteristic of the decade: rather, it was the surge of creativity in all regions, seemingly all at once, that made for the staggering musical diversity of the period. It is little wonder, considering that this widespread diversity allowed for nearly every taste, from crude to slick, from blues to pop, from Anglo-American ballad to big-band instrumental, from fiddle breakdowns to modern love songs, that the music spread so widely.

The decade began with the four major strains discussed earlier; they soon evolved and branched into a dozen or more. In the overview, the influence of Jimmie Rodgers was perhaps the most powerful of all; it must be remembered that the Mississippi Blue Yodeler spent a full half of his short six-year professional career in the 1930s a major portion of his most influential records coming after 1930 (although the effects of the Depression curtailed his total sales, as they did those of every other artist).

Of his songs, it has to be said that some are so rooted in their own time as to be hopelessly dated, while others are American classics. Probably his greatest legacy was his influence on young up-and-coming singers, who adopted his blues style before devel-

Jimmie Rodgers.

oping their own. His black-derived twelve-bar blue yodels were tremendously influential and frequently heard in the early part of the decade —far more, in fact, than his sentimental songs.

Gene Autry, for example, perfected the Rodgers style to the degree that their voices are virtually indistinguishable on record, and in fact the first hit record of many in Autry's long career was "Blue Yodel No. 5." Jimmie Davis was also a blue yodeler at first, recording such racy items as "Tom Cat and Pussy Blues" for Victor (Rodgers' own label!) long before his association with Decca. Bill Carlisle's first popular record was a blues called "Rattlesnake Daddy," and it is well known that both Ernest Tubb and Hank Snow were first influenced by Rodgers yodeling blues. That so many of the following decades' most influential performers began as blues yodelers is a testimony to the massive popularity of Jimmie Rodgers and his popularization of the blues; the fact that in every instance each of these Rodgers devotees went on to develop their own highly individualized styles is further testimony to the creativity of this most creative of decades.

The legacy of Ralph Peer's other August 1927 discovery, the Carter Family, also remained strong throughout the 1930s, although the Carters themselves, because they did not devote themselves to touring or the other necessities of show business, remained merely popular, not spectacularly so. Their main contribution to the music of the 1930s was their songs, which were obligatory in the repertoire of nearly every country act or singer of the era, particularly in the Southeast. Also, the remarkable and innovative guitar style of Maybelle Carter, who above any other single performer encouraged the use of the guitar as a lead instrument among aspiring musicians, was a powerful factor.

There was, in addition, a solo-singer tradition held over from the 1920s that was quite apart from the Jimmie Rodgers style and that is too often forgotten when the credit for turning commercial country music from an instrumental into a vocal form is meted out. Rodgers tends to get all the credit for this rapid reversal of trends, and while the magnitude of his popularity cannot be underplayed, there was a long and influential tradition of solo singers before he ever recorded, from Henry Whitter to Kelly Harrell to Carl T. Sprague to Bradley Kincaid. The king of them all, of course, was Vernon Dalhart, who sold millions of records and recorded thousands of sides under more than a hundred different pseudonyms. The importance of these men (with the exception of Kincaid) diminished in the 1930s, but the tradition they popularized and helped found continued with great vitality: During the 1930s, singers like Wilf Carter, Stuart Hamblen, Zeke Clements, Red Foley, Bob Miller, Tex Ritter, and many others emerged out of a solo-singing tradition (or traditions) quite removed from that of the Mississippi Blue Yodeler.

The fourth musical form at its peak when the decade began was the string band, a sound and a style that were to diminish alarmingly as the decade advanced. The most popular sounds

Arthur Smith and Jimmy Wakely. Courtesy Doug Green.

of the 1920s—provided by the Skillet Lickers, the Leake County Revelers, Charlie Poole and the North Carolina Ramblers, and others—receded very quickly in the face of the onslaught of singers and "stars." In the Southwest, fiddle-band music was quickly transmogrified by its rapid exposure (largely, again, due to radio) to pop, jazz, and blues into western swing; in the Northeast (with the exception of some holdouts in Canada) it disappeared entirely. Only in the musically conservative Southeast did the tradition survive, but we've already seen how rapidly the "Opry" moved away from the fiddle-band format by as early as 1933, and in fact the four major fiddle bands that have endured

the "Opry's" history (two, in fact, are still on the show) were members of the cast by the late 1920s. None has been added since. A couple of these southeastern fiddle bands, Arthur Smith and the Dixieliners and Mainer's Mountaineers, were able to achieve record-selling popularity in the 1930s (although many others, including the Skillet Lickers, were to remain local radio favorites).

Smith's sound was bluesy and unique, and he left a very important legacy to country music in his soulful fiddle style. He was assisted—at least in his years on the "Opry"—by two of the ablest old-time musicians in the business, Sam and Kirk McGee. A more versatile (and ambitious) man than his early Bluebird records and "Opry" appearances may have made him appear, Smith later went on to lead the backup band in several of Jimmy Wakely's singing cowboy films, playing surprisingly hot fiddle and even singing a tune or two.

Mainer's Mountaineers came out of North Carolina and were headed by the two Mainer brothers, a fiddler who went by his initials J.E., and his banjo-playing younger brother Wade, whose sprightly two-finger banjo style presaged the bluegrass music of a decade later. Although they were a fine breakdown fiddle band of the old school, Wade's banjo playing gave them a distinctive sound, and his clear, strong, evocative mountain voice was the factor that really accounted for the popularity of the band (at least on record). As Mainer's Mountaineers they had several popular records, among them "Wreck of the No. 9" and an old Carter Family gem, "Maple on the Hill." As brother acts often will, they eventually split, and Wade Mainer, with a new band called the Sons of the Mountaineers, was one of the last of the string bands to have a major hit record in the 1930s: "Sparkling Blue Eyes" in 1939. It is a fine performance of a fine song, and its success in that year is even more remarkable considering that it competed against a host of much more modern and slick records: Bob Wills' "San Antonio Rose," Autry's "Back in the Saddle Again," and Jimmie Davis' "It Makes No Difference Now."

The only string band to stay strong in the thirties and outlast Wade Mainer into the forties (although Mainer was active in that period, recording a host of fine sides for King) was one that achieved popularity late in the decade: Roy Acuff's Smokey Mountain Boys. But like Mainer's band, the emphasis was heavily on the singing. That Acuff, a tremendously popular singing star by 1940, should have chosen an old-fashioned string band for backup says more about him than it does about his success—he had the voice and the material that were right for the times, and would probably have been a success on record with any unobtrusive backing. In all fairness, however, he had long been a champion of traditional mountain

Mainer's Mountaineers. Courtesy Doug Green.

music, and he did have a superb old-time band whose powerful in-person musical and comedic effects were great aids to his stage shows.

While Acuff and the others mentioned above continued the pre-1930s traditions, however, others were at work developing the music. This, in fact, was the main thrust of the thirties.

There was, for example, the development of the mandolin-guitar duet style in old-timey music. Before 1930 there was very little of this tradition, the only significant activity being that of two blind musicians named Lester MacFarland and Robert Gardner, known professionally over WLS as Mac and Bob. Their simple, homey (though slightly stiff) sound—old or old-sounding songs, sung in harmony, accompanied by rhythm guitar, with the mandolin playing brief turn-arounds between verses—was, however, tremendously influential, and they were quickly followed at WLS by Karl and Harty (whose full names were Karl Davis and Hartford Connecticut Taylor), who played basically the same style, but composed some of the best and most successful traditionally oriented songs of the decade: "I'm Just Here to Get My Baby out of Jail," "The Prisoner's Dream," and "Kentucky."

The effects of this music were not lost on two Kentucky youngsters working in Chicago-area refineries, who eventually went with the WLS road show not as musicians but as square dancers in the early 1930s. They were Charlie and Bill Monroe, who created some of the most innovative, exciting, and certainly most popular duet music

The Monroe Brothers. Courtesy Doug Green.

of the middle 1930s. Bill's mandolin work, in fact, revolutionized the use of the instrument entirely—after his powerful, energy-charged, and lightning-fast solos were spread around on record, the instrument graduated from simple turn-around work to being a virtuoso instrument in and of itself.

Although Monroe himself continued to develop so rapidly as a musician that to this day, nobody has really been able to challenge his mastery of the instrument, he was challenged in the thirties. The challenger was Jethro Burns of Homer and Jethro, whose popular cornball humor sometimes effectively disguised brilliant and sophisticated musicianship. Jethro's mandolin style—syncopated, rhythmic, heavily influenced by jazz, and spacing notes in short, trumpetlike bursts—differed radically from Bill's approach, which was smooth, fluid, and above all played at a breakneck pace that left other musicians in awe.

The Monroe Brothers were popular for more reasons than Bill's revolutionary use of the mandolin, however. Their singing was high and forceful, and they played a great many of their tunes at racing tempos, a stirring contrast to the deliberate pace that characterized most comtemporary duets. Their voices did not express as much feeling—in the sense that the country singer uses that word—as musical excitement, an excitement in the music they were creating and an implicit challenge to others to try to top them (nobody ever accused either brother of being short of ego). Much of this same feeling pervades bluegrass (which Bill was to create after the Monroe Brothers split up in 1938) today. Although the Monroe Brothers recorded for only two short years (1936–38), much of their material influenced old-time and bluegrass bands of the future profoundly. They had one considerable hit record, "What Would You Give in Exchange for Your Soul?" in 1936.

The Blue Sky Boys (Bill and Earl Bolick) were influenced by the Monroe Brothers very directly—Bill Bolick was forced to take up the mandolin simply because of the many listener requests to feature the instrument, so greatly had Bill Monroe popularized it—but their approach to the same form and type of music was radically different from that of the Monroes. Concentrating on religious songs, sentimental songs, and some exceedingly lovely Anglo-American ballads, their tempos were slow and their voices were mournful, and they produced some of the most haunting music of the era. In fact, Bill Bolick has made some revealing comments about the audience they played to in the Depression-wracked South of the time: "People ask, 'Why did you sing so many sad songs?' Well, people weren't in the mood to hear a bunch of crazy junk all the time. There wasn't a heck of a lot of happiness then." The Blue Sky Boys were one of the few duets to remain popular throughout the 1940s (they officially retired in 1951), although World War II disrupted their career for five full years.

Another duet that first achieved popularity in the 1930s and managed to maintain it well into the next decade was the Callahan Brothers. Like the Blue Sky Boys, Homer and Walter Callahan were from North Carolina, but unlike the Bolicks, who never compromised their material, the Callahans adapted with the times. Moving steadily westward (Asheville, Knoxville, Cincinnati, Louisville, Tulsa), they settled in Texas, changed their names to Bill and Joe, and made a career playing the more swingy music of that region well into the 1950s. It is fascinating that the two duet teams that lasted the longest were those that used entirely different means to accomplish it: one, the Blue Sky Boys, holding a loyal following by refusing to adapt; the other, the Callahan Brothers, by adapting skillfully to changing tastes and regions.

Although there were several other fine duet teams—the Morris Brothers, the Shelton Brothers, the Allen Brothers—two youngsters from Limestone

The Blue Sky Boys with Red Hicks. Courtesy Doug Green.

County, Alabama, named Alton and Rabon Delmore formed the only 1930s duet team to gain contemporary parity with the Monroes, the Blue Sky Boys, and the Callahans. Among the first of the transition groups on the "Grand Ole Opry" who attempted to make a living at their music, they created an eclectic style with elements of blues, boogie, hymns, and old-time country. The opposite of the rural string bands, their music (played on rhythm and lead tenor guitar) was intricate, precise, smooth, and polished. They were among the first of the soft singers, and as Charles K. Wolfe points out in his *The Grand Ole Opry: The Early Years*, their acceptance as soft singers was made possible by technological improvements in microphones. They were extremely popular both on the "Opry" and after they left it, and their controlled, careful approach to performance set high musical standards that other duets and bands attempted to emulate. They were also prolific songwriters; "Brown's Ferry Blues," "Freight Train Boogie," "Blues Stay Away from Me," and many other classics came from their pens.

More than most of the other musical forms of the decade, the mandolin-guitar (or, in the case of the Delmores, the guitar-guitar) duet was based, in sound and repertoire, on traditional forms. Most of the other new music of the 1930s was more innovative, but even so, all of it relied heavily on the country music with which the nation entered the decade. For instance, western swing music—the history of which is detailed in Chapter Four—was a merging of the fiddle-band tradition with the jazz feel and repertoire of Jimmie Rodgers, with the addition of drums, brass, and reeds from pop music, the newly developed electric and steel guitars, and the psychological need for Depression-era rural America to get up and dance.

Similarly, the cowboy songs that originally came out of Texas were the very real bases for the traditionally oriented cowboy hits of the early 1930s: "Texas Plains," "The Strawberry Roan," and others. To this was added a suddenly booming film industry which, caught in the tremendous demand for singing-cowboy films, needed original cowboy songs badly. Into this void stepped many talented songwriters who, taking traditional cowboy songs as bases, wrote many of the classics of the era: Johnny Bond ("Cimarron"), Ray Whitley ("Back in the Saddle Again"), Eddie Dean ("Banks of the Sunny San Juan"), Tim Spencer ("Rainbow over the Range"), Jimmy Wakely ("Song of the Sierras"), Foy Willing ("Sing Me a Song of the Prairie"), Johnny Marvin ("Rainbow on the Rio Colorado") and even Fred Rose, who before his celebrated move to Nashville wrote dozens of songs for Gene Autry movies, one of which—"Be Honest with Me"—was nominated for an Oscar. Another Tin Pan Alley songwriter, Billy Hill, deserves a good bit of the credit for getting the whole western song boom rolling, for his

pop-oriented western songs quickly became cowboy classics: "Wagon Wheels," "The Last Roundup," and the like.

No mention of western songwriters would be half complete without the name Bob Nolan, one of the handful of the truly great country songwriters. It is a shame, in a way, that a songwriter's greatness is too often tied to number of record sales, for Bob Nolan's greatness has been partially hidden because western songs, despite their popularity on the screen, have traditionally been unexceptional sellers on record. And Bob Nolan's songs have, in overwhelming proportions, been western in theme. Still, no other country songwriter outside of Hank Williams and Fred Rose (together and apart) has come up with so many songs of such exquisite lyric and mel-

Bob Nolan. Courtesy Bob Pinson.

ody. Among the most memorable of the hundreds of his compositions are "Cool Water," "Tumbling Tumble-weeds," "A Cowboy Has to Sing," "Way Out There," "I Still Do," "Love Song of the Waterfall," "Blue Prairie," "Song of the Bandit," "Chant of the Wanderer," and "When Payday Rolls Around." Without question, Nolan is one of the underrated geniuses of country music.

Honky-tonk music was another form that developed in the 1930s. Like western swing, its creation and development are inextricably entwined with the state of Texas, and are dealt with in detail in the following chapter. Although the music achieved its greatest popularity in the 1940s and the 1950s, its roots are firmly planted in the late 1930s, when Al Dexter ("Honky-tonk Blues"), and Ted Daffan ("Headin' Down the Wrong Highway" and "Born to Lose") began to explore the problems that would so obsess postwar America. It was also in the Texas of the thirties that Ernest Tubb developed the honky-tonk style he would bring to the "Grand Ole Opry" in 1942, popularizing it in the Southeast as well as in the Southwest.

Cajun music also took its first steps toward national prominence in the 1930s, although it too had roots going back to the 1920s and long before. In one sense it was being influenced—modernizing, in a way—with the mixing in of instruments associated with western swing and other musical forms outside Cajun culture during the thirties, but at the same time it was influencing the musical styles in areas that surrounded it. The band that best symbolized this emergence

was the Hackberry Ramblers, which was probably the first and certainly the most popular Cajun band to mix other musical styles and repertoires with their traditional folk music. Recording western swing, pop, jazz, and straight-ahead country in a unique mixture of string band and traditional Cajun sound, they sang both in English and in Cajun French. Their popularity was regional, but at the same time their music was both influenced by and influential to the broader scope of country music and of American music in general.

Another ethnic music that played a role in the country music in the 1930s—albeit smaller and even more localized than Cajun—was the music of Mexico. Just as record companies formed budget-priced sublabels for blues and country (or, as they called these genres, "race" and "hillbilly"), they also had sublabels for Mexican recordings. For instance, Bluebird, a sublabel for Victor, had a subsub-label for their Mexican series, the lovely and familiar buff-and-blue Blue-bird label remaining the same in design but changing colors to buff and light green. The influence of the Mexican recordings was far from overwhelming, but they were very popular along the Texas border. They had a definite influence on western swing musicians who grew up in southern Texas, and made a distinct addition to the western swing repertoire, the standards "Cielito Lindo" and "La Golondrina" being the most famous of the Mexican tunes.

At the other end of the scale from these ethnic musics was the increasingly important self-conscious folk music beginning to appear among intellectuals and activists in New York City. These people were the first urbanites to succumb to the spell of what today might be called the John Denver syndrome among city dwellers: a romantic and unrealistic longing for country life and its supposed simplicity. Spurred on by the arrival of Woody Guthrie in 1938, urban folk music flourished, with singers like Burl Ives, Cisco Houston, and later Pete Seeger joining the fray. Although heavily political in overtone, this self-conscious folk music genuinely introduced thousands to folk, country, and country-like music, although the strength of this introduction was not to be felt until some twenty years later, when the legacy left by these people erupted in the "folk-song revival" of the late 1950s. This revival—the intellectuals' reaction to rock 'n' roll—had a tremendous revitalizing effect on traditionally oriented country music, and the effects are still very much in evidence.

While urban folk music was in its early stages an entirely different musical form was being born, and it too began to flourish in and outside the Southeast. This was country-oriented gospel music, music based on and taken from the hymns of the old Vaughan or Stamps-Baxter singing schools, then modified and blended with traditional country music styles. It was a trend that was to accelerate rapidly in the 1940s, but its original boom began in the 1930s with a group called the Chuck Wagon Gang. Although their first couple of sessions featured nonreligious songs ("Take Me Back to Renfro Valley," "Okla-homa Blues"), their repertoire from then to the present has been exclusively religious in nature. Their music, however, has always featured guitar, mandolin, and other instruments not at all associated with the traditional quartet-and-piano sound of gospel music. In this the Chuck Wagon Gang was unique, and this can be seen as a direct result of southwestern influences. While the repertoire of most southeastern bands was heavily dominated by religious material, the southwestern bands were different; twenty-eight of the Monroe Brothers' sixty recorded songs were sacred in nature, but Bob Wills recorded only one sacred song in his entire career, and the rare sacred songs of the singing cowboys were not traditional hymns but new compositions that reflected the outlook of the synthetic screen characters and/or a romanticized west. The Chuck Wagon Gang, operating mostly in the Southwest, was musically in tune with the country music of the Southwest, but lyrically sacred in the southeastern tradition.

A final innovative byway taken by country music in the 1930s was one we tend to think of as strictly a modern phenomenon (which goes hand in hand with the other common misconceptions about the regionality and supposed purity of country music in the era): the singer-songwriter. As country music became a real business in the 1920s, with more and more bands and singers recording, the limited reservoir of traditional material simply ran out. Also, as the nostalgia-oriented barn dances became more and more a showcase for the emerg-

The Chuck Wagon Gang. Courtesy Charles Wolfe.

ing stars, the public demand for new individualized material from these stars increased.

Jimmie Rodgers had enlisted the songwriting help of his sister-in-law Elsie McWilliams in the 1920s, and Carson J. Robison had migrated to New York City from Kansas mainly to become a songwriter, beginning a long and fruitful association with Vernon Dalhart upon his arrival. Dalhart's 1925 recording "The Death of Floyd Collins" had sparked a (still thriving) tradition of "event songs," and this too was part of the impetus toward more and more new original material. In fact, many of the biggest stars of the thirties wrote, co-wrote, or bought the material that made them famous; Gene Autry's "That Silver-haired Daddy of Mine" and Jimmie Davis's "Nobody's Darling" and "You Are My Sunshine" were examples of this phenomenon. Other popular bands and singers featured a high percentage of new material written by themselves; Bob Wills and Roy Acuff are good examples. Also, singer/songwriters like Rex Griffin ("The Last Letter") began to come to the fore, and it was in this area that Bob Nolan forged an entire country music genre almost single-handedly and Red River Dave began his career of "event songs" with "Amelia Earhart's Last Flight."

Country music in the 1930s, then, was nothing if not diverse—diverse in region, diverse in sound, diverse in personality. It was indeed the most creative single decade in the music's history. Yet for all this remarkable creativity, there were a great number of things that tremendously influenced and changed the music that were not in any way related to the genius of individual musicians or the greatness of certain bands. There were a host of interrelated technological innovations and business decisions that abruptly changed and altered the course of country music many times in many ways. An examination of country music in the 1930s would not be complete without at least a cursory look at technology and economics.

The influence of radio in the Depression has already been seen as a factor of primary importance in spreading the sound of country music, as much in the Midwest as in the South. In fact, the technological innovations of radio and record may well in themselves account for the tremendous surge of creativity that characterized the 1930s, for suddenly, aspiring musicians were able to hear varieties of music vaster and broader than they had ever imagined. As an example, Bob Wills' Texas Playboys recall that in their barnstorming days in the 1930s when they played the radio it was not to listen to country songs—those they knew well enough —but to tune in fresh and inspiring big bands and blues singers. Radio and records suddenly disseminated an enormous quantity and variety of music an open-minded musician was quick to use as building blocks for his development as a musician and eventually synthesize into his own style.

The increasing sensitivity of microphones during the 1930s was also a factor in changing the style of both radio and records. Combined with improvements in home receivers and speakers, this development made it possible for relatively low-volume, subtle singing to be recorded successfully and reproduced as adequately as louder, more dramatic singing. Thus during the thirties, the big-voiced exhortative singers of the 1920s (the Carters and Dalhart, for example) gave way to the gentler singers like Autry and the Blue Sky Boys. The shift in style was as much a result of improving technology as it was a product of musical creativity or changing public taste.

Nowhere is the implication of technology more evident than in the development of electric string instruments, which by the end of the decade radically changed the sound of country music. Although the technology needed to produce electric instruments was advanced enough by 1925 that an ex-Gibson engineer named Lloyd Loar marketed electric violins, mandolins, and basses, electric pickups on guitars weren't really used in pop, jazz, or country music until the middle 1930s. It is generally held that Bob Dunn, the innovative jazz-oriented steel guitarist for Milton Brown's Musical Brownies, first attached a crude pickup to his Martin Hawaiian guitar, thus bringing the electric steel guitar to western swing and eventually to all of country music. Leon McAuliffe of the Texas Playboys was not slow to follow Dunn's lead, and soon the sound of the electric steel was as indigenous to country music as that of the fiddle.

It was in the late 1930s that the electric guitar—played upright, as opposed to the steel—got hooked up as well, and soon western swing bands were all featuring electric rhythm and lead (which, like the steel, was not pioneered but popularized by another Texas Playboy, in this case Eldon Shamblin). Again, this sound spread rapidly to country music at large.

The spread of country music can be attributed to yet another set of technological advances: the increasingly well-built automobiles and the improved roads on which to drive them. For both band and fan, the simple existence of well-made cars and good roads made extensive touring both practical and profitable: The performer could better reach his public,

and, as importantly, his public could reach him as well.

The greatest economic/technological factors in country music's rapid spread during the thirties, however, were the new media, radio and records. Radio's sudden boom period was in large part due to the inability of a large segment of the population to purchase luxuries like records, which at the time sold for $.75 each, with some artists commanding as high as $1.25 per disc. Before the Depression, certain sublabels sold for as low as $.25, but not until 1934 did a brand-new company called Decca settle on a price of $.35 per disc, seriously undercutting the other labels since they featured their first-line artists (Bing Crosby, for example) at this price. This was a major breakthrough, which had an immediate effect on the rapid, healthy growth of the Decca company and put considerable pressure on the other labels to also cut their prices (Victor's Bluebird line, originally a reissue label, suddenly became the haven for their country, blues, and dance bands, and came out with a purchase price of, you guessed it, $.35). Decca had a healthy country catalogue throughout the 1930s (Jimmie Davis, Tex Ritter, Rex Griffin, Milton Brown, the Carter Family, the Shelton Brothers, Eddie Dean, the Sons of the Pioneers), but their main contribution was in driving the price of popular records down, making them affordable to the segment of the public that had given them up as an unnecessary luxury. Decca's move revitalized a sagging industry, and once again the important singers and groups of the era were recorded extensively on wax.

A second major reason for the revitalization of the once nearly moribund record industry (and one that gave a strong boost to western swing and virtually gave birth to honkytonk) was the development and promotion of the jukebox, which shortly after its introduction around 1935 became a national institution in taverns, truck stops, and restaurants. Jukebox operators bought thousands of records mainly western swing, for the big beat was easily heard on the contraption—and it did not take long before songs aimed at the jukebox's listeners appeared: Al Dexter's "Honky-tonk Blues" (1937) and Ted Daffan's "Truck Driver's Blues" (1939). The jukeboxes not only bolstered the record industry, but also did a lot to shape, change, and inspire an increasingly large part of country music style, taste, and form for years to come.

A third reason for the revitalization of the record business has to do with the playing of records over the radio, a phenomenon taken totally for granted today but one that met with intense resistance in its day. In fact, for years radio and records considered themselves rivals for the public's entertainment dollar, and often bitter rivals at that. Each side was resistant and competitive, their last thought that of co-operation. Radio saw its advantages lying in its spontaneity, having no need for anything so mechanical as records, while the record industry saw air play of their records simply as lost sales: Why would anyone buy a product they could hear for free? Hence the small print found on numerous records of the 1930s:

"Not Licensed For Radio Broadcast."

In the late 1930s, somewhere around 1937–38, this began to change. Radio men discovered the obvious economic advantages of paying one man to spin records rather than paying half a dozen to sing the same hit songs, and record men found, quite to their surprise, that far from damaging sales, air play boosted sales tremendously. Suddenly the record and radio industries, adversaries since 1920, found themselves scratching each other's backs. The result was greater profit for radio stations and greater profits and sales for the record companies. The proliferation of labels in the years that followed was a direct result of this Johnny-come-lately co-operation. The only people who lost out were the poor live musicians, who increasingly had to become recording artists to succeed.

With all these creative and technological changes conspiring together, the 1930s was truly a hotbed decade for country music. It was a decade that demanded, and received, escapist entertainment and dreamy musical romanticism, and the sources for the music were scattered all across the nation. The road to Nashville was embarked upon during this decade, but it was a road that came out of a thousand different paths. It was not until the "Prince Albert Show," featuring Roy Acuff and the Smokey Mountain Boys, went on network radio in 1939 that the "Grand Ole Opry" and the city of Nashville began to indicate their future dominance of the country music field.

Chapter Four

Music from the Lone Star State

Now, Texas is a big state: big in area, big in population. Still, its contributions to country music over the fifty-odd years of its recording history are far greater than its large size and numerous inhabitants.

There is a lot of talk these days about "Texas music"—its popularity has created a full-fledged cottage industry for journalists—but too often that talk ignores the fact that Texas music has been influencing country music from the very beginning. The list of accomplishments by sons and daughters of the Lone Star State is enormous, and includes the first country music recording, the first country music million seller, and five of the thirty members of the Country Music Hall of Fame: Autry, Reeves, Ritter, Tubb, and Wills. And Texas has produced major stars in every major form of country music with the exception of bluegrass, and has been the birth-place of many of them: singing cowboys, honky-tonk, and western swing.

Why the Lone Star State has produced such a magnificent lineup of country music's major stars, from Eck Robertson and Vernon Dalhart right on up to the creative, energetic Austin scene and the world-reknowned Willie Nelson Fourth of July Picnic, is a matter for conjecture. Regardless of the reasons, real or supposed, Texas' current vanguard position is not at all new to the state. It has been in the forefront of country music from the beginning.

Ethnic diversity, in and of itself, does not make for a thriving country music heritage; if it did, New York, Detroit, and Chicago would be active country music centers. But there is, on the other hand, little doubt that many musical cultures were influential in the development of Texas music. The state is a melting pot of vari-

A *Texas couple listening to the radio.* Courtesy Charles Wolfe.

ous ethnic strains, many of which survive even today, many of which were incorporated into Texas music, the variety called "western swing" in particular.

The most obvious of these ethnic strains and influences, the one that is the foundation for all of country music, is the Appalachian musical tradition of Anglo-American folk song and minstrelsy, a tradition brought over from the mountains of the Southeast to the plains of Texas by its first settlers. These musical ancestors of both Bob Wills and Bill Boyd were, like Davy Crockett and Sam Houston before them, transplanted Tennesseans. With them these settlers brought their fiddles, songs, hymns, and love of square dancing, and given this background—although time has altered the style—it is little wonder that the fiddle tradition was (and is) so strong in Texas. Bob Wills, for all his audible and visual antics, was a prize-winning old-time fiddler: his first-rate old-time fiddling was merely upstaged by the hot jazz of the super fiddlers he loved to employ.

This influence from the Southeast was far from a pre-1900 phenomenon, either: A popular mountain duet along the lines of the Monroe Brothers or the Blue Sky Boys named Homer and Walter Callahan were North Carolinians by birth and upbringing, but like many others of their era became enchanted with western music. In their early years they played in groups like the Cliff Dwellers and Frankie More's Log Cabin Boys; later they toured with singing cowboys Ray Whitley and Jimmy Wakely, and ended up their career in the late 1940s and early 1950s in Texas, among the stars of the "Big D Jamboree" in Dallas, where by then, for some peculiar reason, they had changed their names to Bill and Joe.

Of course, southeastern mountain-style fiddling and singing were far from the only influences. Texas has long had a heavy settlement of German, Bohemian, and other central European peoples, who brought their love of polkas, schottisches, and waltzes with them, forever to become associated with Texas music. In fact, it is they who left the squeeze-box accordion, a small affair capable of but one key and two chords, with the Cajuns on their way through Louisiana to Texas in the nineteenth century, contributing to the rich, distinctive sound of that musical style. At any rate, the German and Slavic influence has been especially strong in south-central Texas, where waltzes and polkas have been perennially popular among country bands and country fans.

The classic case is Adolph Hofner of San Antonio, still an extremely busy entertainer playing four to five days a week, never venturing across the state line. Hofner's career goes back to the 1930s and is thoroughly western swing in outline, but throughout he has recorded and performed in Bohemian as well as English, and one of his big-gest records, "Green Meadow Waltz," was sung in Bohemian. Today his band includes trumpets, fiddles, and accordions, and he blithely says, "If they want mariachi we give them that; if they want the Slavic we give them that; and if they want plain country we give them that too." He shrugs off his role as a living example of the mixing of three rich musical cultures in the music of Texas. The mixed tradition continues to this day with other performers: Young RCA recording artist Dottsy (real surname Brodt, the German word for bread) is from proud old German central Texas stock.

The Cajun of Louisiana, which owes at least the accordion to the German immigrants, has been another strong influence on the music of Texas, especially the bordering area of southeastern Texas. Cajun music was and is extremely popular in southeastern Texas, as popular as in the bayou country, and in fact the legendary Cajun fiddler Harry Choates spent most of his time in Texas: He did the majority of his recording in Houston, and died in the Austin jail in 1951. A Hank Williams-like figure, Choates died after a short, wild life at the age of twenty-eight, a regional celebrity, especially after his 1946 hit "Jole Blon."

Several figures moved interchangably between the worlds of Texas and Cajun music: Moon Mullican was a country star, a swing pianist, a blues singer, and one of his hits was "Jole Blon," which was also a hit for Red Foley and Roy Acuff and a bigger one yet for Choates. And the music itself was mixed and mingled as well, for while "Opry" singers sang "Jole Blon" in traditional Nashville style, Harry Choates borrowed instruments and styles from western swing, and one extraordinarily popular Cajun band of the 1930s, the Hackberry Ramblers, used instrumentation similar to southeastern string bands of the same era, with, of course, the exception that they sang in that curious patois known as Cajun French. And they were unafraid to venture outside familiar musical genres: One of their more popular records was "Fais Pas Ca," simply a Cajun version of the old blues classic "Trouble in Mind."

So Cajun gave to and took from country music in general and Texas music in particular, adding yet another ingredient to the rich ethnic stew that composes its sound.

Another such ingredient was the Norteño music of northern Mexico, which lent its distinctive sound to a region obviously eager to accept and adapt differing musical sounds. Aspiring musicians growing up in southern Texas were bound to be affected by this music, if not for its own compelling musical merits, then simply by having been so surrounded by it.

Different from the mariachi brass sound, which also had a profound effect on Texas music, the Norteño market was treated by the major labels much like "race" and "hillbilly" music were in their infancy, with specialty sublabels manufactured specifically for the Tex-Mex audience. Victor's lovely buff-and-blue Bluebird label, for example, was a familiar sight to most country record buyers, who picked up the Monroe Brothers, the Delmore Brothers, the Blue Sky Boys, the Prairie Ramblers, and Bill Boyd;

Moon Mullican. Courtesy Doug Green.

similarly, the buff-and-green Bluebird label was as popular in many parts of Texas, only here the stars were Lidya Mendoza and Narciso Martinez.

The sound was close harmony, twelve-string guitar, bass, and accordion, once again introduced by the German and Slavic settlers. And so close was the relation between Anglo and Norteño music at times that, for example, the Tune Wranglers, a country swing group of the 1930s, had several songs coreleased on Bluebird's

Mexican series as Tono Hombres, "Ye Old Rye Waltz" becoming "Centenos Vals" and "Rainbow" becoming "Arco Iris." Conversely, Mexican artists like El Ciego Melquiades (The Blind Fiddler) and Bruno Real had occasional records released in the standard U.S. series.

So the Tex-Mex music of late is really nothing new to native Texans, and while the coming of Johnny Rodriguez and Freddy Fender may seem to many country fans as the opening of new doors and the breaking of old taboos, it is old hat to the creators of Texas' music, who assimilated long ago this Norteño music as well as mariachi, German, Appalachian, Slavic, the blues, and many other strains to form the many thriving, energetic forms of the music of the Lone Star State.

Yet another field to which Texas has contributed significantly has been gospel music, especially in the persons of the Chuck Wagon Gang, consisting of D. P. (Dad) Carter and three of his children, Rose, Anna, and Ernest, whose odd combination of cowboy (or at least frontier) image and gospel material made them popular for decades. They were first formed in Lubbock around 1933, but made their greatest impact in the Fort Worth area. In fact, their radio show —sponsored by Bewley Mills—went on the air over WBAP just before the Light Crust Doughboys' program, sponsored by Burrus Mill. Although their first recording sessions consisted of both secular and sacred material, they soon switched to an all gospel format, for which they became best known.

A trio called the Herrington Sisters (Winnie, Ida Nell, and Olga) had a similar approach, doing about half gospel and half country, folk, or sentimental material. Based in Wichita Falls, they boomed out over the entire central United States on that strange chapter in the history of Texas and of commercial radio, the Mexican border stations.

One of the most famous names in gospel music, the Stamps Quartet, originated in the Lone Star State as well. They became popular over KRLD in Dallas, and, interestingly, some of their early (about 1929) Columbia recordings featured guitar, although they soon settled into the piano/vocal quartet formation that was to become the hallmark of gospel quartets for years to come.

Yet all of these influences are but part of the story, for while they are important ingredients indeed, they are still added ingredients, spices for the two basics of Texas music: the songs of the singing cowboy and the music of the square-dance fiddle band, which not only formed the foundation for the music of the Lone Star State, but that are still dominant today.

Cowboy music and song began as early as the first settlers in the Alamo days of the 1830s, although the occupational songs of cowboy life with which we are familiar today did not really come into being until after the Civil War, when the West began to develop rapidly. What the settlers brought with them were the popular songs of the East and the folk songs and tunes of their particular ethnic culture, particularly England and Ire-

The Herrington Sisters. Courtesy Bob Pinson.

land, from where, in fact, many of the original cowboys had emigrated.

The lonely, if romantic, image of the cowhand and his guitar crooning his cattle to sleep is largely a figment of the imagination of writers of Western novels, films, and songs. In actuality, the guitar was a relative latecomer to the West, and it was certainly an impractical instrument to carry around on horseback—too large and too fragile. The cowboy did indeed sing, both to his cattle and to occupy his time, but except in rare instances the songs were, much like his work, monotonous and dreary, his voice rough (a turn-of-the-century writer said, no doubt with accuracy, "whatever voice he had to begin with he lost bawling at cattle"), and his vo-

calizing unaccompanied by any instrument.

Well before the turn of the century it became the practice of newspapers in the West to publish the poems of would-be bards of the West (among whom were some genuine cowboys), and some of these verses caught on with the public. Usually put to an old tune, they were quickly assimilated into folk repertoire. It was here that the classic ballads of the West were born, these poems set to one of the handful of tunes that made up the bedrock of the cowboy repertoire. And many were to become classics: "Little Joe the Wrangler," "Utah Carroll," "The Zebra Dun," "The Strawberry Roan," and many others.

Although cowboy song was a thriving tradition in Texas, no authentic versions were actually recorded until 1925, when upon the mammoth success of "The Prisoner's Song," a Texan named Carl T. Sprague ventured to the Victor Company in New York to see if he just couldn't do as well trying his hand at this newish business of recording. His "When the Work's All Done This Fall" was to sell some nine hundred thousand records beginning with the following year, and from that point on cowboy songs were here to stay.

The 1920s saw a rash of cowboy songs sung by Texans: Dalhart himself, although hardly a cowboy singer, had a significant number of western songs in his repertoire, "The Dying Cowboy" and "Home on the Range" among many others. Others, like Sprague, stuck almost strictly to cowboy songs: Jules Verne Allen and the Cartwright Brothers, for example. And, in his early period, even Stuart Hamblen's first recording nickname was "Cowboy Joe." Hamblen was to become famous in the 1930s with songs like "Texas Plains" and "My Mary," and after his celebrated conversion at a Billy Graham crusade, for sacred and semisacred songs like "This Ol' House" and "It Is No Secret (What God Can Do)." So dramatic was the conversion, in fact, that the former hell-raiser ran for President on the Prohibition ticket in 1952.

The cowboy image proved a popular one on record, and even the Mississippi Blue Yodeler, Jimmie Rodgers, recorded several cowboy songs such as "When the Cactus Is in Bloom," "Cowhand's Last Ride," and "Yodel-

ing Cowboy," and had at least one publicity photo made of himself in full cowboy regalia—ten-gallon hat, chaps, and all. His glamorization of the cowboy and cowboy life certainly helped move cowboy music farther into the realm of mainstream country music, and his widely heralded move to Kerrville has increased his identification with the state of Texas throughout the years, despite his Deep South roots and raising.

Texas' cowboys moved right into the 1930s as well, as Tex Owens became a major country-music star with his version of "Cattle Call," and Cowboy Slim Rinehart became the king of the border stations, that peculiar, even bizarre, segment in radio's history. Yet by far the greatest glorification of Texas music and cowboy music came not via record but via film, and it was Texas singers who, for by far the largest part, were so influential in the creation and propagation of the popularity of that colorful bit of Americana known as filmdom's singing cowboy.

Easily the most authentic of these heroes of the silver screen was Woodward Maurice Ritter, who learned to love authentic cowboy songs and ballads from noted scholar J. Frank Dobie while attending the University of Texas in Austin. Ritter spent a year at Northwestern University Law School near Chicago before heading for New York for a career on the stage, where he appeared in some half-dozen stage productions (acquiring the nickname Tex in the process) starring in an extremely popular radio series called "Cowboy Tom's Roundup," and hosting a country-music barn dance called the WHN "Barn Dance" before heading West to pursue a career in films.

Tex's first recordings—for ARC (the American Record Company) in 1933—are probably as close to authentic cowboy performances as were ever commercially recorded: Sung with deliberate lack of sophistication (Ritter later proved himself to be a far better singer), with little attention paid to time or meter, and only a rudimentary guitar accompaniment, it is easy to see why these records ("Good-bye, Old Paint," "A-riding Old Paint," "Every Day in the Saddle," and "Rye Whiskey") didn't sell. But they are a fascinating look into an authentic re-creation of a sound.

Ritter was to become one of America's most popular film stars of the 1930s, and in the 1940s he decreased his recording of cowboy songs and recorded a barrage of hit country love songs: "There's a New Moon Over My Shoulder," "You Two-timed Me One Time Too Often," and "Jealous Heart" among them.

Although his screen career pretty much ended in 1945, he maintained great visibility throughout the 1950s through his hosting of "Town Hall Party" in Los Angeles, his recording a set of children's records of cowboy songs that seems nearly ubiquitous among those who grew up in that era, and for his Academy Award-winning rendition of the theme song of the 1953 film *High Noon*. A great lover of authentic cowboy and country music, Ritter was one of the guiding forces behind the Country Music Hall of Fame and was throughout his long career one of the most visible,

accessible, and knowledgeable proponents of Texas music the Lone Star State ever had.

But Ritter was not the first film singing cowboy by any means. He was preceded on the screen in that role as early as 1930 by Ken Maynard in *Song of the Saddle*. Maynard sang, fiddled, and strummed banjo and

Tex Ritter. Courtesy Doug Green.

Ken Maynard. Courtesy Doug Green.

guitar in many of his films, providing musical interludes between the action sequences. Maynard even did a bit of recording in 1930, the old black Columbia label reading "Ken Maynard (The American Boy's Favorite Cowboy)." However, his career on records was neither long nor particularly distinguished.

One of the many western harmony trios also had roots in Texas: Although long-time Autry backup band The Cass County Boys all met in Los An-geles, they took their name from lead singer Fred Martin's home county of Cass in, of course, Texas.

Although Maynard was technically the first cowboy to sing, the first singing cowboy brought into film specifically in that role—whose action sequences were, as opposed to Maynard's, simply interludes between songs—was yet another Texan named Gene Autry. Born on a ranch near Tioga, Autry actually spent his teenage years in Sapulpa, Oklahoma, but in both locations he became a good rider and developed his talents as a singer and entertainer as well. Although for quite some time he had no serious plans of a career in music, he had at least flirted with the idea: He ran away from home while still in high school to join the Fields Brothers Marvelous Medicine Show.

Autry foundered for a style for a time; rumor had it that he even auditioned with Al Jolson's "Sonny Boy" on his first round of record-company tryouts, and was told to go back to Oklahoma (where he was employed as a telegrapher) and practice his guitar and to try to learn some tunes like this hot new sensation named Jimmie Rodgers. Autry returned the following year (1929) apparently having taken this advice to heart: His early records for Grey Gull, Okeh, Gennett, and Victor are virtually indistinguishable from Rodgers. However, around 1930 Autry began to develop his own style and to exploit his authentic western background by surrounding himself with the trappings of cowboy regalia. He obtained a spot on WLS in Chicago as Oklahoma's Yodeling Cowboy, and there he had the first of his many megahits, "That Silver Haired Daddy of Mine." By 1933 he was firmly in the cowboy mold, and he introduced such songs as "The Last Roundup" (1933) and "Tumbling Tumbleweeds" (1934) to country audiences via record, and they responded warmly (Chapter Five describes Autry's career in detail).

Meanwhile, in Hollywood, studio head Herbert J. Yates and producer Nat Levine had come up with the concept of a singing cowboy in a film series, and the popular young singer with the cowboy image, the blond hair, and the flashing smile was chosen. It is said that while casting that they found actors who could sing but couldn't ride, and actors who could ride but couldn't sing, before settling on Autry, the singer who could ride but couldn't act.

If anything, however, his naïveté and ingenuousness before the camera made him somehow more appealing, and he was not just a hit, he was a sensation. The success of his first few films not only delineated a new country-music genre in and of itself, but also opened the floodgates for the horde of singing cowboys who poured in from all over the nation in the next decade: Ritter from Texas via New York, Ray Whitley from Alabama also by way of New York, Roy Rogers from Ohio, Bob Baker from Colorado, Eddie Dean from Texas by way of Chicago, Jimmy Wakely and Johnny Bond from Oklahoma, Monte Hale from Texas, bandleaders Bill Boyd and Art Davis from Texas, Rex Allen from Arizona by way of Chicago, and on and on.

Two place names keep cropping up here: Chicago and Texas, for the "National Barn Dance" and WLS were not only the training grounds for Autry, but for Dean and Allen as well; and Texas, in the vanguard of this movement to begin with, provided a host of musicians and actors for the industries of film and of record.

Eddie Dean had teamed with his brother Jimmie (no relation to fellow Texan Jimmy Dean of "Big Bad John" and pork sausage fame; these Dean Brothers were born with the surname Glosup in Posey, Texas) and apprenticed on the "National Barn Dance" before heading West. Eddie appeared in many Tex Ritter films before starring in his own series for PRC in 1946–49, while Jimmie never got the breaks as an actor but was an essential part of several groups as a singer and musician, notable among them the popular band led by yet another Texan, Foy Willing and the Riders of the Purple Sage. Eddie achieved his greatest fame as a songwriter, however, not an actor, his "One Has My Name, the Other Has My Heart" and "Hillbilly Heaven" the best known among many.

Foy Willing's Riders of the Purple Sage were similar (although far from identical) to a group whose close harmony singing defined the style for all western groups to come: the Sons of the Pioneers. Often associated with Texas, none of the cofounders were from anywhere near the state (Bob Nolan from Canada, Len Slye—later known as Roy Rogers—from Ohio, and Tim Spencer from Missouri), but two extremely important later members were indeed Texans, Hugh and Karl Farr, the fiddle-and-guitar brother team whose sound was integral to that of the Pioneers.

Bill Boyd and Art Davis approached Hollywood from a different angle but were nonetheless from the Lone Star State, Boyd the guitar playing leader of a band called his Cowboy Ramblers (best known for "Under the Double Eagle" and "Lone Star Rag"), while Davis, himself an ex-Cowboy Rambler, first joined Gene Autry as his fiddle player before going into films himself, and, in the early 1940s,

fronting his own western swing band, the Rhythm Riders.

On the other hand, a Texas singing cowboy who was mostly an actor was Monte Hale. Although he sang in many movies (he was hired as a backup to Roy Rogers, should Rogers defect from the studio or make difficult contract demands, much as Rogers had himself been hired during a disagreement between Republic Studios and Gene Autry) and recorded for MGM and other labels, he never really caught on with the record-buying country-music audience. Nevertheless, he enjoyed a brief heyday in films. Like many talented singing cowboys, he entered the field as its popularity was waning, and having had the possibility of being a major star had he been born a decade before, he simply is treated by most film histories as an also-ran. The genre had few years left when he, Rex Allen, and even Jimmy Wakely to an extent made their bids for screen stardom.

One of Texas' most colorful singing cowboys was (and still is) Red River Dave McEnery of San Antonio, who became a popular singer of cowboy songs in New York, recorded for Decca and Continental, and also appeared in Miami, Florida, and throughout Texas on various radio stations, basing for the most part in San Antonio. After a retirement of nearly two decades, McEnery—now bedecked with gold boots and leonine silver hair and goatee—is making a comeback as one of Nashville's most prominent characters.

McEnery made a few movies, but his base in New York City introduced him via network radio to thousands of listeners nationwide. And on a more local level, it introduced him to one of the most important figures in the history of country music, a sturdy, deep-chested fellow Texan named Vernon Dalhart. Although past his prime when he recorded McEnery's composition, "Johnnie Darlin'," at his last recording session in 1939, Dalhart had been country music's first recording star, and the man who sang country music's first million seller.

Vernon Dalhart was born Marion Try Slaughter in Jefferson, Texas, and aspired at an operatic career, in furtherance of which he moved to New York around 1915. By 1916 he had already made his first recording, and was for several years to have quite a successful career on Broadway and in light opera. Among his specialties—especially on record—were the southern "darky" songs that were extremely popular for some time around and after the turn of the century. Dalhart's biggest hit had been, in fact, such a number: "Can't Yo' Heah Me Callin', Caroline?"

Dalhart apparently felt that country tunes could be as popular, especially given the success of Henry Whitter's "Wreck of the Southern Old 97" in early 1924, but few of the record companies with which he dealt (and there were many, for the practice of signing artists to exclusive contracts, taken for granted today, was rare in Dalhart's day, and he was free to record as much for any number of companies on per-record contracts) agreed with his judgment. Eventually he persuaded Edison to try it in May of 1924, and then recorded "The Wreck of the Old 97" again in Au-

gust for Victor, backed with a tune he and his cousin composed, "The Prisoner's Song." The accompaniment was pure country—guitar, harmonica, and voice—and what happened is the stuff from which legend is made: "The Prisoner's Song" took off like no record before and few since, and estimates on its total sales on the multitude of labels on which Dalhart recorded it run from three million to nine million to twenty-seven million! And thus did Vernon Dalhart become country music's first recording star.

As mentioned, because Dalhart did not have a long-term recording contract with Victor, he recorded for nearly every label then in existence, ultimately using well over a hundred pseudonymns by the time his career was over in the late 1930s; some of them still have scholars guessing.

Dalhart was certainly country music's first star, and his 1916 recordings for Thomas Edison make Dalhart the first country singer to record, but these recordings were not country in sound, style, or intent. The honor of the first genuinely country recordings to be made go to—you guessed it—a fellow Texan, named Eck Robertson, in 1922.

Alexander Campbell Robertson, although actually born in Arkansas, moved to Texas at the age of three and became one of the Lone Star State's champion fiddlers, the winner of numerous contests, and a figure of great local popularity. It was he who took the train to New York, having teamed up at a Confederate Veterans Reunion in Richmond, Virginia, with 74-year-old Henry Gilliland, marched into the Victor Records offices in a full Confederate Army uniform (although he was in fact born over two decades after the end of the Civil War), and demanded to make a record. That they did, and their June 30–July 1, 1922, sessions mark the first in country music's history, consisting of six tried and true fiddle tunes. From here sprung the long fiddle-band recording tradition in Texas music, captured on wax as it had been practiced live for years.

Robertson, in addition to his fearsome reputation in fiddling contests, was active as well in the old frontier tradition of playing house parties—that is, Saturday night gatherings at one home or another at which the rugs were rolled back and dancing lasted well into the morning. The development of dancing at house parties to dancing at nightclubs parallels remarkably the growth of western swing.

A crusty old contemporary of Robertson's was M. J. Bonner, an authentic Civil War veteran (could this be where Robertson got the inspiration for his costume?) who recorded but one session for Victor in March of 1925 as Captain M. J. Bonner (The Texas Fiddler). Like Robertson's, his repertoire was basically composed of southeastern hoedowns. Bonner's little niche in history is well deserved, however, because it was he who hosted the initial broadcast of the WBAP "Barn Dance," the first such program in the nation, on January 4, 1923. Backed by, of all the unlikely groups, Fred Wagner's Hilo Five Orchestra, Captain Bonner played a rousing hour and a half of old-timey fiddling, interspersed with Hawaiian music, and

listener response was so great that the nation's first radio barn dance became a fixture at WBAP for several years thereafter.

Other bands in the early days of recording reflect this hoary Texas fiddle-band tradition as well: Solomon and Hughes, and Steeley and Graham, both from the Dallas-Fort Worth area, made pioneer recordings in the late 1920s, and both duos were exclusively string band in sound. Ervin Solomon on fiddle and Joe Hughes on second fiddle were later joined by a guitar-playing younger brother, Jim Solomon; their only recording consisted of two old string-band classics, "Ragtime Annie" and "Sally Johnson." They continued to play house parties with an increasingly larger band (which even included a steel guitar) well into the mid-1930s. A. L. Steeley and J. W. Graham relied very much on the same kind of material (they too recorded "Ragtime Annie" on Brunswick at the same time Solomon and Hughes were recording theirs for Victor), but were extremely atypical of Texas tradition in that Graham played the five-string banjo. Clearly, at this point at least, the fiddle-band traditions of the Southeast and the Southwest were not far different at all. The division of styles was yet to come.

Another example of this same tradition was the short-lived Prince Albert Hunt, who was one of the first to bridge the gap between breakdown fiddle and what was to become western swing. A fiddler in the old-time tradition, he was also a showman, and not only enlarged his band, but also went from playing house parties to

Prince Albert Hunt. (The owner of the phantom hand on Hunt's shoulder is lost in history). Courtesy Bob Pinson.

playing for dances in dance halls and the small bars that became known as honky-tonks.

His association with blacks and with blues was an interesting and revealing part of his music and his life. Hunt lived "across the tracks" in the black section of Terrell, Texas; he was frequently found on the front porch of his shanty jamming with black musicians, and he recorded several rather strange blues, such as "Blues in a Bottle," with a rough, bluesy fiddle style. His close association with black musicians is more than reminiscent of Bob Wills' famous learning experiences in the cotton fields with black coworkers in his youth.

At any rate, Prince Albert Hunt's move from house parties to dance halls was both historic and symbolic, and was, in Hunt's particular case, the cause of his youthful and bizarre demise in March of 1931. While strolling out of a Dallas dance hall at the conclusion of one of his dances, his fiddle under one arm and a good-looking, overly affectionate lady on the other, he was shot to death in his tracks by the jealous husband of his companion. Dallas was still a frontier town in many ways.

A couple long associated with Hunt were the uncle-and-nephew team of Oscar and Doc Harper, who recorded for Okeh the same day as Hunt and apparently backed him on his session. Oscar, a better fiddler than Hunt, stayed around long enough to make several recordings for the Library of Congress on John Lomax's celebrated field trip of 1942.

The band that bridged the gap between old-time mountain string-band music and western swing more than any other was an outfit called the East Texas Serenaders. Both the size and the musical scope of the group presaged the development of the western swing that grew out of the Texas swing band. They were led by a left-handed fiddler named D. H. Williams, whose parents, like so many Texans, had migrated from Tennessee, and his repertoire was full of mountain square-dance tunes like "Sally Goodin" and "Old Joe Clark." In the late 1920s he teamed up with guitarist Claude Hammonds, tenor banjo player John Munnerlin, and a fellow named Henry Bogan, who played a three-string cello like a string bass, and they called this motley aggregation the East Texas Serenaders.

Their recording career (for Brunswick, Columbia, and Decca) lasted from 1927 to 1934, and probably could have gone on further, but they were never full-time musicians and did not care to travel. In addition, they grew up playing at house parties, and were quite uncomfortable in the honky-tonk/ballroom atmosphere in which dances increasingly took place as the 1930s progressed. However, their four-piece group and their selection of "rag" material ("Mineola Rag," "Combination Rag") were definite steps away from the standard fiddle-band tradition, and steps toward the swing-string music to come. In addition, in later years Williams was to tutor one of the great jazz/swing fiddlers of all time: ex-Texas Playboy and current cream of Nashville's crop of session musicians, Johnny Gimble.

The repertoire of the East Texas Serenaders eloquently demonstrates the shift many fiddle bands were making toward swing, largely because of the awesome influences of both radio and record. Williams recalls that in between the square-dance tunes and the jazzier rags, they frequently sang hits of the day, learned from radio or record, such as "Five Foot, Two" in the early days, and "Rosetta" and "Stardust" later on. The fiddle music of the western frontier, not far different from that of the Southeast for many years, was suddenly exposed to a wide variety of other influences over the airwaves: nearby Cajun and Norteño music, the more distant strains of New Orleans and Chicago jazz, and the increasingly swinging sounds of mainstream popular music. Creative and adaptable musicians were quick to make elements of all these styles their own, and thus was born Texas music's most distinctive offspring: western swing.

It all got under way with a group called the Light Crust Doughboys, who were not all that different from the East Texas Serenaders. Not that this was a swing band—it really wasn't at all—but it was heading that way, and among its graduates are all the early greats of the genre: Milton Brown, Johnnie Lee Wills, Tommy Duncan, Leon McAuliffe, Herman Arnspiger, and, of course, Bob Wills.

The Doughboys were led—maybe directed is more like it—by an ambitious flour executive for Burrus Mill named Wilbert Lee O'Daniel, who although not a musician served as their announcer, boss, agent, and even wrote some of their more memorable songs as well, "Beautiful Texas" and "Put Me in Your Pocket" among them. He heard a group called Aladdin's Laddies on the radio one day, and decided this might just be one heck of a way to sell flour, so he took this band—composed of Bob Wills, Milton Brown, and Herman Arnspiger—and renamed them the Light Crust Doughboys (the name was decided their first time on the air in Fort Worth) after the brand of flour he wanted to promote.

W. Lee O'Daniel was inspired by the tremendous popularity of the Doughboys (a band that, in various permutations, has lasted to the present) to propel his career as a politician, with a similar band of the same sort, the Hillbilly Boys. O'Daniel eventually rose to governor of the state of Texas, and later United States senator, but he was an autocratic and high-handed bandleader, and there was considerable disaffection within the Doughboys band.

The Light Crust Doughboys. Courtesy Bob Pinson.

The first to break away was vocalist Milton Brown; his high-pitched, sweet, pop-tinged vocals sparked the band's sound, and he went on to form the first "real" western swing band, which he called his Musical Brownies. Building on what he'd learned as a Doughboy, he and his innovative musicians (primarily Cecil Brower, Cliff Bruner, Papa Calhoun, Wanna Coffman, Ocie Stockard, brother Durwood Brown, and legendary pioneer steel guitarist Bob Dunn) combined the musical styles of their region with the swing and pop styles of the day to become one of the most exciting and influential bands of the era. Milton Brown's influence was every bit as great as was Bob Wills' in his era, but the promise of a legendary career was cut short by a fatal 1936 auto-mobile accident, and all that remains are some great recordings on Decca and Bluebird, which only hint at the greatness possible.

When Milton Brown left the Light Crust Doughboys, he was replaced by a deeper-voiced singer with a real feel for the blues named Tommy Duncan, and although his sound was rather different, it was just as popular. Still, fiddler and more or less *de facto* leader Bob Wills chafed at the bit, and in the late summer of 1933 he finally left the Doughboys, taking with him his banjo-playing brother Johnnie Lee and vocalist Tommy Duncan. Adding the Whalin brothers, Kermit and June, this fledgling swing band moved to Waco, where they called themselves Bob Wills and his Playboys—the "Texas" was added to the band

Milton Brown (at microphone) and his Musical Brownies. Courtesy Bob Pinson.

name only after they moved to Tulsa, Oklahoma, the following year.

Although always firmly associated with the Lone-Star State, Wills and his Texas Playboys found their greatest success—artistically and financially —during the nine years they headquartered at KVOO in Tulsa. Subsequent moves to California and Texas were never able to rekindle the greatness of that era.

The hot dance music Bob Wills and his Texas Playboys, provided from their very first recording session, caused them to become a local sensation, then a regional one, and eventually a national one, with the 1941 million seller "New San Antonio Rose." Propelled by a swing beat, the band never lost its country feel, with Bob's exuberant hollering a trademark

both on record and in person, and with the ever-present steel guitar of Leon McAuliffe as well. It was a music that somehow outlived its usefulness in the 1950s but that is coming back stronger than ever today.

Still, at about the time the Light Crust Doughboys were still going strong, and Bob Wills was beginning to become a star in Tulsa, and Milton Brown was meeting his untimely death, a host of other swing bands began to crop up all over the state of Texas. It would be easy to brand them as imitators—most were indeed inspired by both the sound and the success of Brown and Wills—but on the other hand, most were exactly like the Brown and Wills outfits: Texas fiddle bands experimenting with the new sounds they heard over the radio and on record, and striving to adapt those strains to their own music. Although none approached the popularity of Wills, a host of such Texas swing bands made their indelible mark on the music of the Lone Star State.

A band that maintained a western swing feel but never went to brass instruments was Bill Boyd's Cowboy Ramblers. While its mainstays over the years were Bill and his brother Jim, the Cowboy Ramblers had a host of illustrious sidemen pass through their ranks, including Jesse Ashlock and Art Davis. Davis had the unusual distinction of cutting Boyd's first hit, "Under the Double Eagle," in 1935,

and his last, "Lone Star Rag," in 1950, although he spent the intervening years touring with Autry, appearing in films on his own, and leading his own western swing band as well.

Extremely close to the traditional fiddle-band sound, Boyd nevertheless adopted the fancy Hollywood cowboy image (he in fact made several films in the late 1930s, and has ever since been confused with William Boyd—Hopalong Cassidy) and sported a host of swingy songs. Still his staples were the fiddle tunes and waltzes that have characterized Texas music from the beginning.

There were other groups: for example, the Hi-Flyers, a Fort Worth

Bob Wills and his Texas Playboys. Courtesy Country Music Foundation.

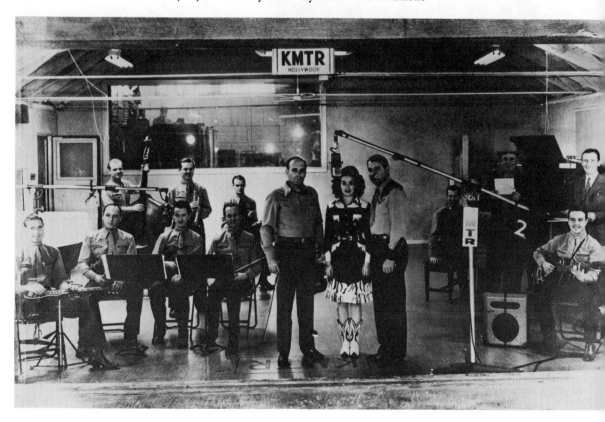

group whose leader, banjoist Elmer Scarborough, claims predates the Light Crust Doughboys. Their progress, too, parallels that of many other pioneer swing bands in that it started small, then grew larger and electrified instruments along the way, their repertoire going from fiddle tunes and reworked pop hits to an increasing number of original songs and tunes as time went on. Perhaps the band's interesting accomplishment was the pairing of Lefty Perkins and the legendary Bob Dunn on twin steel guitars on border station XEPN, a sound that unfortunately was never preserved on record.

An interesting and peculiar band of the period was the Tune Wranglers of San Antonio. Despite two full-fledged hit records (for Bluebird) of the era—"Texas Sand" in 1937 and the novelty "Hawaiian Honeymoon" in 1939—little was heard of them thereafter. They apparently disbanded in 1940 and never reformed. Led by Buster Coward, they claimed to be authentic ranch hands, and their sound was a mixture of string band, swing, and heavy doses of cowboy, although they played down the string-band aspect perhaps more than most, while on the other hand featuring more original material than the majority of their contemporaries. As far as best-selling records go, their moment in the sun was impressive, but it was at the same time surprisingly brief.

A band that delved more deeply into jazz than most was Roy Newman and his Boys, who worked mainly out of Dallas. Recording as early as 1934, their specialities were numbers like "Tin Roof Blues," "Sadie Green, the Vamp of New Orleans," and "Tiger Rag," which shows, if nothing else, the widespread influence of jazz material (spread rapidly by radio and record) on Texas bands. Since Bill Boyd and his Cowboy Ramblers were also playing at WRR in Dallas at the same time, they freely exchanged and shared band members, Art Davis among them. One of Roy Newman's Boys who went on to glory on his own was

Bill Boyd. Courtesy Bob Pinson.

vocalist Gene Sullivan, later to join with Wiley Walker in Oklahoma to become an extremely popular singing and song-writing ("Live and Let Live," "When My Blue Moon Turns to Gold") duet of the late 1930s.

A couple of other bands made contributions to (or at least were reflections of) elements of the burgeoning Texas swing sound, but relatively little is really known about them. The Nite Owls, led by Jack True, were extremely typical of these bands, going from fiddle tunes to blues, rehashed pop, jazz, and even Mexican ("Cielito Lindo," "Rancho Grande") and some original material, none of it unusual enough to make them household words. Their apparent home base of Austin was a bit out of the ordinary, but predates the music scene there by some forty years. Rather the opposite approach came from a West-Texas group formed by Bob Kendrick, but dubbed Bob Skyles' Skyrockets by record producer Eli Oberstein, which was both the brassiest and the corniest of all country swing bands. Working out of Pecos, their sound was sort of a brass version of the Hoosier Hot Shots, and novelty numbers like "Arkansas Bazooka Swing" and "Bazooka Stomp" were their stock in trade.

The far-flung location of the Nite Owls and Bob Skyles' Skyrockets does, however, point out one interesting aspect of Texas swing. While the bulk of the action took place in the Dallas-Fort Worth area, it was a genuinely widespread phenomenon throughout the Lone Star State. Many other swing bands had far-flung locations: Adolph Hofner and the Tune Wranglers in San Antonio, Doug Bine (as well as Bob Wills in his early years) in Waco, Cliff Bruner in Beaumont, Ted Daffan in Houston, and more and more as the 1930s ended and the 1940s progressed.

Another very interesting minor swing band was the Crystal Springs Ramblers, not so much for their own good but unexceptional music as for the band members who came out of the troupe. Link Davis ("Big Mamou"), Bob Wills' longtime left-handed fiddler Joe Holley, and fiddler Leon Selph all were alumni of the outfit, named after the Crystal Springs dance pavilion northwest of Fort Worth, where they were the staff band for years under the direction of Papa Sam Cunningham. Although they had only two recording sessions (both in June of 1937), they were an extremely popular band in person for years.

Although fiddler Leon Selph did not record with the Crystal Springs Ramblers, he was an important member, and he left the band to form an extremely influential group called the Blue Ridge Playboys—a rather odd name for a swing band—in 1935. Two original members later went on to develop the offshoot of western swing known as honky-tonk in the following decade: lead singer and guitarist Floyd Tillman and steel guitarist Ted Daffan. Both were to write songs that sold into the many millions in years to come, and a couple of them (Tillman's "Slippin' Around" and Daffan's "Born to Lose") were to become country-music landmarks in addition to racking up big sales.

The importance of the Blue Ridge Playboys is further underscored by three other members who went on into a honky-tonk rather than in a swing vein: their pianist Moon Mullican, a sometimes vocalist and guitarist named Chuck Keeshan (who was to spend some years with Ted Daffan), and guitarist Dickie McBride, a longtime fixture of the Houston area well into the television age. If the seeds of honky-tonk as a musical style can be said to have been sown somewhere, then it surely must have been with the Blue Ridge Playboys in the 1930s. It was a style created not so much by men as by economics; it was a music for jukeboxes and small bands in roadside dance taverns. With the exception of Ernest Tubb and Al Dexter, every major early figure in the style came out of but one band, the Blue Ridge Playboys.

Still, while this style known as honky-tonk was being birthed from western swing the mother and the rise of the jukebox and the tavern the father, there was still considerable activity in the field of swing, activity that was to span three decades, activity, that despite a period of dormancy, is very much a part of Texas music today.

Another swing band that bridged the gap between the swing and the honky-tonk styles was Cliff Bruner's Texas Wanderers, which has among its many accomplishments the honor of recording and releasing country music's first truck-driving song, a Ted Daffan composition called "Truck Driver's Blues," in 1939. Bruner began his career as a fiddler with Milton Brown's Musical Brownies, participating in Brown's last recording session, and he is still an active performer to this day. Although based in Beaumont, the Texas Wanderers seemed

to borrow band members (Tillman, Mullican, McBride) freely from the Blue Ridge Playboys, which may well explain their propensity toward honky-tonk.

Western swing reached an awkward point in the era after World War II: While for some bands, like Wills and Spade Cooley, it was a financially extremely successful time in their career, on the other hand, a good bit of the music at the grass-roots level was dying on the vine. It was a symptom that accurately paralleled the natonal disaffection with the smooth, dreamy, danceable big-band sound and its concurrent turn to the lonely honky-tonk sound, to songs like "Slippin' Around," and, ultimately, to the simple, direct, southeastern sounds of Hank Williams and Kitty Wells. It was a rough period for Texas in general, and western swing specifically, one from which this particular genre of Texas music was not to recover until the early 1970s.

That swing was fading in Texas after the war is dramatically demonstrable: Most swing bands disbanded during the war, and few reorganized after V-J Day. Those that did (with the exception of Hofner) were unable to get major label affiliation any longer. The exceptions, Wills and Cooley (who was actually from Oklahoma, not Texas), were enjoying considerable success, but not in Texas; both were based in California, and after about 1950 even their big record-selling days were over as well. Bob's younger brother Johnnie Lee Wills also enjoyed considerable success in postwar Tulsa, but despite two hit records— "Rag Mop" and "Peter Cottontail"—

his success was regional. Tastes and fashions inevitably changed, and western swing went quickly out of favor, not to return for two decades.

Still, some new faces appeared in the 1940s, although they had to be extreme diehards or extremely adaptable to survive. An example of the former was an unabashed Bob Wills imitator and admirer named Hoyle Nix, who has led his West Texas Cowboys in Big Spring ever since the late 1940s, faithfully preserving the Bob Wills sound. He was rewarded by a guest appearance on Wills' 1974 album *For the Last Time*. Similarly, a group called the Miller Brothers (real name: Gibbs; Sam Gibbs was later to become Bob Wills' manager) struggled along

in Wichita Falls with a devoted local following, their sound good, traditional western swing.

The other approach was taken by Waco's Hank Thompson, who returned from the Navy to build an extremely successful career with a swing band. He was able to get away with it in the 1950s (while Wills struggled and most of the rest gave up) by a combination of a music much smoother than any of the other swing bands had been able to get, with the occasional exception of Cooley, and also by the use of contemporary material, much of it self-written. It is noteworthy, however, that he achieved his greatest success in Oklahoma, where in fact he still lives. He kept a big band

Hank Thompson (left) and the Brazos Valley Boys (in dark jackets).

until rather recently, and the smooth sound of the Brazos Valley Boys led to their being named the top western swing band for thirteen straight years.

So while Wills endured (his bands dwindling in size until, in the late 1960s, just he and a vocalist were appearing), Hoyle Nix dug in and holed up in a pocket of loyalty, and Hank Thompson adapted swing to meet the demands of the day, an approach also followed with less success by Leon McAuliffe, who had founded his Cimarron Boys after the war. McAuliffe went so far as to record "Sh-boom" in smooth western swing style. Even Ray Price had a fling with western swing, starting out with a small Hank Williams-type band (he in fact used the Drifting Cowboys for a couple of years after Hank's death), then going on to form a big, beautiful swing band in the mid-1950s before settling down to the smaller honky-tonk shuffle band with which he achieved his greatest success.

But for all this, western swing was for most purposes dead by the late 1950s, kayoed by the triple punches of the negative impact of television, the southeastern sound revival of the early 1950s, and the explosion of rock in mid-decade. Still, tastes and fads vary

Commander Cody and his Lost Planet Airmen.

and shift, and music has always been prone to cyclical swings of popularity. What was once discarded is now discovered to be precious, and so western swing has risen once again, riding the pendulum back into popularity. Reunions of the Texas Playboys are big events, and a revamped group of ex-Playboys has been signed to do new recordings for Capitol Records. But time has taken its toll, for during the period of the surging revival of western swing former Playboys Jesse Ashlock, Noel Boggs, Keith Coleman, Sleepy Johnson, and the grand old man himself, Bob Wills, died as the music they created was being reborn.

Much of the impetus for this rebirth came from country-rock bands like Commander Cody and his Lost Planet Airmen, and a group of Austinites (via San Francisco and their native Pennsylvania/West Virginia area) called Asleep at the Wheel, who delved deeply into the Bob Wills sound; they helped introduce this sound to a whole new and enthusiastic generation. An adopted Texan (actually born in Oklahoma) in this same tradition is Alvin Crow, the fiddling leader of his Pleasant Valley Boys, who pursues a half-original, half-revivalist approach to western swing.

At any rate, western swing is back with a vengeance, bigger now than ever before. Of all the Lone Star State's varied musical products, it may very well be the most important.

As has been seen, the history of western swing is closely entwined with that of honky-tonk. The basic thrust of both musical styles is the same—danceability—but as time went on they both took on quite distinct and unique characteristics. For one thing, honky-tonk was usually performed by a small band, with electric guitar and steel lead (to cut through the din of crowded roadside taverns), while the trend in swing was, of course, to bigger bands, full rhythm sections, and often horn sections as well. Thematically the songs differed as well: Western swing songs were for the large part beautiful, danceable melodies, with dreamy, unspecific lyrics generalizing on the subject of love lost or found. Honky-tonk, however, was directed at the patrons of these roadside taverns and the realities of their lives, and as the years went by they became increasingly honest, even harsh, in dealing with the problems that beset honky-tonkers directly: excessive drinking, slipping around, frustration in life and in love. It is a style that has never died: For every Ray Price who changes stylistic horses in midstream there is a Johnny Bush or a Moe Bandy to take up the honky-tonk banner. The music appeals to something in a rather large percentage of country music's populace.

The rise of honky-tonk as a musical style parallels the rise of the honky-tonk as a social gathering place. With the advent of the jukebox, dancing in small taverns became possible, and dancing, it must be remembered, was a national pastime of major proportions in the era; certainly it was the basis for western swing and for honky-tonk first and foremost. But the crowd who did the two-step to the jukebox or the three-piece band was a different one from those who paid to dance at Cain's Academy or the Crystal Springs Pavilion. Hard drinkin' and easy lovin' increasingly became the themes of honky-tonk songs.

As noted before, most of the early honky-tonk greats came out of the Blue Ridge Playboys: Ted Daffan, Floyd Tillman, and Moon Mullican. And that this is one of the purest forms of Texas music is self-evident. All were Texans by adoption if not by birth, as, indeed, were the two honky-tonk greats who were not ex-Blue Ridge Playboys, Ernest Tubb and Al Dexter.

Daffan came out of Houston (although actually born in Louisiana), a Hawaiian guitar player who joined the Blue Ridge Playboys on country steel. Even if he didn't start with country he had what it took, and he was to write more than one country-music classic:

Ted Daffan. Courtesy Bob Pinson.

Well Howdy Folks!!
Sincerely
Ted Daffan

Ted Daffan

His first session with his own band contained the jukebox instrumental favorite "Blue Steel Blues" as well as the perennial "Worried Mind."

Daffan went in for big bands, usually recording with six to eight musicians, sometimes as many as twelve; in fact, *Billboard* reported in the late 1940s that he was planning to build a twenty-two-piece orchestra on the West Coast, but there is no evidence that his plans ever materialized. However, even with large bands Daffan's approach was far more honky-tonk than swing. The band rarely swung, but instead concentrated on the lyrics of his songs, many of them—"Heading Down the Wrong Highway" the classic in this case—speaking directly to the honky-tonk patron.

Ted Daffan's Texans reached their peak at their February 1942 session for Okeh Records: Here the extremely popular "No Letter Today" was cut, as was the anthem of country music's dispossessed, "Born to Lose." It was a song that on its face dealt with hard luck and lost love but that took on a pervasive meaning to those who floundered and struggled in the perplexing war years, thrust into a faster-paced world for which they were ill prepared.

Daffan's career, like that of most big-band leaders, slid sharply after the war. After a fling in California he returned to Houston, where he lives today. His song-writing powers stayed strong, however: "I've Got Five Dollars and It's Saturday Night," "Tangled Mind," and "I'm a Fool to Care" became postwar hits for Faron Young, Hank Snow, and Les Paul and Mary Ford, respectively.

Daffan's old bandmate with the

Blue Ridge Playboys, Floyd Tillman, also distinguished himself largely as a songwriter, although he was a singer of great popularity, his strange, looping voice one of the most distinctive in country music. Although actually born in Oklahoma, he moved to Post, Texas, as a child, and has ever since been closely associated with Texas music. Today, where with bushy white sideburns he is a popular denizen of Austin, he is known affectionately as the original cosmic cowboy.

"I Love You So Much It Hurts Mc," "Each Night at Nine," and "It Makes No Difference Now" are Tillman's best-known compositions, along with another of country music's true landmark songs, "Slippin' Around." One of the first songs to face the issue of infidelity head on, without apology or moralizing, it was daring in its day and has proved to be a landmark in country music's history, although the way had been paved by Eddie Dean's "One Has My Name, the Other Has My Heart." Jimmy Wakely and Margaret Whiting's version of "Slippin' Around" was a quick million seller in 1949–50 and was symptomatic of the postwar mood, speaking to millions not only in honky-tonks but outside them as well.

Aubrey "Moon" Mullican was at once both more and less honky-tonk than his two fellow Blue Ridge Playboys. His bluesy, bawdy-house piano style was in and of itself closely entwined with the honky-tonk sound, and because of it his association with honky-tonk was natural and inevitable. On the other hand, he was a performer who was a master of a great many styles—blues, Cajun, straight

Floyd Tillman. Courtesy Doug Green.

country, pop, honky-tonk, Dixieland, ragtime, and many more—who, like Daffan and Tillman (although to a lesser degree), was well known for his song-writing as well, "Pipeliner's Blues" and "Cherokee Boogie" among them. Still, this East Texan's greatest contribution was his dynamic, exciting piano style, which has had a profound effect on Jerry Lee Lewis and many other rockabillies, who forged from Moon's style their own hybrid creation.

It should, however, be pointed out that the roots of honky-tonk are not solely with the Blue Ridge Playboys among early Texas musicians. For example, the Shelton Brothers were an extremely popular and influential pre-honky-tonk band, recording as early as 1933 with Leon Chappelear as the Lone Star Cowboys. They grew to string-band proportions, then whole-

Al Dexter. Courtesy Bob Pinson.

heartedly adopted the honky-tonk sound in the late 1930s, with songs like "Rompin' and Stompin' Around." Their two most popular songs—"Deep Elem Blues" and the ubiquitous "Just Because"—helped pave the way for the honky-tonk sound.

But the two real kings of honky tonk, as the form became more and more popular in the 1940s, were Jacksonville's Al Dexter and Crisp's Ernest Tubb, who brought the sound to the Southeast when he joined the "Opry" in 1943.

Al Dexter (born Albert Poindexter) began recording in 1936, and late in that decade began what turned out to be an extremely successful flirtation with the honky-tonk style. Al Dexter

and his Troopers were basically a small honky-tonk band, and the term "Honky Tonk" shows up early in his work: "Honky Tonk Blues" in 1936 (which may well be the first use of the term in a song title), "Honky Tonk Baby" in 1937, and "When We Go A-Honky Tonkin'" and "Poor Little Honky Tonk Girl" in 1940. He wrote and recorded the wartime smash "Pistol Packin' Mama," a humorous and unabashed description of the perils of honky-tonk life. Dexter was capable of writing other fine country material ("Guitar Polka," "Rosalita," "Too Late to Worry, Too Blue to Cry"), but his brief but glorious moment in the sun revolved around the honky-tonk sound that had made him famous and that he, in turn, helped popularize on a national level to a far greater degree than ever before.

Less explosively popular but with a career of far greater durability was Ernest Tubb, who began as a Jimmie Rodgers imitator on Bluebird records (he still owns Rodgers' rare old Martin 000-45 guitar, given to him by Jimmie's widow, Carrie). Tubb later developed his own very distinctive style, becoming well known in Texas while being sponsored by—you guessed it—a flour company, as the Gold Chain Troubador. He began recording for Decca in 1940, and had his first big hit with "Walking the Floor Over You" in 1943, which brought him to the "Opry." His sound has always (with the exception of his very early Jimmie Rodgers period) been pure honky-tonk. Perhaps the "Opry" was groping for a successful, up-to-date sound when they hired him; at any rate, he was an immediate success, and

Ernest Tubb and family. Courtesy Country Music Foundation.

he helped spread the sound into the roadhouses and jukeboxes of the Southeast.

Tubb was not the first to bring an electric guitar onto the hallowed stage of the "Grand Ole Opry" (Sam McGee, Pee Wee King, and Paul Howard all claim the honor), but he was the first to make it a major part of his sound, especially after Jimmie Short made that little four-note guitar lick an integral part of the Ernest Tubb sound. Often working with just the electric lead guitar, a steel, and a bass, Tubb's approach was pure honky-tonk: straightforward, loud, direct, unsubtle, with the lyrics focusing on drinking, dancing, and the honky-tonk life. Apparently the man doesn't know the meaning of the word rest: Although he nominally lives in Nashville, he rarely sees the town, still touring over a hundred thousand miles a year of grueling one-nighters.

Ray Noble Price, of Perryville, fell right into this mold as well: Up until his celebrated image change in 1967, he had been known as the Cherokee Cowboy, and his band sound—with the exception of his all too brief fling with western swing—was hard-nosed Texas honky-tonk. In fact, more than anyone he defined the honky-tonk sound of the 1950s: walking bass, heavy-handed drumming, and song after song in the two-step shuffle: "City Lights," "Crazy Arms," "Release Me," "My Shoes Keep Walking Back to You," "Heartaches by the Number," and many more. With Willie Nelson's bluesy composition "Night Life" in 1963, Ray Price at once got as deep into honky-tonk as anyone ever had, and yet hinted strongly at the mellow-voiced, resonant, country-pop Price of "For the Good Times" and beyond. It was a turning point for him, but he left behind him a host of imitators to fill the void (Johnny Bush the most conspic-

Ray Price. Courtesy Doug Green.

uous and easily the best), and the legacy of the greatest honky-tonk music of the 1950s.

Although his peak years came later (they are probably, in fact, occurring now), George Jones of Beaumont was also into the honky-tonk/Hank Williams mold pioneered by Price in the 1950s. In fact, while stationed in northern California while in the Marine Corps (about 1952) Jones appeared on a local basis. Frequently his repertoire exclusively consisted of Hank Williams' songs. Born in Saratoga, Texas, Jones first hit on the Starday label in 1955 with "Why, Baby, Why?" and had a long string of hard-core honky-tonk hits. But George Jones has always been extremely intimate with a song, and has drifted away from the raucous honky-tonk sound into something very personal and unique of his own. If anything, this explains the remarkable phenomenon of his growing popularity, even after a full two decades in country music.

Honky-tonk was a style that wouldn't die: The southeastern sound revival of the early 1950s helped knock off cowboy music and western swing, but it couldn't knock off honky-tonk, nor could the rock 'n' roll phenomenon later in the decade, nor could the ultra-slick Nashville sound of the sixties. And through it all, true to form, it was Texas that carried the honky-tonk banner through good times and bad.

A pair who helped it weather the rock years were Charlie Walker, of Collin County, and Johnny Horton of Tyler. Walker went the time-honored route of disc jockey to singer, and scored biggest in 1958 with "Pick Me Up on Your Way Down." Horton, on

George Jones. Courtesy Country Music Foundation.

the other hand, gave up a promising career in music, having been a high-school singing star, to become a professional fisherman, but drifted back into performing on the West Coast. He returned to the area of his native East Texas* in 1955, joining the cast

* It is a peculiar historical quirk that nearly all the greats of Texas music are from the eastern part of the state, from Vernon Dalhart to Willie Nelson. It's hard to account for the unusual musical fertility of this area, other than the relatively sparse population of the more desolate middle and west of the state. The southeastern part of Texas has always had the seaports and good farmland (as well as oil later on) to support a large population. Then, too, in a musical sense, it was a location where the mixture of various cultures—hillbilly, black, Cajun, Mexican, German, and others—were able to mix and intermingle very freely.

of the "Louisiana Hayride" (Shreveport is just over the Texas/Louisiana border), and his career from that point on was spectacular but all too short: He was killed in an automobile accident on November 5, 1960.

Horton was firmly in the honky-tonk tradition—in fact, "I'm a Honky Tonk Man" was an early hit for him —but drifted into a semifolk/historical-song vein, of which he quickly became king with "Johnny Reb," "Springtime in Alaska," "North to Alaska," and the two superhits "Sink the *Bismarck*" and "The Battle of New Orleans."

It is a debatable point, of course, and purely a subjective one, but per-

Johnny Horton. Courtesy Doug Green.

haps the greatest of them all was an ex-boxer and oil-field worker from Corsicana named William Orville Frizzell. From romping paeans to the honky-tonk life ("If You've Got the Money, I've Got the Time") to gushy sentimentality ("Mom and Dad's Waltz") to straight country love songs ("I Love You a Thousand Ways"), Lefty had a spine-tingling sincerity to his voice, a voice capable of spectacular yet emotive vocal effects, a voice of tremendous warmth and intimacy, a voice that has had a remarkable effect on all who have followed. It was a sound so new (although instrumentally and thematically it was pure honky-tonk, through and through) that Lefty exploded with four songs in the country top ten at one time, a feat never since duplicated. But after the novelty wore off, Lefty couldn't seem to sustain this success, his personal life marred by bouts with the bottle, his records all too often wasting his magnificent voice on nondescript material, although when he found the right song later on ("Long Black Veil," "Saginaw, Michigan"), public response was there. It's a shame he didn't live up to his awesome potential, but even as it is, he ranks in the pantheon of the handful of all-time greats of Texas music.

Although Lefty died all too young (at forty-seven in 1975), the honky-tonk tradition lives on, with the likes of Billy Walker, one of the fine underrated singers of our time; Willie Nelson, a great writer and performer in the honky-tonk style before his outlaw days; and Moe Bandy, whose songs of low life, loose women, and hard drinking are both a throwback to classic honky-tonk and a sure sign that it is as strong a musical form as ever.

Ernest Tubb's move to the "Opry" in 1943 signaled the beginning of another movement that was, in the 1950s, to accelerate rapidly. This was the migration of many Texas entertainers to Tennessee (reversing the steps of many of their ancestors)—more specifically to Nashville and the "Grand Ole Opry" (or at least to the Nashville sound). If there is a decade in which Texas' importance can be said to be minimal, it certainly must be that of the late 1950s to late 1960s. While the state never really fully dominated the entire spectrum of country music—although it made a heck of a run at it during the simultaneous height of western swing and singing cowboys—Texas always was, and currently is, a major force in the movement of the music. But this force was little felt in the rock/Nashville sound decade, blunted by these two extremely different but extremely powerful musical sounds.

Texas-in-Nashville describes this era as well as anything, for after Tubb came Price in 1950, then George Jones, Goldie Hill (one of the few women singers Texas has produced until very recent years),† and Billy Walker, who took that time-honored route of moving from the "Louisiana

Lefty Frizzell. Courtesy Texas Hall of Fame.

Hayride" to the "Opry" after serving time in what might be called the high minors.

Easily the most important influence in the Texas-in-Nashville movement was Jim Reeves, who despite many years in the Lone Star State (he was born in the same county as Tex Ritter) came out of it without a touch of Texas in his smooth, romantic, appealing voice. An ex-disc jockey and aspiring baseball player, Reeves turned his attention to singing while working on the "Louisiana Hayride" as an announcer, and with the success of "Mexican Joe" and "Bimbo" moved to the "Opry" and to a full-time career as a singer.

But if there was any performer ready to shuck the good-ole-country-boy image it was Reeves, who was quite

---

† Others include singer-songwriter Cindy Walker, Texas Ruby (Tex Owens' sister) and Laura Lee McBride (Tex Owens' daughter and Dickie McBride's wife), who was Bob Wills' first girl singer. In the past decade Jeannie C. Riley, Barbara Mandrell, Billie Jo Spears, La Costa and Tanya Tucker, and Dottsy Brodt have helped change that imbalance.

Jim Reeves. Courtesy Doug Green.

eager to go along with the emerging Nashville music, the slick "country-politan" sound that developed when rock all but killed the hard southeastern sound of the early 1950s. Although Reeves never lost his country image to many country fans—including the South Africans and English who revere him today as much as ever —he clearly made a conscious effort at invading the country-pop territory mined so successfully by Eddy Arnold, who pretty much had the field to himself. Unafraid to tackle smooth, popular material, Reeves and the burgeoning Nashville sound helped pull the

town and the music through the lean rock years.

The Texas-in-Nashville phase continued in the early and mid-1960s‡ with the arrival of Willie and Waylon, but by then the character of the movement was beginning to change, and the seeds for the upcoming Texas revival were being sown. But in the meantime there was precious little to say for Texas, for the late 1950s and

‡ It's a trend that continues: One of the "Opry's" newest members, Larry Gatlin, is a native of the West Texas town of Seminole. Likewise, Don Williams hails from the Plainview, Texas, vicinity.

early 1960s saw—other than Reeves, whose sound was not remotely a reflection of Texas, and already established stars like Tubb and Price—few landmark performers or sounds emanate from the Lone Star State. One exception was Plainview's Jimmy Dean (born Seth Ward), who began recording as early as 1953, with "Bumming Around" on 4-Star. Solidly in the Texas-Nashville mold, Dean actually didn't move to Music City, but instead was based out of the Washington, D.C., area for his local television show, and New York for his CBS daytime network television show, and his ABC network show in the evening in the early 1960s.

Country music seemed to take a dramatic shift toward the southeastern sound in the 1950s. It had begun in the late 1940s with Hank Williams, and continued with Kitty Wells and Webb Pierce, and Ray Price and Hank Thompson, two Texans who tried to fuse the styles of the Southeast and the Southwest. Gone was interest in the jazzy complexity of western swing and the dreamy romanticism of the singing cowboys, and here was hard, harsh, direct, simple, gutbucket hillbilly. The southeastern-sound revival lasted only a few years, and country music's shift to the Southeast rebounded westward after a few years, settling instead in the Memphis-northern-Mississippi-Arkansas area, with the powerful phenomenon known as rockabilly, a fusion of the hillbilly soul of the southeastern-revival and the energetic, dynamic, powerful music of the blacks, which had fascinated and inspired western swing musicians for so long.

One of Texas' major rockabilly figures was Roy Orbison, born in Vernon in 1936. His first real band was formed in Wink, Texas, and was known as the Wink Westerners, a band that became prominent through a radio show. Although he was one of the early Sun Records rockabillies, Orbison's high, strained, liquid, totally unique voice and style drew little from country music or Texas music, and gave little to it in return, although partly because of its very uniqueness it has made him extraordinarily popular—particularly overseas—for years.

Texas' contribution to rockabilly was impressive, but not on the magnitude of Memphis. There was a pretty popular band called Sid King and the Five Strings, and Bob Loman, who, after his "Let's Think About Living" rockabilly days became a died-in-the-wool Texan-in-Nashville. Fort Worth native Charles Erwin "Mac" Curtis was successful, as was the Big Bopper, a huge, crewcut bear of an ex-disc jockey named J. P. Richardson, who scored with "Chantilly Lace" before that celebrated plane crash ended his career and his life. And there was that other passenger on that small plane: Buddy Holly.

Born Charles Hardin Holly in Lubbock in 1936, Buddy Holly showed an early interest in performing, singing tenor in a country duo in high school, which became his first professional job after graduation. Known as Buddy and Bob ("western and bop"), their style was a blend typical of the emerging rockabilly style: Western and bop—that somehow seems to sum it up. When they were scouted by

Decca Records, however, it was Buddy who was signed, not Bob, and Holly did his first recordings—unsuccessful recordings, as it turns out—in Nashville, backed by Nashville studiomen. When he caught on, however, it was explosive, creating a legend in less than two years. "That'll Be the Day" was released in June 1957, and Holly died (along with singer Richie Valens and the Big Bopper) in February of 1959. Holly's music was alive and innocent and bursting with energy and sounds, which, for all his hiccuping mannerisms, are not so terribly dated today.

Two of his sidemen were to join him on that plane that night as well, but gave up their seats to the headliners. Both fellow Texans, they have each gone on to make large impressions on country music themselves. The lead guitarist was Oklahoma-born Tommy Allsup, whose roots were so deep into western swing that he played with Art Davis' Rhythm Riders as well as Holly, and cut several "countrypolitan" guitar albums as well. Today an occasional session musician in Nashville, Allsup is a well-known producer who has recorded Hank Thompson, neoswing stars Asleep at the Wheel, and the master himself, Bob Wills, late in his career.

The bass player was a youngster from Littlefield named Waylon Jennings, who put together a lot of the elements of Texas music to become one of the leaders of the Texas revival and one of the most influential performers of our day. With a touch of cowboy and a dollop of rockabilly and a great large helping of pure, old-fashioned honky-tonk, Jennings has,

after an uncomfortable Texas-in-Nashville period of country/folk in the mid-1960s, blossomed into a leader of the highly publicized outlaw faction—singer-songwriters going their own way, doing their own music, flaunting—and succeeding at flaunting—the established Nashville way of doing things.

The *de facto* leader of the outlaw movement (although it can be said, in some ways, to have begun with a sometime Texan, Kris Kristofferson) is Willie Nelson, who stepped out of the honky-tonk genre into the Nashville scene in the early 1960s and astonished the professional world with his awesome song-writing abilities: "Night Life," "Crazy," "Hello Walls," "Ain't It Funny How Time Slips Away," and many, many others. Although he tried extremely hard to fit into the up-and-comer's role (especially as the Nehru-jacketed featured vocalist on Ernest Tubb's syndicated television show), his singing was just too odd, too different, too jazzy and strangely toned and phrased, and his successes as a singer were rather limited, despite the continued successes of his songs.

Fed up with being a Texan-in-Nashville, tired of limited success, feeling he was going nowhere, Willie moved back to Texas around 1970, and the results were explosive: Somehow the Texas counterculture was ready for Willie's musical adventurousness; somehow he was able to appeal with remarkable strength to longhair and redneck alike, and in bringing together these cultures brought about the energetic and vital musical interplay loosely called the Austin sound.

Not that what Willie was doing was all that new: The three biggest hits of his outlaw period were songs not any more recent than twenty-five years old: "Blue Eyes Crying in the Rain," "Remember Me," and "If You've Got the Money, I've Got the Time," which was even done in the same key and in the same tempo as Lefty Frizzell's original! Yet, as always seems to happen, whenever the music gets too complicated, too sophisticated, too formulaic, somebody —be it Jimmie Rodgers or Hank Williams or Elvis or Willie Nelson— comes up with music of urgency, of intensity, and most of all, of simplicity. It is the cyclical nature of music demonstrated once again. This time it was Willie who did the trick.

The rise of Austin and its attendant culture and sound, and the faddish national interest in cowboy song, life, and culture all point to Texas as, if not the new capital of country music, then the place where most of the action, energy, and creativity are. In a way it is true, and few would disagree that it has been a healthy, invigorating, stimulating thing for country music in general. And it also points to the remarkably long-term contribution of Texas on country music as a whole. From Eck Robertson's first recording to Willie Nelson's latest No. 1, the Lone Star State has contributed a great deal more than its share of sound, style, inventiveness, influential men and women, and most of all creativity to the world of country music.

The Singing Cowboys

The legend of the cowboy is unique in the annals of American history, the one purely American tradition. Thus, to look at the legend of the cowboy in his travails through the "dime novels" of the late 1800s and the movie Westerns from their beginning to the present is to look not simply at the cowboy as he really was but at the cowboy as a series of narrow reflections of the country's most basic (and changing) wants and needs embodied in one continuing character.

There are certain basic qualities in the legend of the cowboy that have become universal despite the changes wrought upon him through the passing of time. In the simplest possible terms, the legend of the cowboy created a man of destiny. He was a free man, unencumbered by the encroachment of pending civilization, although each act he performed brought that same civilization one step closer to its

final result: the cowboy's total demise and the full domestication of the Old West. That is the one inescapable fact. In the legend of the cowboy, settlers involved in the civilizing process needed the cowboy much more than the cowboy needed civilization. He was a loner, independent, self-reliant, existing in a violent, untamed world. He was deadly when crossed. His struggle with the elements, whether they were man-made or products of nature at her most awesome, was not a civilized one, but rather an archetypal struggle of sheer survival in the terrifying midst of the unknown, and it was not a struggle to be easily shirked. If there was a challenge, the challenge must be met with all that was available to him, and those tools, too, were largely elemental: courage, skills of survival, an understanding of the land and its untold dangers, and a dogged determination. There was little else at his beck and call, and if he failed, the one reality was his death. It was that reality that lent him a certain awareness of his own mortality and insignificance, but at the same time managed to elevate his struggle for survival to a position of greater importance than the mere meaninglessness of his life. The struggle was everything, because there was no reward but his own destruction. The tools of survival that he mastered were rendered obsolete as the homesteaders and the barbed wire localized him and drew him further and further into the world of domestication.

The cowboy provided a terrific legend that lent itself perfectly to the dreams and fantasies of a people finding the restraints of growing modernity binding and claustrophobic. The cowboy, with his sense of freedom and simplicity of action, offered not only the hope of escape, but also the realization that if the cowboy got his job done, we would all have warm beds to come home to each night. You couldn't ask more of any legend.

But who was the real cowboy, and what was on his mind? As one scholar noted: "The cowboy needed no particular ability except to sit on a horse and pay attention." If we are to believe *authentic* accounts of the life of a cowboy, his was a lot that was more tiresome than heroic and more boring than romantic—or as a cowboy himself said: "There are more cows and less butter, more rivers and less water, and you can see farther and see less than any place in the world."

Following the Civil War, with the South in ruins and overrun with carpetbaggers, and the North attempting

Roy Rogers.

to restructure a total society, there were thousands upon thousands of young men who had nothing to return to. Houses, farms, and cities were gone. Families had been torn apart, if not destroyed, and the broken pieces were simply too scattered to put back together. So many men— soldiers, freed slaves, the displaced, the restless, the adventurers, and more than a few renegades—went West. With them all went the rivalry of the Blue and the Gray, complete with the legacy of violence and chaos, as they all began carving out a new life west of the Mississippi.

That life was based on the long-horn cattle that were descendants of animals brought to Mexico by the Spanish in the 1600s. By 1800, these hardy beasts numbered in the hundreds of thousands as they roamed at large over the southern plains. The use of the animal for its tallow, hide, bones for fertilizer, and meat constituted the wealth of the land, but the cattle trade was disorganized and monopolized by shippers on the Gulf Coast.

It was not a major industry by any means, and the Civil War put a further crimp in its development by drawing off the manpower and closing many markets. The situation changed abruptly when the war ended; the men returned to civilian life, and a peacetime economy opened markets back up again.

In 1867, Abilene opened up as the first stockyard to which cattle from all over Texas were driven, then shipped North by rail to the slaughter- and packinghouses of Chicago. The use of the train was a revolutionary idea, both in its efficiency and its introduction of beef to the diet of Easterners. The man who put it all together was Joseph McCoy, a young Chicago livestock trader who knew that cattle on the hoof on their own range were worth but four bucks a head. McCoy offered forty bucks a head for all cattle delivered to Abilene, while promising Chicago that he would deliver two hundred thousand head within a decade. Within the first four years of operation, however, he shipped two million cattle North, exceeding even his wildest dreams, and thus gave rise to the term "the real McCoy."

It was the cowboy's role to cover the entire range where the cattle roamed, to brand new calves, to drive the cattle into herds, and then to herd the cattle to the railroad. Suffice it to say that it was rough out there. The cowboy's life was hard and lonely, the elements unrelenting whether it was winter or summer, the food awful, and his only real companion was the wretched (but perfectly suited) little pony he rode. The dangers were real enough, ranging from irate settlers fearful of their plowed land being trampled, to irate Indians, to being thrown from a horse and mangled in one of the frequent stampedes. For the most part, however, his life was one of simple and constant drudgery, except for the infrequent stops at the end of a drive in one of the famous cowtowns. There the cowboy indulged himself in all the luxuries of civilization: gambling, loose women, poison whiskey, and fast guns. Given that the days in such towns were few in comparison to the days in the saddle, the hell-raising was a release valve for the endless solitude of the range. And they really blew it off.

East of the Mississippi, those who stayed behind to reshape the broken remnants looked West with keen interest. With the completion of the Transcontinental Railroad in 1869, the western expansion of the telegraph, and the growing number of roving correspondents for the eastern papers, the people were kept more than simply abreast of western developments. They were force-fed the details of the Indian wars, the shootouts, the cattle drives, and life out West in general. And the Easterners loved it. Simple interest quickly grew into rapture, and the legend of the cowboy was born.

To nurture that rapture, the "dime novel" was created to glorify the West, and the "details" that whetted the Easterner's interest soon turned to heroics fraught with gross exaggeration and misinformation. It was, however, just the tonic that the East needed to revive the spirit of a nation staggering through a postwar depression, revealing as it did (and in the most romantic of terms) a united nation turning the combined energies of the Blue and the Gray into a glorious decimation of a common enemy: the redskin. The conquering of the West was to be our salvation, and to conquer an enemy in print, heroes were necessary.

William "Buffalo Bill" Cody was the initial focus of the eastern adulation (although interviews with and stories of Wild Bill Hickock were also quite popular). Cody had established his credentials as a genuine western hero early. He was left the man of his family at eleven, and worked on a number of wagon trains that took him as far as Fort Laramie. There he met the great trapper Jim Bridger and the great pathfinder Kit Carson, from whom he learned sign language as well as the language of the Sioux. Before Bill was fifteen he had trapped, panned gold, and ridden for the Pony Express. He returned to Kansas and worked as a general roustabout, fought with the Jayhawkers conducting a guerrilla war against Quantrill's Raiders, served as an Indian scout for the cavalry, and woke up one morning to find that he'd enlisted in the Union forces while under the influence of a terrific drunk. In

fifteen months he rose from recruit to full private, and was discharged honorably as a hospital orderly. Following the war, Bill returned to scouting, and then, in 1868, was hired to kill buffalo to feed the workers laying track on the Kansas Pacific Railroad. In 18 months, at $500 per month, he killed 4,280 of the dumb beasts, carving off only the hump and the hindquarters and leaving the rest to rot in the sun. It was this feat that garnered Bill Cody his first public notice, and from that point on "the noted guide" would forever be known as Buffalo Bill.

When Ned Buntline, the leading "dime novelist" of his time, went West in 1869 to find a new hero, Buffalo Bill was ready and waiting. The legends of Daniel Boone and Davy Crockett had long since ceased to interest the East. All eyes had turned toward western expansion—the *new* West—and Bill fit the bill perfectly. Within a year he was a national hero by virtue of a few meager facts, an assortment of tall tales, the racial arrogance of an Anglo-Saxon nation that truly believed in "Manifest Destiny," and last, but not least, the mass production and distribution of the "dime novels" following the widespread use of the continuous-roll printing press introduced in the mid-1860s. It's said that in the first meeting between Buntline and Cody, Buntline took a snippet of conversation from here, a callous boast from there, a few humble homilies, and turned each into a rugged, stirring adventure with such titles as *Buffalo Bill: The King of the Border, Buffalo Bill's Best Shot, or The Heart of Spotted Tale,* and *Buffalo Bill's Last Victory, or Dove Eve,*

The Lodge Queen. They touched a vital chord.

In 1894, Bill cashed in on yet another brand-new entertainment sensation: Thomas Edison's Kinetoscope, the hand-cranked peep-show machine that gave each viewer five different but short examples of the magic of the moving picture for a quarter. Edison himself took Bill, Annie Oakley, Lost Horse, and Short Bull (the latter one of the few Indians who had both seen the Indian Messiah and learned the Ghost dance from Him) into his studio in West Orange, New Jersey, and made the first Western Kinetoscopes: Bill and Short Bull "talking" in sign language; Annie's sharpshooting skills; Lost Horse performing the Buffalo Dance. Eventually, Edison also filmed *The Parade of Buffalo Bill's Wild West Show, The Procession of Mounted Indians, The Buck Dance, The Ghost Dance,* and other staged mini-documentaries. These little flash films played coast to coast as penny arcades sprung up in city after city. In a not so prophetic aside to Bill during one shooting, Edison confided, however, "The development of the big screen will spoil everything. We're making these peep shows and selling a lot of them at a profit. If we put out a screen machine, there will be use for maybe about ten of them in the whole country."

Nonetheless, the silver screen full of moving images bigger than life *did* develop (and with Edison at the forefront, naturally, whistling a different tune), and its unveiling in New York in 1896 created a sensation; people could sit in a chair and watch Fatima dancing at the World's Columbian Exposition at Chicago, or Sarah Bernhardt perform the dueling scene from *Hamlet,* or the *Pennsylvania Limited* roaring, at sixty miles an hour, straight at them (which sent men, women, and children screaming for the nearest door the first time they saw it). It was an unprecedented and godlike experience, and by 1906 *Billboard* reported: "Store shows and five-cent picture theaters might properly be called the jackrabbits of the business of public entertaining because they multiply so rapidly."

The year 1903 was a turning point for movies in general and the Western in particular when Edison released *The Great Train Robbery,* a film often regarded as the first feature (a grueling ten minutes long) *and* the first Western (a disputed claim). It was a true narrative film, and established once and for all the basic Western formula of crime, pursuit, showdown, and justice, in addition to highlighting the Western movie staples of fist fights, saloons, horse chases, gunplay, and plenty of action. It was a well-paced film, and the fact that it was filmed in New Jersey with men who rode horses as if the beasts had been invented yesterday didn't bother theater patrons one bit (as if they really knew). *The Great Train Robbery* was a giant success, and is credited as being *the* reason why theaters were established in many towns and cities. For a high percentage of Americans, it was the first moving picture they had ever seen, and they were in awe. The movie industry had a major bankable commodity. Imitations of *The Great Train Robbery* proliferated, and sometimes those imitations were a scene-by-scene ripoff with nothing changed except perhaps the calendar date hanging on the wall of the stationmaster's office. Edison even produced a tongue-in-cheek version called *The Little Train Robbery*, featuring a cast of children on ponies.

The one essential missing ingredient, however, was the star, the hero, the source of audience identification. Buffalo Bill was dead (he died broken and practically penniless, a casualty of modern times and technology, in 1917). It was time for the cowboy legend to be transferred from print to celluloid, and the man who embodied the transition came, strangely enough, from the cast of *The Great Train Robbery*. He became not only the first cowboy movie star, but also the first movie star of any kind.

G. M. Anderson (born Max Aronson), a big, beefy former model who had once posed in dude cowboy gear for the cover of *The Saturday Evening Post* in the midst of a singularly unsuccessful vaudeville career, was cast in *The Great Train Robbery*, but when he revealed he couldn't even get on a horse, much less stay on one, he was pushed into the background. Anderson, however, didn't really care, because he was only interested in making a few bucks. A few months later, however, when he wandered into a theater to see the movie, he was amazed at the tumultuous reception the film received, and from that night on the possibilities of the film medium excited him. He wasn't interested simply in performing in front of the cameras, but rather wanted to produce and direct. He moved to Chicago and got into the business, pro-

ducing and directing rather undistinguished one- and two-reel Westerns and early Ben Turpin comedies. Then, in a strange and unplanned twist, Anderson packed up and moved West to Niles, California, twenty miles south of San Francisco, to launch a West Coast studio. It wasn't exactly Hollywood, but it was the first production unit in the Golden State.

Once again, Anderson set out to make Westerns, taking advantage of the rolling hillsides and the frost-free weather. He also had something else in mind, something brand-new: a cowboy hero with a distinct personality. Stars, however, were difficult to come by in Niles, and finally he chose to play the hero himself. It would be nice to say that it was a wise and calculated move, but as it turns out, it was merely a matter of circumstance. There was just no one else.

Anderson was still big, still beefy, not terribly handsome (but then there were no Robert Redfords or Roy Rogers to compare himself with), but he did have a certain sincerity, and that, in addition to a fumbling but ingratiating awkwardness when it came to dealing with the ladies (on the screen, of course) and the ability to throw his brawn around effectively in a fight, made him an instant hit. The first film was *Broncho Billy and the Baby*, a sentimental tale in the "dime novel" tradition in which Broncho Billy, a "good-bad man," gives up his chance for freedom to save a child who finally reforms him. Anderson had no idea just how successful the film was to be, but three months later he realized that he would forever be a Broncho Billy in the minds of moviegoers. He capitalized on that new identity, and by the time he called it quits seven years later, he had "starred" as Broncho Billy in 375 one-reelers, close to 100 two-reelers, and even a few features toward the end. The final result was cinematic history, for he had created the first Western hero, the first Western series, and had opened the West Coast as the new Mecca for film production.

"Broncho Billy" Anderson solidified the notion of the hero in his peppy, adolescent action films, but the sharp edge of a carefully defined hero was left to be honed by a resolute former stage actor, William S. Hart. Hart knew the West from his childhood, and his films tried to capture the sordid and dismal realism that he remembered, while also including a strain of idealism that complemented an evangelical mood growing within the country as it embarked on its first sacred quest: freeing the world from the Hun.

Hart's films have been called the first "adult" Westerns, and rightfully so. They were brilliantly done, and they raised provocative questions regarding the growing complexities of a rural nation suddenly beset by urban challenges. His hero's ultimate question was always whether to follow the Law of the Gun (the one rule in the Old West) or to follow the Laws of Civilization (the new rules that the Easterners had brought with them to tame the Old West). The films were very heady affairs, and extremely popular, until the Great War in Europe proved to be anything but a spiritually uplifting experience. In fact, it was damned bloody, and no fun at all.

The warriors came home weary and wanting only to forget, and they forgot Bill Hart rather quickly. He was much too serious, especially when there were so many other things to think about and do, like have fun. And there were now so many ways to implement that idea. In 1915, there were only two million cars in the United States and no radios. By 1929, that figure would mushroom to over twenty-five million cars and twelve million radios. In those fourteen years, the country loosened up. Modern young women in once-forbidden silk stockings and rising hemlines were getting into model *T*'s everywhere along with smooth and experienced young men just back from *over there*, and together, armed with a hip flask of bathtub gin, they drove their older parents crazy as they raced wildly into the Roaring Twenties, stripping away all remnants of the Victorian Age. It was all devilish good fun and high-spirited action, and it was an attitude that spawned Tom Mix movies.

Tom Mix had all the credentials of a celluloid hero, including a real past that was a publicist's dream. He saw action in the Philippine Insurrection, the Boxer Rebellion, the Spanish-American War, and the Boer War, and served as a cowboy, a rodeo performer, a Texas Ranger, and a U.S. marshal (not to mention his experience guiding Theodore Roosevelt through blackest Africa). His movies were just as action-packed as his life, and featured a Western landscape where anything went as long as it went *fast*. In his lavish "streamlined" Westerns, Mix combined the best of the Old West with modern niceties like racing cars, sleek stallions, airplanes, ocean liners, trains, tanks, pretty girls, good, snappy direction and camera work, beautiful locations (he was fond of using national parks), and crisp, tailored cowboy outfits—in short, anything that would make a good, fast show. Mix quickly became the biggest cowboy star of all. By 1925 he was earning seventeen thousand dollars a week at Fox, and had given rise to a whole host of self-styled imitators like Hoot Gibson, Tim McCoy, Buck Jones, Ken Maynard, and many other lesser stars. Every major studio had its own cowboy stars, and Westerns were being churned out by the hundreds. The more they made, the cheaper and more formularized they got. But in the world of silent films, they were still paying bills.

Sound wiped all that out. By 1929, all the major studios (with the exception of Universal) had axed their cowboys. The formula Western didn't seem to justify the production expenses that sound required. Thus a lot of cowboys were out of work. That's when the independents of "Poverty Row" took over.

"Poverty Row" was a stretch along Gower Street in Hollywood between Sunset and Santa Monica Boulevard where most of the independents— Puritan, Resolute, Beacon, Majestic, Crescent, Victory, Mascot, Monogram, and more—worked out of bungalows. They were all run by guileless hustlers who had no capital, no equipment, and no sound stages, but who assumed the task of delivering the specialized films that the majors abandoned with the onset of sound: serials, action adventures, and cheap Westerns. They rented cameras, sound equiplent, costumes and stage properties, and hired whoever was cheap and available and willing to work long, hard hours. Following 1929, that meant a lot of people. John Wayne was one of them.

By 1933, Duke Wayne had already starred in Warner's first major Western effort, *The Big Trail*, but it bombed at the box office and Warner's dropped him. He signed next with Columbia, but boss Harry Cohn heard a rumor on the grapevine that Wayne was "foolin' around" with the young starlets (specifically one in whom Cohn himself was interested), and although the accusation proved false, Cohn still put Wayne through some humiliating times and pictures before spitefully dropping him. In a matter of three years, Duke had gone from being a promising actor at Warner's to walking up and down "Poverty Row" in search of any job that would pay the bills.

In those days, "Poverty Row" was an ever-changing parade of fading stars, fading beauties, lovely young starlets fresh from the Midwest, rangy stuntmen, midgets and other assorted freaks, and, of course, cowboys. The cowboys, in full Western regalia, all hung out at Gower Gulch (the center of which was the Columbia Drugstore at Sunset and Gower—and thus the term "drugstore cowboys"), so named because everything a cowboy needed could be found within easy walking distance. Sometimes they even found work. John Wayne did.

In the late summer of 1933, Wayne signed with Monogram Pictures' Lone Star Production to do a series of eight

Westerns (twenty-five hundred dollars per picture, a very good deal considering that Lone Star turned out a movie in *five* days!). In September the first five-reel feature hit the screen: *Riders of Destiny*. John Wayne starred as Singin' Sandy, the singing secret agent of the U.S. Secret Service. Wayne wasn't the first singing cowboy. That honor went to Ken Maynard in 1930 in the Universal film *The Wagon Master*, in which Maynard sang "The Lone-star Trail" and "Cowboy's Lament" (both of which he recorded for Columbia Records). Wayne's role as Singin' Sandy, however, was the initial attempt by a studio to create a singing cowboy from scratch, even though John Wayne was already a known figure at the Saturday matinees.

At first, Wayne put up with the singing as a gag, figuring that anyone who sounded like he did wouldn't be singing too long (some Western buffs insist that it wasn't Wayne singing at all, but was dubbed by a real cowboy singer named Smith Ballew). Much to Wayne's chagrin, however, the singing formula stirred audiences, especially in the South, and before he knew it the singing had become a staple in his films. He didn't like it.

"They finally got up to four songs in one picture," Wayne recalled, "and before you know it, they had me going on public appearances, and over the top of my horse crappin' on the stage, everybody's screamin': *Sing! Sing! Sing.*"

By the time Wayne's contract with Lone Star was up in 1935, many of the best of the "Poverty Row" enterprises had merged under the leadership of a former Wall Street executive, Herbert J. Yates, and formed Republic Studios, the studio that would soon bring the B Western to full fruition. Yates himself was a shrewd moneyman (intent primarily on tripling his money each year) and didn't know the first thing about movie production. He did know, however, that there was money to be made if Westerns could be made cheaply enough, because there were still five thousand theaters across the country showing them. He seldom if ever read scripts, seldom saw movies, and cared little about his actors. He only knew what sold. He was out to make money, not art.

In late 1935, Republic released its first film, *Westward Ho*, starring John Wayne. It was a nonsinging John Wayne, though, because when Duke signed his new contract, he was most explicit about that issue when he faced Yates. "I've had it," Duke said. "I'm a goddamned action star, you son-of-a-bitch. I'm not a singer. Go get yourself another cowboy singer."

The question that eventually must be asked is: *Did the real life cowboy really sing?* In a manner of speaking, the answer is yes, the cowboy did sing. Out on the endless rangeland, herding and tending the wild, long-horned beasts that were his charge, the cowboy learned early that the sound of the human voice, no matter how rude, had a soothing and reassuring effect on the skittish herd. The animals tended to stampede at the howl of a wild animal, a bolt of lightning, or absolutely nothing at all, and a stampeding herd meant both lost time and weight. So the cowboys sang to the cows as they kept their long, solitary vigil through the night. The songs they sang were usually traditional hymns and camp-meeting songs they remembered from childhood or from poems printed in newspapers. As time passed, both the tunes and the lyrics became more vague, and the cowboys resorted to mixing and matching different tunes and lyrics, and then creating their own lyrics. Most cowboys, in fact, based their whole repertoire on two or three melodies, and developed an endless number of verses. One of the favorites was "The Old Chisholm Trail," and in the thirty-plus years that the cowboy worked the range from Texas to Montana, literally thousands of verses were passed orally from cow camp to cow camp. "Sam Bass" was another favorite, recounting in homespun verses the legend of the famous outlaw. Instruments on the trail were virtually unheard of, but if there was an instrument, it was something as simple as a Jew's harp, or a rude fiddle carried in the chuck wagon. The guitar as an instrument of accompaniment did not become popular until the 1900s, and even then the picture of a cowboy with a guitar strapped to his horse is pure hokum. For the most part, it was simply the voice of the cowboy singing or humming low as he moved slowly through the long, black night on his wiry little pony.

With the disappearance of the real cowboy in a domesticated West, his songs were incorporated into larger body of folk and traditional songs performed by folk and hillbilly singers. There was a group who called themselves "cowboy balladeers" in the 1920s, capitalizing on both the romance of the West and the phonograph boom before the Depression hit. These artists included "Mac" McClintock, Jules Allen, and Carl T. Sprague, but by the time these men recorded their "authentic" cowboy ballads, there was relatively little market for such sparse stylings, and for the most part they were regarded as cultural oddities. After all, it was the Jazz Age. Thus the Western music that the American public was to hear throughout the next decade had almost nothing to do with the music that the real cowboys had made. In fact, it is safe to say that except for an occasional song, the real cowboy had virtually no influence either vocally or instrumentally upon the development of popular or country music.

With John Wayne out as a singing cowboy, Herbert J. Yates' right-hand man at Republic, Nat Levine, went looking for someone to replace him. By 1935, singing and dancing had become a staple of the Hollywood film, and Busby Berkeley had developed the big production number to a high and lavish art. People all across the nation flocked to their local theaters to see the "all-singing, all-dancing, all talking" extravaganzas as a simple way to escape the realities of the Depression as it settled in for a long stay. Levine meant to cash in on all that.

Levine had received many letters requesting auditions, but one young singer from the WLS "Barn Dance" in Chicago was most persistent. He claimed he had sold millions of records and was America's most popular cowboy singer. Levine finally consented to the audition and brought him West. The cowboy's name was Gene Autry.

Gene Autry seemed like an unlikely candidate for a new type of singing cowboy, and executives at Republic tried to talk Levine out of even considering him. As they saw it, Autry was pleasant-enough looking but hardly handsome, and the only way he looked halfway slim was when he stood next to his rotund sidekick, Smiley Burnette. Also, he had never acted before, and besides that, he had a definite aversion to horses. What then, other than a slightly nasal voice that kept on tune, did he have to offer? It was a question that was to be asked many times, but five years later the question proved to be purely academic as Autry's popularity and money-making capacity ranked him in Hollywood with Clark Gable, Gary Cooper, and Bing Crosby.

Gene Autry was born in Tioga, Texas, in 1907, and his early upbringing indicated little interest in the Texas tradition that would later make him famous. His earliest dream, in fact, was to be a major-league baseball player. It wasn't until his early teens that he became interested in music. By the time he was fifteen, he was making fifty cents a night singing popular ballads at a Tioga nightspot, followed shortly by a three-month stint with the Field Brothers' Medicine Show.

Gene's father bought a cattle ranch in Achilles, Oklahoma, a short time later, and one of Gene's duties was to drive the cattle a short distance to the railroad yard. The bustling railroad station interested Gene far more than

the business of moving cattle, and at the urging of one of the station hands he learned how to operate the telegraph machine and soon became the regular operator for the graveyard shift. To while away the long, slow hours of the night, Gene began playing a guitar he had picked up in trade for his old saxophone (at one time he wanted to be a singing saxophone player), and he sang popular and traditional songs. He became so good that he drew an official rebuke from the Frisco Railroad because the operators up and down the line were listening in while Gene sang into the company telephone.

One night a stranger walked into the office with a telegram he wanted to send. He saw the guitar and asked Gene if he was a singer. Gene nodded and the man requested "They Plowed the Old Trail Under." Gene obliged, and then the stranger himself sang "Casey Jones." For the next hour, the two men traded songs until finally the caller had to go—but not before he offered Gene some final words of encouragement: "You've got something, boy. Work hard, and you may go somewhere." The man was Will Rogers.

Three years later, Autry headed off to New York with his guitar in hand. His first stop in the Big Apple was at the Victor offices, the company that recorded Jimmie Rodgers. Autry had fallen under the Rodgers' spell and had developed a soft tenor much like that of his idol, plus the very popular and distinctive blues yodel. By the time Gene hit New York in 1929, Rodgers was already the most popular hillbilly singer in rural and small-town

America, especially below the Mason-Dixon line. Gene's repertoire included many of Rodgers' songs, and Victor, therefore, seemed to be the right label for Gene.

Gene sat politely in the anteroom for several hours waiting to sing for anyone who would listen, but to no avail. Finally, he pulled his guitar from the case and began to sing for the secretary. A Victor official passed by and liked what he heard, and gave Gene his first official audition. It was short and bittersweet. "You've got a voice," he told Gene, "but you haven't had enough experience with a microphone. Go home, get a job on the radio, and work hard. Come back in about a year."

Gene traveled home to Tulsa and got work on KVOO (*sans* pay) doing his own show, but within a year he had moved on to the WLS "Barn Dance," originating from Chicago. The WLS "Barn Dance" was different from most of the radio barn dances because it included many pop tunes and sentimental "old favorites" in addition to the basic hillbilly music. It thus allowed Gene to branch out into different musical categories. Gene returned to New York in 1930 and, under the tutelage of Art Satherly, recorded his first records for the American Record Company, which leased the masters to many smaller companies. One label to carry Gene's records, naturally, was the Sears label, which sold its records through the Sears catalogue, and, of course, Gene sang all his releases on the Sears-owned WLS "Barn Dance," whose powerful beam reached almost the entire nation.

Few of the songs that Autry sang

were of a western nature; his repertoire was drawn from the southern rural tradition in both selection and performance. He had also taken to writing songs, and one of his first compositions (written with friend Jimmy Long) was "That Silver-haired Daddy of Mine," which sold thirty thousand copies during the first three months of its release (it would eventually sell far more than a million copies) and

Gene Autry. Courtesy Country Music Foundation.

established "Oklahoma's Yodeling Cowboy" as the nation's best-known cowboy singer. His records were prominently displayed in the Sears catalogue, followed shortly by a number of Gene Autry songbooks and guitar instruction manuals, and finally a Gene Autry "Roundup" guitar, along with a reminder that Gene had become a star by simply "learning how to play the guitar while on the ranch."

Roundup? Ranch? Oklahoma's Yodeling Cowboy? In a master stroke of image building, Gene had taken on the guise of a cowboy (*B* Western variety, very streamlined), because it was in rural America that the legend of the cowboy loomed largest, and it was in rural America that the Sears Roebuck catalogue was only second in importance to the family Bible. By 1934, Gene's popularity in small-town America was unparalleled, whereas in New York and the other sophisticated metropolitan areas (even as late as 1940, by the way), the name Gene Autry mean very little. That in itself might explain why Hollywood was somewhat dubious about a singer who almost invited himself to the big audition. *After all,* you can almost hear the film moguls saying, *if we don't know him, how can anyone else?*

In Nat Levine's mind, however, Autry was the man, and he signed him for a hundred dollars a week, along with his sidekick, Smiley Burnette, for seventy-five dollars a week. Levine figured that since Autry had already sold a few million records and had been appearing on one of the nation's biggest barn dances, he must have a built-in audience out there in the hinterlands, and that was exactly where the *B* Westerns were going. Half the battle for acceptance seemed to have already been won.

Autry was first cast in a Ken Maynard vehicle, *In Old Santa Fe,* and appeared somewhere in the middle of the movie for a ten-minute musical interlude between fist fights and horse chases. Maynard even sang a song, but it was clear from the mail response that there were indeed Gene Autry fans out there, and they wanted *more.*

Gene was next seen in the Maynard serial *Mystery Mountain,* but only in passing, because behind the scenes at Republic the studio was working diligently with Gene to make some sort of an actor of him. The big test came with *Phantom Empire,* Gene's first solo vehicle. It was a twelve-chapter serial that immediately guaranteed Gene at least a twelve-week stay at all the local Saturday matinees across the country, and, in Levine's shrewd mind, a sure way to get the Gene Autry message across. The most unique feature of the film, however, was that it not only starred Gene Autry but also represented Gene playing *himself,* an unprecedented but quite calculated move. Levine was hoping to capitalize on his star's established popularity, and if that wasn't enough, he portrayed Gene as a singing-cowboy *radio personality.* The movie itself was a strange science-fiction epic about the subterranean civilization of Murania, which was located directly underneath Gene's Radio Ranch. The Muranians, led by Queen Tika (who had a hankering for Gene's body), feared that the people above ground would find the secret entrance and destroy the subterranean city. Therefore they wanted Autry out of the way so that they wouldn't be disturbed. And as if that weren't enough, Gene also had to contend with above-ground criminals who wanted to get rid of him and take over the ranch because they had discovered deposits of radium. Gene's one real mission, however, seemed only to escape in each episode in order to get back to the ranch and make his broadcast. And if the kids still didn't get the message about just who this guy Gene Autry was, Gene sang "That Silver-haired Daddy of Mine" in eight of the twelve chapters. The serial was a great success.

Autry's fourth film and first starring feature, *Tumbling Tumbleweeds*, established him as the most important newcomer in Western films, in addition to providing him with yet another giant hit record, the title tune "Tumbling Tumbleweeds." Republic was ecstatic, and quickly put more money (within Yates' limits, of course) and energy into the Autry films. Within two years, Autry was the kingpin of the studio and of *B* Westerns in general. In short, he was a giant, and he was changing the shape of the industry. Republic made a few Autry films with historical settings, but that mode proved too cumbersome to showcase Autry's talents, so the studio quickly reverted not only to "streamlined" Westerns, but also to "ultrastreamlined" *musical* Westerns. Action, which had always been the staple of the *B* Western, gave way

to a certain extent to a new emphasis on musical numbers, and to a new world in which those numbers were performed.

The Depression turned the world upside down and created a modern villiany—the city, seat of evil incarnate, breeding ground for sedanloads of sharp-eyed smoothies wearing pencil-thin mustaches whose only goal was to separate the trusting rural rubes from their just dues. That was the prevailing attitude toward the city in rural America.

Autry plugged into that attitude in virtually all his movies, and always found himself at the end of the final reel as the vanquisher of the evil and the savior of the populace. Somehow it was always the result of his songs or his singing, and given the bizarre problems he had to face, it's little wonder that the world in which this character lived came off as a little beyond the pale. *Mexicali Rose* is a good example (and is also another film with a title tune that became the most popular "hillbilly" record of 1936, but which, like most *B* Western film titles, had absolutely nothing to do with the movie itself). In the movie the city slickers had once again hit town. This time they were selling phony oil stock to the good honest local folk, including an orphanage in deep financial distress. They hired Gene to promote the stock by singing its praises on the radio. He did so, and everybody in town invested everything but their milk money. Gene, however, soon suspected some chicanery, and did a little detective work (with the help of a darling pair of orphans, of course). He discovered the ruse and *sang* a sensational exposure. In a neat twist, however, it turned out that there really was oil on the land, and the good people not only held onto their money, but also apparently got rich.

In addition to phony oil stocks, similarly fraudulent schemes were hatched: Various films featured helium wells, superdams, a fake Sun Valley, dude ranches, a threat of hoof and mouth disease, dairy farming, sleazy politics, and so on. When World War II began, Gene also fought Nazis, spies, and submarines, and always with a song at his lips. The mind-boggling incongruities of the traditional Western motifs (horse chases, fast gunplay, knock-down, drag-'em-out fist fights) and the thoroughly modern motifs (glamor gals in cute-as-a-button cowgirl miniskirts parading down the town streets carrying placards reading "Autry for Sheriff," racing cars, and music, music, music) combined into one slick, entertaining piece of film fare that disarmed the critics and put the Autry films into an enchanting ozone of their own. If one doubted that, the final proof was the word from the box offices, and the word was SRO.

In the never-never land that Autry created, a new type of song was needed, one that evoked images different from those offered by the southeastern hillbilly songs then dominating country music. Autry's own songs prior to his movies were basically within the hillbilly genre, but with his growing cinematic success they began to change. Traditional song sources were forsaken in exchange for Tin Pan Alley tunesmiths and a growing body of writers influenced by both the movies and the newer country sounds coming out of the Southwest. Mountains and green valleys soon gave way to blue prairies and purple canyons and whatever else could be mustered from the scenic myth of the New West, and these new songs jibed perfectly with the picture of Autry dressed in his form-fitted and neatly trimmed cowboy suits. The music and instrumentation changed little, however, but with Autry's success, the term "hillbilly music" was soon supplanted by the term "Western music" in the mind of the nation. "Hillbilly" had long been a pejorative term, not only to those who played and listened to it, but to an even larger audience of those who sneered at it. Autry's success, however, opened up a brand-new audience and proved that it wasn't so much the music as the hillbilly style usually *surrounding* the music that turned off a greater audience. Thus the hillbilly musicmakers followed Autry's lead by simply changing their dress code. Straw hats and patched overalls were quickly replaced in many quarters with white Stetsons and starched and spangled cowboy outfits. It's been that way ever since, although there have been some staunch holdouts (Roy Acuff has always maintained that his Smokey Mountain Boys are "a country band, and do country music, and thus dress like country people . . . not cowboys!")

For the first five years of his movie career, Autry had it all his way in Hollywood Western circles, although most studios tried to capitalize on his success by producing their own singing cowboy. It was rare, in fact, that any cowboy of any reknown didn't take at least one shot at warbling, but those who actually stayed with it in a continuing series of Westerns were few. Dick Foran was Warner's entry, and he was a lusty baritone who was often backed by The Sons of the Pioneers, but even that wasn't enough. The high point of Foran's career was when he introduced the pop standard "I'll Remember April" in Abbott and Costello's *Ride 'Em Cowboy*, years after he'd washed out of the singing-cowboy competition. Fred Scott had a nice husky voice, but it was apparent he wasn't a cowboy. Jack Randell, on the other hand, was a fine action actor, but his voice was so bad that often when the film distributors got their Randell films back from theaters, all the vocalizing had been neatly excised. Bob Baker was a tall baby-faced kid, who, like Autry, had come from the WLS "National Barn Dance," but his films were under-budgeted and he never had a chance. Tex Ritter's films suffered from the same budgetary problems, and it wasn't until he gave up the film industry that he went on to become the country music legend he now is.

The first real threat to Autry's popularity occurred in 1937 when he decided that he wasn't sharing in enough of the financial rewards his pictures were providing for Republic. Studio head Yates, however, was still a tough man with a buck at the bargaining table, and he remained unswayed by Gene's astute and businesslike arguments at contract time. So, in 1938, Gene simply took a walk when his option came up again. Yates' reaction

was typical: *To hell with Autry! We'll just get another singing cowboy!* It was an odd statement considering the number of existing singing cowboys who were barely getting by. Autry's strength was based not simply on his movies, but also on his continuing succession of hit records. No other singing cowboy could claim to have that advantage. Yates, however, would not relent, and the search for a new singing cowboy was on. Strangely enough, Yates didn't even have to leave the Republic lot to find his next star. He was there begging to be discovered. His name was Leonard Slye. Two weeks later it had been changed to Dick Weston, and then again a few months later to Roy Rogers. It never changed again.

Roy Rogers was born in Cincinnati in 1912, the son of a shoe factory worker, but from age seven on through his teens, he lived on a small farm in Duck Run, Ohio, raising vegetables and farmyard animals and "developing the bottoms of my feet like elephant's hide." Roy's family was musically inclined, and by the time he was ten, he was the best square-dance caller in the county. A few years later he added a little guitar-playing and technique to his act, plus the yodeling techniques he too had heard on Jimmie Rodgers records.

When the Depression hit big, Roy's dad found himself out of work, so he took the two hundred dollars the family had saved, packed up everybody in the '23 Dodge truck, and drove to California to visit one of Roy's married sisters. She was living in Lawndale, then a small agricultural town just south of Los Angeles. It seemed

Roy Rogers and Dale Evans.

like heaven on earth compared to the bitter cold of Ohio. The days were warm, clear, and breezy, but after four months the family returned to Ohio, much to Roy's disappointment.

Two months later, however, he hitchhiked back and moved in with his sister. He worked around Los Angeles at a series of odd jobs, including moving sand from the ocean beaches to the sand traps at the golf course by the Hollywood race track, picking fruit, and boxing in the back room of a bar for a couple of dollars a round. At night he would sit on the back porch and sing to the sound of the crickets while his sister tried to convince him that he should try singing on the radio. Roy finally gave in to her gentle but persistent demands and joined a hillbilly group called the Rocky Mountaineers. They were older musicians, and Roy was the only vocalist, so he ran an ad in a local paper: "Singer wanted." He got two replies, one from a young Santa Monica lifeguard by the name of Bob Nolan, and the other, by coincidence, from a friend of Nolan, Bill Nichols. They both joined Roy in the Rocky Mountaineers, and soon found their harmonies quite acceptable, but since playing dates were rare for the group, Nolan quit to become a caddy at the exclusive Bel-Aire Country Club.

Undaunted, Roy ran another ad, and this time Tim Spencer answered it. Again Roy had a trio, but following a short and unsuccessful barnstorming tour of the Southwest, the band broke up altogether. Connections, however, had been made.

Roy then joined Jack and His Texas Outlaws on Los Angeles radio station KFWB, and, again displeased with the vocal quality of the group, he called on his old partners Spencer and Nolan and offered to share his meager fifteen-dollars-a-week salary if they'd join him. They both accepted, and soon were ensconced in a Hollywood boardinghouse practicing their precise harmonies day and night. Their arrangements became quite tight, especially on "The Last Roundup" (a big Gene Autry hit), and one morning in the Los Angeles *Herald Examiner*, noted columnist Bernie Mulligan in his "Best Bets" column wrote, "If you want to hear the best arrangement of 'The Last Roundup,' tune in 8–9 on KFWB and listen to the Pioneer Trio." That impressed the KFWB brass, and soon the trio had their own show and a new name: The Sons of the Pioneers.

The Sons of the Pioneers' popularity grew quickly, and in short order they were appearing in Western movies with Dick Foran, Charles Starrett, and Gene Autry, and playing such places as the Texas Centennial. The group moved from KFWB to KNX and Peter Potter's "Hollywood Barn Dance." Soon they were recording for Decca Records and had expanded the group to six men. By 1937 they were the pre-eminent "Western" group in the nation.

Roy, however, had other plans. He was in Glendale one afternoon having his Stetson cleaned when an actor rushed in looking for a new hat to wear to try out for the singing-cowboy audition at Republic. It was the first Roy had heard about it, and his ears perked up: *a new singing cowboy?* The next day, in his full cowboy regalia, Roy too was at the Republic gate, but without a pass, and the guard wouldn't let him in. He finally sneaked in with a group of carpenters, and wasn't more than fifty feet inside

the gate when someone tapped him on the shoulder.

"What are you doing?"

Roy turned to find himself looking at Sol Seigel, the very man conducting the auditions. "Looking for you," he answered. Within the day he was auditioned, within the week he was screen-tested, and within two weeks he was signed.

From the beginning (discounting the Dick Weston days), Rogers had all the earmarkings of success, and prexy Yates, in an obvious slap at the delinquent Autry, lavished all the care usually accorded the original singing cowboy, including Republic's best writers, directors, and the usual bevy of beauties, on the Rogers films. Roy proved to be an instant hit from his very first starring role, *Under Western Skies*, and by the end of 1938 he was a proven star and the equal of Gene Autry. Rogers' films were more action-oriented than the Autry vehicles (*Variety* noted in a scurrilous review of Autry's *Gaucho Serenade*, a sixty-six-minute film, that the first horse wasn't mounted until the forty-four-minute mark, the first fist was not heaved faceward until the fifty-minute mark, and the first gunshot was not heard until the fifty-six-minute mark!), but the musical interludes by Rogers and his pals, usually coming within the last ten minutes of the film, were basically the same "Western" stylings. Autry himself, somewhat taken aback by the newcomer's meteoric rise, soon returned to the Republic fold, and as the country headed into World War II Republic could lay claim to the two biggest cowboy stars in the business.

The sheer visibility of Autry and Rogers in the public's eyes commanded the attention of country music performers all across the nation. Not only had the acceptance of Roy and Gene changed the clothing style of country music performers (in addition to influencing the musical styles), but also many established country artists saw Hollywood and the movies as a means of extending their own popularity. Thus, throughout the 1940s, many made the almost obligatory trek West to the soundstages and rolling hills surrounding the San Fernando Valley to appear in the proliferating B Westerns. Roy Acuff, Ernest Tubb, Hank Snow, Bob Wills and the Texas Playboys, Lulu Belle and Scotty, Jimmie Davis, Red Foley and his Hoosier Hotshots, and many others made the trip. For the established country recording artists, the lure of Hollywood was a passing fancy, but for the unknown artists Hollywood seemed like the new Mecca, and in the minds of many aspiring young country artists the notion of making it in Hollywood became the ultimate dream. They didn't, however, come to California alone.

Just as the United States was the melting pot of the world at the turn of the century, California had become the melting pot of the nation by the late 1930s and on through the 1940s. During the Depression, thousands upon thousands of dispossessed laborers and farm people from the Midwest, the South, and the Southwest had migrated to California looking for a brand-new start and a new direction in life as hope gave out elsewhere. That constant westward flow of people continued through the war years as soldiers and sailors and war workers found themselves leaving from, stationed at, or working on the sunny southern shores of the Golden State. There were the migrant workers of the blossoming San Joaquin Valley, the shipyard workers of San Pedro and Oakland, plus the supporting cast working in industries that maintained the war effort, and, of course, the enlisted men simply passing through by the tens of thousands on their way to the Pacific Zone, but staying on permanently once they had returned and were discharged. The state had opened its arms to all, and nowhere was that more true than in Southern California, with its developing industrial and technological facilities. The incredible growth of the Southland generated a whole new musical audience whose roots were steeped in country music of every possible variation, and the crosscurrents of those musical stylings flowing into each other dispensed with hard-line traditional attitudes. If there is one thing that can be said of the country music that developed in Southern California, it is that it was undefinable, a product of the traditional country singers, Western singers, western swing, honky-tonk, novelty, and a heavy dose of pure popular music. Musical divisions blurred as it became the first country music sound created in a somewhat sophisticated and growing urban environment for both pop and country audiences. California, it might be said, spearheaded the first commercial movement in modern country music.

Gene Autry and Roy Rogers were undoubtedly the most prominent singing cowboy stars, but their success created the opportunity—and the fashion—for others. By 1940, the Wakely Trio had arrived in Hollywood with the promise of Gene Autry still ringing in their ears: "If you boys ever get to California, look me up." Gene had first heard the Wakely Trio on their own local radio show on WKY in Oklahoma, and had been quite impressed. The boys—Jimmy Wakely, Johnny Bond, and Scotty Harrel—had been equally impressed with Gene's promise. They almost beat Autry back to California, and within months had joined him on his new Sunday afternoon national CBS radio broadcast, "The Melody Ranch

Roy and Trigger.

Show." It was a fortuitous move for Wakely, Bond, and the development of a country music scene in California.

The Wakely Trio was an immediate hit on the national airwaves, and within two years the two principals, Bond and Wakely, had broken up the trio and moved on to broader horizons.

Johnny Bond signed with Columbia Records and became a mainstay for that label for the next fourteen years, also appearing in *B* Westerns with Autry (both singing and accompanying Gene on guitar), Charles Starrett, and others. He also became popular in the lively Los Angeles country ballroom scene that was developing, and was usually backed by the Cass County Boys, Gene Autry's own touring band. He wrote over four hundred songs, and in 1950 became the emcee for the popular country music television show on Los Angeles' KTTV, "Town Hall Party."

Jimmy Wakely, a smooth and handsome fellow who patterned himself after Autry, formed his own band after leaving "The Melody Ranch Show" and moved into promotor Foreman Phillips' popular "Los Angeles County Barn Dance" on the Venice Pier, one of the major stops for touring country music stars. Wakely soon became so popular that he formed a backing trio, The Saddle Pals, was featured in more than thirty *B* Westerns, and was eventually signed with Monogram Pictures to star in his own Western series. He turned his band-leading chores over to a rising young western swing bandleader from the Northwest, Spade Cooley.

In California the Spade Cooley Band, featuring Tex Williams on lead vocals, soon became as popular—if not more so—as the Bob Wills congregation, and Spade took to calling himself "The King of Western Swing." In the late 1940s he moved from the Venice Pier into his own ballroom in Santa Monica, and he was regularly drawing crowds of six thousand on Saturday nights in addition to the SRO crowds he drew when he took his band on the road. His band backed up both Roy Rogers and the Sons of the Pioneers on many of their recordings, and was featured in many Western movies as both the posse and the purveyors of that good ol' Western music. Bob Wills moved his base of operations from Tulsa to California in 1944 (even Wills was lured West by the movies, appearing first with Tex Ritter in 1940, and later in a series that starred ex-Hopalong Cassidy sidekick Russell Hayden in *Wyoming Hurricane*, Wills actually engaged in a rough-and-tumble barroom brawl), but even with Wills in the area, Cooley's popularity remained undiminished through the early fifties. In 1949, Cooley even starred in a mediocre Western, *The Silver Bullet*. He also recorded many successful sides for Columbia Records.

Tex Williams had achieved celebrity status by 1946 as Cooley's vocalist, and in that year, Tex formed his own twelve-piece band, The Western Caravan, and not only played to giant local crowds in such places as the American Legion Hall in Placentia, the Foster Park Ballroom in Ventura, and the Harmony Park Ballroom in Anaheim (ballrooms at that time dotted the entire state), but also traveled as far away as the Aragon Ballroom in

Johnny Bond, left, with Pat Buttram and Gene Autry.

Chicago. In the late 1940s he also appeared with his band in fifteen Universal Western-musical shorts, as well as being featured in films starring Charles Starrett, Buster Crabbe, and Judy Canova.

In 1942, two local giants of the Southern California record business decided that it was high time there was a major label on the West Coast. Decca, Columbia, and Victor had offices in Los Angeles, but there was little action coming out of them, considering how fast the West Coast music scene was growing. Glen Wallach, owner of Los Angeles' largest retail music store, Wallach's Music City, and Johnny Mercer, one of America's foremost popular tunesmiths (in 1936, Mercer had written the tongue-in-cheek standard "I'm an Old Cowhand" for the Bing Crosby film *Rhythm on the Range*, in which

virtually the entire cast, including Bing, Martha Raye, Louis Prima, and the Sons of the Pioneers, then still led by Roy Rogers, took turns at the song), combined forces and started Capitol Records in offices located above Wallach's Music City at the corner of Sunset and Vine (just three blocks away from the original Gower Gulch).

Capitol Records' first country music signee, Tex Ritter, was a blockbuster. Tex had recorded for both Decca and Columbia, but it wasn't until he recorded with Capitol that he established himself as a country legend, beginning with his very first release, "Jingle, Jangle, Jingle." His success opened the doors of Capitol Records to other country singers, which in turn led Capitol to sign Cliffie Stone as their country-Western musical consultant. Stone was a man who was to figure prominently in California music circles for the next twenty-plus years.

Cliffie Stone was a local product (born and raised in Burbank) who first became interested in country music in 1935 under the tutelage of Stuart Hamblen, a longtime country performer and disc jockey in Los Angeles. Cliffie was only seventeen when he became a local DJ and country-bumpkin comedian on KFVD's "Covered Wagon Jubilee." Within ten years, however, he had become a top-rated country DJ (in the mid-1940s he emceed twenty-eight Western radio shows a week!) and was both a respected country musician and one of the most knowledgeable authorities on the burgeoning California country scene—he had played with virtually all the new country singers making names for themselves, in addition to fronting his own band. By the time he joined Capitol Records, he was known as a man who could make careers. He proved that at Capitol almost immediately by signing Jimmy Wakely, Tex Williams, Merle Travis, and a few years later Tennessee Ernie Ford (another local Los Angeles DJ and country comedian) and Hank Thompson to the label.

With Cliffie's help the head of Capitol's country division, Lee Gillette, soon established Capitol as a major country label, although theirs was not an exclusively country audience. From the beginning, Capitol was willing to take a few chances as it sought out the largest audience possible for its country artists. One result was a style of music that could easily be called "pop-Western," which featured modern musical arrangements, including string backgrounds; it predated the lush modern Nashville sound of the early 1960s by more than ten years. It was a sound that generated as much interest in pop as in country circles.

Jimmy Wakely scored one of the big pop-country hits of the 1940s when he was teamed with popular singer Margaret Whiting on "Slippin' Around," and then later with "I'll Never Slip Around Again," "Till the End of the World," and more, while also establishing the pop-Western duo genre later repeated by George Morgan and Dinah Shore, Tennessee Ernie Ford and Kay Starr, and even Ernest Tubb and the Andrews Sisters. As a solo artist Wakely hit big with "One Has My Name, the Other Has My Heart," "I Love You So Much It Hurts," and many more.

Tex Williams exploded on the pop and the country charts with his third Capitol release, "Smoke! Smoke! Smoke! (That Cigarette)" and it became the label's first million seller.

Merle Travis, the legendary guitar player and singer-songwriter from Kentucky, was discovered by Stone after Merle was discharged from the Marines and settled in California. Travis was an integral part of Stone's popular radio shows and band, and in the late 1940s Travis's Capitol hits included "Divorce Me C.O.D.," "So Round, So Firm, So Fully Packed" (an offshoot of "Smoke! Smoke! Smoke! [That Cigarette]," which Travis had written with Tex Williams), "No Vacancy," and "Cincinnati Lou." Travis also wrote "Sixteen Tons," which was one of the best-selling hits of all time when recorded by Tennessee Ernie Ford in 1955. The guitar playing of Travis has also been singled out as being probably the most influential of any in the entire history of country music.

Other successful ventures in the developing pop-Western vein at Capitol Records were the tongue-in-cheek efforts of Red Ingle and His Natural Seven featuring Cinderella G. Stump (in reality Jo Stafford) on rousing pseudohillbilly versions of "Temptation" and "Them Durn Fool Things."

Both records became pop hits, and also created a country music backlash when country DJs refused to play them on the grounds that they sullied the name of country music. Popular songstress Helen O'Connell also had a big hit with her fun-filled pop-country version of "Slow Poke." It was the success of these records that paved the way for other labels (notably Columbia, under the leadership of Mitch Miller) to provide the first commercial "covers" of country material to the pop market in the early

Merle Travis. Photo by Arthur Maher.

1950s. In those years Tony Bennett recorded Hank Williams' "Cold, Cold Heart" and sold 1½ million copies; Jo Stafford had a big hit with "Jambalaya"; Rosemary Clooney scored with "Shotgun Boogie" and "This Ol' House"; Frankie Laine hit with "Kaw-Liga"; Guy Mitchell hit with "The Yellow Rose of Texas"; and Joni James hit with "Your Cheatin' Heart." It was country music's big entree into pop music—or vice versa. Whatever the case, it was definitely a product of the rise of country music in California.

By the end of the 1940s the B Westerns had long since seen their best days and were nearing a much-needed retirement. They had become rather shoddy as the budgeting in the studios become more and more restrictive and production costs rose. Rogers had succeeded Autry as the new "King of the Cowboys" during Gene's three-year stint overseas in the Army Air Force during World War II, but upon his return the title didn't really mean much, anyway. Gene's recording career at Columbia, however, resumed, and soon he was selling more records than at any time in his career—usually around Christmas, when he had a series of pop-novelty-pseudocountry hits including "Here Comes Santa Claus," "Rudolph, the Red-nosed Reindeer," "Frosty, the Snowman," and (let's throw in Easter) "Peter Cottontail." Roy Rogers also scored with a few minor hits at that time, including "Don't Fence Me in" and "Blue Shadows on the Trail," featuring the Sons of the Pioneers from Walt Disney's *Melody Time*. Roy, however, didn't sell nearly the number of records Gene did, but then he never had. In 1951, Roy made his last feature film, *Pals of the Golden West*, and called the movies quits (other than for a long cameo in Bob Hope's *Son of Paleface* and a quick flash in another Hope comedy, *Alias Jesse James*). In 1953, following *The Last of the Pony Riders*, Autry called it quits with the movies, too. Both, however, moved quickly into television. Roy did the popular "Roy Rogers Show" ("Happy trails to you. . . .") for a few seasons, and Autry did his own show, "The Gene Autry Show." Autry's company, Flying A Productions, also produced early-TV favorites "Annie Oakley," "Buffalo Bill, Jr.," "The Range Rider," and "Champion" (starring, of course, Champion), but it was never the same. Television was in fact *the* prime mover in the destruction of the B Western, and by the time that Rex Allen was making the very last B Western at Republic in 1954, the early films of Gibson, Maynard, Jones, McCoy, and even Gene Autry were already appearing on Saturday-morning television.

The legacy left behind by the singing cowboy, however, is immeasurable. It goes far beyond the oversimplified stale-popcorn/Saturday-afternoon-matinee-at-the-local-Bijou stuff by which most people fondly remember him today. In the twenty-plus years that he sang and galloped across the silver screen, the wildly popular singing cowboy changed the shape and the scope of country music. He made country music at least palatable to a "sophisticated" audience that had previously jeered at it, and thus he laid the groundwork for the greater popularity to follow. "Hillbilly" was out; "Country and western" was in.

The singing cowboy injected a certain mythic quality into the music by changing the stylistic elements of the songs; he also changed the appearance of the musicians so that a developing nation weaned on the legend of the cowboy (the one true American legend) became more comfortable with the sights and sounds of a music that in reality had little to do with the Old West. The singing cowboy also gave established stars a new form of exposure in his films, and he gave rising new stars a new venue in which to achieve stardom. And, perhaps as important as any one other thing, he opened up the West Coast as a new and creative focal point for both playing and recording that was far more important than Nashville in the 1940s. The singing cowboy represented the first popular commercialization of country music and a grand and sweeping scale.

Chapter Six

The Road to Nashville

If the 1930s were a decade of explosive creativity and expansion in country music, the 1940s were a period of problems and confusion. The decade was characterized overall by a shifting pattern of power and influence within the industry, culminating in a lessening of influence from Chicago and Hollywood and a rush to Nashville as the new country music center; additionally, there were problems with the unions and, of course, the complex of troubles brought on by the Second World War.

As the decade began, Nashville was relatively insignificant as a production center for country music. The "Opry" was still lagging behind Chicago's "National Barn Dance" in the race for the top radio-show spot, and there was practically no recording or music publishing coming out of Nashville. Chicago, on the other hand, seemed well set up; it was the home of the na-

tion's leading country radio show, and had both recording studios and publishing companies. Even so, it seemed in 1940 that if any single city was going to emerge as a center for country music it would be Hollywood. All the ingredients that were eventually to make Nashville the home of the country music industry were present in Hollywood at this time: the stars, the studios, the presence of major labels, the songwriters, the radio programs, the musicians, the demand for music by a large populace, and a major barn dance. However, it never happened and the reason is a matter for conjecture. Perhaps the relative success of country music seemed pale in the glamorous shadow (and Hollywood in this era prized glamor above all else) of success in films. Perhaps the "tinseltown" image repelled the average country music record-buyer. Perhaps there was not the kind of in-studio creativity and flexibility that was to draw musicians and producers to Nashville late in the decade. Whatever the reason, it just never happened, and it took only some impressive public relations by the Nashville-based Country Music Association to steal Hollywood's thunder entirely and create the impression that Nashville had always been at the center stage of country music.

The country-music boom on the West Coast had begun in the 1930s, when the migration to the supposed land of milk and honey began in earnest, thousands of dust-bowl farmers straggling across the country in barely running old Fords, a picture straight out of *The Grapes of Wrath*. Some found a home in the West; some did not. Most—like the parents of Merle Haggard—brought with them a love for country music and the desire to hear more of it. And more than anything, it was western swing they wanted to hear. Popular bands that normally played just jazz and swing found themselves having to include country tunes in their repertoire or lose their audiences. The second great influx of country-rooted people, brought on by the wartime demand for labor in the California defense plants, pushed the California music scene farther in the direction of country and western swing music, and it wasn't long before a well-known California promoter by the name of Foreman Phillips had built a string of some half-dozen country-swing ballrooms to cater to public demand. Foreman's most famous venue was the Venice Pier ballroom. Foreman did not have the market to himself,

however; the leader of one big country dance band that played in Phillips' ballrooms went out on his own and opened a ballroom in Santa Monica. The place was soon drawing five thousand people every weekend, and the name Spade Cooley rose to prominence. In 1945, Cooley had the No. 1 record of the year, "Shame on You." He went on to assemble the biggest western swing band of all time— twenty-five musicians, including a large string section and even a harp player.

As the ballroom phenomenon continued to grow—even after the war— bandleaders from Texas were imported in droves, and existing bands broke up into multiple aggregations as successful band-members formed their own bands. One such graduate was Tex Williams, the vocalist for Spade Cooley's band who left to form his own Western Caravan and record the

giant hit "Smoke! Smoke! Smoke! (That Cigarette)" in 1947.

Ray Whitley and Jimmy Wakely fronted big bands of the era, Whitley's Rhythm Wranglers and Wakely's Cowboy Band. Whitley's band featured the likes of Merle Travis and fiddler Jesse Ashlock, while Wakely's band produced the lovely Colleen Summers (who can be heard harmonizing on "One Has My Name, the Other Has My Heart"), later known as Mary Ford of Les Paul and Mary Ford fame. Merle Travis led his own band for a while, as did Wesley Tuttle and Wade Ray, a transplanted Chicagoan who had been the Prairie Ramblers' fiddler on the "National Barn Dance."

The California scene drew musicians from all over the country—Foy Willing and Art Davis from Texas; Spade Cooley, Jimmy Wakely, and Johnny Bond from Oklahoma; Hank Snow from Canada; Merle Travis from Kentucky by way of Cincinnati; and Joe Maphis from Virginia. The "Opry" even lost a member to the lure of Hollywood—Zeke Clements, "The Alabama Cowboy," who headed West to be the voice of Bashful in Walt Disney's *Snow White and the Seven Dwarfs*.

Besides the dances, the film industry was an inducement for many, for while the singing-cowboy films ensured places for certain stars there was also a constant need for backup groups who could provide musical interludes for films starring action cowboys and augmentation for the singing cowboys. The Sons of the Pioneers were followed by similar harmony groups like Foy Willing and the Riders of

the Purple Sage, the Cass County Boys, Andy Parker and the Plainsmen, and others. There was also room for singing sidekicks like Ray Whitley, who was featured in a series of Westerns with Tim Holt and George O'Brien, and Bob Wills (with an abbreviated band of Texas Playboys) who costarred in some eight films with Russell Hayden. Wills doubled as a semicomic sidekick, usually in the role of top hand of a bunch of cowpokes (who of course seemed to have steel guitars and fiddles packed away in their saddlebags). In one case, 1943's *Riders of the Northwest Mounted*, Wills played a sergeant in the Mounties.

Radio—much of it network—was also a factor on the West Coast in the golden age of that medium. Gene Autry's "Melody Ranch," sponsored by Wrigley's Gum, began in 1939, and was to run into the late 1950s, an American Sunday afternoon tradition. "All-star Western Theater" was another popular show of the time, featuring many guest stars (Ritter, Wakely, Dean, even Eddy Arnold) as well as Foy Willing and the Riders of the Purple Sage, the staff band. "The Hollywood Barn Dance" was not a network show, but was a popular local program, and television programs like "Town Hall Party" in Compton began in the 1950s as that medium began to gain popularity.

With all this activity it is not surprising that recording studios were relatively commonplace, Columbia doing a great deal of cutting in their Hollywood studio. Capitol, whose tower was to dominate the West Coast music scene for so long, had the bulk of their recording roster on the West Coast in the 1940s: Tex Ritter, Jimmy Wakely (with or without big-band singer Margaret Whiting), Tennessee Ernie Ford, Tex Williams, and Merle Travis.

In 1942 California was going strong, Chicago was waning, and the "Opry" had yet to begin the talent hunt that would eventually launch it toward a position of absolute prominence in the field. It was in 1942, however, that a serious problem hit the entire country music business. This was what was commonly called the recording ban or the Petrillo ban, and it began when James C. Petrillo, president of the American Federation of Musicians, called a general strike on August 1, 1942. The main issue was that the proliferation of jukeboxes and radio stations (all playing prerecorded material) were, according to Petrillo, forcing musicians out of "live" work. Petrillo demanded the creation of a fund, supported by the record companies, for unemployed musicians. The demand was not met, so the union called the strike, thereby ending all recording.

The negative effects were immediate: Without recording income, it became hard for bandleaders to keep their big bands together—but the effects on posterity were worse: Many of the best and biggest versions of the big bands went completely unrecorded, star soloists entering and leaving the bands while the ban was in effect. Bob Wills' largest version of the Texas Playboys, for instance—twenty-two pieces—was never recorded at all. The immediate effects on country music were serious indeed. The

available backlog of recordings was quickly used up, and performers found it difficult to sustain both their popularity and their income without the help of new records.

Decca became the first company to give in to the demands of the musicians' union, signing the desired agreement in September of 1943. When, in November of that year, Victor and Columbia caved in, the strike was for all intents and purposes over. Petrillo called yet another strike in 1948, and its main effects were the same: More benefits to musicians, but much important music was left unrecorded in the hiatus. Bob Wills, for example, did not record from November 12, 1947, until May 5, 1949, and many others had similar stories: Bill Monroe was not recorded from October 28, 1947, through October 22, 1949; Johnny Bond from December 29, 1947, until March 18, 1949; and Al Dexter from December 15, 1947, until September 27, 1949.

Another purely business decision, completely out of the hands of the musicians, was the creation of BMI as a rival to ASCAP in 1940, and the subsequent war of sorts between the two that added to the confusion of the era, although it was ultimately of enormous benefit to country music, musicians, and songwriters.

The beginnings of the rift go all the way back to 1914, when the American Society of Composers, Authors, and Publishers—ASCAP—was formed to protect songwriters from unlawful use of their material. Called a licensing agency, it registered the compositions of songwriters and collected the fees due to them and their publishing companies for the use of their songs. At the time of ASCAP's formation, sheet-music publication and performance royalties were the main sources of income. ASCAP's territory was extended to cover sound recordings when that medium came along, then, later, to the playing of material over radio.

Formed mainly by and for Broad-way composers for their own protection, ASCAP as an organization tended to think of minor music forms —like "race" and "hillbilly"—as both musically and financially unworthy, and so many fine country songs, unless in the hands of an honest publisher big enough to insure collection, went unprotected, earning their authors little or nothing. The problem came to a head in 1940 when ASCAP announced that they were raising their rates for radio play. Broadcasters, having forseen the problem on the horizon, had begun their own licensing organization, Broadcast Music Incorporated—BMI—in October of 1939. The contract with ASCAP expired on December 31, 1940, and as of January 1, 1941, radio stations no longer played any ASCAP material, and the resultant confusion was immense. Big bands, for example, had to play either public-domain material (hence the astonishing surge in Stephen Foster material at the time), or the work of young, often unknown writers not affiliated with ASCAP, and even had to change their well-known theme songs as well.

Truth to tell, BMI's catalogue was pretty scanty at the time, but they had two things going for them. First, they were open and eager to have a minority catalogue, including country

and blues; second, they began to add some very important songwriters to their list of supporters. Pop publisher Edward B. Marks was the first to switch over to BMI, followed by two of the giants in country music, Peer International and M. M. Cole of Chicago, which published hundreds of songbooks in the 1930s and 1940s. Perhaps the most important individual to switch was an old Tin Pan Alley songwriter named Fred Rose, who had written pop hits like "'Deed I Do" and Sophie Tucker's "Red-hot Mama." About him much more will be said later.

ASCAP and the broadcasters patched things up in October 1941, but by that time BMI had a firm foothold in the publishing world, and soon most popular country music writers were publishing through BMI-affiliated companies (as they still tend to, although ASCAP has made great strides in broadening its base, going so far as to open a branch headquarters on Music Row in Nashville). BMI gave the country songwriter a chance, and it gave them the opportunity to be fairly and adequately compensated for their work. But more than this, it gave them—and country music in general—a respectability long denied it by serious musicians and popular composers. On a more mundane level, it was an acknowledgment of the growing financial stature of the music.

This growing financial power led to another confusing business development that marked this decade of confusion: the proliferation of record labels. As with many other industries, the Depression had pretty much wiped out most of the old companies, with only the biggest surviving. As the 1940s began there were a few small labels, but the vast majority of country music performers recorded for Victor (usually on their subsidiary Bluebird), Columbia (usually on their subsidiary Okeh), or on the relative latecomer (1933), Decca. There was, however, big money in country music, and as the last strains of the Depression faded away, more and more people wanted some of it. Easily the most successful new label of the decade was Capitol, founded in 1942 by Johnny Mercer, which became a "major" almost immediately. Their first country signee was Tex Ritter, an indifferent seller on Decca who suddenly supplied them with a long string of No. 1 records in the 1940s: "Jingle, Jangle, Jingle," "There's a New Moon over My Shoulder," "Jealous Heart," and "You Two-timed Me One Time Too Often." He was followed by Merle Travis, who did the same with "Divorce Me C.O.D." and "So Round, So Firm, So Fully Packed." Later in the decade came supersellers

Tex Ritter in the 1940s. Courtesy Tex Ritter Official Fan Club.

like "Smoke! Smoke! Smoke! (That Cigarette) by Tex Williams and "One Has My Name, the Other Has My Heart" and "Slippin' Around" by Jimmy Wakely. Capitol got on its feet early, and has remained strong in popular and country music ever since.

Another company to join the fray was MGM, which organized in 1947 and immediately went after the best, signing Hank Williams and Bob Wills right off the bat. In fact, they had the honor of having the last hit of Carson J. Robison's long and illustrious career. A song-writing pioneer who began with Vernon Dalhart in the 1920s, Robison had a big seller in 1948 called "Life Gets Tee-jus, Don't It?" Mercury had entered the field a year earlier, with Rex Allen heading up a stable that included Lulu Belle and Scotty and the Prairie Ramblers, among others.

There were many other labels as well. Some of them went on to prominence while others faded away to become prized items for collectors only. Majestic, in New York City, came into the field as a pop label, yet important country acts like Eddie Dean, Foy Willing and the Riders of the Purple Sage, and Pete Cassell graced the label, while Rich-R-Tone in East Tennessee first recorded such staunch and important ultratraditional groups as the Stanley Brothers and Wilma Lee and Stoney Cooper. Regional location seemed to mean little to new labels, either. Detroit's Fortune Records had Skeets MacDonald, the York Brothers, and Skeeter Davis (with Betty Jack Davis as the Davis Sisters), while Texas was the home base of several small labels including Macy's,

which released early records by Jim Reeves, Bluebonnet, which at one time had both Hank Thompson and Sheb Wooley, and Globe, on which Hank Thompson's first records were released.

Back in the Motor City, some of the most unusual records ever produced were first released in the 1940s —Vogue's picture records. Implanting a photo image in wax was not new: Victor put out a Jimmie Rodgers memorial record shortly after his death with a photo of the late Blue Yodeler in all his glory. But Vogue went a step farther, using full-color depictions of the events in the song, done in maudlin *True Confessions* style, full of bold motion and bright colors. The process, as might be expected, was prohibitively expensive, and the Vogue picture record did not last terribly long, although they had at least one substantial hit in Lulu Belle and Scotty's "Have I Told You Lately That I Love You?"

One of the most important of the new labels was King, a Cincinnati-based outfit that at one time had the largest country catalogue of any record label. As one who was present at the creation, Grandpa Jones (then a star of the "Boone County Jamboree") described how King got its start: "The last part of 1943 there was a man by the name of Sydney Nathan, who had a record shop close to WLW, and he came over one day and said he was going to start a record company and he wanted some of us to record for him. We were all eager to record, at least the ones like me who hadn't recorded before. So one day Sydney took Merle Travis and I up to Dayton. He said there was a studio up there he could use as he didn't have one yet and knew there was none in Cincinnati. I remember we recorded upstairs over the Wurlitzer Piano Company. We cut a few sides and coming back Sydney said, 'What will we call the company?' We decided on King Records: 'King of them all,' Syd said."

Besides Travis and Jones (whose first record was released under the pseudonym the Sheppard Brothers), Syd Nathan quickly signed up a host of country music stars, many of whom were to have big hits on the label: Cowboy Copas, the Delmore Brothers, Moon Mullican, Paul Howard, Mainer's Mountaineers, and others, including the superb gospel singing of the Browns Ferry Four, which consisted of Jones, Travis, and the Delmore Brothers. No one record put King Records on the map as much as Clyde Moody's "Shenandoah Waltz," King's only gold record. King remained a factor in country music into the 1970s, but actually much of its vitality had disappeared with the

Ernest Tubb on stage. Photo by Gary Parker.

death of Syd Nathan years before. Still, of all the labels that started as shoestring operations, King was the most successful. With no outside backing and removed from recording and publishing centers, Syd Nathan built a label that often rivaled the true majors in sales and popularity.

Two West Coast labels also came to prominence in the 1940s. Although based in the West, Imperial did a great deal of recording (both blues and country) in the Texas-Louisiana area, one of their first country artists being the remarkably adaptable Adolph Hofner, who recorded for them both in English, and in Bohemian, a great deal of his popularity being with the large middle-European community scattered throughout Texas. Hofner's "Green Meadow Waltz" was one of Imperial's first records. In the 1950s Imperial was to have big hits in three fields, with Slim Whitman in country, Fats Domino in rhythm and blues, and Ricky Nelson in pop.

Another thriving label—which after many changes of management and ownership is still active in Nashville today—was the (originally) California-based 4 Star. It got its start as a specialty label, recording only Mexican material, but was taken over shortly after its formation by a country music sharpie named Bill McCall, who turned it, for the most part, into a country label (although some blues and Mexican music were still recorded). Their lineup of talent in the 1940s included Smokey Rogers, Buddy Starcher, the Maddox Brothers and Rose, and the first recordings of Hank Locklin. But their big gun was T. Texas Tyler, "the man with a million friends," who had a nationwide hit with Scotty Wiseman's "Remember Me" (which became his theme song) and who scored again in the early 1950s with "Deck of Cards." McCall also hired a young apprentice named Don Pierce, who went on to bring a small Texas-based label called Starday to Nashville and to prominence in the 1950s by presenting the vitality of supposed old-timers like Cowboy Copas and Johnny Bond, proving they still had muscle when it came to record sales.

The final small label to make its mark in this era was based, interestingly, in Nashville. Bullet Records—owned by ex-"Opry" announcer Jim Bulleit—began in the mid-1940s, and his December 1945 recording of Sheb Wooley was the first Nashville studio recording produced neither on portable equipment nor in WSM's studio.

Bullet Records flourished for a while, and their roster—on and off—included some important people indeed: Ray Price (who did his first recordings there), Clyde Moody, Leon Payne, and Wally Fowler, among others. Their big country sellers, however, were both by a non-"Opry" act, Bob Wills' younger brother Johnnie Lee Wills, who scored twice with "Rag Mop" and "Peter Cottontail." Their best seller of all was, however, a purely pop record: "Near You," by Francis Craig, a Nashville hotel bandleader. Jim Bulleit also recorded a lot of fine blues artists, B. B. King among them. Still, as the 1950s progressed, Bullet Records lost most of its vigor, and except for scattered releases has not been heard from much since the early 1950s.

Bullet was as much a sign of the times as anything: It showed that by 1945 there was enough first-rate talent in Nashville to make recording feasible, and it showed the desire to improve upon and expand the extremely limited recording facilities that existed in what was to become Music City at the time. Bullet Records was hardly a threat to Capitol, but it was one of the first of many harbingers that accurately foretold the decline of the West Coast and the ascendance of Nashville as country music's home.

Still, as disruptive as any one of these sources of confusion might have been, all were cast deep in the overwhelming shadow of world war, which disrupted musical life every bit as much as it did the lives of every American. The effects of the war were numerous, varied, and complex, and are still being felt. Some were major, some minor; some helped country music grow, some retarded its progress. One thing is for sure: Country music was never the same.

One (maybe the least) of the deep effects of war can be summed up in one word: shortage. Restrictions on gasoline and rubber (for tires) made travel increasingly difficult for both entertainers and fans, who might have driven miles to hear a favorite singer or group before the war. The vinyl shortage was even more severe. Columbia A&R man Art Satherley recalls that during the worst years of the war he was not only forbidden to sign new artists (thereby missing Eddy

Arnold, a loss he has regretted ever since), but also he was allowed to record only the Big Three of his huge Columbia stable: Gene Autry, Roy Acuff, and Bob Wills. In addition, Satherley turned over his entire enormous collection of records (many of which dated back to his days with Edison) to the war effort as scrap vinyl, a priceless collection lost forever.

The hardships of shortage were obvious: A performer who can do only limited traveling, plays before smaller audiences, and has no records released or available is a performer with problems. During the war, such artists' only consolation must have been that they were not alone.

A far more serious hardship was the draft. Musicians in general were young and often single, and were prime prospects as soldiers, and the spirit of patriotism ran high, causing a great many to volunteer. A classic case was Bob Wills' famous vocalist Tommy Duncan, who strode into the studio of KVOO in Tulsa for the Texas Playboys' regular noon broadcasts on December 8, 1941, and announced to the band: "I don't know about you guys, but I'm going to join 'this man's Army' and fight those sons-of-bitches!" He and several other Playboys were gone by Christmas, followed shortly by Leon McAuliffe, the steel player whose sound was so much a part of western swing; he became an Army Air Force pilot. Wills himself was drafted at the age of thirty-seven in 1943, totally dismantling the Texas Playboys until late the following year.

No career was more visibly affected than Gene Autry's: He enlisted in the

Air Force as a pilot and spent much of the war ferrying supplies in Burma. Autry left as America's most popular country singer and one of its favorite actors, and returned to find Roy Rogers as "The King of the Cowboys," and could muster only a handful of hit records after the war—with the obvious exceptions of the multi-million-selling seasonal classics "Here Comes Santa Claus" and (at nine million sales) "Rudolph, the Red-nosed Reindeer." Another seriously damaged career was that of the Blue Sky Boys, who split up in 1941, separating for a full five of their best years by war, and reuniting in 1946 to play before a new and changed public. In fact, the draft so decimated the ranks of musicians that several bandleaders, faced with this and the difficulty of travel, simply disbanded for the duration. The Sons of the Pioneers lost half a group, and Bob Atcher left for years, as did Merle Travis and Jack Guthrie, who reportedly contracted malaria (a disease that may well have contributed to his untimely death of tuberculosis in 1948) in the Philippines. The list goes on and on.

There is a case to be made, however, for positive effects of wartime on country music, especially the long-held theory that in bringing southern soldiers in contact with northern, a taste for country music was spread and new fans made where none would have otherwise existed. A similar situation existed among civilian defense workers in the North and the West who were exposed to the music by the Southerners and the Southwesterners who migrated there in search of work in the plants. While it has been ade-

quately demonstrated that country music was a nationwide phenomenon long before World War II, there is no doubt that the music was spread by such contacts. An illustrative and well-documented case in point occurred in occupied Germany, where GIs were polled as to their favorite singer, and Frank Sinatra was nosed out by Roy Acuff. A country music radio program was begun immediately.

At any rate, country music was quick to respond to the exigencies of wartime with appropriate music, and hardly had the war begun before such records as Johnny Bond's "Draftee Blues," Cliff Bruner's "Draft Board Blues," and the Sons of the Pioneers' ironically prophetic "They Drew My Number" were available in record stores. Patriotic feeling was also strong, as Denver Darling's "Cowards Over Pearl Harbor" attests, and the war provided material for a legion of songs, many immediately forgettable, some country music classics. The theme of patriotism rang out in "Smoke on the Water," a hit for both Red Foley and Bob Wills, and in Carson Robison's "1942 Turkey in the Straw" and the Sons of the Pioneers' "Stars and Stripes on Iwo Jima." It was a theme sometimes expressed in a comic vein, as with Johnny Bond's "*Der Führer*'s Face." Most common among the wartime themes, however, was loneliness; the love of a girl for her faraway soldier or the concern of a GI in a far-off land over the faithfulness (or lack of it) of the girl he left behind. From the female side, Judy Canova used Patsy Montana's "Goodnight, Soldier" at the end of every wartime broadcast, and Bob Wills expressed the sentiment definitively in his "Silver Dew on the Bluegrass":

Soldier boy so far from me
How I wish that you could see
Silver dew on the bluegrass tonight

From the male viewpoint, Ernest Tubb wondered plaintively (in one of his greatest songs) "Are You Waiting Just for Me, My Darling?" while Gene Autry received the bad news by letter in one of the last of his big hits, "At Mail Call Today." And, of course, there was the recurrent theme of the son who did not return, as in Ernest Tubb's "Soldier's Last Letter," revived by Merle Haggard during the Vietnam conflict. Even the aftereffects of war were examined in country songs, from Roy Acuff's story of a young lady "Searching for a Soldier's Grave," to two looks at the fearsome technology of the atom age that was born at Hiroshima and Nagasaki, the Buchanan Brothers' "Atomic Power" and · the Louvin Brothers' "Great Atomic Power."

The king of all war songs was, of course, Elton Britt's "There's a Star-spangled Banner Waving Somewhere," a corny but moving tale of a crippled mountain boy trying somehow, in some way, to help the war effort. "Let me show my Uncle Sam what I can do, sir/Let me help to take the Axis down a peg," he begged his draft agent. Britt's multimillion seller was in fact awarded country music's first gold record. Although there had been million sellers in country music going all the way back to Dalhart's "The Prisoner's Song" in 1925, the practice of awarding a gold record for

Elton Britt. Courtesy Doug Green.

sales in excess of a million did not arise until Columbia gave one to Glenn Miller for "Chattanooga Choo Choo." The award was given fitfully for a few years, and it was Britt's 1943 hit that was granted gold-record status for the first time in the country field.

Country music's songwriters, singers, and A&R men have always demonstrated a remarkable flexibility when it comes to reacting to a national mood. The patriotic and "lonely soldier" songs were one example of this phenomenon; the sudden and wholesale change in the nature of the music after the war was another. Where prewar America was dreamy, romantic, impulsive, and escapist, postwar America was just the opposite: Hardened by the grim reality of war, the soldiers who returned wanted music that honestly reflected life's realities regardless of how unpleasant they might be. In truth, reality was often unpleasant: Consumption of alcohol rose rapidly during the postwar period, and many returned to wives and sweethearts as changed by the effects of war as they were themselves. The result frequently was divorce, loneliness, and anomie, often assuaged by the bottle. Postwar America saw a time of alienation, confusion, and an increasingly "wild side of life," a time of adjustment and adaptation that was not always easy or successful, and just as country music had been quick to respond to the feelings of America at war, it also was quick to express the difficulties of the war's aftermath. The story of one song in particular, "One Has My Name, the Other Has My Heart," exemplifies the rapidity with which these changes took place.

The song was written by singing cowboy Eddie Dean with his wife Lorene ("Dearest") and Hal Blair. Dean shopped both it and himself around to the major record labels but none would touch it, infidelity being quite taboo as a subject for records, especially infidelity as explicit and unrepentant as in Dean's song: "So I'll go on living my life just the same/ While one has my heart, the other has my name." Dean recorded it himself on a small label called Crystal (over the heated objections of the morally offended owner), but even with the finished product in hand he found he couldn't get disc jockeys to play it: "It's a great record, Eddie, but you know we can't play that kind of song over the air!" The climate had changed so much by 1947, however, that Capitol Records, remembering the song, got one of their own singing cowboys, Jimmy Wakely, to cut the song, and it was one of the biggest hits of the following year. So it was that "One Has My Name" became the song that got the whole "cheatin' song" genre under way.

Wakely followed this release with a Floyd Tillman song that has proved to be the classic of the style, a pure country duet with big-band singer Margaret Whiting called "Slippin' Around." It was an immediate million seller. It set a tone of resignation, not regret—"Oh you're tied up with someone else/And I'm all tied up too"— and placed the problem right out in the open.

The changes in taste were evident in all forms of music—the big bands, for example, at their peak a few years earlier, were all but extinct by 1950. Gone was the blithe optimism of the 1930s ("You Are My Sunshine") and the willingness to drift into the dreamy escapism of cowboy songs and danceable ditties like "San Antonio Rose." Here to stay was a certain cynicism, a certain hardness, and an implicit demand for songs that were straightforward, honest, and about the very real, very pervasive, very painful events which were an increasingly large part of life in postwar America.

Another historically significant record also appeared in 1948, and it too spotlighted the new morality (or at least the new honesty about the old morality) of the time. It was one of Bob Wills' first releases on the MGM label, "Bubbles in My Beer," and it

Bob Wills. Photo by Bill Ward.

treated the old "born to lose" theme with frankness, dealing with drunkenness without apology or moralism: It was a radical departure from country music of the past. Like all Wills' tunes, "Bubbles in My Beer" was above all danceable, featuring twin fiddles, steel, and Tommy Duncan's mellow vocalizing, but Cindy Walker's pointed and poignant lyrics ("I know that my life's been a failure") opened the door to the deluge of frank honky-tonkin' songs that followed, epitomized by the Webb Pierce classic of the 1950s, "There Stands the Glass."

In point of historical fact, the honky-tonk genre had begun before the war, with songs like Al Dexter's "When We Go A-Honky Tonkin'" and "Honky Tonk Blues." Ernest Tubb championed the sound throughout the 1940s, more or less introduc-

ing it to the Southeast via his position on the "Opry," but Dexter was the unquestionable leader of the pack. Although capable of beautiful love songs like "Too Late to Worry, Too Blue to Cry," he had one of the top songs of the entire decade with "Pistol Packin' Mama." Yet any song beginning with "Drinkin' beer in a cabaret/ Was I havin' fun. . . ." is a song with strong comic overtones, and "Pistol-packin' Mama," like most early honky-tonk songs, was basically comic. Therein lies the difference between them and "Bubbles in My Beer," a landmark song because of its willingness to face the problem in a manner both serious and straightforward. America had changed forever, and country music changed with it.

It is indicative of the complexity and variety of country music that a third major country music form was developed in the 1940s beside the cheatin' and honky-tonk genres. This was bluegrass, a music both traditional and innovative, which in one sense was a late manifestation of a line of development that began in the 1930s, yet also presaged the southeastern-sound revival of the early 1950s. Bill Monroe clearly stamped the music as his own as early as 1939, when he and his Blue Grass Boys (hence the name of the music) joined the "Grand Ole Opry" and let loose with their wild new blend of galloping tempos, unique rhythms, and "high, lonesome sound." The creative music of one man—Monroe—became a whole new genre with the arrival of Earl Scruggs (who joined the Blue Grass Boys at the age of nineteen) in 1945, for Scruggs' unique and dramatic approach to banjo playing, when combined with Monroe's sound, galvanized the sound and electrified "Opry" audiences.

After the war, country music on the West Coast was probably stronger than it had ever been, and for some, like Bob Wills, it proved to be the financial peak of their career. In retrospect, however, the writing was on the wall for big bands such as the Texas Playboys, and, indeed, for the whole West Coast scene, for national interest turned away from singing cowboys at about this time. The focus of West Coast country music seems to have been too narrowly based on film stardom and dance bands, and when public interest turned from those two forms the Coast was, in a way, left high and dry. (This is, of course, a relative statement, for the California country music scene has remained tremendously important, particularly in the clubs, in the location of Capitol Records, in the studios of Los Angeles, and in the tremendous influence of Californians like Wynn Stewart, Merle Haggard, and Buck Owens, who was to build a mini-empire in Bakersfield in the 1960s.) This trend was not obvious at the time, however; in fact, the country charts were dominated by West Coasters from 1945 to 1949—that is, until the coming of Hank Williams, who accelerated the shift to Nashville. In that pre-Hank period the big stars were Merle Travis, Gene Autry, Spade Cooley, Johnny Bond, Tex Williams, and especially Jimmy Wakely, whose two big hits of the era had, as we have seen, consequences far greater than their record sales alone.

Still, these were Wakely's last big

hits, and he wasn't alone. Even the prewar king of the West Coast, Gene Autry, didn't have a huge hit after his 1945 war song "At Mail Call Today," although he did have a few lesser hits in the later 1940s (excluding, of course, "Here Comes Santa Claus" and "Rudolph," which were country neither in sound nor intent). Much the same is true of Bob Wills, who was extremely successful for a time in the fading ballroom scene on the West Coast, but who didn't have a hit after his 1950s "Faded Love" until his 1960s "Heart-to-heart Talk." By the early 1950s the charts were all Hank Williams, Hank Snow, and Red Foley, with an occasional Texan like Lefty Frizzell or Hank Thompson occasionally thrown in; except for a few hits by Tommy Collins, and Tennessee Ernie Ford's "Sixteen Tons" in 1955, the West Coast scene was pretty much out of the charts until Buck Owens began the California comeback in 1959.

The West Coast was of tremendous importance throughout the decade, and no trumping up of Nashville or the "Grand Ole Opry" can deny it. But despite the dominance of California in this era, the slippage of influence eastward to Nashville is apparent with the convenient hindsight time gives, and the foundations of the West Coast dominance had been so fragile (or so narrowly based) that it took only the power of one southeastern "Opry" singer, Hank Williams, to tip the balance forever.

Chicago was another story altogether. The king of the barn dances throughout the 1930s, the "National Barn Dance" lost ground so rapidly in the 1940s that it had become nearly insignificant in the 1950s. Rock 'n' roll was a hard storm to weather, but Nashville and the "Opry" did just that, while WLS eventually dropped the "National Barn Dance" altogether in 1960, the entire station switching to a rock format that year (although the show hung on, a shadow of its former self, over WGN until 1970). In retrospect, the reasons seem obvious: While the "Opry" went out and signed a host of singing stars, moving right along with the trend toward solo singers and away from the big-band sound, the "National Barn Dance" stuck with its tried-and-true format and lineup of stars. As popular as Lulu Belle and Scotty, Arkie the Woodchopper, Doc Hopkins, Karl and Harty, the Hoosier Hotshots, and the Prairie Ramblers were—and they *were* extremely popular—without an influx of the "hot" new talent the lovable old "National Barn Dance" grew stale. In the 1940s they added only two major stars to their roster: Bob Atcher, who although a major artist had long been a Chicago fixture; and Rex Allen, whose stay was relatively short, for he fled to Hollywood to become the last of the singing cowboys when film roles were offered.

Even as the "Opry" overtook the "National Barn Dance" as the leader in the field, the "Louisiana Hayride" down in Shreveport, relying on the star system alone, appeared late in the decade to move quickly into second place behind the "Opry." The acts that began on the "Louisiana Hayride" are impressive indeed: Webb Pierce, Johnny and Jack, Faron Young, Red Sovine, Goldie Hill, and, of course, the greatest of them all, Hank Williams. The only reason the "Hayride" didn't come to dominate the more traditional "Opry," in fact, was that the "Opry" had so quickly and so firmly developed the image as the No. 1 country show that in every case performers jumped the "Hayride" to join the "Opry" at the first opportunity. Ultimately the "Hayride" became known as the "cradle of the stars," a sort of farm club where talented entertainers matured before joining the big leagues at the "Grand Ole Opry."

By 1950 the "Opry" was at the top of the heap, and it is fascinating to see how they did it. A study of the "Opry" in the 1930s quickly reveals that Roy Acuff was not the first singing star of the show, but simply that he was the first to hit with powerful national impact. His success on the "Prince Albert Show" (the "Opry" program carried nationwide on the NBC Blue Network in the 1940s) not only assured his continuing stardom and first accelerated the process that would give the "Opry" the No. 1 position among barn dances, but also sent the venerable institution on a massive talent hunt for new singing stars. Many were successful, some have been forgotten, and the Acuff-type magic didn't work again until Hank Williams joined in 1949, but the result was that the "Opry" became stuffed with singing stars in the 1940s.

Ernest Tubb was among the first, joining in 1943 with his electric guitars and honky-tonk sound, two innovations with powerful ramifications for the future. Drums made their first appearance on the "Opry" in 1944 during a guest shot by Bob Wills and his Texas Playboys, although they weren't to become steady "Opry" fare for well over a decade—in fact, Wills' drummer was forced to play behind a curtain, so the offensive instrument wouldn't be seen by the audience.

Predating Tubb were Paul Howard, who joined the "Opry" as a solo singer in 1940 and ended up building the "Opry's" only western swing-type band during the mid 1940s, and Pete Pyle, a graduate of Bill Monroe's Blue Grass Boys, who brought a gentle country sound to the "Opry" for a few years. Before them came two major stars who joined in 1939: Bill Monrone, a major star then and now, and Zeke Clements. It was after the coming of the Texas Troubador, however, that the floodgates seemed to open, beginning in 1944 with the brightest new star of country music—Eddy Arnold, whose plaintive, evocative voice was a marvel of heartbreaking ingenuousness, the crystal, achingly beautiful tones never really captured on record. At the same time one of country music's true pioneers was added to the cast: Bradley Kincaid, a tremendously influential entertainer who has never received the historical attention he has deserved. And he was, of course, a solo singer.

In 1945 the "Opry" scored a major coup by hiring Red Foley to host the "Prince Albert Show," replacing a disgruntled Acuff, who then left the "Opry" for a while in disgust. Foley was a big name, having starred on the "National Barn Dance," the "Renfro Valley Barn Dance," and the "Boone County Jamboree," although he had not had much success on record ex-

cept for "Old Shep." The boost the "Prince Albert Show" gave his career, plus the burgeoning skills of Nashville musicians and studio technicians, which would in following years make the town a national recording Mecca, changed his fortunes. After years of recording he suddenly seemed to get the Midas touch, and sold millions upon millions of records in the 1940s and 1950s.

Clyde Moody stepped out of Bill Monroe's Blue Grass Boys to a solo spot with Roy Acuff before joining the "Opry" on his own in 1945, and the Midas touch worked for him for a while, too: His "Shenandoah Waltz" was to sell well over a million records in the decade.

In 1946 one of the "Opry's" longtime favories, a solo singer with a western flavor named Cowboy Copas, joined the cast on the strength of his big hit "Filipino Baby." Copas was almost universally liked by his castmates, but more importantly brought a western image which, the "Opry" seemed to feel, would add some of the glamor of the singing cowboy to their image, particularly since Zeke Clements, the Alabama Cowboy and the only "Opry" performer other than Tubb who affected western dress at the time, had recently departed from their ranks. The flashy western fare of another Alabama cowboy named Hank Williams, and the even gaudier outfits of his protégé Ray Price just a few years later, show that the "Opry" not only went along with a trend toward western clothing and western songs, but in many ways helped perpetuate it. The names of the bands—from the Smokey Mountain Boys and the Blue Grass Boys in 1940 to the Drifting Cowboys, the Cherokee Cowboys, and the Rainbow Ranch Boys in the early 1950s—reflected this change.

The need for an Eddy Arnold-type singer was considered great by "Opry" brass, for Arnold, their most popular star during the second half of the decade, left the show in the late 1940s. Already persuing a pop market (as he

Eddy Arnold. Photo by M. L. Fallwell, Jr.

was to do with such great success in the 1950s), he had consciously changed his style, and the Eddy Arnold with the high, plaintive voice was superseded by a more mellow-voiced version with slick pop phrasing, the "tingaling" sound of Roy Wiggins' steel replaced with a smoother background, even the Hugo Winterhalter Orchestra.

The search for an Arnold replacement yielded a young George Morgan, who was brought in on the heels of his 1948 hit "Candy Kisses." His style—high, with a touch of yodel and a restrained vibrato—was reminiscent of Arnold's but was clearly his own, and although Morgan never had another hit like his first record, he was, like Copas, one of the best-loved of the "Opry" cast, and continued as an integral and important part of the show until his death.

The same year also saw the signing of Jimmy Dickens, a fine singer of throbbing heart songs who was best known for his comic ditties like "Sleeping at the Foot of the Bed" and "Take an Old Cold Tater and Wait." It was June Carter who described him, upon seeing one of his outlandish outfits on his four-eleven frame, as "Mighty Mouse in pajamas."

As 1950 dawned, the star-gathering process was still very much in evidence. Both Hank Snow and Carl Smith joined that year, and both were to be constant hitmakers throughout the 1950s. Very much in tune with the melding of cowboy look and country sound, which was becoming increasingly fashionable, Snow (a Canadian), Smith (from East Tennessee), and Dickens paraded a succes-

Hank Snow. Photo by M. L. Fallwall, Jr.

sion of dazzling western outfits—made by the famous Nudie of Hollywood, of course.

The biggest addition, however, was Hank Williams, who moved to the "Opry" from the "Louisiana Hayride" in 1949, and returned to the "Hayride" in 1952 in disgrace. His career and the multitude of effects he had on country music past and present are explored fully in Chapter Seven, but for the moment it is important to see that his appearance on the "Opry" was part of a logical progression that had begun about fifteen years earlier. Just as Roy Acuff happened to be the entertainer with enough charisma to become the singing star the "Opry" had been hoping for since 1933, so Hank Williams became that sort of massive star in the late 1940s and early

1950s, and accomplished the feat (toward which the music appeared to be heading anyway) of making Nashville the nation's country music capital. With a western image and hillbilly songs (again, a combination common to the "Opry" in general at this point), Hank was the performer and songwriter who put it all together, and put Nashville on top to stay.*

* It is interesting in this regard to note that the "Opry," in addition to adding a host of solo singers to its roster, also went heavily into comedy during this period, far more than before 1940. Minnie Pearl, Rod Brasfield, and the Duke of Paducah all joined in 1942, Lonzo and Oscar entered the picture in 1944, and the following year Stringbean left his job as Bill Monroe's banjo player to team with Lew Childre. Clearly the push the "Opry" made for dominance in the field was broader in nature than reliance on singing stars alone.

To give Hank or even the "Opry" all the credit for country music's postwar swing into the Southeast is unrealistic; the course of events was taking this direction anyway and would probably have produced the same outcome with or without Hank. His role, important in terms of visibility and as a catalyst who speeded up the process, was really more symbolic than anything else; the rise of Nashville as a center was due to a complex web of circumstances of which Hank and the "Opry" were only parts.

First and most obviously there was the decline of both Hollywood and Chicago. The decline of national interest in the singing cowboys, ballroom dancing, and the big bands was obviously a severe blow to the mainstays of West Coast music; Hollywood's narrowly based concerns were unable to support a full range of country music, while Nashville's broader focus was able to pick up the slack. Then, too, Hollywood's noted disdain for "losers" (what Johnny Bond called the "Yeah, but what have you done *lately?*" syndrome), compared to the traditional ultraloyalty of "Grand Ole Opry" fans in the Southeast, had a lot to do with it; Nashville was (and is still) very much in the center of the heartland, and in many ways it was a much more friendly, easygoing place in which to begin a career. None of this meant that California became moribund as a musical center. Far from it. Hollywood stayed active as a country music scene, but by 1950 it was clearly secondary to Nashville.

Another reason for Nashville's growing prominence was the rise of publishing companies in that city. In

Carl Smith.

1940 there was not a single music publisher in Nashville; by 1950 song-publishing was a big business there. The man chiefly responsible was Fred Rose, one of the greatest country songwriters of all time. Rose had written hits for Sophie Tucker on Tin Pan Alley (" 'Deed I Do," "Honestly and Truly") before drifting into drink and despair. His career foundering, he spent some time in Nashville as a pop pianist in the 1930s before singing cowboy Ray Whitley took him under his wing, and soon the two of them began cranking out movie scores for Gene Autry, as well as many hit records: "Ages and Ages Ago," "Lonely River," "I Hang My Head and Cry," and others, as well as many the reformed Fred Rose wrote by himself (often on Whitley's piano), such as Autry's "Be Honest With Me," which was nominated for an Academy Award.

Having developed a feel for country music, Rose returned to Nashville in the early 1940s, and having quit ASCAP to join BMI, decided to set up his own company, the first country music publisher in the Southeast. With financial backing from Roy Acuff (for whom Rose had already written hits like "Fireball Mail" and "Low and Lonely"), Acuff-Rose Publishers opened its doors in 1943 and has since become an international giant thanks not only to Rose's monumental genius and productivity (his output was so enormous that not only have every major country and many pop artists recorded Rose's songs in styles from blues to western swing to bluegrass, but also most have had hits with them, right up to Willie Nelson's 1975 "Blue Eyes Crying in the Rain"), but also to his ability to recognize talent in others. Hank Williams is the obvious example, but there are plenty of others: Felice and Boudleaux Bryant, Marty Robbins, Jenny Lou Carson, the Bailes Brothers, the Louvin Brothers, and hundreds more (right up to Mickey Newberry) first wrote for Acuff-Rose. Fred's major coup of the 1940s was obtaining the songs of Pee Wee King and Redd Stewart, which included the million seller "Slow Poke," standards like "Bonaparte's Retreat" and "You Belong to Me," and the all-time, most-recorded, most-sold country song, "Tennessee Waltz."

Huge sales like these don't go unnoticed, and although other companies didn't have Rose's genius to fall

Fred Rose. Courtesy Charles Wolfe.

back on, Acuff-Rose soon found itself far from alone in the country music publishing field. Quick to follow his lead was Hill and Range, who, with the bait of big advances, lured a number of country music's biggest stars into their fold: Bob Wills, Bill Monroe, and Hank Snow, who remains a Hill and Range writer to this day. Soon most of the major publishers with an interest in country music— Peer, for example—set up offices in Nashville, and many companies founded on shoestrings in the 1940s and 1950s—Tree, Cedarwood, Pamper —became worth millions within a few years. So publishing came to Nashville, and in a synergistic relationship with all the other factors that caused Nashville's ascendance, grew into a major industry in and of itself.

Another main factor in Nashville's

rise is perhaps the most obvious: the growth of the recording industry. Yet its existence would not have been possible without the nearly simultaneous occurrence of the other factors. It all began rather slowly after the war when three engineers named George Reynolds, Carl Jenkins, and Aaron Shelton took it upon themselves to set up a crude but workable studio in WSM's smallest and least often used radio studio. It was there that Jim Bulleit recorded Sheb Wooley in December of 1945, which may well give Bulleit the honor of producing the first recording ever done in Nashville by a Nashville company. (To Victor goes the honor of having produced the first Nashville recordings of any sort—a result of their 1927 field trip during which DeFord Bailey, the Crook Brothers, the Brinkley Brothers, and others were recorded. Victor may also claim the first Nashville studio recording—Eddy Arnold's sessions in the makeshift WSM studio in December 1944.)

The position of the enterprising WSM engineers soon became somewhat uncomfortable—they were, after all, using their employer's premises—so they moved their base of operations to a suite in the old Tulane Hotel in downtown Nashville and called their outfit Castle Studios. The name is now legendary. Castle Studios opened in 1947, and the very first recording done in the Tulane Hotel location was a jingle for Shyer's Jewelers, sung by Snooky Lanson (later of "Your Hit Parade" fame on television) and backed by Owen Bradley on piano, Harold Bradley on guitar, and the ex-head of the Nashville local of the American Federation of Musicians, George Cooper, on bass.

For all their pioneering efforts, Castle Studios had something of an old-fashioned and inflexible attitude —they refused to add an echo chamber as that sound was becoming popular because of the expense of the device, for example—which to a large degree led to their eventual demise. In addition, of course, they were still employed by WSM, and Castle Studios was pretty much a part-time affair from the beginning. Yet on the other hand, although the recording scene was only in its barest infancy at the time, Castle Studios was the only game in town. It stayed that way until 1948, when two brothers from Mis-

Roy Acuff. Courtesy Country Music Foundation.

souri moved to town and built the Brown Brothers Transcription Service near the corner of Fourth and Church in downtown Nashville. RCA's Steve Sholes much preferred the Brown Brothers' sound and attitude, and so all of RCA's recording was done there for some time, while Castle did the majority of the rest of the work. The Brown Brothers eventually called it quits and moved back to Missouri, selling their concern to Cliff Thomas, who continued to record acts at the Cliff Thomas Studio, but RCA eventually took their business to the Methodist Publishing Company for a while before finally building their own studio about 1957.

RCA was, however, preceded by some years on Music Row (their setup was and is on Seventeenth Avenue South, recently renamed Music Square West) by the farsighted Owen Bradley and his younger brother Harold, now the dean of the Nashville session musicians. They had opened a studio known as Bradley Film and Recording Studio on Second and Lindsley as early as 1952, and moved to a location in Hillsboro Village (not far from the Hillsboro Theater, where the "Grand Ole Opry" was held in the 1930s) a year later, finally building the famous "Quonset Hut" studio behind a residence on Sixteenth Avenue South in 1955. It was from that point on that the recording boom became an avalanche, and Nashville became the undisputed center of country music.

Although this came to fruition in the 1950s and especially in the 1960s, all the groundwork was laid in the late 1940s. It was pretty obvious by the end of that decade that recording was quickly becoming Nashville's domain, for before 1950 these studios had already produced a giant pop hit ("Near You" by the Frances Craig Orchestra), and a giant country hit ("Chattanoogie Shoe Shine Boy" by Red Foley), and a host of lesser but still substantial sellers. It was a trend that was to increase, to mushroom, and eventually to develop into a giant industry, certainly the most visible and glamorous of all Nashville's businesses. It was the kind of enterprise that helped itself grow as well, for more recording meant more money for the studios, which went for better equipment, hence better recording, hence more recording, and the cycle began again. In addition, it drew thousands of musicians into the city. This influx created the nucleus of talent that was to explode into the Nashville sound during the 1950s and eventually lead to the renaming of the large southern town as Music City, U.S.A.

The 1940s was a period of confusion, conflict, and catharsis for country music as well as the nation at large. The creativity of the 1930s became attenuated during the decade, and the arrival of Hank Williams toward its end pushed country music into a sharp and unexpected turn toward a new traditionalism—but while the 1940s pale in comparison to the decades that preceded and followed them, they saw the establishment of Nashville as a major creative center, and they set up the equipment for the boom that was to follow.

Chapter Seven

Hank the Great

Raw-boned and semiliterate Hank Williams hit country music like a cyclone in 1949. What he did, quite simply, was rise to the top of the business faster than anyone has ever risen, before or since, and become in the process the finest songwriter, one of the finest performers, and the most influential figure country music has ever produced. That he then fell as fast as he had risen has detracted not a bit from the love that popular-music enthusiasts feel for him. Indeed, his flameout at the age of twenty-nine served to frame the greatness of his work in a solid-gold legend.

"Hank Williams," Johnny Cash said not long ago, "is like a Cadillac. He'll always be the standard for comparison." Cash noted the "beautiful simplicity" of Williams' lyrics, a simplicity that "effectively communicates heart-to-heart ideas." The esteemed jack of all pop-music trades, Mitch Miller, expressed a similar idea several years ago, calling Williams "an absolute original" and classing him with Stephen Foster as the best American songwriter. "So indelible, so timeless" are Williams' songs, Miller added, that "they can take any kind of musical treatment." And take it they have, including much that should be called abuse, from crooners and wailers and orchestras and choruses and rock bands and God knows what else. In 1976, twenty-three years after his death, Hank Williams' own recordings reappeared on the country music best-seller charts. His albums—many of which have remained on the market—have always sold well, but here was a Williams *single* on the charts. It was the bouncy "Why Don't You Love Me?," a cut from the newly released album *Hank Williams Live on the "Opry" Stage*. At the same time both *Hank Williams Live* and

Hank Williams. Courtesy Doug Green.

Hank Williams' 24 Greatest Hits were earning places on *Billboard*'s album chart, along with a *Me and Hank* album issued by his onetime protégé, Ray Price. In all it was a remarkable showing for an artist dead nearly a quarter century.

Born in 1923 in south-central Alabama, Williams grew up in an era of country music giants whose influence spread across the United States: Jimmie Rodgers, the Carter Family, the young Roy Acuff. Rodgers, the "Blue Yodeler" and "Singing Brakeman," was the rage during the years when young Hank was trying to break in as a professional musician. Jack Cardwell, now a Mobile songwriter and disc jockey, grew up in the same time

and place, and Cardwell remembers Jimmie Rodgers with awe. Cardwell and his brother played the guitar as youngsters, copying Rodgers shamelessly: "Momma taught my brother three chords plus the words to 'My Old Pal of Yesterday.' He started playing for the buses that came in, so as soon as I learned that song I lit out for the bus station, too." Yet neither Jimmie Rodgers nor the Carter Family had a perceptible impact on Hank Williams. He didn't yodel or imitate the very imitable Rodgers. Nor, with the possible exception of a few of his sacred songs, did he pattern himself at all on the Carters. Williams said years later that his style was something of a cross between Acuff and Tubb—the wailing sound of Acuff and the phrasing of Tubb. The singer who influenced him most, however, was unknown outside of south-central Alabama. He was a black street singer whom everyone called Tee-tot. He played on the sidewalks of Georgiana and Greenville, the towns in which Hank lived, and he taught the white boy for a few dollars or a good meal. From Tee-tot Williams learned all he needed to know about basic country guitar, blues rhythms, and how to put across a song.

Williams the songwriter owed nothing to anyone. Although his songs are wholly in the country genre, they are indelibly, uniquely his own. One indicator of Williams' songwriting talent is the fact that he sang very few compositions by other writers; better indicators are the adaptability of his songs, which today are almost as well known by pop as by country fans, and the permanent place so many of them have found in the enduring repertoire of American popular music. No other country writer can boast a comparable list: "I'm So Lonesome I Could Cry," "Cold, Cold Heart," "Hey, Good Lookin'," "Jambalaya," and "Your Cheatin' Heart," to name the most obvious examples. ("Jambalaya" enjoyed a striking resurgence in western Europe in 1976, when Hank's original recording of it went to the top of the charts in several countries.)

Hiram Hank Williams was the son of a lumber-camp worker who spent

Cowboy Copas, George Morgan, Hank Williams. Courtesy Doug Green.

most of Hank's formative years in a Veterans Administration hospital. The boy was raised by his mother, Lilly, a resourceful, overbearing woman. Hank steadfastly resisted formal education, daydreaming through some classes and—after playing a show date the night before—dozing through others. Eventually he dropped out of high school to go for broke on a country music career. Except for an interlude as a shipyard laborer, Williams never worked at anything but country music. His lack of education and marketable skills would have made any other kind of good job hard to find. He consistently mangled the English language and did not possess even a rudimentary knowledge of business affairs or social niceties. He suffered from poor health as well: hookworm as a child, a bad back as a young man and again in his later life, and a variety of ailments either induced or aggravated by alcohol and drugs.

By his late teens, Williams was a scarred survivor of southern Alabama's blood buckets. He broke his hands fighting on a couple of occasions, broke guitars over antagonists' heads on a couple of others, and, in a honky-tonk brawl, lost "a plug outta my eyebrow, hair and all" to a man who sank his teeth into it. From age thirteen on, he had his own band, a sometimes-shifting collection of musicians who always played under the name he first gave them, the Drifting Cowboys. Without exception, they were country boys, and as instrumentalists they were all more talented than he. (Williams never attained proficiency on the guitar; his only other instrument

was the fiddle, which he played poorly and hardly at all after he reached the big time.) But as with all "backup" men, in country music and elsewhere, they did not have the leader's inventiveness and charisma.

The Drifting Cowboy's basic personnel were Jerry Rivers, fiddle; Don Helms, steel guitar; Bob McNett and then Sammy Pruett, lead guitar; and Hilous Butrum and then Cedric Rainwater, bass. Helms was the key to the band's instrumental sound—Williams valued his ability on the steel guitar and gave him unusual latitude to improvise in the midst of otherwise set arrangements. As Butrum notes, "The lonesome sound of Don's steel playing fit right in with the lonesome sound of Hank's singing." In the tradition of country-band bass players, Butrum and Rainwater filled the roles of comics, complete with baggy pants. When Rainwater joined the group in 1950 it marked the last change in the Drifting Cowboys' ranks until Williams left Nashville. Since his death, the band has re-formed, with its original members, a tribute to their skill and to the durability of the Williams image.

During the band's early years, Lilly Williams served as treasurer and paymaster—and, at times, as first-aid administrator and booster of fragile teen-age spirits. Later that job fell to Audrey Mae Sheppard, a country-pretty, southern Alabama blonde who became Hank's wife. Although she was a better bookkeeper than singer, she never lost her desire to be a star, and the couple recorded a number of mostly forgettable duets. As almost every Hank Williams fan knows, Au-

Hank, Audrey, and the Drifting Cowboys. Courtesy Doug Green.

drey played a critical and often dramatic role in his life. Their turbulent relationship and her goading, status-seeking personality provided the flint against which Williams struck his creative genius. The sparks eventually consumed the marriage, but they also led directly to many of his best songs.

Williams reached Nashville in the fall of 1946, a bony, almost gaunt twenty-four-year-old with an open manner, a winning smile, and a look that melted some women. Comedienne Minnie Pearl, who first saw him at about this time, vividly remembers

his "haunted and haunting eyes . . . deep-set, very brown, and very tragic." Williams came to Nashville not to play the "Opry"—he was far too green for that—but to get a start as a commercial songwriter. He'd been turning out songs, especially what he called hymns, for ten years. None of them, however, had been published; what country music publishing existed in those days was to be found in Nashville. Williams went straight to a firm that had earned a reputation for honest dealings with songwriters: Acuff-Rose.

Legend has it that Williams wowed Rose and his son Wesley by writing, in their studio and on demand, the hit "Mansion on the Hill." In fact, Williams sang a half-dozen songs he had written already, and the Roses promptly signed him to a contract. He then recorded, at WSM's primitive studio, four sides for Sterling Records: "My Love for You," "Never Again," "Wealth Won't Save Your Soul," and "When God Comes and Gathers His Jewels," and armed with these recordings, Fred Rose secured a contract with MGM Records. Then he secured a spot on the "Louisiana Hayride." After a decade of grinding anonymity, Hank Williams was on his way to country music immortality.

Red Foley and Hank Williams. Courtesy Doug Green.

A couple of years on the "Hayride" —and off it, when his worsening drinking problem got out of hand—earned Williams a shot at the "Grand Ole Opry." On June 11, 1949, he sauntered up to the microphone in Nashville's Ryman Auditorium and made "Opry" history with a performance of "Lovesick Blues." Since Williams had made a well-received recording of the song, he was expecting some response to it, but nobody expected the response he got: a standing ovation when he began singing and a commotion when he tried to stop that obliged him to take a half-dozen encores and to sing the closing lines—*"I'm lo-o-onesome, I got the lovesick blues"*—over and over. Jerry Rivers recalls that the applause and cheers lasted at least five minutes after Hank and the band finally returned to the dressing room. (Ironically, "Lovesick Blues" was not Williams' own song but a forty-year-old Broadway-type tune recorded by numerous other country singers without notable results.)

Although they were worried about Hank's drinking and tendency to miss show dates, the "Opry" managers couldn't keep him from becoming an "Opry" regular after that sensational debut. For the next three years, except when bouts with alcohol sidelined him, he was an "Opry" headliner, playing there for peanuts on Friday and Saturday nights in order to build a demand for his recordings and show-date appearances. In less than a year his price for a show date went from $250 to $1,000, a modest sum today but top dollar for a country performer at that time.

Meanwhile, Fred Rose concentrated

on making him a hit songwriter. Rose started with a daring premise: that Williams' songs, sung by pop artists, could be as successful in the pop field as in the country field. Rose took a handful of the best songs to New York pop-music executives, who turned him down flat, but when he got to Mitch Miller, then director of popular music at Columbia Records, his luck changed instantly and permanently. Miller snapped up "Cold, Cold Heart" and placed it with an up-and-coming singer called Tony Bennett. That turned out to be one of the most fateful moves in the course of American popular music. Bennett's recording of "Cold, Cold Heart" sold over a million copies and became No. 1 on the pop charts. In the process, it broke the artificial barrier that for so long had separated the pop and the country forms, and as often happens with seemingly impregnable barriers, once broken it proceeded to dissolve. "Hank," says Wesley Rose, who is now president of Acuff-Rose, "was the first writer on a regular basis to make country music, national music."

What made Hank Williams' songs such a powerful crosscultural force? One cannot readily distinguish them from other good country songs because the difference is a matter of degree. The best country music is simple, sincere, lyrical, and catchy if not pretty. The best of Williams, rated on a scale of one to ten, would score at least nine in each of those categories, with a ten-plus for lyricism. In one of the wondrous transformations that art brings about, the man who was crude and inarticulate in conver-

Courtesy Bob Pinson.

sation became, with a pencil in his hand and a song on his mind, a folk poet. His oft-quoted opening lines to "I'm So Lonesome I Could Cry" are worth quoting again: "Did you ever see a robin weep/When leaves began to die?/That means he's lost the will to live/I'm so lonesome I could cry." One could ponder the meaning of these lines indefinitely, but nobody could deny their lyrical beauty. (Typically, Williams was so unsure of their worth that he asked a fellow songwriter, after reading the verse aloud, "D'you think people will understand what I'm tryin' to say?") Country music fails if it does not pluck familiar, personal chords deep within the breasts of its listeners; Hank's songs did that with a consistency unmatched by other writers.

"Hank Williams had a way of reaching your guts and head at the same time," Mitch Miller has said. "No matter who you were, a country person or a sophisticate, the language hit home." That was probably Williams' single most important talent: the ability to elevate basic English—the only kind he knew—to folk poetry. Vic McAlpin, a Nashville songwriter who used to swap songs with him, says that Williams concentrated on lyrics and "didn't worry about melody.... Three or four of Hank's songs were taken from the same melody. The meter and tempo, and the lyrics, of course, are different."

Hank carried the country songwriter's practice of creating songs directly out of his own experience to new lengths; if it seems facile to say that his finest songs—the ballads of love and loneliness—were musical vignettes taken from his life, that is nonetheless the case. His eight-year marriage to Audrey, with its endless series of emotional highs and lows, yielded an unknown number of songs and song themes—unknown because he seldom talked about his marital difficulties. Some songs were obviously spawned by spats with Audrey: "I Can't Help It (If I'm Still in Love with You)"; "Cold, Cold Heart"; "My Love for You"; "Your Cheatin' Heart"; and, perhaps the most direct product, "Mind Your Own Business," a pointed rebuff to Nashville gossips who liked to talk about the latest Williams family battle. Not directly connected with Audrey, but premonitory as well as autobiographical, was "I'll Never Get Out of This World Alive," composed not long before his death.

And it must be added that not all of the Audrey-based songs were anguished or doleful; Hank had good years and good times with Audrey, and some of his early, exuberant songs reflected them.

Williams liked to make fanciful comments about writing in bursts of inspiration. He once said of his hymns, "I just sit down for a few minutes, do a little thinking, and God writes the songs for me." Inspiration did play a part in his writing, but it was inspiration of a very earthly sort. "I Saw the Light" owes its title and basic idea to a chance remark made by his mother when she and the band were returning from a show date in the small hours of morning. Weary from the night's work, she spotted the lights of the Montgomery airport, only a few miles from home, and exclaimed, "Thank God, I saw the lights." Williams awoke with a start, asked her to repeat what she'd said, and settled back in his seat. By the time everybody was climbing into bed, he had worked out the structure and many of the words of his best hymn.. He was a resourceful songwriter. Struck by an event or a remark or a chance acquaintance, he would scribble a note to himself on a piece of paper and tuck it away for future use. He stored these scraps, ranging from titles to complete verses in old shoeboxes. Years afterward they would be resurrected and carefully evaluated by Acuff-Rose, then turned over to Hank Williams, Jr., for expansion into full-fledged and highly salable songs.

When Hank, Jr., was still in diapers, Fred Rose was doing a more complex but less publicized kind of song en-hancement for Williams. Rose was a master craftsman of popular songwriting. He worked with many of Williams' songs, reconstructing, polishing, adding a twist here or a different word there. The most notable example is "Kaw-Liga," which Rose turned from a banal tune about love between a couple of Indians into a memorable number about unrequited love between *wooden* Indians. It is doubtful that any other country star of the first rank has had such an important accomplice. Rose personally supervised all of Williams' recording sessions as a kind of super A&R man. Rose alone decided when and how the records would be released. "My father never came back to the market with the same kind of song," Wesley Rose says. "He went from a blues to a ballad to something else." The Country Music Hall of Fame elected Williams and Fred Rose to membership together in 1961, although the citations on both of their plaques diplomatically avoid mentioning Rose's singular contributions to Hank's success.

Rose also influenced what seem to be the most personal of Hank's songs, the "Luke the Drifter" recitations that he recorded now and again. Although Hank's name was not publicly associated with the recitations, everyone in the business knew they were his. For the most part they were small sermons on homely virtues set against a mournful, three-quarter-time musical backdrop. A couple of the recitations carried a muffled social message; for example, one called "The Funeral," based on a Negro funeral procession he once happened upon, cites "the wisdom and ignorance of a crushed, undying race." That line is so foreign to his old-southern attitude toward blacks, and to his choice of words, that one automatically suspects the hand of Fred Rose.

All of Hank's attitudes came out of a time and place that now, in the era of the New South, seem terribly remote. Williams was pure country in dress, speech, humor, even food (he doused everything with ketchup). A celebrated maker of malapropisms, he once told a disc jockey inquiring about the abundance of sad situations in his songs: "Yes, I guess I am kind of a sadist." Williams was a generous man and, in his high-riding days, an easy touch for down-and-out members of the country music fraternity. Money was less important to him than the cheers of audiences and the acceptance of his songs; he did, however, love being rich. In one uncharacteristic display of childlike greed, he drew some four thousand dollars in one-dollar bills from the bank and stacked them in piles in his den. Scooping up handfuls of bills and scattering them onto the floor, he told Vic McAlpin, "I was so poor most of my life, I've always dreamed about being able to do this."

Even as a star, Hank was less vain than might be expected. Bob McNett, lead guitarist with the Drifting Cowboys, recalls how the boss would goad his band members into playing their solos so well that the audience applauded in the middle of them. "Hank really wanted us all to shine, not just himself," McNett says. Also, beneath his easygoing manner he bore a fierce pride, a legacy of his years of anonymity and hard work. Jack Card-

Audrey, Hank Thompson, Hank Jr., and Mrs. Stone, Hank's mother. Courtesy Bob Pinson.

well recalls that when Hank came to Mobile as an "Opry" headliner, he took a room at the best hotel in town and went straight over to the leading radio station with a sizable crowd on his heels. "He walked into the boss's office and told him, right in front of all of us, 'When I was in Mobile before, I tried to get on this station. I wasn't good enough then. I reckon I still ain't good enough.' He turned on his heel and went over to the other station and went on the air there."

The dominant components of Hank's personality, however, were an instinctive openness and a naïve delight in things around him. They helped make him a great stage performer. In today's hyped-up world of country music, one is never certain whether the Johnny Nashville at the microphone is the real Johnny or someone milking the now-bountiful country market. With Hank Williams, there was never a doubt. What you saw and heard was the genuine article. It was not just that Hank didn't know any other style; he wouldn't have used it anyway. Country musicians who have seen scores of

Nashville stars invariably cite sincerity and an ability to "make people feel he was one of them" as the hallmarks of a Williams performance. "You could hear a pin drop when Hank was working," says Little Jimmy Dickens, who shared many stages with him. "He seemed to hypnotize those people. You couldn't put your finger on the reason. Simplicity, I guess. He brought the people with him, put himself on their level."

Beyond sincerity was what Minnie Pearl has described as "a real animal magnetism." Says Pearl: "I was so proud to be onstage with Hank. He destroyed the women in the audience. They just had to have his autograph and get close enough to touch him. It wasn't sex per se, like with some artists. He appealed to their maternal instincts a lot." Hank would doubtless have been embarrassed by the suggestion that he appealed to maternal instincts, but after he'd blushed he would savor the notion of his having animal magnetism. Throughout his adult life he was a persistent—and by most accounts frustrated—woman chaser. Well before Elvis Presley came along, Hank used swaying, suggestive, Presley-like body movements onstage. To get really into a song, Hank hunched over the mike, buckling his legs and turning his hips, fixing the first few rows of the audience with the dark, haunted eyes that so impressed Minnie Pearl. The effect was often spellbinding. "Now and again," recalls Don Helms, the steel guitar player, "he'd close his eyes and swing one of those big long legs, and the place would go wild."

Hank's voice was a large part of his appeal as a performer. It must rank as one of the memorable country music voices, and like the man himself, it was genuine. He used no vocal tricks and no studio gimmicks. Also like the man, the voice was rough and unpolished. It was capable of sustaining notes across a broad range, and it was ideally suited to the material he performed. His successes with such songs as "I Saw the Light," "Lovesick Blues," and "Your Cheatin' Heart" stemmed largely from his stunning vocals. He adopted a distinctly country characteristic in his singing—the "tear," or quick sobbing warble, that Nashville singers inject into their songs. His sloppy speech patterns did not hurt his singing any more than they inhibited his writing; he enunciated cleanly and with a professional's sensitivity to the material. "Lovesick Blues," a vocally demanding piece, is an excellent illustration of his singing talents.

Williams fell from country music's heights as quickly as he had ascended them, ruined by inner torment and the abuses of his body to which it led. He had been a drinker since his early teen-age days around Alabama lumber camps, and what began as a boyish game became an incurable habit. He went to extreme and sometimes comical lengths to conceal the bottles and the effects their contents had on him. People who might have been expected to help him were disarmed by his lovableness as a drunk and, more important, by his insistence on keeping a certain distance from everyone. Hank had no close friends, no one who could pierce his shell of lonely discontent. Audrey tried, if only in her own interest, but failed. The pill popping began later, apparently as a legitimate palliative for his bad back and other physical discomforts, but it quickly got out of hand, and toward the end of his life he used pills, as well as alcohol, indiscriminately. Gradually, both the country music promoters and their audiences became fed up with Hank's offenses: appearing onstage too drunk to perform decently, often not appearing at all. Nashville promoter Oscar Davis remembers an ugly incident in Peterborough, Ontario, that should have shaken some sense into Hank but didn't. Hank had gotten drunk in his hotel room and had told Davis he wasn't going to play the date. Davis put his star under a shower, then pushed him onto the stage, and immediately wished he hadn't bothered. "Hank stumbled on the steps, crawled up to the mike, and began singing. He repeated the lines to songs a dozen times. Finally he fell down, and we had to drag him off the stage. The crowd was furious. They really wanted to get him. We called the Mounties, and they escorted us all out of town."

In August 1952, the "Grand Ole Opry" had had enough. It tossed Hank off the show. Six weeks earlier, Audrey had been granted a divorce, getting not only a hefty share of their assets but also one half of all his future royalties from song-writing and recording—a provision that was to make Audrey, who died in 1976, a wealthy woman. Hank went to the "Louisiana Hayride," supposedly to shape up for a return to the "Opry," but he was a broken man. His last few months were a wild kaleidoscope of scenes

and characters: Billie Jean Jones Eshlimar, a stunning young woman from Shreveport who traveled with Williams and eventually married him in two "performances" at the New Orleans Municipal Auditorium (the validity of the marriage has been contested ever since); Toby Marshall, a medical charlatan, who, in the guise of treating Hank's alcoholism, gave him all the "bennies" and Seconal he wanted; Hank's mystic sister, Irene, who says that just after midnight on New Year's Eve 1953, she clutched her throat and cried out, "Hank just died!"; and Charles Carr, a Montgomery teen-ager who was driving Williams to an Ohio show date when his famous passenger died quietly in the back seat, the victim of alcohol-induced heart failure.

The funeral was the biggest seen in the South until the one accorded Martin Luther King, Jr., fifteen years later, and the lawsuits that followed have been among the most complex and prolonged in the annals of the entertainment industry. Literally millions of dollars have been at stake in suits involving the renewal of publishing rights to Hank's songs and the guardianship of Hank, Jr. (who came of age in 1967 and—after a serious and disfiguring accident—rebuilt his own country-music career). In the two decades between 1953 and 1972, Hank's work generated royalties of well over five million dollars. With the man's recordings constantly on the charts and with fragments of lyrics remaining to be turned into complete songs, the commercial future of the long-dead Hank Williams and his music have no foreseeable limits.

Photo by Penny Weaver.

As with any great artist, however, Hank Williams will live not just in sales receipts and commercial promotions, but also in the esteem of his audiences. There are many millions of Hank Williams fans, and the number has grown rather than diminished in the years since his death, even though at this point a large segment of his fans are too young to have seen the man perform or even to have listened to his records during his lifetime.

Hank Williams has never been simply a cult figure. His appeal has been more enduring and more broadly based than that—more so, it appears, than that of any other long-deceased figure in the history of American popular culture. "The thing with Hank gets bigger and bigger," said Wesley Rose of Acuff-Rose Publishing in late 1976. "It could go on forever."

Chapter Eight

The Mountain Sound Revived

Always the quickest musical form to react to national moods, whims, fads, and attitudes, country music groped and floundered stylistically—while enjoying tremendous popularity—in the postwar years, until an Alabama boy named Hank Williams, with his raw, unpolished, and intensely moving mixture of mountain blues and delta soul, brought hard country back in a big way.

Of course, Roy Acuff was still immensely popular in those years, as was Molly O'Day, the classic white mountain singer with a big voice full of exhortation one moment and pain the next, but the big records came, for the large part, from anywhere but the Southeast. On the West Coast Gene Autry and Jimmy Wakely (especially in his duets with big-band singer Margaret Whiting) were big sellers. The Southwest brought the honky-tonk hits of Al Dexter and Ernest Tubb,

and the smooth-yet-hot sounds of Bob Wills and his Texas Playboys (who transplanted his band to the West Coast at this period). New York-based Elton Britt, maybe the sweetest-voiced of all, was also in his prime after the wartime hit "There's a Star-Spangled Banner Waving Somewhere," and even in Nashville, on the "Grand Ole Opry," that bastion of country music conservatism, the stars of the show were smooth-singing Red Foley and the rising young singer fresh out of Pee Wee King's band, Eddy Arnold, having hit after hit singing in a relaxed, easygoing voice.

There were a few besides Acuff and O'Day carrying on the mountain style —Bill Monroe, the Bailes Brothers, the Bailey Brothers, and more—but country music had gone pretty slick. The flirtation with pop music—as active then as now—had begun as early as 1940, when Bing Crosby began recording hit after hit like "San Antonio Rose," "You Are My Sunshine," and "Pistol Packin' Mama." But in general postwar interest in the mountain style of country music was definitely on the wane: It was an old-fashioned sound even then, and seemed doomed to obscurity—that is, until Hank Williams, who drew heavily from the mournful Acuff sound and fused with it more than a touch of blues and his monumental songwriting talent. By the time he hit his stride in the late 1940s and early 1950s, he was singing a sound America apparently wanted to hear—simple, unpretentious, eloquent, intensely moving.

With Williams came the rebirth of the mountain sound. Hank wasn't really a mountain singer, and he was modern enough to use electric instruments and even a hint of percussion, but in comparison to the Crosby-like sounds of Jimmy Wakely and Eddy Arnold and George Morgan and the big-band sounds of Wills and Cooley and Tex Williams, he was hard, hard country: no fancy frills, just raw repressed emotion, classic southern country soul. His impact was not lost: He not only spawned a host of imitators—most bad parodies, some who grew to prominence after developing in their own style—but also he opened the ears of all the record companies and the public in general to the rebirth of the mountain sound.

It was a fantastic rebirth, for the updated "hillbilly" singers almost literally blew the sweet singers off the map. Perhaps it was a return to conservatism in the country at large (the Eisenhower years were just around the corner); perhaps it was a market that had largely been overlooked. Perhaps it was weariness with the too-slick sounds that had increasingly dominated the previous decade, or maybe the expression of a war-scarred, no longer naïve America that now sought the raw, the gritty, the genuine in its music. For whatever reasons, the doors swung open for the high, tight, emotional-yet-repressed sound that dominated the next decade until the coming of rockabilly.

Perhaps the most important—and certainly for a time the most popular—singer for whom these doors opened was a native of West Monroe, Louisiana, named Webb Pierce. Although his sound seems dated today (as Hank's, for example, does not), Webb racked up a mind-boggling row of twenty-one No. 1 records in the early and middle 1950s, and was, with Hank Snow, the most distinctive country stylist of the era: Webb's tight vibrato and throat-busting always-at-the-very-top-of-his-range vocal style gave his voice instant recognizability. The 1950s were studded with his hits like "Wondering," "Backstreet Affair," "In the Jailhouse Now," "More and More," "I Ain't Never," and the honky-tonker's anthem: "There Stands the Glass."

Pierce's hit "Slowly" was a landmark for more reasons than simply being his second big hit. It sent scores of steel guitarists drilling holes and attaching coat hangers to their instruments trying to hook up jury-rig methods of duplicating the mind-blowing sound of the pedal-steel guitar as introduced on record by Webb's steel player Bud Isaacs. Although Isaacs didn't invent the pedal steel by any

Ryman Auditorium. Courtesy Charles Wolfe.

means, his was the first prominent use of the instrument's note-bending possibilities. Its sliding, tearful, evocative sound was an instant ear catcher for not only the steel guitarists but also the record-buying public in general.

Like so many of that period—including Hank Williams—Pierce came up through the ranks at the "Louisiana Hayride" in Shreveport, where he began performing for free while selling shoes at the local Sears, Roebuck store. Three No. 1 singles in a row—culminating with "There Stands the Glass"—brought him to the "Opry" and to superstardom, at least until rock 'n' roll took the wind out of country music for several years. Despite a big crossover hit of the era—"I Ain't Never"—Webb's glory days were over by the early 1960s, although

after a decade of semiretirement he recently switched labels from Decca (MCA) to Shelby Singleton's Plantation, and is back in the performing limelight. Still, he is best remembered for his hits of the 1950s and the symbols of success: the guitar-shaped swimming pool and the silver-dollar and leather-encrusted Pontiac.

A protégé of Pierce's was a cocky youngster named Faron Young, who came to Nashville and the "Opry" at around the same time as his mentor. If Hank Williams opened the door for a singer like Webb Pierce, who had already fashioned his own unique style, then he made a direct impression on Faron Young. It's hard to imagine it, but the mellow, crooning Faron Young we know today started out sounding as nearly identical to

Hank Williams as imaginable. Fortunately, a string of good material—especially "Five Dollars and a Saturday Night"—established Faron's identity despite his derivative style, and by the late 1950s this too had become unique and his own. Now an established and long-popular singer, who long ago gave up the fringed suits and note-shaped rhinestones à la Hank, Faron Young now sings everything from honky-tonk to nightclub pop,

Roy Acuff. Courtesy Country Music Foundation.

Webb Pierce. Photo by Jack Gunter, courtesy Nashville *Banner*.

and has been one of the few performers who has consistently been able to flirt with the pop market and pop sound while retaining a firm identity in country music.

The Williams influence goes on: Carl Smith, from Roy Acuff's hometown of Maynardville, Tennessee, was yet another singer who was strongly influenced by Hank's style. Like Faron Young, he was careful enough to come out with unique material that became associated with him, from old-timey-sounding songs like "Are You Teasing Me?" to the prerockabilly "Hey Joe" to western swing like "Deep Water." Yet the stylistic derivation from Hank Williams is clearly marked on songs like "I Overlooked an Orchid" and "If Teardrops Were Pennies."

Carl Smith makes no big waves in country music today, but he racked up some eighteen No. 1 records on Columbia in the early 1950s. He even hosted his own TV show on Canadian television, but like many of the post-Williams hard-country singers, his career was hobbled when rock 'n' roll eroded country music's audience later on in the 1950s.

While on Canadian television,

Smith went on to a much bigger band than usual, a move also made by Jimmie Dickens, whose big, loud band featured twin guitars, steel, and heavy, heavy drumming. Although we remember Dickens for his comedy songs like "Sleeping at the Foot of the Bed," "Take an Old Cold 'Tater and Wait," and "May the Bird of Paradise Fly up Your Nose," he was actually an emotionally moving singer in the best country tradition, with a catch in his intense, throbbing voice best displayed on "We Could" and other weepy love songs, highlighted by a crying, brittle steel guitar.

The man who was most successful in fusing the styles of the Southeast and the Southwest was, oddly enough, a close friend and confidant of Williams in Hank's later years: Ray Price. A college graduate out of Texas, Price was heavily influenced by Hank Williams, yet Price also brought to Nashville a love for the Bob Wills music he'd grown up on. The result—exemplified by early performances like "I'll Be There"—was a curious and extremely exciting amalgamation of eastern and western country music styles: The wailing, breaking, and certainly unpolished Hank Williams-style vocals were backed by three fiddles and the heavy beat derived from Bob Wills and the Texas Playboys (in fact, Price recorded a tribute album to Wills in the early 1960s; it took him until 1976 to record a tribute to Williams).

As years went by, Price eventually developed a tense vibrato, and his music became characterized by a Texas shuffle, a southwestern-style fiddle, and classic honky-tonk songs, a combination that made for hit after hit

Ray Price.

after hit in the late 1950s and early 1960s: "City Lights," "Heartaches by the Number," "The Other Woman," "Invitation to the Blues," and "Crazy Arms." The formula was so successful for Price that he was reluctant to abandon it. Still, as the 1960s progressed, the rhinestone-bedecked Cherokee Cowboy transformed himself through a series of records— "Night Life," "Danny Boy," and "For the Good Times"—into the tuxedo-clad countrypolitan crooner we know today.

Another who followed this course, although quite independently, was Texan Hank Thompson, who began his career just as the mountain-sound revival began. For years Hank never compromised on his big western swing band, providing, by the late 1950s and early 1960s, nearly the only taste of it still available nationally. His singing owed nothing to Hank Williams;

it was full, rich, and strongly reminiscent of Merle Travis. What Hank Thompson did have that allowed him to walk the thin line between East and West with such agility was good material. Beginning with "Humpty-Dumpty Heart" and then the classic 1952 weeper "Wild Side of Life" (often best known by the first line of its chorus, "I didn't know God made honky-tonk angels"), Thompson was able to appeal consistently to both musical regions, for despite his ultra-smooth big band, his songs (many self-written) were always pure hard country. Thompson had a gift for words, and his lyrics, whether tearful or catchy, were in the simple, easily understood southeastern-sound mold. To this, Thompson added a strong honky-tonk flavor, which matched well with postwar America's willingness to accept songs about going out, getting drunk, and raising a little hell without moralizing. Hank caught this mood, and it served him well down through the years.

But Hank Thompson and his big band were really something of an anomaly, as, in some ways, was Ray Price. A Texan who did not go the big-band route but stuck with striking fidelity to the sound of Hank Williams early in his career was George Jones, whose early Starday records reflect an amazing resemblance to Williams' sound of just a few years earlier, not at all the tortured, closed-mouthed, choked-throated voice with which we identify Jones today. Rarely (with the possible exception of Gene Autry) has an artist's maturation in vocal style been so well documented on record.

Still, perhaps the greatest legacy left by Williams was not the imitators who became stars with their own songs and their own—although derivative—styles. It was, rather, the opening of eyes and ears to songs not so smooth, so jazzy, so dance-oriented. Words—lyrics—were back, and back in a big way. A plaintive catch or a throaty throb in the voice were once again the mark of a country singer, not how smoothly he might sing. This is the gut-wrenching country music many of us grew up on; today, many people think of it as "pure" country music, whatever that most indefinite of terms means.

Maybe the greatest of the "pure" country singers was Muriel Deason, known professionally as Kitty Wells. After several years of alternating between housewife and featured singer with her husband's band, Johnny and Jack, she took the country-music world by storm with her answer to Hank Thompson's "Wild Side of Life" called "It Wasn't God Who Made Honky-Tonk Angels," a lonesome, plaintive, yet angry look at the not often seen woman's point of view. High-pitched, quivering, curiously unexpressive while intensely moving in classic Appalachian-repressed style, Kitty's homespun voice, which spoke of pain and woe, was a voice America was longing to hear in the early 1950s.

Her string of hits, including "Poison in Your Heart," "Whose Shoulder Will You Cry On?" and "Making Believe" made her the reigning queen of country music, a reign unbroken until the rise of Loretta Lynn a decade and a half later. Kitty Wells represents, in a way, the very best of the mountain sound revived: Unashamedly sincere, heartrending and emotive yet repressed, with the glimmering of a woman's consciousness, she moved men and women alike, all the while retaining a shy dignity befitting her royal stature.

Yet the field at the time was also open to other innovators and innovations, provided they pretty much stuck to the Williams format: songs that tell a story, songs of heartbreak, songs heavily laden with "feelin'," songs told on a personal one-to-one, drinkin'-buddy basis, rather than the lovely but impersonal and lovestruck lyrics of the bigger bands and the previous era's country crooners.

Two singers with a strong Irish influence first came to the fore during this era: Slim Whitman and Hank Locklin. Their sky-high tenors and rich vibratos wrung tears across the heartland of country music, and if their voices were unusual for the period it didn't prevent their successes. In fact, Whitman's biggest hit was probably the most surprising of the decade: an arcane old pop tune popularized by Jeanette MacDonald and Nelson Eddy called "Indian Love Call." It should come as no surprise

Kitty Wells and her husband, Johnny Wright.

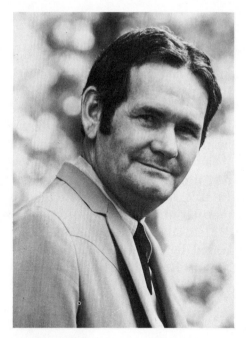

Hank Locklin.

that as late as the 1970s both Locklin and Slim Whitman were, despite a lack of recording successes in this country in some time, still big big stars in England and Ireland. In a way, this Irish influence was not new to country music. In fact, at its roots, it was the basis for much American music from the first days of the colonies.

The birth of bluegrass as a modern form for the most traditional of mountain and country music was another milestone of the 1940s. Bill Monroe, father of the movement, remained popular in the 1950s, when he produced some of the best music of his long career. Meanwhile, other bluegrass stars enjoyed tremendous popularity. Mac Wiseman was Dot's biggest seller until Pat Boone came along, and Lester Flatt and Earl

Scruggs became popular enough to join Columbia Records, eventually moving to the "Grand Ole Opry" in 1955.

Speaking of bluegrass, it is interesting that one of Don Gibson's early 78s with RCA was backed by a bluegrass tune of his own composition called "Carolina Breakdown," featuring the banjo and mandolin work of the Brewster Brothers, long a staple of the Knoxville bluegrass community. Gibson's early sound was strictly mountain—although, with the exception of "Carolina Breakdown," not bluegrass—and this and his monumental song-writing gift brought him hit after hit in the late 1950s and early 1960s, including "Sweet Dreams," "I'd Be a Legend in My Time," "Blue Blue Day," "Oh Lonesome Me," "I Can't Stop Loving You," and one that he did not write, "Sea of Heartbreak." After a decade-long dry period, Gibson again showed chart muscle with a No. 1 song in 1973, "Woman (Sensuous Woman)."

Yet another traditional form, the male duet, was enjoying its last years, perhaps given something of an extended life by the southeastern-sound revival. Having begun with Mac and Bob in the early years of recording risen to glory with the Monroe Brothers and Blue Sky Boys in the 1930s, continued with the Bailes Brothers and Bailey Brothers in the 1950s, and more or less ended with the Wilburn Brothers of recent times, the male duet reached surprising heights in this Hank-to-rockabilly era.

One of these last atavistic holdovers consisted of Johnny Wright—Kitty Wells' husband then and now—and

Jack Anglin, who had been known as Johnny and Jack for years. Popular "Opry" members until Jack's death in 1963, they scored big with Caribbean-flavored numbers like "Poison Love" and "Ashes of Love," as well as with straight country heart songs like "I Can't Tell My Heart That."

Like Johnny and Jack, the Louvin Brothers had a sound and a repertoire steeped in tradition. What set the Louvin Brothers apart was their powerful song-writing and their intense, emotion-filled, awe-inspiring harmony. Considering their brilliant singing, there is much justification for those who have called the Louvins the greatest of the brother duets. Charlie was (and is) a fine singer with a powerful yet supple voice, but Ira must be considered one of the greatest country singers of all time. Sky-high, filled with repressed pain so intense it was almost palpable, Ira Louvin's voice embodied Appalachian soul, and the pure mountain sound has perhaps never been captured on record as well as on such Louvin Brothers' cuts as "Too Late," "My Baby's Gone," and especially "When I Stop Dreaming."

The revival of the southeastern sound brought on a tremendous migration of traditional-minded musicians to Nashville, and Music City became something of a Mecca where a career could be born for a singer with style and song laden with tradition. Nobody came farther than Hank Snow, a native of Nova Scotia who had been hacking his way across Canada for nearly fifteen years and recording a string of successful but not overwhelming records for Canada's RCA subsidiary. Snow, a Jimmie Rodgers

devotee, was persuaded by Ernest Tubb to try it in the States. He went broke trying in Texas and in Hollywood before coming to Nashville in 1950. Hank joined the "Grand Ole Opry," and, almost as if by magic, the hits rolled in: "I'm Moving On," "Rhumba Boogie," "Now and Then There's a Fool Such as I," "Bluebird Island," and "I Don't Hurt Anymore." In fact, he, Williams, and Lefty Frizzell just about dominated the country-music charts in the very early 1950s.

Unquestionably, Hank Snow was and is a traditional singer, although his Canadian accent, back-of-the palate tone, and precise diction make him perhaps the most easily recognized—and imitated—country singer alive. Still, with his backup of fiddle, nonpedal steel, and his own acoustic guitar picking, there is little that is "uptown" about Hank Snow. He was one of the first to benefit from the trend toward traditional music in the early 1950s, and, due to his relatively early success in the 1947–57 decade, he did a great deal to further strengthen and solidify this trend.

The honky-tonk tradition from the Lone Star State that had spawned Al Dexter and Ernest Tubb was important in this period as well. The two major newcomers with this style to emerge in the 1950s—Lefty Frizzell and Johnny Horton—used the more intimate and more Spartan Hank Williams-like four-piece band, forsaking the big-band Bob Wills sound entirely. Just as important, they were also careful to sing the kind of straightforward one-on-one lyrics that the temper of the times demanded. Whether this was a conscious decision or whether they were in turn effected by their era is a moot point; whether it was the chicken or the egg, it served them well in this prerockabilly era.

Horton struggled for years on the "Louisiana Hayride," his unusual voice—high, emotion-filled, with a touch of a growl borrowed from T. Texas Tyler—eloquent on love ballads like "All for the Love of a Girl," raunchy on prerockabilly songs like "Honky Tonk Man." He really hit his stride around 1960, cashing in on the brief if powerful vogue for historical songs, with "Battle of New Orleans," "Sink the *Bismarck*," and "North to Alaska."

Lefty Frizzell burst on the scene in the early 1950s, racking up hit after hit and turning a trick yet to be duplicated: four records simultaneously in *Billboard*'s top ten. The string of Frizzell classics includes "Always Late," "I Love You a Thousand Ways," "If You've Got the Money, I've Got the Time," "Long Black Veil," "Saginaw, Michigan," "Mom and Dad's Waltz," and "I Want to Be with You Always." As with Hank Williams, sudden wealth and fame were difficult—in many instances impossible—to deal with for this uncomplicated Texas boy from an impoverished family, and Lefty spent the next twenty-odd years in a battle with the bottle, marked by occasional flashes of the greatness that was so obvious. He seemed, in a way, to once again be getting hold of himself—having written or cowritten a score of chart records within a period of a few months—before his untimely death of a stroke in 1975. He was only forty-seven years old.

As the years go by, Lefty Frizzell has emerged not only as a true original in country music—that is already self-evident—but also as a very powerful and widespread influence on others as well. His sliding, drawling phrases and rich vibrato can be heard in the singing of Merle Haggard—an admitted admirer—and Johnny Rodriguez and a dozen more, and the way country singers have had of saying "wie" for "way" (listen to Buck Owens, for example) traces back to the strange, innovative, and unique phrasing and pronunciation of Lefty Frizzell. More than this, Lefty Frizzell could be *intimate* with a song. He wasn't a smooth singer in the cowboy or western swing tradition, and he wasn't a singer with a big, emotive voice like Roy Acuff or Hank Williams. There was an immediacy and warmth and a depth of subtle feeling to Frizzell's voice that was spellbinding. It could literally send shivers up your spine.

An interesting anomaly of the period was an Arizonian named Marty Robbins, whose style was unique and not derived from any particular tradition or artist, except, perhaps, the early Eddy Arnold or two underrated smooth singers of the 1940s, Pete Cassell and Zeke Clements. Marty Robbins' voice was so superb—flexible, expressive, and warm—that he was welcomed with open arms into the country-music establishment and hailed as one of the new breed of country singers. His singing was overwhelming in those days—strong, caressing, punctuated by high, clear

Marty Robbins.

yodels, breaking and crooning, inspiring his early nickname, "Mr. Teardrop." He played this role to the hilt in these early days—he joined the "Opry" in 1953—with magnificent country songs like "Time Goes By," "At the End of a Long Lonely Day," and "Sing Me Something Sentimental."

Robbins is probably the most versatile country singer of all, and began to expand his repertoire widely in the early years of rock, scoring the first of his No. 1 hits with "A White Sport Coat and a Pink Carnation," and re-

cording several other rockabilly sides like "Mean Mama Blues" and even Chuck Berry's "Maybelline." Rockabilly was but one of his numerous flirtations with widely different musical styles. For example, he recorded two Hawaiian albums (highlighted by Jerry Byrd's tender touch on the steel) that are among the best of that genre, and he chalked up a big hit with the voguish calypso sound with "Devil Woman" in 1961. And, of course, he is noted as one of the few to ever have big-selling cowboy records, with his back-to-back hits "Big Iron" and "El Paso," both of which were included on *Gunfighter Ballads and Trail Songs*, one of the earliest country albums to be awarded gold-record status.

Marty Robbins eventually recorded three albums in the cowboy style, which are testament to the power of his rich, versatile voice: The great majority of the cuts feature only the voice of Marty Robbins, the powerful harmony singing of the Glaser Brothers, a rhythm guitar and a bass, the absolutely brilliant gut-string guitar work of Grady Martin. These forays into other fields did not keep Robbins from having hits with pure country love songs like "Don't Worry 'Bout Me" and "Singing the Blues." Somehow he has always kept his identity with the country fans, who never seemed to desert him despite his wide-ranging musical explorations, and Marty Robbins remains one of the most popular contemporary stars.

Another factor as important as the careers of these stars (and in many cases directly related to them) was the growth of the industry during this period and the increasing dominance of Nashville as the center of the industry; much of this growth can be traced directly to the impact of Hank Williams and the "hard country" revival he launched.

One of the most visible figures in this growth was the Rose of Acuff-Rose. Founded in 1943 by Roy Acuff and ex-pop/Tin Pan Alley/Hollywood songwriter Fred Rose, this firm became the first publisher of country music in the South, and grew rapidly as popular "Opry" acts like Acuff, the Bailes Brothers, and Pee Wee King and his Golden West Cowboys began producing hits for them, including the King-Redd Stewart contribution "Tennessee Waltz," which has proven to be the top-selling country song ever. Overall, of course, the leadership in business and song-writing was that of Fred Rose, who was one of the finest, most prolific songwriters country music has ever known, producing reams of hits for Autry and Wills and Acuff and scores of others at an astonishing rate. With the coming of Hank Williams, Acuff-Rose really hit its stride. Fred Rose took the young singer and songwriter under his wing, helped polish Hank's vast, raw talent with his own tremendous experience, and attempted to guide the career of the wild and rangy young man, who became a country music legend. It was Fred and his son Wesley (head of Acuff-Rose since his father's death in 1954) who realized the potential for wide appeal in Hank's supposedly hard-country songs, and Tony Bennett's version of "Cold Cold Heart" became a big pop hit thanks to the efforts of the Roses.

Even after the deaths of Fred Rose and Hank Williams within a little more than a year of each other, Acuff-Rose flourished, always seeming to sign the right writer at the right time: Marty Robbins, Don Gibson, and Doug Kershaw published their early works through Acuff-Rose, and the outfit seemed to pull the best work from several fine writers like Leon Payne ("I Love You Because," "Lost Highway"), Jimmy Work ("Making Believe," "Tennessee Border"), and Melvin Endsley ("Singing the Blues"). In fact, a young couple named Felice and Boudleaux Bryant helped Acuff-Rose weather the rock boom as much as any other single factor. Their "Wake Up, Little Suzie" and "Dream" were among the best-selling records of the era.

It took little imagination to see —even before Hank Williams—that country publishing could be a lucrative field, and in the late 1940s two Swiss-born brothers named Aberbach formed Hill and Range Music, using large cash advances to lure some of country music's biggest stars, including Bob Wills, Bill Monroe, and Hank Snow, who has remained a Hill and Range writer ever since, to sign with them. Although the Aberbachs—and Hill and Range—were headquartered in New York, they have maintained a strong Nashville presence to this day, although they were absorbed by the vast Chappell Music empire in the mid-1970s.

When "Opry" manager Jim Denny and country music's then biggest star, Webb Pierce, formed Cedarwood Music in the mid-1950s, they added further impetus to Nashville's continuing growth as the center of the industry and set the stage for a group of publishers to open shop in what was becoming known as Music City, U.S.A.: Tree Music, Pamper Music, Combine Music, Central Songs, and many others became associated with Music Row and built million-dollar catalogues from the pens of country songwriters. Within a decade of the founding of Acuff-Rose, country music publishing was a major business concern; within two decades it was a multinational, multimillion-dollar industry.

A second major business development was the rather sudden growth of recording studios in the city. Although Victor made an exploratory field trip into Nashville in 1928, recording many pioneer "Opry" performers like De-Ford Bailey, the Crook Brothers, Theron Hale and Daughters, the Binkley Brothers Dixie Clodhoppers, Dr. Humphrey Bate's Posum Hunters, and others, there was no other recording activity in what was to become Music City until veteran "Opry" announcer Jim Bulleit recorded Sheb Wooley on his newly formed Bullet label (about which more will be said later) on December 29, 1945. The first major label to begin recording in Nashville with some regularity was Decca (now MCA), whose first effort was an Ernest Tubb-Red Foley session at Castle Studios, an independent operation run by a few WSM radio technicians.

Nashville's centralized location and the presence of the "Opry" would seem to have made it a logical recording center long before, yet it was not. It may be indicative that when Blue-

bird recording artist Pete Pyle joined the "Opry" in the early 1940s, he, Bill Monroe, and Roy Acuff were the only members of the entire cast who had recording contracts at all. Recording took place most often in New York, Chicago, or Los Angeles, with a few regional field-trip recordings made in Dallas, Atlanta, and Charlotte a couple of times a year.

Not long after the Decca experiment—and prodded by the success of Bullet Records—most of the other major labels of the time (excluding the fledgling West Coast-based Capitol and the new Cincinnati-based King) began to use the Castle Studios facility frequently. An interesting exception was RCA, whose A&R man, Steve Sholes, preferred the Brown Brothers Transcription Service just a few blocks away.

If any record label deserves credit for a major role in the proliferation of recording studios in Nashville, it must be the now largely forgotten Bullet label, which produced Nashville's first million seller, "Near You," a pop recording by a longtime local dance band, Francis Craig's Orchestra. The success of "Near You" allowed Bullet's owner, Jim Bulleit, to delve deeply into country, producing a great number of important country records for Nashville and non-Nashville performers alike: Johnnie Lee Wills (whose "Rag Mop" was Bullet Records' biggest country hit), Ray Price, Clyde Moody, Minnie Pearl, and others. Bulleit proved there was a wealth of recording talent in Nashville, and, more important, that first-rate recordings could be made there, and he has the dubious honor of being

an unsung pioneer in drawing the attention of the major record companies
to Nashville's available facilities and
talent.

From this point on, all the major
companies began, with increasing frequency, to use Nashville's studios. It
was inevitable, after all this, that
someone would set up a studio built
specifically for record-making. That
man was Owen Bradley (a 1975 elec-
tee to the Country Music Hall of
Fame). Bradley was a popular local
piano-playing bandleader who was
guaranteed a hundred sessions a year
by Decca if he would build such a
facility. With the help of his younger
brother Harold (now one of Nashville's top studio guitarists), he built
three in rapid succession, the third
and most famous being "the Quonset
Hut." Bradley, of course, went on to
become a major figure in Nashville's
music community, producing most of
Decca's country acts in the 1950s and
1960s and discovering Patsy Cline,
Loretta Lynn, and others. In fact, an
oft-repeated Nashville claim is that it
was the strength of the country catalogue (which in addition to the newer
discoveries included stalwarts like
Tubb, Monroe, Pierce, Wells, and
Foley) that kept Decca from folding
during the onslaught of rock.

RCA was also a pioneer major label
in Nashville, largely due to the insistence of Steve Sholes, who is highly
credited in the industry with helping
make Nashville a major recording
center. Initially he recorded at Brown
Brothers' Transcription Service, but
before long RCA had its own studio,
where Sholes recorded acts as varied as
the Blue Sky Boys and Elvis Presley.

Steve Sholes. Courtesy Charles Wolfe.

Sholes made an appointment of ex-
traordinary wisdom when he hired as
his assistant and Nashville co-ordina-
tor a fine guitarist who had helped
him line up musicians and lead the
sessions themselves as far back as the
field-trip days at Brown Brothers. His
name was Chet Atkins, and his lesser-
known contributions to the music industry have changed, affected, and influenced the course of country music
every bit as much, if not a great deal
more, than his contributions as a
musician.

Columbia was a bit later in settling
in Nashville, but under the leadership
of Don Law, the label had some of the
top acts of this period: Frizzell, Robbins, Dickens, Cash, Horton, Flatt
and Scruggs, Smith, and others. Like-
wise Capitol joined in late, and although they have never had their own

studio in Nashville, they began increasingly to focus on Nashville as a country music center. This process culminated years later in the moving of the country division of the label from Los Angeles' Capitol Tower to Nashville in the mid-1970s.

The role of Starday Records (which originated in Texas) was also considerable. While continually acting in the role of underdog, Starday had a great deal of success with records by established artists who were no longer on major labels, banking on both the loyalty of their fans and on their inherent talent. The formula was occasionally a successful one, with No. 1 records like Cowboy Copas' "Alabam'" and Johnny Bond's "Ten Little Bottles" outstanding. They also had the first hits of George Jones, who sounded frighteningly like Hank Williams in those days, but who went on to become one of the most influential singers in country music from that time on.

The "Grand Ole Opry" was, of course, of overwhelming importance in the changing voice of country music in this era, and most of the credit can be given to Jack Stapp and Jim Denny, the men who wrested control of the "Opry" away from "The Solemn Old Judge" in the early 1940s, determined to "modernize" the "Opry." In a way this was not an easy period for performers, but Stapp and Denny's efforts turned the "Opry" from a popular barn dance into a star-studded supershow, packed not with high-spirited fiddle bands but with singing stars. The cast grew enormously, and most of the major recording stars of the period became "Opry"

members, turning the show into every performer's ultimate goal.

Under Stapp and later Denny, the "Grand Ole Opry" lost its barn-dance flavor and became a showcase of stars, having lost something on one hand and gained something on the other. The judge, confined to a figurehead role, left the show in 1953, fifteen years before his death, as new star after new star—all featuring those hated electric guitars and increasingly gaudy outfits—was added to the show: Williams, Pierce, Price, Smith, Young, and more.

This changing of the order at the "Opry" was a difficult thing, but momentous in its time and increasingly so later, for it not only made the "Opry" the major country music show, but also made it easier for major record labels to justify setting up studios in the "Opry's" home city. Increasingly it was where the stars were and the musicians were, and rather than sending field men out to Chicago, Charlotte, Atlanta, Knoxville, and Dallas, setting up and tearing down equipment at each stop, they simply set up shop in Nashville, where all the hot talent seemed to be anyhow.

The later contribution of the Country Music Association to the tremendous growth of country music—and, for a time, its survival—was enormous. Although the formation of the organization came late in the 1950s—beyond the scope of this chapter—the constant and effective public-relations promotion of country music and of Nashville as *the* country music city by the CMA has strongly affected our vision of that era and its importance.

That the persistent boosting by the CMA did as much—perhaps more—than anything to pull country music out of its 1960s doldrums is without doubt, but it is also a fact that despite the efforts of the occasional West Coast-oriented Board member like Tex Ritter or Gene Autry or Johnny Bond, the CMA encouraged a decidedly pro-nashville outlook from its inception. This boosterish attitude gave a Nashville bias to the histories that began to pour out of the organization in the early 1960s. To read those documents, one would think that Nashville had been the center of country music since the word "go." This is not, in fact, the case: Nashville began its real-life struggle to the top of the heap in the late 1940s and the 1950s, not before.

The southeastern-sound revival that began this rise was, like all musical movements, a complicated meshing of gears, a bewildering combination of energy, drive, vision, and blind luck on the part of a host of businessmen, boosters, and entertainers who worked together (often without any common goal at all) to make both the southeastern sound and Nashville itself the dominant forces in country music. The southeastern sound of this period is a style remembered fondly today (and even, it seems, showing signs of another revival), but at the time it became instant history with the coming of rock.

Chapter Nine

Rockabilly!

The decade following World War II was a period of great growth within the recording industry. In 1940 there were but three major record companies in America: Columbia (founded in 1889), Victor (founded in 1901), and Decca (formed in 1933) as the American subsidiary of British Decca). In the forties, new majors began to appear. Capitol Records began in Los Angeles in 1942. MGM Records was formed by its parent film company in Los Angeles in 1946. Mercury was founded in Chicago in 1947.

More important than the new majors, however, were the many smaller, independent companies that blossomed during this period. In 1942, Ike and Bess Berman started Apollo Records in New York City, and Herman Lubinsky formed Savoy Records in Newark, New Jersey. In 1945 came Al Green's National Records in New York City, Sydney Nathan's King

Records in Cincinnati, and three Los Angeles labels: Art Rupe's Specialty Records, Jules and Saul Bihari's Modern Records, and Eddie and Leo Mesner's Philo Records (which became Aladdin Records the following year). In 1946, Jim Bulleit founded Bullet Records in Nashville. The next year, Leonard and Phil Chess started Chess Records in Chicago, and Lew Chudd started Imperial Records in Los Angeles. In 1948 came Jerry Blaine's Jubilee Records and Herb Abramson's and Ahmet and Nesuhi Ertegun's Atlantic Records, both in New York City. In 1949, Don Robey formed Duke/Peacock Records in Houston. In 1950, Randy Wood started Dot Records in Gallatin, Tennessee. The following year, Al Silver formed Herald/Ember Records in New York City, Lester Bihari started Meteor Records in Memphis, Lillian McMurry and Johnny Vincent started

Trumpet Records in Jackson, Mississippi, and Sam Phillips started Sun Records in Memphis. In 1953, Ernie Young formed Excello Records in Nashville as a branch of the Nashboro gospel label, George Goldner formed Rama Records in New York City as a subsidiary of Tico Records (a company that specialized in Latin music), Archie Bleyer started Cadence Records in New York City, and Vivian

Carter and James Bracken started Vee-Jay Records in Chicago. There were these and many others in operation in the year of Hank Williams' death, 1953.

The independents—or "indies," as they were called in the music business —often issued products that the major companies would have no part of. Theirs was, and is yet, an avant-garde of economic necessity. It was no major company that released the first Hank Williams records in 1946, but Sterling Records, a New York City indie so ill secured that it changed its telephone number at least five times in three years. (Nor, later, was it a major label that issued the first Beatles records in America, but Vee-Jay, a Chicago indie that dealt primarily in rhythm-and-blues.)

Although many of the independents, such as Aladdin and Vee-Jay and Chess, employed mostly black artists, and others, such as Dot and Cadence, employed mostly white artists, the indies discovered that artistic miscegenation often led to profit. Thus Savoy released not only jazz records, but also ersatz hillbilly records, and its artist roster included both Charlie Parker and The Texas Top Hands. King issued some of the finest jump blues records ever made, and also some of the finest country records. Jubilee Records put out anything available, from Jewish *schtick* records to street-corner doo-wop. Bullet Records issued B. B. King's first record, and also Owen Bradley's.

Every major American record company today makes most of its money from rock 'n' roll sales. In the beginning, however, they wouldn't touch the stuff. Columbia had Benny Goodman, Victor had Perry Como, Decca had Bing Crosby, Capitol had Frank Sinatra. What need they with this reprehensible new "nigger music"? It was the indies that gave rise to rock 'n' roll.

It is impossible to discern the first rock record, just as it is impossible to discern where red becomes yellow in the color spectrum. The phrase itself was nothing new to music. In a 1934 film called *Transatlantic Merry-Go Round*, The Boswell Sisters sang a song called "Rock and Roll," written by Sidney Clare and Richard A. Whiting, both of whom were born in the 1890s. There are quite a few records from the 1940s that can be comfortably described as early rock 'n' roll. In 1947, Roy Brown cut his song "Good Rockin' Tonight" for Deluxe Records, and in the summer of the following year Wynonie Harris had a hit version of the same song on King. Harris's version of "Good Rockin' Tonight" was, like Brown's original, a jump blues, the most popular type of music among urban blacks of the 1940s. But it was markedly rawer, less mellow than the usual jump-blues records. It rocked. The following year, Imperial issued Fats Domino's first record, "The Fat Man," and it sold well. Black music began rocking strong, and in 1951 there were several pure and unmistakable rock 'n' roll records: "Sixty Minute Man" by The Dominoes on Federal (the biggest rhythm-and-blues hit of the year), "It Ain't the Meat" by The Swallows on King, "Rocket 88" and especially its

sequel "My Real Gone Rocket" by Jackie Brenston and His Delta Cats on Chess.

There were also more than a few hard-rocking country records in this period, records that must be separated from the bulk of hillbilly boogie records due to their extremism. The Delmore Brothers, like Moon Mullican and Arthur Smith, pioneered hillbilly boogie, but in such King releases as "Freight Train Boogie" (1946) and "Whatcha Gonna Gimme?" (1952), they went beyond boogie into an effervescent sort of country rock. Freddie Slack and Ella Mae Morse's hip country recording of "House of Blue Lights," released by Capitol in 1946, was such a fine primitive rocker that Chuck Berry covered it twelve years later. Red Foley's "Tennessee Saturday Night" on Decca was one of the biggest country hits of 1948, and it rocked. "Rootie Tootie," Hank Williams' third MGM record, cut in 1948, is a jivey rocker, full of nonsense lyrics, funky call-and-response, and hot instrumental licks. A handful of Tennessee Ernie Ford's early records on Capitol, such as "Smokey Mountain Boogie" (1949), "Shotgun Boogie" (1950), "Blackberry Boogie" (1952), and "I Don't Know" (1953), are among the best, and strongest, examples of country music's gropings toward rock 'n' roll.

While these rumblings from country music circles pointed to new directions, the full-scale rush toward rock 'n' roll was begun by three individuals: disc jockey Alan Freed, singer Bill Haley, and recording entrepreneur Sam Phillips.

In 1952, twenty-nine-year-old Alan Freed was hosting his "Moondog Rock and Roll Party," a nightly show broadcast from WJW in Cleveland. Freed's programming of black music for white kids, one of the most revolutionary media moves in the twentieth century, was actually the idea of Leo Mintz, an acquaintance of Freed who operated the biggest record store in Cleveland. In March 1952 Freed promoted his first concert, which he called a Moondog Ball, at the Cleveland Arena. The Arena had a capacity of ten thousand. There were nine thousand tickets sold in advance. On the night of the show, between twenty thousand and thirty thousand kids showed up. They bashed the doors open, stomped the outnumbered police, and screamed. "Everybody had such a grand time breaking into the Arena," said Freed, "that they didn't ask for their money back."

William John Clifton Haley was born in the Detroit suburb of Highland Park in 1927. At the age of seven, Haley's family moved to Booth's Corner, a small town in southeastern Pennsylvania. During his high-school years in Pennsylvania, Haley started playing country music, and in 1951 he and his band, Bill Haley and The Saddlemen, had their first record issued by Holiday Records, a Chester, Pennsylvania, label operated by Dave Miller. Bill Haley's country roots were deep and strong. In the late 1940s, he had billed his group as Bill Haley and The Four Aces of Western Swing. His 1952 recording of "Icy Heart" on Essex was obviously derived from Hank Williams. The saxophone work of Rudy Pompelli, which

Bill Haley. Courtesy Doug Green.

Haley added to his later records, is very similar in sound to that of Texas saxophonist Bob Herrick, who played in the band of Texas Playboys alumnus Leon McAuliffe, and was featured in such McAuliffe records as "Plaintalkin' Man from the West," released by Majestic in 1947.

Curiously, the debut recording of Haley's group was a version of Jackie Brenston's recent "Rocket 88." On his new Essex label, Dave Miller continued to issue Haley's records under the new group name of Bill Haley and His Comets: "Rock the Joint," "Real Rock Drive," and then, in 1953, "Crazy, Man, Crazy." There had been rock 'n' roll records on the rhythm-and-blues charts, some records that could be called rock 'n' roll on the country charts, but "Crazy,

Man, Crazy" was the first rock record to become a national pop hit. Those weird glimpses of something new in the music of such men as Wynonie Harris and The Delmore Brothers, the outright fiery newness of Jackie Brenston's rock 'n' roll rocket, were smuggled into the backyards of America by Bill Haley. Some called it a fad, a passing silliness, but it was an irreversible and uncontrollable energy that would rule and haunt for decades.

Bill Haley, the first white rock 'n' roll singer, was the man who brought rock to the top of the pops, but Haley was more an entertainer than a rock 'n' roll madman. Vernon Dalhart's 1923 Victor record of "The Prisoner's Song" was the first million-selling hillbilly record, but there is no way Dalhart himself can be termed a hillbilly singer. He was a pop singer, and his interpretations of hillbilly music betrayed this with their schmaltzy affectations of folkiness. Haley was something similar: he was a country singer, a pop singer when he wished to be, but not a rock 'n' roll singer. His singing was clean, gelt, manicured. It is significant that his biggest and most remembered hit, his 1955 Decca record of "Rock Around the Clock," was written by Max Freedman and Jimmy DeKnight. Freedman, the Tin Pan Alley author of "Sioux City Sue" and "Blue Danube Waltz," was born in Philadelphia in 1895. Jimmy De-Knight was really Jimmy Myers of Myers Music, Inc., who published the song.

Like Alan Freed, Haley spread interest in modern black music so that by the close of 1954, every hip kid in America was into rock 'n' roll. Freed was doing in the biggest city in the nation what he had done in Cleveland. His first New York "Moondog Rock 'n' Roll Party" (later simply "Rock 'n' Roll Party") was broadcast over WINS on the night of September 8, 1954. In the November 6, 1954, issue of *Billboard*, in an article titled "R&B Music Success Sends Major Diskers Back to Field," it was noted that black music was showing up increasingly in white-area jukeboxes.

Monday, July 5, 1954. The most popular albums in America are Jackie Gleason's *Tawny* on Capitol, Frank Sinatra's *Songs for Young Lovers*, also on Capitol, the film soundtrack of *The Glenn Miller Story*, and the television soundtrack of *Victory at Sea*, both on RCA/Victor. The No. 1 song on "Your Hit Parade" is "Three Coins in the Fountain." The biggest-selling rhythm-and-blues artists are The Midnighters, and the biggest-selling country artist is Webb Pierce. Although rock 'n' roll is a widespread phenomenon, only one white rock singer has yet achieved any success: Bill Haley. On this summer day, something is happening down in Memphis that will eventually change the course of American music. Within the Sun Record Company at 706 Union Avenue, Sam Phillips is cutting a first session on a local kid named Elvis Presley.

Sam Phillips got into the record business by way of radio. Born in Florence, Alabama, in 1925, he began working as a radio announcer after dropping out of high school in 1941. At night he studied engineering, podiatry, and embalming. In 1942, he became a disk jockey at WLAY in

Sam Phillips. Photo by Marshall Fallwell, Jr.

Muscle Shoals, and the next year at WHSL in Decatur. In 1945, he worked at WLAC in Nashville, and from 1946 to 1949 at WREC in Memphis. In Memphis, he also promoted shows at the Hotel Peabody. With the money he had saved as a disk jockey and promoter, Sam Phillips opened a recording studio at 706 Union Avenue in 1950. There he made recordings of southern blacks and leased them to the independent record companies: Chess, Modern, Meteor, Trumpet, and others. He also recorded weddings and club meetings, and transcribed them onto single-faced LPs, charging nine dollars a shot.

One of the earliest records Phillips cut and leased was Jackie Brenston's "Rocket 88," recorded in March 1951. Some of the record's success as a rocker should be attributed to Phillips. He added extra amplification to Willie Kizart's guitar work, and in doing so added much brash dimension to the final product. Other bluesmen recorded by Phillips were Bobby Bland, Little Milton, James Cotton, Sleepy John Estes, Earl Hooker, Walter Horton, Howlin' Wolf, B. B. King, and Joe Hill Louis.

In 1952, Sam Phillips decided to start his own record company. He took his brother Judd on as partner and paid a commercial artist on Beale Street to design a label for his company, which he called Sun. The early months of Sun Records are unclear. The first known Sun record, "Blues in My Condition," (*B* side, "Selling My Whiskey") by Jackie Boy and Little Walter, is Sun 174, recorded on February 25, 1952. It is not known, however, when this record was released, if indeed it ever was. Sun started as a blues label. Walter Horton, Joe Hill Louis, Rufus Thomas, Memphis Ma Rainey, The Prisonaires, and Junior Parker were among the first Sun artists.

The first country record issued by Sun was "Silver Bells" by a quartet from Ripley, Tennessee, called The Ripley Cotton Choppers. The record was released in October 1953, with HILLBILLY stamped in red upon its yellow label. With subsequent releases, it became obvious that Sam Phillips was trying to coax a new sound from his country sessions. "Boogie Blues" by Earl Peterson, a country singer from Michigan who had known Sam since his disk-jockey days, was issued in March 1954. This record, a wry, uptempo cut featuring a yodel-trimmed vocal, also bore the HILLBILLY stamp. Peterson was basically an old-line country singer (there were traces not only of Hank Williams, but also of Jimmie Rodgers in his style), but "Boogie Blues" possessed a lively, youthful edge.

Hardrock Gunter's "Gonna Dance All Night" was released in May of the same year. Sidney Gunter had been recording since the 1940s, and was best known for his 1948 "Birmingham Bounce" on the Bama label. Gunter continued to record for small labels right on into the 1960s, when he worked for a time as a disk jockey at WWVA in Wheeling, West Virginia, before retiring to Golden, Colorado. When he recorded for Sun, Gunter was a member of the WWVA "Jamboree." "Gonna Dance All Night" and its flip, "Fallen Angel," were indeed a new sort of country music. "Gonna Dance All Night" was not merely an uptempo country song, it also bordered on rock. Sam Phillips added a saxophone to Gunter's sound, obviously influenced by the work of Rudy Pompelli in Bill Haley's recent records, and the combination of country honky-tonk, rolling saxophone, and lyrics such as *"We're gonna rock 'n' roll while we dance all night"* wrought a strong effect.

A side recorded the same day as "Gonna Dance All Night," and released in June of 1954, came closer to country rock than anything Phillips had previously produced: "My Kind of Carryin' On" by Doug Poindexter and The Starlite Wranglers. This was a country record, but barely traditional. It fluttered and jarred like a creature flirting with madness. It was a great record, but it was Poindexter's only Sun single. In 1955, Arkansas-born Poindexter retired from the music business following the breakup of his band. His lead guitarist, Scotty Moore, and his bassist, Bill Black, had joined up with a new singer. Today, Doug Poindexter works for an insurance company in Memphis.

Monday, July 5, 1954, Sam Phillips, Elvis Presley, Scotty Moore, and Bill Black are in Sun's poky, thirty-by-twenty-foot studio messing with "Blue Moon of Kentucky," a song Bill Monroe and His Blue Grass Boys had recorded for Columbia in 1945. It isn't a country song they're trying to set down on tape, nor a rhythm-and-blues song in the Haley mode, but a weird bastard sound that Phillips has been carrying in the dampness of his brain. Finally the sound is in the air, its configurations caught on magnetic tape. Sam Phillips grins. "Hell, that's different," he says. "That's a pop song now, Little Vi. That's *good*." These are perhaps the most apocalyptic words in the history of American music.

Born in Tupelo, Mississippi, on January 8, 1935, Elvis Aron Presley was nineteen that July day in Memphis. Six years earlier, in 1948, his family had moved to that western Tennessee city, and in the spring of 1953 Elvis was graduated from Humes High School there. His photograph in *The Herald*, the Humes High School yearbook, shows a boy with sideburns, Corinthian pompadour, and a hint of acne. He had participated, his yearbook caption says, in ROTC, Biology Club, English Club, History Club, and Speech Club. The summer after graduation, Presley went to work for the Precision Tool Company. He left that job after a short while and began work at the Crown Electric Company, where he was paid forty-two dollars a week to drive a truck.

On a Saturday afternoon in late

Scotty Moore, Elvis Presley, and Bill Black. Courtesy Doug Green.

1953, Elvis made his first visit to the Sun studio. As a sideline operation to Sun, Phillips still maintained his Memphis Recording Service, administered by Marion Keisker, the former Miss Radio of Memphis. It was to the Memphis Recording Service, not Sun Records, that Elvis came that afternoon. He paid Keisker the four-dollar charge, entered the studio with his acoustic guitar, and recorded two songs directly onto a double-sided ten-inch acetate disk. On the one side Elvis cut "My Happiness," with which The Ink Spots had hit on Decca in 1948. On the other side he did "That's When Your Heartaches Begin," a mawkish ballad written by Zeb Turner and recorded by Bob Lamb on Dot in 1951.

Struck by Presley's voice and raw acoustic guitar work, Marion Keisker recorded the end of "My Happiness" and the whole of "That's When Your Heartaches Begin" on a length of used tape. Seventeen years later, she told Elvis biographer Jerry Hopkins, "The reason I taped Elvis was this: Over and over I remember Sam saying, 'If I could find a white man who had the Negro feel, I could make a billion dollars.' This is what I heard in Elvis, this . . . what I guess they now call 'soul,' this Negro sound. So I taped it. I wanted Sam to know."

Marion also took note of Presley's address, 462 Alabama Street, and when she next saw Phillips she played the tape of Elvis's performance. Sam seemed mildly impressed, but did not pursue the matter. Several months later, on January 4, 1954, Elvis visited the Memphis Recording Service again. Marion Keisker was not in, but

Sam Phillips was. They spoke, Sam calmly and plainly and easily, Elvis nervously. Elvis gave Sam four dollars and cut another acetate, "I'll Never Stand in Your Way," a 1941 country song written by Clint Horner, and "Casual Love Affair," a song of unknown origin that may have been quickly learned from a demo Phillips played for Elvis.

In the early summer of 1954, about eight months after Elvis had first visited the Sun studio, Sam's mail yielded a demonstration record of a composition called "Without You," recorded in Nashville by an unknown black singer. Sam was so impressed by the demo that he wanted to release it on Sun. He called Nashville in search of the singer, so that he might obtain permission to issue the record. He was told that nobody knew who the kid was, that he had just happened to be hanging around the studio when the song arrived. Phillips decided he must find someone else to cut the song in a hurry. "What about the kid with the sideburns?" suggested Marion Keisker.

Elvis was contacted that same Saturday afternoon, and he rushed to the studio. Phillips played the demo for him. Elvis sang it. By all accounts, it was horrible. He tried again, then again, and still it was bad. Phillips forsook "Without You," suggesting that Elvis try "Rag Mop," a song written by Johnnie Lee Wills and Deacon Anderson. In 1950, Johnnie Lee Wills (Bob Wills' brother) had a top-ten country hit with his recording of the song on the independent Nashville label Bullet; that same year, The Ames Brothers had a million-sell-

Elvis. Courtesy Doug Green.

fevered glossolalia. In the end, Elvis remarked he was looking for a band.

Sam contacted Winfield Scott Moore, better known as Scotty, the twenty-two-year-old guitarist who had recorded with Doug Poindexter several weeks before. That Sunday, Independence Day, Elvis and Scotty got together at Scotty's home, where they fooled with several recent country hits such as Eddy Arnold's "I Really Don't Want to Know" and Hank Snow's "I Don't Hurt Anymore," both on RCA/Victor, and a few of jazz singer Billy Eckstine's MGM sides. After a few hours, bass player Bill Black, Scotty's neighbor who had also played at Doug Poindexter's session, dropped by for a few minutes. Black was not impressed with the goings-on. Nonetheless, the next evening, July 5, Black found himself in the Sun studio with Phillips, Presley, and Moore. It was Sam's idea for Scotty and Bill not to bring the rest of the Starlite Wranglers with them. No fiddle, no steel guitar. It was obvious that Sam had a different kind of country session in mind.

That first recording of "Blue Moon of Kentucky" was never released legally. "Blue Moon of Kentucky," as released on Elvis's first record, Sun 209, is surer, tougher than the earlier take. Like a young boxer after his first professional knockout, Presley is dizzy with the confirmation of his prowess. "Blue Moon of Kentucky" is daring to the point of insanity. It is Elvis walking on iron blades, through fire, invincible with the knowledge he sees in Sam's eyes, hears in his own voice, and feels in his own flushed meat; the knowledge that right now,

ing pop version on Coral. It seemed a fairly easy song, but again Elvis failed.

During a break, Sam, a bit disturbed, asked Elvis just what it was he could sing. "Oh anything," Elvis replied. Do it, Sam said. And then it poured forth, a crazy rush of disparate sounds: gospel (earlier in 1954, Elvis had almost joined The Blackwood Brothers, a gospel quartet who performed regularly on the WMPS "High Noon Roundup"), hard-core country, rhythm-and-blues, middle-of-the-road pop. For hours it went on, no cool Apollonian eclecticism, but this instant, he, Elvis Aron Presley, is the greatest singer in Memphis and the universe.

After "Blue Moon of Kentucky," Elvis and the boys cut "That's All Right," a song originally recorded by Mississippi-born bluesman Arthur Crudup (better known as Big Boy Crudup) for Victor in 1946. As Elvis performed it, it was no more a blues song, and no less a country song, than "Blue Moon of Kentucky." Where Bill Haley's versions of rhythm-and-blues songs were playfully mimetic, Elvis's were frighteningly creative.

The first Elvis Presley record, "Blue Moon of Kentucky" (B side, "That's All Right"), was released on July 19, 1954, a Monday. Sam Phillips took a copy of the record to Dewey Phillips, the disk jockey who hosted the "Red Hot and Blue" show on WHBQ, and he broadcast "That's All Right." Listeners called in their enthusiastic reactions. On station WHHM, disk jockey Sleepy Eye John began playing "Blue Moon of Kentucky." The record took off, and as the weeks passed "That's All Right" became the No. 1 country record in Memphis.

That is when rockabilly became fact, and Elvis became its god. On September 25, Elvis's second record was issued, a coupling of "Good Rockin' Tonight" and "I Don't Care if the Sun Don't Shine," written by Mack David, author of "Bibbidi Bob-bidi Boo" and "La Vie en Rose." Elvis made his debut on the "Grand Ole Opry," a guest on Hank Snow's segment, where he sang both sides of his first single. On October 16, Presley played the "Louisiana Hayride,"

where he went over so well that he was brought back the following week to become a regular member. The third Elvis record, released on January 8, 1955, was "Milkcow Blues Boogie," originally cut by Kokomo Arnold on Decca in 1935 (and done in a country swing version by Johnnie Lee Wills in 1941, also on Decca), and "You're a Heartbreaker," a strong country weeper, closer to a honky-tonk performance than any of Elvis's other Sun sides. "I'm Left, You're Right, She's Gone," written by a Sun session man, steel-guitarist Stan Kesler, and "Baby Let's Play House," which had been a minor rhythm-and-blues hit for Arthur Gunter on Ex-cello earlier in the year, comprised Elvis's fourth single, issued on April 1, 1955. For the first time, one of Presley's records hit the national country charts; "Baby Let's Play House" rose to the No. 10 position. As "Baby Let's Play House" was high on the charts, Elvis's last Sun disk was issued: "Mystery Train," a rhythm-and-blues song Junior Parker had cut for Sun in 1953, and "I Forgot to Remember to Forget," another Stan Kesler song. The record became a double-sided hit, and rose to the No. 1 position on the country charts. Elvis Presley, rock 'n' roll madman, had the best-selling country record in the nation.

Late in 1955, Elvis signed with RCA/Victor. On January 5, 1956, in Nashville, Elvis cut his first sides for his new label. Now, in addition to Scotty and Bill and drummer D. J. Fontana (who had joined the group early in 1955), there were Nashville cats involved: guitarist Chet Atkins, pianist Floyd Cramer, and the vocal group The Jordanaires. Elvis's first RCA/Victor recording, "Heartbreak Hotel," was released in February 1956. It became the No. 1 song on the country and the pop charts. "Heartbreak Hotel" was a superlative rockabilly song, full of austerity, sex, and stone-hard rhythm. For the next two years, Elvis continued to cut strong rockabilly material on RCA/Victor: "Don't Be Cruel," in 1956, "Jailhouse Rock," in 1957, "Hard-headed Woman," in 1958. But with each new session, Elvis grew farther from rockabilly. By the time Elvis was drafted into the Army in 1958, the golden days of rockabilly had passed.

All things that contain more creativity than formula, more emotion than intellect, cannot be precisely defined, and this is true of rockabilly music. As the word implies, rockabilly is hillbilly rock 'n' roll. It was not a usurpation of black music by whites, as Haley's rock 'n' roll might justifiably be termed, because its soul was white, full of the redneck ethos.

Country music and the blues are two tributaries of a common source. Nothing in traditional American music is as white as it might seem, or as black. Waylon Jennings' album *Dreaming My Dreams*, released in June 1975, has a song on it called "Waymore's Blues," credited to Waylon and Curtis Buck. The song ends with this couplet:

I got my name painted on my shirt;
I ain't no ordinary dude, I don't have to work.

Now go back a bit, to 1951, when Harmonica Frank Floyd, the first white singer to record for Sun, cut a song called "Rockin'-chair Daddy," in which you can hear:

Rock to Memphis, dance on Main,
Up stepped a lady and asked my name.
Rockin'-chair daddy don't have to work,
I told her my name was on the tail of my shirt.

Search back another couple of decades, to Jimmie Rodgers' 1930 recording of "Blue Yodel No. 9":

It was down in Memphis, corner of Beale and Main.
He says, "Big boy, you'll have to tell me your name."
I said, "You'll find my name on the tail of my shirt,
I'm a Tennessee hustler, I don't have to work."

To stop here in the genealogy of this perennial country lyric would be misleading. In 1928, blues singer Furry Lewis cut his two-part "Kassie Jones":

Had it written on the back of my shirt:
Natural-born eastman, don't have to work.

Two decades earlier, when there were neither blues records nor country records, folklorist Howard Odum collected a song in the field and later published it in his 1925 book, *The Negro and His Songs*:

I got it writ on de tail o' my shirt:
I'm a natu'el-bohn eastman, don't have to work.

Going back farther, you enter the lyric's prehistory. Was it ultimately invented in 1901 or 1855? Was it a black man or a white man who invented it?

The first blues, of course, was sung in a white man's language, played on a white man's instrument. Both Leon McAuliffe's steel guitar and Elmore James' slide guitar are descended from the music of vaudeville's Hawaiian guitarists. The searcher of ethnic purity in popular American music finds little.

Black versions of country songs are not uncommon. Darrell Glenn cut the first version of "Crying in the Chapel" (whch his father wrote) for Valley Records in the summer of 1953. Rex Allen covered it on Decca and had a top-ten country hit on it. The most widely known version of the song, however, is that of the rhythm-and-blues group The Orioles, who cut it for Jubilee. The Pearls, another black group, covered Hank Williams' "Your Cheatin' Heart" for Onyx Records. Eddy Arnold's 1947 hit "It's a Sin" was cut in 1961 by Tarheel Slim and Little Ann on Fire Records. "Jealous Heart," the Al Morgan country hit of 1949, was covered that same year by King artist Ivory Joe Hunter (who returned to country music in his records shortly before his death in 1975). Solomon Burke's first successful recording, on Atlantic in 1961, was "Just out of Reach," a country song. Bobby Comstock cut both "Tennessee Waltz" and "Jambalaya," the first on Blaze in 1959, the second on Atlantic in 1960. Wynonie Harris's big 1951 rhythm-and-blues hit, "Bloodshot Eyes" on King, was

a cover of the western swing original cut the year before by Hank Penny on the same label. Bullmoose Jackson, another black King artist, covered both Wayne Raney's 1949 "Why Don't You Haul Off and Love Me" and Moon Mullican's 1951 "Cherokee Boogie." Blues guitarist Earl Hooker, at a 1953 session in Memphis, cut not only Leon McAuliffe's "Steel Guitar Rag" but also the perennial "Red River Valley."

When Elvis cut Big Boy Crudup's "That's All Right," he was no more usurping black culture than Wynonie Harris was usurping white culture when he cut Hank Penny's "Bloodshot Eyes" three years before. Presley's version of "That's All Right" is better than the original, just as Harris's version of "Bloodshot Eyes" is better than its original.

There was an affinity between rockabilly and black music of the 1940s and 1950s, as there had been an affinity between western swing and black music of the 1920s and 1930s, but it was not, really, more than an affinity. Of the sixteen known titles Elvis recorded as a Sun artist, five were derived from rhythm-and-blues records: "That's All Right," "Good Rockin' Tonight," "Milkcow Blues Boogie," "Baby Let's Play House," and "Mystery Train." (Two of these, in turn, were derived from country records: Arthur Gunter's "Baby Let's Play House" from Eddy Arnold's 1951 hit "I Want to Play House with You," and Junior Parker's "Mystery Train" from the Carter Family's 1930 "Worried-man Blues.") During his Sun years, as during the decades since,

Elvis derived the bulk of his music from country and pop sources.

What blackness there was in rockabilly in no way constituted an innovation in country music. The black enculturation in the music of old-timers such as Jimmie Rodgers and Bob Wills was far greater, far deeper. Nor was there much of a technical nature in rockabilly that country music had not known before. The slap-bass technique, one of the watermarks of classic rockabilly, can be heard in country records of the prewar era: Listen to bassist Ramon DeArmon in the Light Crust Doughboys' 1938 Vocalion record "Pussy, Pussy, Pussy." The echo effect heard in many rockabilly recordings had been used by Wilf Carter in such sides as his 1935 "Sundown Blues," and, more recently, by Eddy Arnold in his 1945 "Cattle Call."

What made rockabilly such a drastically new music was its spirit, which bordered on mania. Elvis's version of "Good Rockin' Tonight" was not a party song, but an invitation to a holocaust. Junior Parker's "Mystery Train" was an eerie shuffle; Elvis's "Mystery Train" was a demonic incantation. Country music had never known such vehement emotion, and neither had black music. It was the face of Dionysos, full of febrile sexuality and senselessness; it flushed the skin of new housewives, and made teen-age boys reinvent themselves as flaming creatures.

Although Elvis was the god, the unforgettable boy-daddy of rockabilly, there were others. In Memphis, and across the South, burning ever

North, they drove country music berserk.

Carl Lee Perkins was born on a welfare-supported tenant farm near Tiptonville, Tennessee, on April 9, 1932, the second of three brothers. His early years were spent on a plantation in Lake County, Tennessee, where his family were the sole white sharecroppers. In 1945, the Perkins family relocated in Bemis, where Carl began working as a laborer in a battery plant, then at a bakery in nearby Jackson.

Musically, Carl was reared on a mix of country via Nashville's WSM, and rhythm-and-blues via sharecropper neighbors and black radio broadcasts. In 1945, Carl won a talent show in Bemis. He taught his brothers, Jay B. and Clayton, to play guitars, and together the three began performing locally as the Perkins Brothers Band.

Late in 1953, after Carl and his Mississippi-born wife, Valda Crider, moved to Parkview Courts, a government-subsidized housing project in Jackson, Carl began sending demo tapes to various record companies in Nashville and New York. In December, 1954, after several unsuccessful attempts, he had an audience with Sam Phillips at Sun. Several weeks later, in February of 1955, Sam issued Carl's first record on the Flip label (a Sun affiliate): "Movie Magg," which Carl had authored in 1945, and "Turn Around," a straight country piece. In "Movie Magg," it became immediately apparent that Perkins was a consummate rock guitarist, given to rapid-fire high-note runs on his Les Paul Gibson. The Flip record got decent disk-jockey response in Memphis, as had Elvis's first records during the previous seven months, and Sam signed Carl on as a regular Sun artist.

Over the next years, until Carl left Sun in 1958, there were only seven of his singles released, or less than two a year. This is odd, considering the fact that four of these records were country hits, and three of these four crossed to the pop charts. (One of Carl's records, the giant "Blue Suede Shoes," was a top-ten hit on the country, pop, and even rhythm-and-blues charts.)

Like Elvis, Carl Perkins sometimes used black material, as in his 1957 record of "Matchbox," a hard-edged version of Blind Lemon Jefferson's 1927 "Matchbox Blues" (which had been covered previously by several country acts: Larry Hensely in 1934, Joe Shelton in 1935, Roy Shaffer in 1939, and Roy Newman and His Boys also in 1939). Unlike Elvis, however, Perkins was a consummate songwriter who was at his best in songs such as the 1956 "Dixie Fried," a raving whorl of whiskey and violence, and the 1957 "Put Your Cat Clothes On" (unreleased until 1971), an anthem of redneck rock.

From Sun, Perkins went to Columbia; then, in 1963, he went to Decca.

Carl Perkins. Photo by Marshall Fallwell.

Jerry Lee Lewis. Photo by Tom Hill.

After Decca, he signed with Dollie, and in 1968 he returned to Columbia, where he remained until 1973, when he joined Mercury, with whom he released only one album and a handful of singles.

Born in Ferriday, Louisiana, on September 29, 1935, Jerry Lee Lewis signed with Sun late in 1956. Of all rockabilly artists, Jerry Lee projected the most hellish persona. To some he was a redneck prince, the spirit of southern rock 'n' roll; to others he was sin itself, the most despised and feared of the 1950s pop heroes.

Jerry Lee's debut record was a coupling of "Crazy Arms," the Ray Price hit that was still on the charts when Jerry Lee cut it in the fall of 1956, and "End of the Road," an original piece. Although he did not pursue the writing aspect of music in subsequent years (of the several hundred titles

he has cut in the past two decades, only five bear his signature: "End of the Road," "High School Confidential," and "Lewis Boogie" on Sun, "Lincoln Limousine" and "He Took It like a Man" on Smash); in "End of the Road" Jerry Lee proved himself a masterful evoker of lurid mood and dark thirsts, and it is precious, and poetically just, to consider the song a statement of purpose, an existential anthem of the career to follow:

Well, the way is dark,
Night is long,
I don't care if I never get home:
I'm waitin' at the end of the road!

Jerry Lee had the two biggest hits in Sun's history: 1957's "Whole Lot of Shakin' Goin' On," which had originally been cut by The Commodores on Dot in 1955, and the 1957–58 giant "Great Balls of Fire," written by Otis Blackwell, the rhythm-and-blues singer and author of "Don't Be Cruel," "All Shook Up," and others. "Whole Lot of Shakin' Goin' On" rose to No. 1 on the country charts, No. 1 on the rhythm-and-blues charts, and No. 3 on the pop charts. "Great Balls of Fire" hit No. 1 on the country charts, No. 3 on the rhyhm-and-blues charts, and No. 2 on the pop charts. In 1958, Lewis's "Breathless" again went to the top ten in the country, rhythm-and-blues, and pop charts. In the spring of that year, however, something bad happened to Jerry Lee.

In England on a promotional tour in May 1958, Jerry Lee became the victim of a sensationalistic press that smarmed and tsk-wailed the fact that Lewis's wife, Myra, was his thirteen-year-old cousin. With his customary *élan*, Jerry Lee responded to the British press: "Myra and I are legally married. It was my second marriage that wasn't legal. I was a bigamist when I was sixteen. I was fourteen when I was first married. That lasted a year, then I met June. One day she said she was goin' to have my baby. I was real worried. Her father threatened me, and her brothers were hunting me with hide whips. So I married her just a week before my divorce from Dorothy. It was a shotgun wedding."

Jerry Lee's British tour was canceled after three shows, and he returned home to Memphis. The publicity did not wane. In the June 9 issue of *Billboard* appeared a full-page advertisement titled "An Open Letter to the Industry from Jerry Lee Lewis." It began, bluntly: "Dear Friends: I have in recent weeks been the apparent center of a fantastic amount of publicity and of which none has been good. . . ."

Jerry Lee's next record, "High School Confidential," from the film of the same name, reached No. 9 on the country charts, No. 16 on the rhythm-and-blues charts, and No. 21 on the pop charts. It was Jerry Lee's last appearance in the top ten of the country charts until 1968 and his last appearance, period, in the top twenty of either the rhythm-and-blues or the pop charts.

But Jerry Lee kept pumping away. In 1968, he rose anew with a series of country hits that began with "An-other Place, Another Time" on Smash. Of the Sun rockabilly triumvirate, Jerry Lee is the only one still making rockabilly-based music.

Jerry Lee recorded for Sun from 1956 to 1963. When he left the label, the days of Sun were already numbered. After "Carry Me Back to Old Virginny," Lewis's twenty-third and last Sun record, Phillips issued only eleven more records; then, after a decade, it was over. In 1952, the world's first Holiday Inn had opened, in Memphis. By the end of the 1950s Holiday Inn was one of the fastest-growing, wealthiest operations in the nation, and Sam Phillips, who as a small-time Memphis businessman had invested in Holiday Inn, emerged as one of its major stockholders.

Sun began to dissolve in 1958. The previous year, Johnny Cash, Bill Justis, and Jerry Lee Lewis had given Phillips great crossover hits (Justis's hit "Raunchy" was on the Phillips International label). By the fall of 1958, Justis and Lewis had ceased to have hits, and Johnny Cash had signed with Columbia. During the same period, Judd Phillips, Sam's brother and partner at Sun, faced payola allegations for his promotional activities, and the brothers broke their relationship. (It was then that Judd founded his own Judd label.) Early in 1959, producer Jack Clement, who had been at Sun since 1955 and had been responsible for much of Sun's most imaginative work in the late 1950s suddenly left the company.

Early in 1961 Phillips opened a studio on Seventeenth Avenue in Nashville and started using many of that

Johnny Cash. Courtesy Bob Pinson.

city's pop-country musicians at his sessions: Floyd Cramer, Hank Garland, Buddy Harmon, Bob Moore, Pig Robbins, Billy Sherrill, and others. But Phillips did not succeed in making Sun a part of the ever more lucrative Nashville sound and the company languished. In 1966, Sam closed his company, Phillips International. From 1964 to 1968, Sun released only twenty singles, most of them bad. In 1968 Sun Records ended. On July 1, 1969, Nashville entrepreneur Shelby Singleton, Jr., acquired from Phillips 80 per cent interest in the Sun catalogue and became the major stockholder in a newly formed Sun International Corporation. Since 1969, Singleton has released a steady flow of budget-line Sun reissues.

Presley, Perkins, and Lewis were

the three most famous, most successfull rockabilly artists. Others, less enduring, less famed, made music often as good, sometimes better.

Vincent Gene Craddock, more widely known as Gene Vincent, was born in Norfolk, Virginia, on February 11, 1935. Gene served in the Navy during the Korean War. He was severely injured in combat, and it was thought that his leg would have to be amputated. Vincent did not permit the amputation, and instead wore a leg brace through the rest of his life. Thin, wan, crippled, Vincent was an unlikely pop star, but a pop star he nonetheless became.

After performing on radio station WCMS, Vincent and his band, the Blue Caps, went to Capitol Records, and in the spring of 1956 his first disk was released: "Bee-bop-a-Lula," written by Vincent and Sheriff Tex Davis (and inspired by a "Little Lulu" comic book), and "Woman Love." On the country charts, "Be-bop-a-Lula" hit No. 5, and on the pop charts No. 9. It was a strong song, and a unique one. Vincent delivered its basically light, cute lyric with a febrile psychopathy. It was a perverse, gothic performance, and one of the perfect rockabilly records. "Woman Love" was an obvious emulation of Elvis, but it possessed that powerful sense of the macabre that came to be Vincent's trademark. It is one of the most overtly sexual recordings of its time, roiled full with Vincent's unceasing flow of orgasmic pantings.

"Be-bop-a-Lula" was Vincent's only country hit, and his only top-ten pop hit. Capitol issued nineteen singles by Vincent before he left the label in

1961. During the next ten years, Vincent recorded for Challenge, Forever, Dandelion, and Kama Sutra, all without commercial success. On October 78, 1971, Gene Vincent died in California from internal hemorrhaging. He was thirty-six.

Of the major rockabilly artists, Buddy Holly alone never had a hit record on the country charts. Born Charles Hardin Holly in Lubbock, Texas, on September 7, 1936, Buddy's musical heritage was hard-core country, but by the mid-1950s he had developed an interest in black music.

After several years of playing in clubs and on radio in the Lubbock area, Holly was signed to Decca early in 1956, and on January 26, in Nashville, Owen Bradley produced Holly's first session. In April, a single was released: "Blue Days, Black Nights" and "Love Me." Four more disks followed, including the classic "That'll Be the Day," but little happened. In March 1957, Buddy Holly and The Crickets were signed to Brunswick/ Coral, and late that year "Peggy Sue" became Holly's first hit, eventually rising to No. 3 on the pop charts.

Buddy Holly (playing guitar). Courtesy Doug Green.

The Everly Brothers. Courtesy Doug Green.

Within the next two years, Holly had five more pop hits, but none entered the top ten.

On February 3, 1959, near Fargo, North Dakota, an airplane carrying Holly, Richie Valens, and The Big Bopper (J. P. Richardson) crashed, killing all aboard. Waylon Jennings, who was in Holly's band at the time, had given his seat to The Big Bopper at the last minute.

Although Holly was a rockabilly artist, he was very different from the rockabilly mainstream. His was a softer music. His records sounded less neurotic, effervescent instead of turbulent. Buddy Holly was the gentleman of rockabilly, the first soft rocker. In Holly's records, rockabilly can be heard deflecting from country music toward a more refined, Apollonian form, perhaps best exemplified by the music of The Everly Brothers.

Don Everly was born in Brownie, Kentucky, on February 1, 1937; his brother Phil followed on January 19, 1939. The duo cut their first sides for Cadence in early 1957, and they were received immediately and enthusiastically by both pop and country audiences. "Bye Bye Love," "Wake Up, Little Suzie," "All I Have to Do Is Dream," "Bird Dog," and "(Till) I Kissed You" were top-ten records in the late 1950s on both the pop and country charts. In 1960, The Everly Brothers left Cadence for Warner Brothers, and their first release on that label rose to No. 1 on the pop charts: "Cathy's Clown." Although the duo disappeared from the country charts after 1961, they continued to have moderate success on the pop charts through the late 1960s. In 1972, The Everly Brothers left Warner Brothers for RCA; in the summer of the following year, they announced their breakup. The historical importance of The Everly Brothers is not to be overlooked. With their harmonious sound and rosy-romantic material, The Everly Brothers were the pivotal rockabilly act, rooted more deeply in pop than in country.

It was the final, inevitable step, the homogenization. With Buddy Holly, the mania had ebbed. Now it was merely an echo in the blood.

Chapter Ten

The Nashville Sound

For journalists in the 1960s, nothing seemed to capture their feeling of excitement in the discovery of country music as much as in the elusive, heady phrase, "the Nashville sound." It became a shorthand means of explaining the rise of country music from the ruins left by rock, and the increasing dominance of the form all through the 1960s.

On the surface the concept of the Nashville sound is simple. Nearly everyone has heard the phrase—it conjures images of Chet Atkins, late-night recording sessions in dim studios, and creative camaraderia. The term is actually quite complex, however, for it has multiple meanings; it refers to a specific style of recording, to an era in the development of Nashville as a recording center, and finally to a mystique that grew up around the city in the years when the marriage of pop and country music was consummated.

Something about the Nashville sound—the actual sound itself, not yet burdened by historical or mystical overtones—made singers want to record in Nashville, made people want to buy records produced there, and brought country music to the mid-American public for the first time since the days of Gene Autry and Bob Wills. Because even musicians found it hard to define with any precision, those who discovered Nashville and its sound called it "loose," "jazzy," "swinging," "subtle," and applied a host of other vague adjectives. Growing out of the jamming of sophisticated musicians (this in itself was a great surprise to many who "discovered" country music around this time), it was all this and more, and like any sound or combination of sounds, it had its magnificent moments and its excesses, ranging from the sublime to the ridiculous—but at a time when "hard," traditional country music was stone-cold dead, the Nashville sound pulled country music (and the city that came to be called Music City, U.S.A., as a direct result) out of terrible doldrums. Whether the resulting music helped improve the quality of country music or helped destroy it—there are persuasive spokesmen presenting both extremes—it saved the industry when things looked bleakest, and that is the dominant legacy of the Nashville sound.

The Nashville sound was the result —as many things seem to be in retrospect—of a succession of fortunate accidents, a whole series of the right people being in the right places at the right time. Historically speaking, the growth in number and quality of recording studios in Nashville gave as much impetus to the development of the Nashville sound as anything else, for it was this proliferation that gave rise to a group of studio musicians who played so often and so smoothly together that they made recording in Nashville easy, relaxed, and incredibly efficient. They were disciplined and creative at the same time, musically sophisticated and co-operative; they knew each other's music by feel, and were able to work out stunning arrangements in a matter of minutes. In the 1970s a lot of criticism was leveled at the mechanical, business-like, sound-alike approach this technique produced, but when the approach was new it was a thrill for both

the artist who found a superb, solid, creative band behind him (so different from many road bands) and for the producer who could enter the studio and cut four or five musically strong sides in just three hours. It created substantial savings, too, in both time and money, and there existed always the assurance of high quality. The Nashville musicians had built a better mousetrap, and in that light it is easy to see why singers, studios, and record labels began falling over themselves to get to Nashville, particularly when they couldn't seem to make a hit recording in New York or Los Angeles.

Certain informal rules came into being in the Nashville recordings of the early years. First, a single group of talented sidemen moved from studio to studio and worked on the sessions of many singers on many different record labels. This approach stood in contrast to that practiced in New York and Los Angeles, where sidemen were frequently connected with the work of a single company-owned studio. Second, Nashville sidemen did not usually read music on recording sessions. They were all sophisticated musicians, and many could and did read music when it was necessary, but most played instruments that were frequently learned "by ear" and thus found an "aural" approach to arrangements more comfortable than reproducing sounds indicated on a written chart. Because it was derived from folksong, country music has always placed its greatest emphasis on the message of the song—the text. The basic musical structure was fre-

Hank Garland. Photo by Arthur Maher.

quently simple: A basic 1-4-5 progression or perhaps a 1-4-2-5 progression would handle many country songs. Such chord changes were repeated verse after verse, so detailed charts for an entire song were rarely needed; similarly, time signatures were unnecessary because country songs rarely changed tempo once begun. It was, then, the simplicity of much of the music, combined with the "by ear" orientation of many Nashville musicians, that kept the strict classical notation pretty much out of Nashville studios.

Instead, a musical shorthand was substituted for "notes," and for most sessions today the system remains in use. In "Nashville notation" the musician simply records the chord progression of a song when he first hears it (usually when it is played for him on tape at the beginning of a session). He writes down a number for each measure in which a particular chord is played and makes his lines of numbers conform to the phrasing of a song. It looks like this:

$$1 \quad 1 \quad 4 \quad 4$$
$$5 \quad 5 \quad 1 \quad 1$$

If the numbers were translated into chord names in, for example, the key of C, the same diagram would look like this:

$$C \quad C \quad F \quad F$$
$$G \quad G \quad C \quad C$$

If the musician played one measure of these chords in 4/4 time, this pattern could serve, for example, as accompaniment for Ernest Tubb's "Walking the Floor Over You," or, for that matter, "The Great Speckled Bird," or "There's a Star-spangled Banner Waving Somewhere," or country music's first hit, "The Prisoner's Song," or one of its more recent: John Denver's "Back Home Again."

This type of notation merely provides a framework—the barest skeleton—for a musical performance. The individual sidemen improvise parts that fit this skeleton, either playing chords or appropriate melody lines. The frame is, in fact, so open to invention that the specific background arrangement evolves as the sidemen rehearse in the recording studio, and when musicians are familiar with the system and comfortable with each other, a complete arrangement will emerge after four or five run-throughs of the song. And if the musicians are creative, and if they're not tired or bored, their individual ideas will equal or surpass an arrangement written out in advance; each musician contributes something very individual to what ultimately becomes a well-structured

and homogenized unit. The payoff is that musicians who are friends as well as coworkers, playing in an environment in which their ideas can find a place on every record and in which every arrangement is considered to be evolving, should be able to produce relaxed, creative, fresh-sounding recordings.

A unique instrumentation was also a part of the Nashville sound, and Music City was (and is) strongly oriented toward the sounds of the rhythm section and particularly toward the sound of the guitar in each of its many incarnations. The "standard" Nashville recording team in the 1960s consisted of bass, drums, piano, sometimes a fiddle, and guitar (or, more properly, guitars); one and sometimes two acoustic guitars were strummed for rhythm. If two were used, one usually had a special set of high-pitched strings to produce a brilliant ringing of the chord toward the high end of the audio spectrum. Usually one electric guitar played "lead" lines—either single notes or simple intervals—and the ubiquitous pedal-steel guitar fulfilled a number of functions, sometimes sounding like a standard electric guitar and at other times playing slurs more suited to the fiddle. Often a six-string bass guitar—a little-known electric instrument tuned one octave below a guitar and one above a string bass—was used in conjunction with an upright string bass to double the bass line and contribute the crisp bass "punch" associated with Nashville recording. The standard four-string electric bass has come into widespread use in recent years, but in the heyday of the Nashville sound the upright/

six-string bass combination was universal.

The manner of the combination of instruments was also unique to the Nashville sound. Restraint is a large part of Nashville musicianship: Country pickers know when not to play, which is most of the time, for their function is to support, to showcase, and to frame the work of a featured vocalist effectively. The New York style—a big-band, wall-of-sound approach to recording in which there is *always* something complicated going on in the orchestra—never worked in Nashville. Nashville players divide playing into three activities: "backing," "filling," and "soloing." Most of the playing is just backing—playing the proper chord in the proper meter in the proper voicing. Filling brings a single instrument out front, usually to "fill" a musical hole left by the singer's phrasing. Soloing is, of course, an instrumental break featuring a lead line on one instrument. Even solos are kept intentionally simple, however, so as not to detract from the lyrics of the song. Playing is simple, only one instrument is out front at a given moment, and all of the instrumental work is subordinated to that of the vocalist. The creativity comes in on the "licks," those little one- or two-beat ideas that knock us out, grab our attention, and fix it firmly on the song. Just as countless great songs have survived mediocre performances, so too many mediocre songs have been saved by catchy instrumental devices. When both are present, the results can be special. Think, for example, of how much that descending Dobro line added to

"Harper Valley PTA," or going farther back, how that unbelievably simple little steel-guitar lick on Webb Pierce's "Slowly" in 1954 not only made the song a sensation (it was the top song of the year), but also excited and inspired so many steel guitarists that the use of pedals on steel guitars became mandatory almost overnight. The Nashville approach to recording provided maximum opportunity for these lucky accidents,* and their presence on country records did much to spread the word about Nashville sidemen to singers in other fields.

Over the years, there has been remarkable continuity in this approach to recording in Nashville, but the sidemen had a rougher, more energetic, more experimental sound in the middle-to-late 1950s when the Nashville-sound approach was being formed. No doubt the sidemen of today—many of whom have worked in the studios for some twenty years—suffer the pangs of success and drift into cliché and repetition from time to

---

* It is surprising but indicative of the Nashville approach that many of these record-selling "licks" were indeed genuine accidents. Drummer Ferris Coursey's thigh-slapping occured in-studio as a whimsical bit of humor while recording "Chattanoogie Shoe Shine Boy" in 1950. By the time the song was rehearsed that way, so the legend goes, Coursey's thigh had grown so tender he switched hands and recorded the song with left hand slapping left thigh. Similarly, the now-commonplace but then-striking fuzz-tone guitar on Marty Robbins' "Don't Worry" (1961) was the result of guitarist Grady Martin plugging into a studio amp with a blown speaker. Instead of putting the amp in the corner and using one in good shape, he began experimenting with the strange, rasping sound, and a hit record was born.

time. In general, however, the Nashville approach to rhythm-section recording remains the city's hottest commodity. Some of the musicians who backed Jim Reeves in the late 1950s played for Bob Dylan a decade later as the Nashville sound came to symbolize relaxed creativity in recording.

If the Nashville sound is a style, it is also an era. In the late 1950s, Nashville was still the provincial capital of a small country music scene; ten years later it was recognized internationally as a recording center coequal with New York and Los Angeles. In the late 1950s Nashville had two studios; by the late 1960s it was home to dozens. The decade of the Nashville sound made reality of the dreams of the 1950s. Major record labels opened offices and major executives emerged to lead the Nashville music community. Nashville's musicians placed a distinctive stamp on the city's recordings, and their success eased Nashville into a decade of unprecedented growth.

The proliferation of studios was a major cause of Nashville's success, and is in itself a fascinating study. As noted in Chapter six, RCA began recording at WSM radio's smallest studio, which was run by three staff engineers — George Reynolds, Carl Jenkins, and Aaron Shelton—on their off hours. It was there that they recorded Eddy Arnold as early as December 1944. The three then opened up their own facility, Castle Studios, in 1947, and this studio became the location for much of Nashville's recording for the next decade (although RCA's allegiance switched to the Brown Brothers' Transcription Service, Castle Studios' only real competitor in those dawning years).

The impetus toward expansion in the number and quality of recording studios came when Castle Studios began to lose popularity due to the engineers' unwillingness to change, modernize, or invest in their business (they had proved reluctant to purchase an echo chamber, for example, when that sound came into vogue). Into this obvious gap stepped a popular local society band leader and his guitar-playing brother — Owen and Harold Bradley, respectively—who decided to build a new studio for producing not only records, but also films for that hot new medium, television. They built their first studio not on what is called Music Row today, but on the second floor of the Teamsters' Union office at Second and Lindsley. The year was 1952, but the location didn't last long. The Teamsters, knowing a good thing when they saw it, tripled the rent on the Bradleys the following year, so they moved to a small building on Twenty-first Avenue South behind Hillsboro Village, just south of the Vanderbilt University campus. The place is now Acme School Supply, but in its heyday it was host to numerous sessions for Mercury, Dot, and Decca. Still, the ceilings were too low, the space too limited, and the sound not really first-rate. Finally Decca A&R man Paul Cohen considered moving the bulk of his company's country recording to Dallas, so Owen promised to build a whole new studio if Decca would guarantee him one hundred sessions a year. The agreement was made, and the search for a new location was on. Finally, Sixteenth Avenue South was chosen, and a Quonset hut was put up in back of an old home on a quiet residential street. Originally meant for film use (the first recording studio was actually in the house's basement), the Quonset hut was soon adapted to recording. It was sold to Columbia records in 1961, and although a large modern building has been constructed around it, Columbia's studio B, as it is now known, is still very obviously the old Quonset hut with the addition only of updated equipment.

The Quonset hut is in many ways typical of the Nashville studios that were to follow; they were and are well suited to the music made in them. By and large they are far more intimate than those in other recording centers, somewhat smaller and inclined toward burlap and wood in earth tones for decor. The studios themselves have become legendary, and in the 1970s this same old Quonset hut remained the most popular single studio in Nashville. Its interior is taken to be magical; everyone always feared to remodel it in case that special sound might be lost. Back when Columbia Records first bought the hut from the Bradleys, the CBS president, Frank Stanton, made his first visit to Nashville and naturally examined Columbia's new acquisition, the Quonset hut. The hut had a tattered interior —old drapes covering part of the ceiling and burlap covering the rest. Stanton looked around with cold efficiency and allowed that "the studio is fine, but we must remodel immediately, of course. Tear down all these old curtains." Stanton's Nashville staff blanched, gulped, and quietly ushered their leader from the hallowed room. The old studio was already a star, and deserved protection.

Paralleling the growth and development of recording studios in Nashville was the growth and development of certain key individuals. It is genuinely surprising to find that a movement of this magnitude was the creation of a mere handful of men and women—probably fewer than a dozen, all told, really got it rolling—and this in itself is a telling indication of the lack of direction in the country music community at the time. That so few talented people could take control of the sound of a major segment of American popular music is remarkable, to say the very least. It also shows just how small, in relative terms, the country music industry of the late 1950s and early 1960s really was.

Of these dozen or so prime movers, four stand out as particularly influential, going beyond musicianship and helping to produce, publicize, and sell the sound they created. First among them was Chet Atkins, whose name is as synonymous with the Nashville sound as it is with the sound of modern country guitar playing. Born in an isolated Appalachian hollow near Luttrell, Tennessee, and reared there and in rural Georgia, Chet followed in the footsteps of his elder half brother Jim, a superb musician who was best known as the singer and rhythm guitarist in the Les Paul Trio, a sensation in big-band musical circles in the late 1930s.

Chet worked as a staff guitarist on

Chet Atkins. Photo by Marshall Fallwell, Jr.

many country music radio shows, but in those early years he did not achieve recognition as a soloist. It came when he was signed by RCA/Victor in the late 1940s as competition to Capitol Records' star songwriter/guitarist Merle Travis, but Atkins' early RCA 78s (on which he both played and sang) were not successful, and he returned to radio work as an instrumentalist. He played behind the Carter Sisters and Mother Maybelle on the "Grand Ole Opry," and performed a solo instrumental spot on the network segment of the "Opry," sponsored by Prince Albert Tobacco.

Though Atkins had been disappointed in the results of his first RCA recordings, that early work had brought him into contact with Steve Sholes, the RCA A&R man who cut country records on periodic visits to Nashville. When Sholes was faced with the difficulties of assembling musicians and booking a studio, he fell back on the many talents of Chet Atkins, whose versatility, taste, and faultless execution quickly made him a fixture of the then-budding studio scene, still very much in its infancy. Sholes came to Nashville every few months to produce recordings by everyone on RCA's country roster (although like most of the early A&R men he recorded rhythm & blues, gospel, children's records, and anything else in the grab bag left over from mainstream pop). His Nashville roster varied from the Blue Sky Boys—who recorded their final RCA session at the Brown Brothers' studio in March of 1950—to Elvis Presley, who recorded his first RCA session on January 5, 1955, at the Methodist Publishing Company location RCA used for a time.

Sholes came to rely heavily on Atkins for his organizational ability as much as for his musicianship, and Chet began to spend a good deal of his time setting up sessions, arranging for musicians and studios and the like in preparation for a Sholes appearance in Nashville. The inevitable result, in Chet's own words (from his autobiography, *Country Gentleman*) was: "Steve came to me one day to ask: 'Chet, how would you like to take over the new RCA studio we're building?'" "You mean *me* run it for *you?*" Chet asked. "Sure, you know the business and the people and the songs. It would be a perfect deal for both of us," Sholes replied. Although he made it appear simple, Atkins admitted candidly, "My biggest problem was fear." He quickly overcame that problem on one of his first recording sessions, however, producing "Oh Lonesome Me" and "I Can't Stop Loving You" with Don Gibson: "When we released the recording a few days later—varoom! Both sides were smashes and I was an A&R man."

In his role as head of operations for RCA's Nashville office, Chet produced many of country music's biggest stars for RCA. Traditional country singers like Hank Snow, rockabilly's superstar Elvis Presley, and country-pop singer Jim Reeves all came under his production control in the late 1950s. His ability to succeed with the diverse styles of these singers indicates that Atkins himself was never bound by the stylistic limits of country music. Chet was influenced by—and recorded at one time or another—jazz, pop, and classical mate-

rial; he was as much at home with violins as with fiddles, and was, in the late 1950s and early 1960s, the right man to ease country music away from its traditional regional and cultural audience, and toward greater impact on the popular music scene.

Atkins set out to broaden the scope of country music immediately, adding a fuller, lusher sound—which was, of course, to become part of the Nashville sound—to country recordings in the hopes of making them broadly palatable. His method had a twofold purpose and result. He succeeded in expanding the production values of country music—mainly through the use of strings, horns, and background voices—thereby broadening the potential and actual audience for the music, and, as Bill Ivey wrote in *Stars of Country Music* (Urbana: University of Illinois Press, 1976), "His work with pop entertainers [Perry Como and Al Hirt] convinced New York and Los Angeles record men that Nashville musicianship had something of value to offer noncountry performers."

Add to all this Chet's own efforts in popularizing the mystique as well as the tangible value and effects of the Nashville sound, and the portrait of the man most responsible for its creation, fruition, and widespread popularity appears. In 1976, hindsight led him to reflect on his role in developing the Nashville sound, and his reflections were clearly filled with mixed emotions: "I hate to see country going uptown because it's the wrong uptown. We're about to lose our identity and get all mixed up with other music. We were always a little half-assed anyway, but a music dies when it becomes a parody of itself, which has happened to some extent with rock. Of course, I had a lot to do with changing country, and I apologize. We did it to broaden the appeal, and to keep making records different, to surprise the public."

The second major figure in the creation of the Nashville sound was Owen Bradley, who was born in rural Westmoreland, Tennessee, but did a good bit of growing up just south of Nashville, a city in which he was to become a popular pianist and orchestra leader. He led WSM's radio orchestra from 1947 to 1958 as well as playing the usual run of society dances. Like Chet Atkins a few years later, Bradley was asked by a country A&R man to take some of the load of Nashville recording off his shoulders. The man in this case was Paul Cohen, the record company was Decca, and the year was 1947. Although producing records was far from his only (or even major) source of income, Bradley built the studio above the Teamsters' Union in 1952 just for the purpose of recording Decca sessions with the help of his younger brother Harold (who by the 1970s was the dean of Nashville's studio guitarists). Comparing those days to the 1970s, Owen once said: "When I started there were just three of us fishing from the same hole; now you can hardly find a place to drop your line!"

With his pop-music background, it was no surprise when Decca's Bradley-produced records began to exhibit what was coming to be called the Nashville sound. Although he was able to produce traditional country records by Bill Monroe and Ernest

Owen Bradley. Courtesy Charles Wolfe.

Tubb and Kitty Wells, Bradley was also responsible for the lusher sound of Brenda Lee and Patsy Cline (just as Atkins used Jim Reeves as his main Nashville sound breakthrough artist). In fact, it is an old rumor that the country division was the only thing that pulled Decca through the lean rock years, for unlike other labels, Decca seemed unable to develop a rock or rockabilly artist like Elvis Presley or Chuck Berry or Carl Perkins. The closest they came was Buddy Holly; Bradley in fact produced Holly's first session in early 1956 (it was one of the early Quonset hut records), but the mixture of the burgeoning Nashville sound and raw Texas rockabilly were about as compatible as

STP and water, and the early records went nowhere. Holly was dropped only to be signed by a Decca subsidiary, Coral, where he made his brief but brilliant mark. The point is that while others in the company were running around like chickens short of heads, down in Nashville good ole Owen just kept churning out hit after hit after Nashville sound hit for Decca.

Where Atkins' approach was, generally speaking, characterized by fuller instrumentation—strings and horns—Bradley's tended more toward background voices, as a cursory examination of early Decca Nashville sound hits (Jimmy Newman's "A Fallen Star" or Bobby Helms' "Jingle Bell Rock" are good examples) will show. The voices were usually provided by either the Jordanaires or (more frequently) the Anita Kerr Singers, themselves contracted to Decca for their own recordings. They were led by Anita Kerr, the third member of this quartet of Nashville sound creators.

Originally from Memphis, Anita's talent as a pianist won her a staff job on a local radio station at the age of fourteen. She moved to Nashville in the late 1940s, and by 1951 had put together her acclaimed group and begun recording with Decca. Although mildly popular on record and a frequent guest on television—notably on Arthur Godfrey's show—the group made its mark in the recording studio behind other singers, where they provided the *ooooohs* and *aaaaahs* that enhanced many records of the era (and buried many others). There are few sounds as characteristically Nashville sound as that of smooth voices—

today the staple of dentists' offices and supermarkets—set to country tunes; the close-harmony chorus is the quintessence of the "countrypolitan" sound. Its effects were often overused in the dawning days, the genuinely experimental early period of the Nashville sound, but there can be no question that the use of background voices helped broaden country music's base in an era where it desperately needed all the help it could get.

The final member of this extremely important quartet—and the only non-musician among them—was Don Law, who was Columbia's distributor in the 1930s in Dallas when he met and eventually joined Art Satherley, Columbia's longtime A&R man. Satherley and Law shared both a love of traditional music and British birth. They each produced half of Columbia's country recording in 1945, Satherley cutting everything west of El Paso, Law doing all recording to the east. Upon Satherley's retirement in 1953, Law took over all country recording for Columbia until his own retirement in the middle 1960s.

Law's importance lies not only in the number of important artists he discovered and produced for Columbia —Marty Robbins, Carl Smith, Lefty Frizzell, Flatt and Scruggs, and Johnny Cash were just a few among many—but also in the fact that he was one of the first to begin using Owen Bradley's famous Quonset hut, finding it such an amenable atmosphere that he persuaded Columbia to purchase it when they moved to Nashville in the winter of 1961–62. He was always more than eager to use and develop and promote the Nashville sound—despite the wide variety of styles among his artists—and was the single most important factor in persuading Columbia to open up an office in what was becoming Music City, U.S.A.

The presence of these and other individuals in Nashville in the decade from 1955 to 1965 not only created the Nashville sound, but also helped to make Nashville's music a bigger and bigger part of the pop-music whole. Certainly there was much musical activity in Nashville in 1957, but the scene didn't rival New York or Los Angeles, and showed signs of blossoming importance only to prophets. But then, through business leaders like Chet Atkins, Owen Bradley, and Don Law, Nashville developed divisional offices for major record companies, and with those offices the musical community developed national visibility and clout for what had once been a regional recording center producing records for a minority audience. It must be remembered that before the late 1950s, virtually all recording was done in either New York City or Los Angeles or on location by traveling A&R men who returned to New York as soon as a session or series of sessions was completed. Nashville A&R men, who developed as assistants to traveling producers, gradually convinced New York that it didn't really understand Nashville and country music (as New York-recorded country records by Elton Britt, Rosalie Allen, and others vividly demonstrate); the best technique for the large record companies, they argued, was simply to leave the Nashville offices alone. Atkins and Bradley and Law kept cutting hits, and year by year they carved out greater independence for their respective country divisions. Nashville thus became the first (and only) full-fledged colony of the New York recording companies. Nashville's profits frequently ended up in New York, but with the exception of total fiscal control, Nashville divisions possessed virtual autonomy by the middle 1960s.

It was within this business environment that country music's third generation of stars came along. If the 1920s and 1930s produced artists like Jimmie Rodgers and the Carter Family and Gene Autry and Bob Wills, then the 1940s and early 1950s can claim Eddy Arnold, Ernest Tubb, Red Foley, Hank Williams, Lefty Frizzell, and Kitty Wells. From the late 1950s to the late 1960s the list would include many artists who remain stars today. As Atkins and Law and Bradley solidified Nashville's control over its professional destiny, they asserted their control by producing hits by George Jones, Johnny Cash, Loretta Lynn, Marty Robbins, Patsy Cline, Jim Reeves, Brenda Lee, and Waylon Jennings. Other Nashville producers cut Tammy Wynette, Roger Miller, David Houston, and Faron Young during those same years. The interaction of personality, business independence, and artistic excellence produced an era in which Nashville gained its reputation as *the* place to record, and Chet Atkins, Owen Bradley, and Don Law had the largest definable roles in that drama.

There were many others, of course, who contributed to the growth and

Boots Randolph.

development of the Nashville sound: musicians like bassist Bob Moore and legendary guitarist Hank Garland. There were Boots Randolph, who introduced the saxophone as a solo instrument in country music, and Floyd Cramer, whose "slip note" piano style brought about a great wave of interest in country music and an appeal to what is called today the "easy listening" or "MOR" (middle of the road) market. All had a share, all played a part in creating the Nashville sound.

Just as there were certain producers who effected this change, there were certain performers who symbol-ized it. Probably the best example was James Travis Reeves, who, blessed with a rich, full voice with a lulling vibrato, was the most natural artist to make the switch from hard country to the Nashville sound. His early records like "Mexican Joe" (1953) and "Bimbo" (1954) were solid country, and songs like Jimmie Rodgers' "Waiting for a Train" were staples of his repertoire, but his 1957 hit "Four Walls" marked the change dramatically, for it was total Nashville sound: muted accompaniment (no wailing fiddles or crying steel guitars), cushy backup singing; soft and easy through and through. Reeves joined the cast of the network radio show "Sunday Down South" late in 1957, performing purely as a pop singer, partially out of economic necessity—the rock explosion hurt him as much as any other country singer, and both the price and the frequency of his appearances had dropped rapidly—and partly to expand both his singing style and his audience. He weathered the inevitable criticisms of having "gone pop," and went on to build a new career filled with cross-over hits and epitomizing the Nashville sound.

Although her background, like Reeves', was thoroughly country, Patsy Cline's entire recording career, from "Walking After Midnight" in 1957 onward, was predicated on the Nashville sound, and while she continued to appear on country shows as she became popular, she quickly shed her cowgirl outfits for soft sweaters. Her singing, always reminiscent (although gentler in tone) of Kay

Floyd Cramer.

Jim Reeves.

Starr's, was, like that of Reeves', a natural for the laid-back Nashville sound approach. It was smooth, full, distinctive, and supple, and many of her hits exemplify the sound and style to perfection, particularly "I Fall to Pieces" (1961) and "Crazy" (1962) —the latter, incidentally, written by Willie Nelson.

Three others of the same era were also major forces in the spread of the Nashville sound: Don Gibson, Faron Young, and Hank Locklin. Gibson's early career was filled with frustration, as he was able to achieve success as a writer but made no waves as a singer. As Chet Atkins recounted earlier in this chapter, however, when Gibson cut "Oh Lonesome Me" and "I Can't Stop Loving You" for RCA in 1958, his career as a singer was assured. His unusual voice and sophisticated sense of phrasing no doubt accounted for much of his appeal, but the background over which he sang was once again the subtle instruments and full voices that typify —some might say stereotype—the Nashville sound.

Faron Young came to the style quite another way: A hard-core honky-tonk singer with a voice reminiscent of Hank Williams at the time he scored his first hits—"Going Steady" in 1953 and "I've Got Five Dollars and It's Saturday Night" in 1956— he metamorphosed into a smooth Nashville-sound singer (after a brief and abortive attempt at becoming a teen-age heartthrob) with his classic version of "Hello Walls" (again, a Willie Nelson song), outstanding among many successful Nashville-sound records.

Although his sky-high Irish tenor didn't fit into the standard Nashville-sound mold, the musical background used on Hank Locklin's recordings did, and the combination proved an effective one in the late 1950s as he scored big with "Send Me the Pillow That You Dream On" in 1958 and "Please Help Me, I'm Falling" in 1960. Another tenor whose records were steeped in the Nashville sound was Jimmy Newman, whose "A Fallen Star" was, in 1957, one of the earliest of the heavy-handed Nashville-sound hits.

An interesting historical anomaly of the period was the rash of "epic" or "saga" songs, which appeard first in 1959 with Johnny Horton's "The Battle of New Orleans," Marty Robbins' "El Paso," Eddy Arnold's "Tennessee Stud," and the Browns' "The Three Bells," (although these were all antedated by the Kingston Trio's "Tom Dooley," which won the Grammy award as best country song of the year in 1958, the first year such a category was listed. A rash of such material—apparently country music's answer to the folk-song boom—followed. Horton, an ex-honky-tonk singer, led the movement with "When It's Springtime in Alaska" in 1959, "Sink the *Bismarck*" in 1960, and "North to Alaska" in 1961, before his untimely death at the height of his career in a 1960 automobile accident ("Alaska" was released after his death). Marty Robbins' foray into the genre (with "El Paso" in 1959 and "Big Iron" in 1960, plus an album called *Gunfighter Ballads and Trail Songs*, which earned gold-record status) can now be seen as a stopping point in a remarkably diverse career that has touched upon pure hard country, rockabilly, Western, Caribbean, Hawaiian, pop, and other musical styles. Other landmarks of this genre include Lefty Frizzell's "The Long Black Veil" (of which co-author Danny Dill said, "I got on a kick with Burl Ives songs—those old songs —but I didn't know any, and I had no way to find any at the time, or was too lazy to look. So I said 'I'll write me a folk song'—an instant folk song, if you will") in 1959, and Jimmy Dean's "Big Bad John" and Jim Reeves' "The Blizzard," both in 1961. Lefty's "Saginaw, Michigan" ended this cycle of saga songs, in 1964.

The saga-song anomaly (and the occasional rockabilly foray like "Bye-bye, Love" in 1957 and "Guess Things Happen That Way" in 1958) aside, however, the period between

Elvis and Roger Miller was dominated by the Nashville sound, and its main exponents were Jim Reeves, Patsy Cline, Don Gibson, and, to a lesser extent, Faron Young and Hank Locklin. It was these men and women who took the sound out of the hands of the in-studio creators and presented it to an American public obviously quite ready to receive it.

Chet Atkins, as we have seen, has apologized for his influential role in bringing the Nashville sound's blandness to country music, but in perspective—as much, anyway, as the limited distance will allow—it is clear that country music had to do something desperate and radical to survive. For better or for worse it was the Nashville sound that stepped in, took the lead, and brought success and prosperity where there had been confusion and failure. There were, however, distinctly negative effects of the coming of rock from which many careers would never recover, even with the help of the Nashville sound. as Charlie Louvin said so succinctly when recalling the times, "We [the Louvin Brothers] had made about the first 120 dates with Elvis that he worked, but when he came along, the music changed. The people like Webb Pierce, who had 25 No. 1s, went down the drain, and there was a terrible slump in our kind of music right then, and so it did get lean. It was a living, I'll put it that way, but that's about all it was."

Similar things were happening to traditional country singers and acts throughout the business with the coming of rock. Some, like the Louvin Brothers, toughed it out;

others retired. A few tried to jump on the bandwagon with results that were in a few cases fine, but were generally embarrassing. It was a terribly hard time and, for the traditional act, the advent of the Nashville sound was scarcely more a friend than rock; these acts appeared as antiquated and outmoded by one trend as by the other. Still, although the Nashville sound has fallen into critical disfavor today, there is ample evidence to show that it pulled country music up by its bootstraps—although they were now patent leather and velvet pumps—during these tempestuous times.

Rock 'n' roll hurt country music in two ways. First of all, it drained country music's talent and audience as artists like Elvis, Conway Twitty, Carl Perkins, Jerry Lee Lewis, and Buddy Holly—artists who in another era would have found careers in country music—abandoned country roots for rock and the lure of pop superstardom. The rock era also dragged American popular music toward the black, Afro-American tradition of city blues. For the period between 1957 and 1967, it is fair to argue that mainstream pop music did little more than rework and extend the city blues developed in the late 1940s. With the appearance of Elvis Presley, popular music moved into a flirtation with the black musical tradition unlike that of any other period since the 1930s, when the popularity of jazz linked Harlem and South Chicago with the popular-music scene. Meanwhile, Nashville and country music groped for an antidote to the deadly poison that rock 'n' roll was to them. Some industry leaders argued that country music should retreat into a minority

role, serving fans in the South and in a few urban centers, that its performers should play one-night stands for a few hundred dollars and call any record that sold more than five thousand copies a hit. Another route away from oblivion found greater impact: Take the talent of Nashville's soloists and sidemen, bring in large doses of pop-music style (pop music of the Perry Como/Jo Stafford variety, that is), and compete head-to-head with rock for a portion of the popular market; try to sell country records to individuals who longed for the bland approach to recording taken by popular music in the early and middle 1950s. This survival tactic was pioneered by the leaders of the Nashville music scene in the Nashville sound era.

As the 1960s dawned, the effects were taking hold: Where country music had occasionally reached into the pop market, now the term "crossover" was being invented to describe the success in the pop field of a country record such as Jim Reeves' "He'll Have to Go" in 1960, or the concomitant phenomenon of a pop record selling strongly in the country market, as with Connie Francis' "Everybody's Somebody's Fool" (of the same year), a No. 1 pop record recorded in Nashville (by Danny Davis, long before his Nashville Brass days) with country musicians and with a country feel. With the Nashville sound.

There occurred a palpable quickening of the pulse of this once-moribund city with the rapid success of the Nashville sound and the acceptance of country music by the outside world. The Nashville sound quickly became the sound of country music—not exclusively, of course, but in the public eye—for everybody is eager to jump on a winner's bandwagon, particularly in an era of heavy losers. Nashville sound-alike records began to pour out of Music City, and the league of session musicians expanded to two, then three, then four teams as studios proliferated like rabbits and every label large or small grabbed a piece of the Nashville sound action.

In addition to the forces already explored, there were a number of other, independent factors that played a part in the success of the Nashville sound. All of them seem to point to the ironic fact that at the very time when it looked like there was to be almost no future at all, country music's day was dawning.

As we've seen, the Nashville sound broadened the audience for country music by making it acceptable to new ears. In addition, the term itself gave journalists and critics something tangible with which to explain the strange and rapid growth of what had so recently been called "hillbilly music" throughout the course of the 1960s: The term was short, catchy, and gave the impression of saying so much about country music while actually being quite adaptable to any meaning the writer cared to give it. Phrases like this have a snowballing effect: The more they are used, the more they tend to be used, and it didn't take long before country music and the Nashville sound became synonymous terms to much of the American public. It was not because country music had become a monochrome music—it clearly had not, for the California sound and the rebirth of

bluegrass both occurred at about this time—but simply because the phrase had become so handy, so convenient, so popular. With the phrase so apparently meaningful and so readily at hand, it can be no surprise that Paul Hemphill's interpretive look at Nashville—the book which stood alone for over five years—was entitled simply *The Nashville Sound*. In addition, the term gave direction to an industry plagued by vagueness and indirection and generated excitement, enthusiasm, and even pride, a sense of creativity and willingness to help each other and a bit of the joy of victory and the smell of success: intangible but important assets in the propagation of a sound and an image.

As to the sound itself, the slicker it got, the more it filled a gap. The rock onslaught had left a vacuum in the easy-listening middle of American pop music—Elvis hit New York and Los Angeles just as hard as he hit Nashville—and it was into this space that Nashville ventured. Certain segments of the public wanted a smooth, bland, easily listenable and most of all soothing type of music, and Nashville supplied just that. The tunes were catchy, the pace was slowed to an unthreatening crawl, the rough edges were knocked off and polished to a high gloss, and the music offered enough mildly interesting elements to please without placing any demands on the listener. If this was not exactly an artistic breakthrough—it has been compared to the innovation brought about by twenty-dollar original oil paintings in the 1970s—it was certainly a broadening of the market. In commercial terms, it did not hurt the country music that broke out of it—

the outlaws, western-swing revivalists, rockabillies, and honky-tonk singers of the 1970s—at all, for by the time they revolted against the Nashville sound's excesses, the Nashville sound had built an impressive distribution machine that awaited their use. It is interesting to note, in fact, that the Nashville music business turned to the outlaws in the 1970s for the same kind of reason it turned to Chet Atkins and *his* methods in the 1950s: a larger market for the music and a bigger share of the bucks.

As an approach to recording, the Nashville sound remains strong despite the effects of its excesses and the howls of its detractors. Pound for pound, Nashville sidemen tend to create more quickly, more easily, and with less emotional strain on one another than sidemen in any other recording environment, and so Nashville remains *the* place to record those musical styles and forms that don't require complex written charts. Today that includes almost everything but symphonies, Broadway musicals, and grand opera. Nashville became a national recording center because its musicians were flexible, and it remains so today for the same reason. During the peak years of the Nashville sound, the marketing motives of Nashville's music-business executives created a situation in which the pickers' talents were sorely underutilized, but the commercial success of their records did at least provide work where before there was none and make the existence of a recording community possible. Thus when more "gutsy" music proved to be more commercial yet than the Nashville-sound *style* (as op-

posed to method), the pickers were already assembled—as were the studios, publishing houses, and record-company setups. Today many forms of work are available in Nashville—the opportunity to pursue one's own art exists, but there is also more on-demand, commercial-type work than a flexible professional musician can handle, and the method of recording that generated the Nashville sound is still alive and kicking; today Nashville produces more cheap, easy, country-flavored pop and commercial music than ever. The Nashville sound is by no means dead; it has simply been eclipsed by the success of artists who went beyond it.

The Nashville sound is, however, in critical disfavor today, and it's easy to see why: When it was in control, its successes came close—and sometimes succeeded—in ruining otherwise fine, energetic, moving performances on record. The vice of overproduction made a mockery of normally distinctive and emotive singers. Thus the tyrannical aspects of the Nashville sound left a legacy of bitterness among both performers and fans of "hot" music. Chet Atkins may have felt that he had to apologize in this context, but the fact remains that he and Owen Bradley and Anita Kerr and the rest of the Nashville sound's architects saved country music (all of it) from obscurity and maybe even oblivion. They created a means of survival, kept Nashville working, and thereby ensured that when the time for greater expansion arrived, the Nashville artists, pickers, and businessmen would still be there to take advantage of it.

The Death of Rock, the Rise of Country

It is about three in the morning at Columbia's Studio A—the big, symphony-sized studio buried in Columbia's office complex in the middle of Nashville's Music Row. A bass player and a guitar player sit improvising idly—the atmosphere is stoned—and two drummers sit in opposite corners of the high-ceilinged room. Both play constantly, and now and then they drift weirdly out of phase and then back in again. The star sits in the center of the room on a high stool and reads movie magazines. Every now and then he looks up and makes some remark, and several of the musicians laugh reflexively. The drumming goes on constantly. The star's manager stands in the studio control room. Periodically he takes a quarter from his pocket and flips it, hard, against the acoustical-tile ceiling. The quarters stick. The drummers keep drumming, sometimes in, sometimes

out of phase. This is the building, the *very* building, in which Tammy Wynette and George Jones and Sonny James and Marty Robbins and Johnny Cash record. But this is not a typical Nashville session.

This is Bob Dylan, king of the folkies, an experimenter with rock music, recording in the capital of country music in 1966; the most important musical figure of the decade at work in the hometown of a music known only to at best a third of America's population. Here is America's folk poet, the conscience of a generation, recording in a style long associated with a Neanderthal social outlook and a sometimes ignorant, sometimes devious, sometimes violent culture.

Isolated as an incident out of context, these *Blond on Blond* sessions were, on the surface, improbable and strange occurrences. But with hindsight, Dylan's Nashville sessions stand out as a meeting place for the confluence of trends and directions in the popular music of that moment in American musical history. These were the trends that would not only include country music in the realm of popular music, but also would eventually elevate it to never before dreamed-

Johnny Cash.

of heights of nationwide—even worldwide—popularity. While most of Nashville concentrated on producing Nashville-sound records for the middle-of-the-road pop market, things had been changing across the broader scope of American pop and folk music. Although the threads of this process can be traced back to the beginning of commercial recording, the trends that were to arrive in Nashville in the late 1960s and the 1970s first became truly apparent in the mid-1950s when the youth of middle America, weary, disenchanted, and bored with the monochromatic landscape of popular music of the day, discovered the rich variety of ethnic American music, black and white. Black music found its way into popular music through rock 'n' roll, while white rural folk song became a significant part of the folk-song revival.

The raw, energetic, sexual music of old-time rhythm-and-blues became, when performed by Southern whites like Carl Perkins, Jerry Lee Lewis, and of course Elvis, not only a new hot fad but also a musical force that was to change the face of popular music all over the world. Rockabilly, that early amalgam of black and white rural traditions brought into the space age with electric instead of acoustic instruments, was the real thing. However, it gained the greatest acceptance in watered-down form, the popularity of the music being inversely proportional to the naked energy it exuded.

The ersatz daring and riskiness of black rock, and its concomitant safety and cultural distance when performed by whites, was a compelling attraction to bored middle-class youth. The face of popular music was forever altered when Elvis Presley and Bill Haley captured a massive middle-class audience. But at the very same time another whole set of young people—although a good bit smaller in number—was similarly drawn toward the roots of native American music, toward the Anglo-American folk songs and the traditional blues that formed the underpinnings of rock and of country music. They were drawn to the primitive blues of the Mississippi Delta and to the old-time country music that spoke to them of the dignity, simplicity, and purity of country life (a theme more with us today than ever before). American youth was drawn to these musics out of despair at the blatant commercialism that made up so much of the world around them, a charm that folk music held in common with rock 'n' roll. In this way many young listeners were drawn away from pop music's wasteland to the ethereal purity of the music of the Carter Family, or Bill Monroe, or Lightnin' Hopkins, or Woody Guthrie.

This movement toward traditional music came right on the heels of rock 'n' roll, with the Kingston Trio's 1958 release of "Tom Dooley," though, like rock 'n' roll, popular interest in minority music went back at least into the 1930s (actually, it went even farther back, to the turn of the century with the then-faddish sounds of ragtime and the popularity of minstrel-like "coon songs"). At any rate, this scattered movement toward traditional music popularized blues, calypso, mountain ballads, and any material that seemed to possess cultural

authenticity. It produced enthusiasm on the part of many singers and songwriters for the form, expression, and style of country music; appreciation for the straightforward, person-to-person music sung simply and directly.

The folk-song revival paralleled the early rock 'n' roll era. Fans of music who found even rock too slick and commercial flocked to the Kingston Trio; Peter, Paul, and Mary; the Limelighters; the Chad Mitchell Trio —the list is nearly endless. In the process, many also discovered the "real thing" behind the revival, and became fans of Frank Proffitt, Maybelle Carter, Doc Watson, and Bill Monroe. The revival itself—the spirit of revival—took a generation of American musicians and listeners and carried them into ethnic cultures and lifestyles. Many artists who are important in popular music of today "came of age" musically during the folk-song revival. They learned a particular approach to music, an approach based on detailed imitation of performance, style and, in some cases, the imitation of lifestyle as well.* Many performers who have moved

---

* It is interesting to note, in this regard, that many revivalists—middle-class musicians imitating traditional styles—took on (or attempted to take on) the speech patterns, dress, and values of traditional cultures. In the early 1960's, white bluesmen tried to become black, and imitators of old-time country music began to talk and dress like Appalachian mountaineers. Such extensive cultural borrowing was indicative of the widespread rejection of middle-class values by the youth of the era. Cross-cultural imitation only came to grief in the area of politics, for the often-conservative views of those imitated were frequently at great odds with the generally liberal sentiments of their urban and suburban fans.

popular music toward country music learned to love the material in those folk-song revival days, and learned simultaneously that imitation—often crossing cultural and racial boundaries—was the key to producing vigorous pop performances.

If the importance of folk-song people was obscured by rock's commercial success in the burgeoning days of the revival movement, it is clear that the "folkies" (as they were somewhat derisively called) have, in many ways, come to dominate American popular music of recent years. John Denver, Judy Collins, Gordon Lightfoot, Joan Baez, Joni Mitchell, Paul Simon, and of course Bob Dylan all bore the "folk singer" label early in their careers, and a group of second-generation folkies like Linda Ronstadt, Emmylou Harris, James Taylor, Stephen Stills, Jim Croce, and Gram Parsons followed closely on their heels. Others who achieved less recognition as soloists—Jerry Garcia of the Grateful Dead, Mike Bloomfield of the Paul Butterfield Blues Band—also learned to perform in the revival days. Clearly the folk-song revival "ethnicized" American popular music and in fact changed our definition of what qualified as popular music.

The period of greatest commercial success for folk-song revivalists followed the explosion of rockabilly and rock by about three years, and in the few years just around and a bit before 1960 not only were the Kingston Trio and Peter, Paul, and Mary and the like among the hottest acts in the nation — selling noncommerciality quite professionally—but also authentic country performers also occasion-

ally found success on a national level with records of folk-tinged material: Johnny Horton with "The Battle of New Orleans," Marty Robbins with "El Paso" and "Big Iron," Lefty Frizzell with "The Long Black Veil" and "Saginaw, Michigan," and Tennessee Ernie Ford with "Sixteen Tons."

Rock 'n' roll and the folk-song revival conspired in the ethnicization of American popular music, for while romantic, synthetic ballads and Broadway tunes had dominated the record industry in the decade before 1955, since 1960 it has been rare indeed to find hit records of any given period that have not been derived from some form of American folk music. Only very strong mainstream material—the work of writers like Henry Mancini or Burt Bacharach—has been able on occasion to crack the solid front of ethnic-based music.

Even though rock and folk song brought new energy to the American pop scene, both fell victim to the same undermining forces that crippled jazz in an earlier era. One of the few "givens" within popular music seems to be the tension between minority music and popularity. Folk music—any folk music—is visceral, minority-value-oriented, and disinclined to change, while music that is broadly popular is bland, majority-oriented, and trendy. Thus as soon as rock and folk music captured the imagination of a few, the material and its performance immediately began to deteriorate. In the early 1960s rock had lost much of its early virility and had been replaced in the popular arena by more effete, less visceral forms, such as surf music and the black-controlled but white-aspiring Motown sound. The folk boom—in some ways healthier than rock—also showed a lack of energy in the early 1960s, for overly slick groups like the Limelighters and the Chad Mitchell Trio had turned off much of the early folk-music audience, and television exploitation of the folk movement (on shows like "Hootenanny") drove home the final coffin nails. By 1964 the folk-song revival had lost its grip on the popular-music audience, having become an almost embarrassing parody of itself.

Add to this the difficulty of sustaining the originally high emotionality that any music—or any movement, for that matter—eventually suffers. The folkies found new ways of expressing their anger at injustice, and new injustices—specifically Viet Nam—became their concern. They grew weary of the wide-eyed innocents who tried to change an essentially violent and corrupt world with a song; they had seen how much really had changed through using this method, and in truth it wasn't much. It is a significant indication that only one protest song of any consequence—Tom Paxton's "Talking Viet Nam" came out of the folk-song movement after the middle 1960s. The folkies had either found more forceful means of expression or had simply dropped out entirely.

It was a similar situation, although with far different manifestations, for the rock 'n' rollers, whose rebillion in the late 1950s was so dramatically successful that they were left with literally no place to go. Nobody, by God, was stepping on their blue suede shoes now, and they were for all intents and purposes running the popular-music show. There was no place to go because there was no place for an essentially rebellious music with nothing to rebel against. How, for example, could the rock movement express a sneering view of the establishment when Bobby Darin and Bobby Rydell were playing Vegas, and Frankie Avalon and Fabian were making fools of themself onscreen? And speaking of films, what about Elvis? The tough street punk with the surly voice was now crooning love ballads with a big orchestra and a bigger vibrato in beach movies! What was next? Chuck Berry as Gidget? Jerry Lee Lewis as Mary Poppins? "John Milner" summed it up quite concisely in *American Graffiti* when he said, "Aw, rock 'n' roll's been going downhill ever since Buddy Holly died."

It has always proven difficult for any essentially faddish art to sustain passion and commitment. Because changes in taste have always been cyclical, the era of commitment to the music's message—implied or explicit, rock or folk—was simply coming to an end. There appeared an awkward void in popular music—although the music industry kept churning out these increasingly lifeless songs—for there was really nothing in American music to replace it. Into this void, then, stepped the Beatles, who borrowed from rockabilly, country, English dance hall, middle of the road, blues, and about every other musical form—later including modern electronic invention—to develop an always melodically enchanting music containing a little something for everyone. In a sense, the Beatles (and other such British groups as the Rolling Stones) were the master revivalists, dipping into a worldwide variety of ethnic and popular forms in order to produce a new pop amalgam. Much of their early work was a mere imitation of blues or rock or country performances, and not terribly distinguished imitations at that. What the Beatles lacked at first in musical talent they made up for in presence, in style. They presented an image of boyish rebellion and good-natured defiance that touched the collective heart of American (and European) youth.

Over and above their musical substance and repertoire, the Beatles' influence on American music was powerful indeed. Where less than a decade before the American sound had come to dominate the world, now the English sound—and look—came to dominate America, driving American music into either slavishly imitative or wildly divergent forms. It produced, on one hand, groups like that headed by current Texas country-blues-rocker Doug Sahm, the Sir Douglas Quintet, who were packaged, produced, and marketed as though they were an English band. It also produced the psychedelic excesses of many American West Coast groups, a music "full of sound and fury," but so introverted, contrived, pretentious, heartless, and drug-dependent as to lose all meaning.

For four—nearly five—years, the domination of the American pop scene by the English was nearly complete. The Beatles, Manfred Mann, the Rolling Stones, Freddy and the Dreamers, Petula Clark, the Dave Clark Five, Donovan—all of these and more had hit after hit on American radio. The English look, sound, and style were dominant for what, in retrospect, was only a short time (1964 through 1967), but the extent of that domination was so widespread and total that American music was for a time virtually submerged beneath it. Old-fashioned pop had died, a victim of rock; old-fashioned rock was passé; folk music went underground; American rock splintered. Meanwhile, country music went its own way, a slumbering giant, calmly and methodically (although unknowingly) developing and refining the Nashville sound and studio techniques which would blow the whole town wide open within just a few short years.

As Nashville grew, virtually unnoticed, English rock and the largely imitative American rock scene themselves became slavishly imitative. One group imitated the Beatles, the next imitated the imitators, the next imitated the imitators' imitations, and so on. The Beatles' own later work in electronic experimentation—itself frequently self-indulgent and excessive—created in imitation a flood of overintrospective, overworked, studio-hyped, album-length extravaganzas. English rock began quickly to wither on the vine—a decline hastened by the breakup of the Beatles—setting the stage for the death of rock and the rise of country music.

Just as the impact of the British sound is explainable, so is its rather short life understandable. The English scene was removed—quite literally—from the cultural sources of the music its musicians played. Black American music was still at the headwaters of the rock movement, and the best that can be said of the British rockers is that, most of the time anyway, they imitated their sources well. It is interesting to note that, of the surviving British bands from that era, those that remained closest to imitation and took part in less experimentation maintained greater commercial viability. In 1965 few would have seen the Rolling Stones as the band that would long outlive the Beatles, and fewer still would have guessed that the Stones might one day be seen as having greater artistic impact than the Beatles. Things look different from a present-day perspective.

"Slumbering giant" is as good a descriptive phrase as any for country music between the late 1950s and the late 1960s, for that is exactly what country music had become as the English wrested control of popular music from American musicians. Down in Nashville the studios stayed busy with the Nashville sound, honing the talents of producers, engineers, and the session musicians, which were shortly to become highly prized. And if rock's explosion had made instant anachronisms of Webb Pierce and Kitty Wells and Gene Autry, it did not kill the music completely. It simply forced country music to forge new paths, develop new sounds, and create a new generation of stars. Nashville responded with the likes of Roger Miller (and Kris Kristofferson and Willie Nelson not much later), whose brilliant, foolish, catchy songs were filled with a mad genius for linking words and sounds that shattered long-

held conventions and ways of doing things. But if these songs were hillbilly-intellectual, they were also understandable, resulting in both the wondrous admiration (and imitations, as always the sincerest if least welcome form of flattery) of fellow performers and songwriters, and enormous popular success as well. Miller opened the floodgates for a whole new wave of country songwriters who

Roger Miller.

were not only challenged and inspired by his inventiveness and unconventionality, but also were made aware of the level of sophistication that country audiences could and would accept and enjoy.

It all resulted in Miller's sweep of six Grammy Awards in 1965 (based largely on his success of the previous year), a sweep of categories unequaled before or since and one that inclined the Recording Academy to limit crossover voting in succeeding years. Certainly country music was coming of age, and indeed the era of the "crossover" was about to begin, for from this point on they came in a dizzying rush: "Gentle on My Mind," "Honey," "Harper Valley PTA," "Folsom Prison Blues," "A Boy Named Sue," "Daddy Sang Bass," "Okie from Muskogee," "Sunday Morning Coming Down," "I Never Promised You a Rose Garden," "Help Me Make It Through the Night," "Me and Bobby McGee," and "For the Good Times" the most prominent among them. It was at this time that country developed its new superstars, a whole legion of new talent: Merle Haggard, Tammy Wynette, Dolly Parton, Glen Campbell, Charley Pride, Buck Owens, and the reconstructed rockabillies Conway Twitty, Jerry Lee Lewis, Carl Perkins, and Johnny Cash, who were welcomed back with open arms to the music of their roots.

It is a marvelous bit of irony that it was right at this time that Nashville was really learning big-city ways, aiming for ever lusher arrangements, and yearning for and learning about the rich rewards of the crossover. At the very same time, city kids began to idolize the supposed freedom and purity of the Nashville scene and country music—Gram Parsons formed his International Submarine Band (which may claim the honor of being the first city country music band to record), and the Lovin' Spoonful broadcast far and wide the joys of life in Music City, U.S.A., in "Nashville Cats." The irony lies in the ossification that was at that very time becoming a part of the Nashville music scene, the gradual evaporation of the vitality and energy of the original Nashville sound as it was developed

Gram Parsons.

in the late 1950s as an antidote to rock 'n' roll. It was, within the space of just a couple more years, to cause Willie Nelson to make his celebrated hejira to Austin, disenchanted with the formulaic, closed-minded approach he felt was ingrained in Nashville. To those—like Willie—who were aware of what had been and, even more, what could potentially be, Nashville was a disillusioning place. But for those first discovering country music, first visiting Nashville, it was a town of tremendous excitement. One musician's boredom is another's thrill, and this truism has never been demonstrated with such vivid clarity as in Nashville in the late 1960s.

They flocked to Nashville to record, to play, to write songs, to drink Blue Ribbon at Tootsie's, to eat grits at Linebaugh's, and to snack on Goo Goos and moon pies, all the while glorifying the Nashville studios and musicians, many of whom—Pete Drake, Harold Bradley, Charlie McCoy—became instant cult heroes through their identification as sidemen on the backs of albums by Dylan, Baez, George Harrison, Ringo Starr, Neil Young, and Buffy Ste. Marie.

Many a city musician had fallen under the Nashville spell, and if the bulk of the music they created in Music City was not great, at least it was interesting, and more importantly, it introduced a whole new set of fans and musicians to the sincerity and the simplicity of country music, country styles, country songs, and country life. There was a genuine charm to it, a laid-back feeling and flavor that evoked a more straight-forward, far less complicated age. If the rebellious turn to rock 'n' roll was a bang in the 1950s, then the city kids' turn to country music in the 1960s was more of a murmur—but it was rebellious nonetheless, rejecting the technologically complex (while still, of course, enjoying its benefits) for the age-old serenity of the farm and the country.

But somewhere along the line here, very subtly, the relationship between country music and its traditional audience began to change. On the one hand, country singers and producers had quickly absorbed the values of popular music—production, hits, promotion, crossovers—while the "Opry," on the other hand, became an object of cult love from outsiders, a love that peaked around 1970 when one of the hippest places a celebrity could be seen was backstage at the funky, tumbledown old Ryman Auditorium on any given Saturday night. It happened on many levels, of course, but the overall effect was of popular music pulling away from blues and English rock as sources of inspiration, and edging toward Anglo-American "hillbilly" for that inspiration. City—even foreign—rockers started to dig country music, incorporating it into their performance style. This tended not only to help legitimize country music (a process that had begun in tradisional pop music with Perry Como's and Al Hirt's treks to Nashville to record, as well as Dean Martin's and Ray Charles' dabblings in the genre), but also in fact to lend it a measurable degree of hipness, a process that has come to full flower today with the overwhelming national interest in cowboy culture and in country life. America has been quick to seize upon country life as the last fragment of a gritty and tangible reality in an increasingly plasticized world, much as our mass culture discovered the treasures of black experience and culture just a few years ago.

By the time British rock wound down in psychedelic splendor in the late 1960s, an American alternative had developed in the popular-music marketplace. For some years American pop acts had drawn inspiration entirely from the British scene, but two groups came along who possessed a distinctively American sound: the Lovin' Spoonful and the Mamas and the Papas. The Spoonful, with John Sebastian and guitarist Zal Yanowski, and the Mamas and the Papas, led by John Phillips (who had been the lead singer of a late folk-song-revival group, the Journeymen), both had their origins in the folk-song revival. The Mamas and the Papas were essentially a vocal band, with instrumental invention secondary, even incidental, to their complex vocal arrangements. They were, in an obvious and refreshing way, unlike British pop groups. The Lovin' Spoonful had a different sound but one that was just as distinctively non-British. They drew heavily upon black pop music and country styles, and presented interesting material written by John Sebastian. Their anthem to country music, "Nashville Cats," was an early statement of the growing interest and involvement of pop musicians in the country scene.

It all began in the middle 1960s, when the folk-song revivalists of five years earlier removed themselves from coffeehouse cloisters to challenge the sound of English rock. In head-to-head combat the folkies moved mostly toward soft country, and, ultimately wresting control, set the stage for John Denver and Olivia Newton-John, who would appear nearly a decade later. Folkies were, after all, ideally equipped to regain control of the pop-music scene. They had kept in touch with the rural musics that periodically invigorate pop recording; they had remained onstage in coffeehouses, honing professional skills; and they were experienced in imitation and in performing music drawn from backgrounds other than their own. Not every folk singer, of course, wanted to sing like Hank Snow—Paul Simon has yet to make a move toward Nashville—but Judy Collins, Elvin Bishop, Bob Dylan, Joan Baez, Buffy Ste. Marie, and others did. The impact of these stars on American musical taste helped create an explosion in the popularity of country music that was eventually to reach all corners of the nation.

Of course, it took more than the efforts of a few individuals to create this explosion in country music's popularity. Several things happened at once. Certainly the interest in country music on the part of folk and popular musicians formed a part of the picture. Country music itself was actually in surprisingly strong shape, with the third-generation stars on hand in Nashville and Bakersfield and a group of studio sidemen and industry executives ready to push country music beyond its traditional regional and ethnic boundaries. The vacuum left by the demise of British rock certainly provided opportunity, and the national media suddenly provided mass exposure of country music.

All these forces coexisted at the end of the 1960s, and their combination produced a new set of hyphenated stars. Johnny Cash was country, or maybe "country-folk" or maybe "country-pop." Glen Campbell was "pop-country" (or was that "country-pop"?) and Anne Murray was "pop with a little country." All this groping for appropriate terminology indicated that country music was more pop than ever, growing more pop every day, and that at the same time pop music was leaning more toward white southern music for inspiration and sustenance than ever before. Just as the middle 1950s witnessed the beginning of a decade in which American popular music, through rock 'n' roll, copied and reworked the black urban tradition, the late 1960s witnessed the beginning of an era in which country music would provide a similar sort of inspiration for the popular-music field.

An indicator of the existence of this explosion in country music's popularity every bit as graphic as the trade-publication popularity charts was the appearance of country music on what had become America's great mass medium: television. Syndicated shows (Porter Wagoner's and Flatt and Scruggs' the most memorable) had been with country music for a long time, and even Jimmie Dean and the "Ozark Jubilee" and the "Grand Ole Opry" had made brief network appearances in the 1950s and 1960s. Toward the end of the 1960s, however, came not only appearances by country entertainers on shows like "Today," "The Mike Douglas Show," and others, but also prime-time network shows devoted to country (or what the network executives thought of as country) music. First came "The Johnny Cash Show" in 1969, then "The Glen Campbell Goodtime Hour" on CBS, and "Hee Haw," also on CBS. All appeared within a couple of years of each other, and each offered a different view of what network people thought country music was all about. Johnny Cash's show

Johnny and June Carter Cash.

was essentially a romantic view of country music as the music of the common man, its story told by the hobo/historian with a heart of gold. Campbell's show was full of vapid good cheer, but included some good country picking and occasional glimpses of country authenticity. "Hee Haw" displayed a split personality: On one hand it reinforced the old haybale and barnyard hillbilly image that country music never quite deserved and has long sought to escape, on the other hand it showcased some of the most authentic old-time performers (like Stringbean and Grandpa Jones) available in the country field. The Cash show was canceled in 1971 amid speculation that network interference with Cash's purist approach had hastened

the program's demise. Both Campbell's "Goodtime Hour" and "Hee Haw" were canceled at the same time by CBS. Both shows had high ratings at the time, but were dropped because CBS feared it had developed "too rural" an image (sitcoms "Green Acres" and "The Beverly Hillbillies" bit the dust at the same time). "Hee Haw" went into syndication, where it was seen on more stations than when it was on CBS, and remained a Saturday night staple, throughout the country, perhaps fulfilling the same function as that performed by the "Grand Ole Opry" years before.

The very existence of these shows, and then the long-term success of "Hee Haw," indicate the grass-roots support for country music that existed in the late 1960s. To this day network television is rather uncomfortable with country material and themes, and resists presenting it in unadulterated form. The recording industry seems less reluctant to see music move in a rural direction, and country music's greatest success remains on disc.

Another factor of signal importance in the rise of country during this period was the parallel rise of the country songwriter (which in turn paralleled the rise of singer-songwriters like James Taylor and Don McLean in the pop music field). Although Roger Miller, Kris Kristofferson, and Willie Nelson stand out as particularly influential in this era, the process had begun a good bit earlier. Actually, for years Nashville had but one real professional songwriter, Fred Rose. Singers either sang their own songs, sang standards, covered new

Glen Campbell.

Buck Owens, Roy Clark, and the "Hee Haw" cast. Courtesy "Hee Haw."

hits made popular by other singers on other labels, or did a tune or two or more of Rose's. The complexion changed in the mid-1950s, however, when Opry manager Jim Denny left WSM to form his own booking agency and to go in with Webb Pierce on a new music-publishing company, Cedarwood Music. Here he assembled a staff of writers, among them Mel Tillis, Danny Dill, Marijohn Wilkin, Wayne Walker, and others, and the list of songs they created was awesome: "Detroit City," "Burning Memories," "The Long Black Veil," "Waterloo," and "Slowly."

The staff-writing concept, having been pioneered by Acuff-Rose and given a strong boost by Cedarwood's success, was quick to catch on, and Tree (Roger Miller's publisher), Combine (Kristofferson's publisher), and Pamper Music quickly became multimillion-dollar operations, producing songs and songwriters to fill the needs of the pop-music industry (the First Edition's "Ruby, Don't Take Your Love to Town" to name but one example) as well as the booming country field.

With the overwhelming success enjoyed by Kristofferson came a new wave of singer-songwriters to Nashville. The old image of the feckless, fancy-free, but invariably broke musician hanging out in Nashville looking for a job (usually at Tootsie's) was replaced within a few years by his modern counterpart: the feckless, fancy-free but invariably broke songwriter hanging out waiting to get his songs recorded. The result, of course, was better songs, because despite the high percentage and volume of dross, more writers meant, in the long run, more good songs. So rapidly, in fact, did this trend advance that these people came to be in demand as performers as well. The era of the singer and the song interpreter seemed to be over (although it appeared to show a glimmer of returning in the late 1970s), and the era of the singer-songwriter on record—whether he or she could sing or not—bloomed for a decade.

With many of these songwriters—despite the faded jeans and carefully applied country accent—coming to country music from widely varying backgrounds, it was logical that their material should begin to gain accep-

Shel Silverstein. Photo by Bill Arsenault, courtesy of *Playboy.*

tance among their own peers as well as at least a portion of the traditional country audience. Besides Kristofferson (who had been a Rhodes Scholar and an Army helicopter pilot before becoming a songwriter) there were Chris Gantry ("Dreams of the Everyday Housewife"), Tom T. Hall ("Harper Valley PTA"), and Mickey Newberry ("She Even Woke Me Up to Say Good-bye" and "An American Trilogy"), all of whom exemplify the influx of a host of songwriters from all regions and backgrounds who moved into Nashville in the mid-to-late 1960s.

One of the most interesting—unique, even—was a (pre-Kojak) shaven-headed Jewish ex-*Playboy* magazine cartoonist named Shel Silverstein who showed a remarkable, sensitive, and totally unexpected gift for country songwriting. Although his material—"A Boy Named Sue," "Marie Laveaux," "One's on the Way"—was by and large clever and humorous, he was also to write some more serious songs like Brenda Lee's "Big Four Poster Bed" and Loretta Lynn's "Here I Am Again." That Silverstein fit so neatly into the country music mainstream is not only an indication of his talent, but also demonstrates the breadth of the scope that country songwriting had come to encompass within a very short period of time.

This new dominance of the songwriter/performer on the Nashville scene altered the smooth system that had evolved in the late 1950s and early 1960s with the Nashville sound. In the early days of Nashville's success, the music business consisted of a chain of individuals linking songs with records. Writers brought their material to a publisher; publishers made demonstration records and hired a song plugger to pitch songs to A&R men around town. The A&R man picked material for his artists, helped the singer learn and interpret each new song, and helped hire musicians for a recording session. By the time a country singer actually put a selection down on tape, four or five different links in the chain had been activated, and each had taken (or would be paid from earnings) some kind of fee for its contribution to the overall success of the song.

It was inevitable that some of these functions would be combined, because the more activities that could be concentrated in one individual or corporation, the greater the share of the profits that would stay in one place. Suddenly A&R men were also songwriters, or A&R men owned their own publishing companies, or singers not only wrote but also published their own material, or record companies themselves owned publishing companies. The list of possible combinations was endless, but the results were nearly always the same: The creative process was undermined or circumvented. If a singer is also a songwriter, it follows as the night the day that he or she will tend to record his or her own material. If an A&R man is also a writer, then he too is more than likely to encourage his artists to sing his songs. And if a record company owns a publishing firm, it may require—or at least strongly suggest—that an artist sing material from that

company's catalogue, or may force or encourage new singer/songwriters signed to the label to place their songs in the company-owned publishing house. The pressures and combinations were, again, virtually endless.

With record companies in increasing control of the publishing side of the music business it became, in the late 1960s increasingly difficult for independent publishers—the real heart of the Nashville music business—to place songs with singers. The publishers, then, turned to the singer/songwriter as a solution to the problem of getting material on record. Rather than try to pitch songs to an A&R man or producer, publishers could bring the singer/songwriter himself to the company as a package: "If you want him as a performer, you have to take his songs as well." Thus the increasing concentration of power in the hands of producers and record companies helped reinforce the importance of the singer/songwriter to Nashville. The result was that by the late 1960s the doors of Nashville were simply not open to a singer who didn't have access to a fund of new songs, because the industry had learned that the really big money in commercial music was not so much in records but in publishing. The struggle to control the copyright to a successful song remains one of the greatest areas of conflict in Music City. In the late 1960s it combined with the charisma of new singer/songwriters to make Kristofferson-like images fixtures upon the Nashville scene.

Yet another contributing factor that

must not be overlooked is the Bakersfield phenomenon of the middle 1960s, for just when Nashville seemed locked into the semipetrified Nashville-sound approach, Buck Owens and Merle Haggard and Wynn Stewart on the West Coast were turning out pure hard country, heavy on fiddles and steel guitars (where Nashville had discarded them in favor of strings and background voices) and honky-tonkin' lost-love and heavy-drinking lyrics. The surprising thing is not that this helped win back the country fan who felt his music rapidly slipping away from him, although it indeed had that effect, but that it was in many cases this music that entranced the urban folkies and ex-rockers, *not* the broadly aspiring Nashville sound. Somehow it seemed so much more *country* (what they were searching for was a feeling, a sense, a vision, not a particular style) than the monochrome Nashville sound. Merle Haggard was praised by city listeners and lauded as a folk poet, a modern Woody Guthrie, and it seems to be no accident that it was Owens' "Act Naturally" that struck the ears of the Beatles.

All this activity set the stage for the countryfication (or at the very least the ethnicization) of many pop bands. The Byrds were among the first to exploit country style in a pop context effectively, their *Sweetheart of the Rodeo* album standing as a significant landmark, for not only did it give life to their fading career as folk-rockers, but also it turned many ears previously thought to be immune to hillbilly music toward the country sound. It was not great music—the Byrds'

renditions of older country songs sound especially weak in comparison to the originals—but it was good, interesting, provocative music, and it gave birth to several West Coast groups like the Flying Burrito Brothers and others who delved further and further along the path of pseudo-country, tongue-in-cheek country, and country rock.

It was inevitable, of course, that the best of pseudocountry would become as good as the authentic country it sought to emulate. This is not to say, of course, that country music or its musicians are inherently superior to folk, rock, or indeed to city musicians. But because country music does, to many ears, sound deceptively simple, and because it has often been parodied through third-rate imitation or played for a campy joke, country musicians have been viewed as inferior to those in other fields. In fact, country music demands control, taste, and lifelong familiarity with the southern white culture from which country style and song spring. Few urban musicians have been able to render country music convincingly, but the late Gram Parsons, and even more successfully Emmylou Harris, came to sing country with authority and authenticity. In fact, Ms. Harris has been accepted among country musicians, singers, and fans as one of their own, and she is virtually the first urban revival performer to be so accepted.

Despite Emmylou's background in the country music-rich Washington, D.C., suburbs, the pseudo-country movement was by and large a product of the West Coast. It was in California, for example, that Commander Cody and his Lost Planet Airmen (transplanted from Ann Arbor) and Asleep at the Wheel (transplanted from Ohio and Pennsylvania) first grew to prominence. The West Coast country rock sound of Gram Parsons —heard in the music of the Byrds and the Flying Burrito Brothers, as well as the Dillards in their folk-rock period—was soft, ungutsy, intellectual, characterized by high trio harmony, and was well suited to ears of the late 1960s. The only solidly country aspect of that sound was the use of the pedal steel guitar. Just as the whine of the steel had for years clued pop fans to tune the radio away from some country songs, now the pedal steel was becoming a pop music staple—the most obvious symbol of popular music's new love affair with country songs and sounds. The steel alone failed to completely countrify the West Coast sound, and though Parsons and his followers found a dedicated audience in the pop field, their music remained alien to hard country fans.

Emmylou Harris is clearly the peak performer of this genre, the product of individual talent and dedication combined with years of interaction between popular and country music. Though Emmylou will never be able to claim the role of pioneer in the countrification of popular music, she is nonetheless the first star to attract both soft rock and hard country fans. In an environment in which the "pop" or "country" nature of a John Denver or an Olivia Newton-John can be— and have been—debated endlessly, Emmylou has scarcely a detractor. If a true pop-country consensus has

evolved from a decade of interaction and exploitation, it is certainly embodied in her career.

Emmylou Harris is not the only pop artist working effectively with country material or country performance style. Poco and the Eagles, groups with a sound more analagous than similar, have made use of country imagery in songwriting, and have utilized country instrumentation and vocal harmonies in many recordings. Their work is, however, another example of the countrification of popular music, a widespread trend which affects not only the songs of these groups ("Tequila Sunrise," "Peaceful Easy Feeling," and "Lyin' Eyes"), but those of Kenny Loggins, The Band, Bill Danoff (of the Starland Vocal Band), and, of course, the high priest of urban escapism, John Denver. Though each of these artists has affected country music, their majority audience remains in the pop field.

Country music will remain prominently on the American musical horizon for some time. Partly, this is natural: pop musicians from the middle 1950s to the middle 1960s reworking and extending America's black musical tradition, and it should be little surprise to find popular music in a similar period in which it reworks and extends that country musical tradition which runs back to American and British folk song. This much of the trend makes cultural sense, for America's periodic interest in the music of its roots has been well documented.

Other forces will also conspire to maintain country music in its currently prominent position, but their ultimate effects are less certain and more ambiguous. Though country music helped fill the vacuum left by rock's decline, Nashville in the 1960s mounted a conscious campaign to expand the horizons of country music. The Country Music Association, an industry-wide trade organization, set out to increase the number of full-time country radio stations, and to increase access to country music through the medium of television. Success enjoyed in the pop field by country artists created the expectation of a crossover hit, and artists, producers, and record companies sought to create recordings suited to both pop and country markets. The pressures of expansion and success have created trends acting in various directions upon country music: country music artists want crossover hits, because it increases record sales dramatically, and these in turn increase live concert dates both in price and in number. Thus country artists tend to cut—or attempt to cut—pop-style material, and record companies tend to sign pop-country acts, and these demands of the marketplace affect the sound of country music.

Radio—AM country radio—also has an ambiguous role in the increasing popularity of country music. Stations compete for the largest possible share of the available listening audience; their advertising rates and thus their income is directly dependent upon audience size. Country radio was predictably thrilled and enchanted with the crossover phenomenon, for it allowed country stations to program "head to head" against their generally much larger pop music competitors.

If Johnny Cash had a No. 1 record in both the pop and the country charts, the country station suddenly possessed a great opportunity to lure listeners away from the local pop station. The more "pop" a country station could sound, then, the larger its audience seemed to be, and thus John Denver, Olivia Newton-John, the Nashville Brass, Mac Davis, Glen Campbell, and the like have all been welcomed with open arms by country radio programmers. All of these forces have combined not only to increase the popularity of country music, but also to make it sound more pop; to make it lose some of those characteristics which kept it tied to a minority audience, but that simultaneously gave it a distinct character.

To some this seems all to the good, but some careers—some important individuals—are being caught in the crunch. Pop records (because of the extra instrumentation, production time, and promotional expense) cost considerably more to produce than country records, so crossover records —hits or misses—carry a larger initial investment, and therefore demand greater sales from an artist to keep him (or her) on the label. Sales of 25,000 used to make a country record a hit, but it's not enough in today's pop-country environment. Artists with a small, dedicated following —Ernest Tubb or Kitty Wells or any of a number of bluegrass performers —just can't compete for radio air play with John Denver and just can't sell records like Olivia Newton-John or Linda Ronstadt. The new, pop-oriented approach to recording and radio programming tends, then, to drive out some of the performers and material that sound "too country." Country music thus succeeds by cutting off its own roots. The danger is that, when pop music makes its inevitable turn to some new music—be it reggae or salsa or conjunto or Hawaiian or even back to the blues—country music may be left with nothing. The pop stars will have moved on to another new fad, and the hard core, solid country artists and the fans who helped country music through difficult times in the past will all be gone. In the middle and late 1950s the popularity of watered-down versions of the blues hurt record sales and concerts by traditional bluesmen, and in the 1970s the media explosion surrounding country music may similarly damage the tradition it attempts to exploit. These negative forces are the hidden but ever-present penalties of success.

The effects of the death of rock are varied and extremely fragmented, as are the effects on and within country music itself. For example, while the whole Austin outlaw movement seems to have come out of a deep disenchantment with the Nashville way of doing things, that very way of doing things (or the image of what that way comprised) is what attracted Dylan, Baez, Buffy Ste. Marie, and many others to the Nashville sound. They all came clambering to Nashville even as Willie and Waylon were throwing up their hands and leaving. The countrification of pop songs is yet another effect of the death of rock, the frightening rise of countrypolitan radio another, the revivalist surge of western swing (which began on the West Coast with Commander Cody and Asleep at the Wheel) yet another, and so on.

It was a confusing and bewildering period for country music—all that national press attention—but the ultimate result was little more than a reshuffling of the old deck. Country music today is playing with a new and stronger hand, but is playing in a game with higher stakes than ever before.

Chapter Twelve

Modern Country

During the 1970s country music was being pulled in several directions. On Nashville's Music Row, the trend was toward a slicker, smoother, more popular sound. In the "Grand Ole Opry" the atmosphere was business as usual, with a renewed appreciation of the established modes of the music. It mattered little that some of the "Opry" stalwarts like Roy Acuff and Ernest Tubb hadn't had a hit record for years; the "Opry" and its ritual were flourishing. In Austin and points southwest, the sound was earthier, grittier, more down-to-earth: it was back to basics time, outlaw time. In the southeast, bands like the Allman Brothers and Charlie Daniels were pulling country in the direction of rock—or rock in the direction of country. In the East and border states, bluegrass was attracting millions to outdoor happenings staged in cow pastures, state parks, and town squares,

and old-timers like Lester Flatt and Bill Monroe and Mack Wiseman were telling acres of chanting kids to "keep on supporting that grass." People were suddenly Taking Country Music Seriously, and everyone was trying to figure out its "essence," and everyone was coming up with a different explanation. And no wonder. The music in the 1970s was as confused and as eclectic as it had ever been; it was as if the whole history of country music, with all its neat periods and divisions, had suddenly telescoped itself into one möbius strip decade.

In October 1976, three widely reported quotes set the tone for the widespread tension over the direction of country music. The first was from David Snow, program director for a large country station in Buffalo, New York, one of the top country stations. "We play middle-of-the-road country-

The new "Opry" House at Opryland.

easy-listening country music like Ray Price, John Denver, Olivia Newton-John. No drinking songs, no Hank Snow, Buck Owens, or Stonewall Jackson. I like to listen to those folks at home, but they're not commercial anymore. . . . There are some who are afraid country music is losing its identity, but I think the changes are good. For one thing, they're bringing more people to country. We get letters from doctors and lawyers. Country isn't just blue-collar any more."

David Snow's quote reflected the sentiments of many of the music industry's professional promoters, people who have their fingers on the pulse of the dollars-and-cents popularity of entertainers. David Snow concluded with an even blunter assessment of the music's fabled sense of tradition and continuity. "You can respect people like Roy Acuff and

Ernest Tubb for what they were, but if Babe Ruth were alive today, you wouldn't put him in a ball game."

Country entertainers generally responded in one of three ways to this challenge. Some echoed the concern of Hank Snow, who announced a few days after David Snow's quote that he was considering a change in style. Hank Snow, a legendary performer of over thirty years' standing, is one of the music's most direct links with the lean, spare singing style of Jimmie Rodgers, "I was playing a date in Kerrville, Texas, not long ago, standing there in nearly waist-deep mud, singing for a hundred people. A few miles away Willie Nelson was singing for a hundred thousand. He must know something I don't. My last album hardly sold three copies. They've been warning me about it—Chet Atkins, in particular. They told me I had to modernize a long time ago. I didn't believe it. I thought the old country sound would hold out."

Other members of the Nashville-"Opry" establishment agreed with George Jones and Hank Williams, Jr., who went on record defending the aesthetics and the appeal of the more

Willie Nelson. Photo by Marshall Fallwell, Jr.

traditional country style. But an increasing number were agreeing with Alvin Crow, a Texas fiddler and bandleader prominent in the western-swing revival: "Nashville doesn't like western songs at all. They're trying to sell country music to the Yankees and they want it all watered down, not too outrageous for the Yankees to stomach." Crow, along with Willie Nelson, Waylon Jennings, and Jerry Jeff Walker, has turned his back on the Nashville establishment and has been instrumental in starting a country-music counter-culture centered in Texas.

With such diversity being the rule of the day, it was no surprise that the 1976 Country Music Association (CMA) Awards show was an almost surrealistic panorama of every different country music style and sound. The Awards ceremony takes place in October of every year, and the CMA conducts a massive gathering of country music business types in Nashville. The best country singles are honored, the most popular songwriters are singled out, country disc jockeys from across the nation assemble, and the "Grand Ole Opry" celebrates its birthday. Of all the various country music meetings in Nashville, this one more than any other is the money meeting. At this event, you can tell which songs and which singers are really making money, which are really popular; here there is no room for nostalgia, no room for reputations, no room even for aesthetics and only the barest recognition of tradition. The members of the CMA are bookers, promoters, writers, media men, and performers, not fans; they are tough and pragmatic, viewing country music not as a folk—or even pop —art, but as a product to be merchandised. At these meetings, the reality of the country music business often clashes with its idealism. This was especially true in the mid-1970s, when the CMA Awards became a harsh barometer for the changes shaking the country music scene.

On the 1976 Awards show, "Outlaw" Willie Nelson was introduced as an original and daring country songwriter, but once onstage, he launched into a honky-tonk version of "If You've Got the Money, Honey, I've Got the Time," an old 1950s hit by traditionalist Lefty Frizzell. Happy Roy Clark, whose television guest shots no longer even rate the label "country singer" from *TV Guide*, came dressed to kill and performed a primitive fiddle showoff piece, "Orange Blossom Special." Emmylou Harris, fresh from a pop session with Bob Dylan, performed with a simple, basic country band, while established Nashville singers Crystal Gale and Tammy Wynette used elaborate string arrangements. It was like watching selected scenes from the history of country music, only it wasn't a history show. It was supposed to be a portrait of country music in 1976— *modern* country music. In one sense the eclecticism was refreshing. It's sort of like what Huck Finn said when he was talking about his style of cooking "odds and ends" in an old river barrel: "Things get mixed up, and the juice kind of swaps around, and the things go better." People who don't understand Huck Finn are apt to use the term "synergy" to ex-

plain this kind of process. Synergy is probably a characteristic of modern country music, but isolated components can still be identified and even labeled. The pattern that emerges, however, is like that of a kaleidoscope: It changes whenever you look at it from a new angle.

Still, we can start with two basic images: the smooth and the hairy. The smooth concerns the sophisticated Nashville studio products formulated by producers like Billy Sherril and appealing to the kind of middle-class, middle-of-the-road audience that listens to the top forty, watches prime-time television, and has fun at Opryland. The hairy concerns shaggy outlaws like Kristofferson and Willie Nelson and Waylon Jennings who write their own songs, perform their own rough-hewn, simple arrangements, and appeal to the youth, the working class, and the rednecks and good ole boys who tote their pieces along with them to Nelson's Texas brain fries. The two basic images at times can merge and blur in strange ways, and sometimes they seem to have more in common than not, but on the whole they do form a sort of dialectic for country music of the seventies; they do represent distinct polarities that may emerge as reference points for the confusing image of the music today. And if the hairy image is to be cast in the role of the rebel, then the place to start is with the old aristocracy: Nashville.

A key symbol for the mentality that now pervades the new, pop-oriented Nashville is Opryland. This giant amusement park, which opened in 1972, immediately began to attract the kind of middle-class and upper-middle-class audience to which the "new" country music was aspiring. By the time the "Opry" itself moved there in 1974, the park complex was attracting over 1.5 million visitors a year from all over the nation, not just the South. (In 1971, the "old" Opry had bragged because its attendance had exceeded 400,000 for the first time.) The lessons of the pop appeal were graphically demonstrated by the hordes of northern visitors who trekked through the gates of Opryland, and unlike the fans who had stood in the long lines outside the old Ryman Auditorium to pay homage to their gods, many of these new visitors had only a vague notion of the fundamentals of country music.

The story of Opryland is, in a sense, the story of the National Life and Accident Insurance Company's attempt to merchandise their most curious product, the "Grand Old Opry." By the early 1960s the "Opry" had created a rather embarrassing image problem for the prestigious life-insurance company. The rockabilly stars of the 1950s, including Jerry Lee Lewis, Elvis, Johnny Cash, and the Everly Brothers, had brought to the music (and to the "Opry") unorthodox lifestyles and free-wheeling behavior, and in the late 1950s mainstream "Opry" stars like Red Foley and Ernest Tubb were involved in brushes with the law. Also, the area of Nashville around the Ryman Auditorium had been degenerating into a neighborhood full of massage parlors, tacky souvenir shops, pawn shops, adult-movie houses, and funky old bars. To be sure, many of the tra-

ditional patrons of the "Opry" rather liked this atmosphere, and "Opry" performers enjoyed the convenience of being able to slip across the alley from the Ryman into the back door of Tootsie's Orchid Lounge for a beer or two between shows. But the WSM officials were bothered by "image," and Edwin Craig, the National Life executive who had overseen the founding of the show in 1925, was also bothered by the direction things were going. He had seen the show start out as an informal, genial collection of Tennessee natives playing old-time music; now he saw an unstable coalition of highly professional entertainers specializing in honky-tonk music and songs about lost love. In view of his innate conservatism, Craig realized that something had to be done.

Early in 1962, WSM officials went to California to inspect Disneyland and brought back some ideas for improving the "Opry's" appearance. One of the real problems was the Ryman Auditorium itself. Completed in 1892 as a religious tabernacle, the Ryman by 1960 was restricting the "Opry's" attendance (it held only about 3,500) and making those who did come uncomfortable. The old hall was hot in the summer (there was no air conditioning), cold in the winter, and the seats were the hard wooden pews of the old church; the floor of the balcony was covered with a sort of tar paper that allowed soft drinks spilled in the balcony to drip down on the audience below. The building was only a few blocks from the heart of downtown Nashville, and parking for the "Opry" was a nightmare. Over and over again, polls taken of the audience showed that most of the complaints were about the building itself.

As a result of the Disneyland tour, some attempts to renovate the old Ryman were made. The off-duty policemen who had been serving as ushers were replaced by pretty young girls in hostess uniforms. In 1963 National Life went ahead and bought the old building for about $200,000, and a few further renovations were made. Yet the shortcomings of the structure were becoming even more apparent. The "Opry" was essentially a radio show, and attempts to produce anything beyond radio in the Ryman met with nightmarish complexity; television broadcasting, as Johnny Cash found out when he tried to originate his network show from the Ryman, caused problems at which even network technicians balked. National Life looked at numerous plans to remodel the Ryman, but all would have cost more than the purchase price of the building, and none would have solved the problem of the environment of Lower Broadway.

Meanwhile, a new generation of executives was emerging at National Life; in contrast to the older generation, which felt that the company should restrict itself to the life-insurance business, this newer generation felt that the company should branch out into noninsurance areas. One of these areas was the exploitation of the "Opry" name and the "Opry" image. Thus in October 1968 it was announced that the company had hired the California firm that had planned Disneyland to "study the feasibility of building a new "Grand Ole Opry"

house and creating a tourist attraction around it. The new complex would be called "Opryland, U.S.A." The old National Life people saw this meaning just a new home for the "Opry," but the new generation saw it as a chance to use the "Opry" appeal to generate even more television and tourism and to begin attracting a wider audience.

In fact, the report from the California group argued that such a park could not succeed if it focused only on country music, and recommended that it was worth only a modest investment. "Opry" manager Bud Wendell argued that the Californians did not understand the appeal of the "Opry" name. (He recalled that they admitted that "there is no other park in the country other than Disneyland that has the built-in image acceptance that the 'Grand Ole Opry' represents. It is synonymous with purity, patriotism, the flag, motherhood, and apple pie.") Besides that, though, was the fact that WSM, the radio/television arm of National Life, was not thinking of a park featuring only country music. From the beginning of the project, WSM President Irving Waugh had had the idea to, in the words of "Opry" historian Jack Hurst, "illustrate country music's role as a musical melting pot by surrounding the 'Opry' with live performances of the other kinds of music to which the American people have given rise—blues, jazz, western, folk, and the rest." Also, the California group did not sense what some of the Nashville men did: that country music was appealing to an increasingly wider audience, and that it was threatening to "break out" of its traditional geographical and class appeal.

Thus in 1969 work was begun on Opryland. The location for the park was a few miles east of the Nashville city limits in an arm of the Cumberland River. The initial cost of the park was projected at $16 million, but expenses soon ran to 2½ times that amount. The park was opened in 1972—two years before the new "Opry" House was ready—and it soon exceeded the expectations of its owners, both in attendance and in income. The first two years of its operaion saw the park generate over $6 million in cash flow. Visitors coming to the park saw a number of country music motifs—a roller coaster called "the Wabash Cannonball," characters dressed up as guitars and bass fiddles, Roy Acuff's country music museum—but they were by no means exposed to a steady diet of country music. In addition to taking rides and playing games, visitors could attend any number of free shows throughout the park; one of these was a mountain music show, featuring bluegrass and "folk" music, and one was a country show, but others were rock shows, Broadway-like musicals, and Dixieland jazz bands. Few "name" stars appeared at any of the shows; the musicians comprised a sort of repertory company of young artists chosen from auditions held around the country, from New York to Dallas. Only a few of these singers had any ambitions of becoming "country" stars—most of them wanted to break into Broadway, the movies, or television. The country shows at

Opryland were generally rather trite rehashes of old country hits performed in an imitative style; they were a very watered-down version of real country music, and at times they seemed almost to parody the music. Opryland management, however, felt that these were the best methods by which the increasing numbers of non-country fans at Opryland could be attracted to the music.

Many of the Opryland visitors never see the "Opry" itself. In 1975, three times as many visitors saw the park as saw the "Opry" (though "Opry" attendance was at an all-time high of over 750,000). Undoubtedly Opryland does attract new audiences to the "Opry," and to country music in general, but many other fans get their main impression of modern country music from the park itself. Yet there is no doubt that the center of the park is the new multimillion-dollar "Opry" House itself. The fact that the "Opry" was to dominate the complex was made clear in 1974 when park expert Michael Downs, who tended to see the park as something quite distinct from the "Opry" and from country music, was replaced by former "Opry" manager Bud Wendell. Such a move could be interpreted as suggesting that National Life still sees the park as an attempt to upgrade the image of country music and to attract to the music a national, upper-middle-class audience.

The new "Opry" House was opened on March 16, 1974, and among the guests was the President of the United States. For many fans of country music, the spectacle of seeing the President appear alongside Roy Acuff, and of hearing "Hail to the Chief" played by a fiddle, banjo, and steel guitar, seemed the final proof that the music's long struggle to gain respectability was won. Acuff himself, who had barely twenty years earlier heard a Tennessee governor complain that the "Opry" and the hillbilly image were embarrassing to the state, admitted that he felt that in spite of the later Watergate scandal, Nixon's visit to the "Opry" stage was the greatest thing that had ever happened to country music. To the older musicians like Acuff and Hank Snow and the McGee Brothers, who could remember the years they spent trying to establish their music as a legitimate profession, the President's visit was especially meaningful.

Many of the younger "Opry" members who had always seen their profession as relatively respectable were impressed with the physical aspects of the new "Opry" House. These were signs that the music *was* being taken seriously; the house had an elaborate lighting system, plush seats, superb acoustics, and expensive television facilities. "It's more like a real opera house," one young "opry" member commented. The convenience of running across the alley to Tootsie's was gone, but the dressing rooms were larger and more comfortable than the cramped, confining quarters at the old Ryman. The entire place intimidated audiences so much that at first Grant Turner had to encourage people to cheer and whoop it up like they did in the old

Ryman. The singers, who had thrived on the close audience contact, now complained that they couldn't hear the audience very well. Respectability did have its price.

Opryland can be seen as a symbol for the new type of country music originating from Nashville in the 1970s. Both the "Opry" and the music were eclectic, lush in an artificial sense, based on a wholesome, natural motif, and designed to appeal to the widest possible audience. Opryland called itself "the home of American music," and in 1972 a national television special on Opryland was aired, featuring noncountry performers like Wayne Newton, Leslie Uggams, and Carol Lawrence. This show irritated a lot of "Opry" regulars, who felt it should have featured strictly country music, but the Opryland idea was to merge all types of music. This was in line with the kind of thinking in many of the modern Nashville studios, where the desire to produce a "crossover" hit was so strong that some producers wanted to get rid of the name "country music" and replace it with a broader term like "American music."

Both the "Opry" and the "new" Nashville sound were lush—and artificial. A central quality of Opryland is its very artificiality; one of the rationales for building Opryland, according to WSM President Irving Waugh, was to "go outside the city to a place where we could control our own environment." Opryland can thus be seen, in one sense, as an attempt to create an "other world" environment for the "Opry" that would have none of the real-life prob-lems of the Lower Broadway neigh-borhood that surrounded the Ryman. The park itself is totally fabricated, taking as its natural base only the Cumberland River; the design is so cunning that once in the park, the visitor can detect relatively little of the original natural terrain, and even loses his sense of direction. The mu-sic and shows in the park are like-wise orchestrated, and are often cho-reographed and staged by sophisti-cated arrangers. The thing that made the Nashville music of the early 1970s so distinctive was this same artificial quality—only in the music, it was ac-complished by the use of string ar-rangements, overdubbing, studio en-hancement, and orchestration. The artificiality in both cases was pleas-ant, sophisticated, and easy to assimi-late, yet it was curiously sterile.

The lushness of Opryland, the arti-ficiality, is paradoxically based on back-to-nature motifs. The flowers and shrubs in the park are very real, though part of an artificial design; there are real animals in the petting zoo and real fruit sold from fruit carts, but it is all under the watchful eye of Opryland Enterprises. One re-porter visiting Opryland early in its career noted with some amusement how clean the place was; one of the uniformed park attendants actually followed him around scooping up his cigarette ashes with a little dust pan. Such an environment seems like a long way from Nashville's Lower Broadway, where the bums sleep in doorways and broken glass litters the alleys. In many ways, the "rural sim-plicity" subtheme of Opryland is also

characteristic of the new Nashville music; the melodies and messages of the songs are still rather basic, and the values, for the most part, are still pretty traditional. Opryland has its counterpart in the bucolic image pre-sented by Donna Fargo's "Happiest Girl in the Whole U.S.A.," a good example of the "new" Nashville mu-sic of the early 1970s.

Just as Opryland alienated some of the older musicians, so did the new Nashville music alienate some of the older established country singers. For one thing, the mainstream of the new music was no longer confined exclu-sively to the "Grand Ole Opry" itself. In 1974, for instance, only a third of the CMA Awards winners were mem-bers of the "Opry" cast. Of course, joining the "Opry" does eat into a performer's touring time, but another serious reason is the difficulty of re-producing the sound of elaborate stu-dio recordings on the "Opry" stage. Tom T. Hall, for instance, quit the "Opry" in 1974 over a dispute about whether or not he could use a string section to back his stage performances. The "Opry" wasn't quite ready to make that much of a concession to the new Nashville sound. In spite of its attempts to attract new young country talent, the "Opry" has gen-erally continued to maintain a fairly traditional definition of country mu-sic. Though Opryland itself is quick to embrace the precepts of country-pop, the "Opry" still maintains the spirit, if not the letter, of Judge Hay's famous old law: "Keep it down-to-earth, boys."

This means that the essence of the "new" Nashville sound is not so easy to pin down, to observe; no club, no concert series in town can be seen as a showcase for this sound in the way the "Opry" is for the older sound. This is partly because the new sound is an amorphorus entity that doesn't really exist outside of the studios of Music Row and the recordings produced there. It is hard to find any material touchstone for the music, but one can find several key individuals in Nashville who were the prime architects of the new music. In the early 1970s, probably the most important of these individuals was Epic Records executive Billy Sherrill. If producers like Chet Atkins pushed Nashville in the *direction* of pop music, it was Sherrill who actually pushed country into the pop scene.

This was a shocking and at times painful baptism, and it brought howls from country music purists, but by 1975 it was a historical and economic fact, and Nashville had accepted it and was assessing its implications. Atkins himself later expressed misgivings about his pushing country toward pop, and said he was worried about country music losing its identity, but it is characteristic of Sherrill that he has expressed no such misgivings; he feels the music "improved tremendously" in the years between 1966 and 1975. Much of the change —whether or not one views it as improvement—can be attributed to Sherrill's producing and to his development of a middle-of-the-road music style.

Billy Sherrill in Nashville in the early 1960s, coming from an Alabama background of gospel music (his parents were evangelists, and the young

Billy played piano for their meetings) and honky-tonk dance bands. He got his apprenticeship with Sam Phillips, the founder of Sun Records and developer of rockabilly. (Sherrill was the engineer for Jerry Lee Lewis' hit "What'd I Say?") Phillips was one of the pioneer crossover producers, and much of his attitude and many of his techniques impressed Sherrill. Moving to Epic Records, Sherrill produced a wide variety of music from the bluegrass of Jim and Jesse to the black gospel of the Staples Singers. In 1966 he produced David Houston's recording of "Almost Persuaded," a song he had written with Glen Sutton, and found himself with the No. 1 song of the year. With this Sherrill began an enviable string of hit singles and albums, and within a year he was recognized as one of the most successful and innovative producers in Nashville. Soon he was producing artists like Tammy Wynette, Charlie Rich, Tanya Tucker, Johnny Paycheck, and Barbara Fairchild, and getting many of them wide exposure to a popular audience.

It's difficult, though, to really identify any Sherrill "formula" for this middle-of-the-road music. He himself has admitted that his approach was in part to buck the traditional Nashville-sound formula: "The Nashville sound in my opinion is what you get when you turn the session over to the musicians." In order to really sell, he insists, "a record has to be different rather than pretty." Some characteristics, however, mark Sherrill as different from other Nashville producers; he is, for instance, oriented toward the hit single rather than the

Billy Sherrill.

album. He tries to make a hit single every time he turns the tape on ("That's the baby, that's it. Hit singles are the best concept for albums in the world.") Because of this, he often sees the song as more important than the singer ("Finding the right song is the rough part of the record business. Recording is just the gravy.") He has been known not to record a hot young prospect until precisely the right song is found for that singer. He feels that original material is an integral part of any major success; when an artist comes into his office, "the first thing that comes into my mind is, 'Do you have a source of material?

Are you a writer? Do you have a friend that writes?' " From the days of Jimmie Rodgers and Ralph Peer, original material has in fact been an important part of the really big country singers. So Sherrill was merely reestablishing an old rule. He perceived that the philosophy that was current in country music—that an established singer would sell a limited but steady number of albums solely on the basis of his personality and fan appeal—was not really suited for the more fickle but more lucrative pop market.

Sherrill was also pragmatic about what it took to break into this pop market. He had no idealism about maintaining the purity of the country tradition. "Nobody can ever put down Hank Williams and Hank Snow and Ernest Tubb. But to say we can't broaden the appeal is ludicrous, ridiculous," he once said. "I think people [can] learn how to write better country songs. . . . I don't think we'll lose our identity. I think our identity will grow with people that can do something with a wider range of lyrics, melodies, and instruments. It doesn't necessarily have to be two guitars and a banjo. I don't think you're losing anything, I think you're gaining something." The "wider range" shown on Sherrill's successful recordings included, on occasion, elaborate orchestrations, overdubbing of vocal effects and background harmonies, and the use of horns and piano stylings. Through this kind of arranging, Sherrill was able to form a distinctive aural image for his artists: bland, easy-going, easy-listening music. But against this new style, the songs Sherrill produced (and often wrote) dealt with the traditional country themes of lost love, loneliness, cheatin', and found love. A closer look at the way Sherrill developed his three major artists—Charlie Rich, Tammy Wynette, and Tanya Tucker—reveals even more of his philosophy, and more of the nature of the "new" Nashville sound.

Perhaps the most spectacular of Sherrill's successes was the elevation to stardom of a middle-aged, silver-haired Arkansas singer named Charlie Rich. In the mid-1970s Rich absolutely dominated the country-recording field, producing an astonishing string of hit "crossover" singles and albums. By late 1974 he had three huge hits: "Behind Closed Doors," selling over three million; "The Most Beautiful Girl in the World," selling over two million; and "A Very Special Love Song," with sales approaching one million. In October of 1974, when Rich was voted Entertainer of the Year by the Country Music Association, his album containing "Behind Closed Doors" had been on the charts for seventy-nine weeks—far longer than any other country album. In fact, according to the 1974 *Billboard* survey, Rich led all country artists in sales, with five singles and six albums on the charts. (This was accomplished in spite of the fact that Rich's new recordings with Sherrill were meeting competition from six other labels reissuing old Rich material.) The year 1975 saw Rich's hit album *Every Time You Touch Me (I Get High)* and his winning a string of *Billboard* awards for Best Male Vocalist, Best Male Singles Artist, Best Album Artists, and others. These awards were, of course, in the "country" category, but his songs were also appearing routinely on pop charts. And significantly, Rich himself was still reluctant to describe himself as a "country" singer.

This reluctance was probably due not only to the fact that Rich was selling records to a popular, easy-listening audience, but also to the fact that he himself came from a rich and eclectic musical background. Before he met Sherrill, Rich had spent some twenty years managing to survive as a pianist, singer, and songwriter. Much of this time was spent in northwestern Arkansas, where he grew up listening to the blues played

Charlie Rich. Photo by Alan Whitman.

by black sharecroppers on his father's plantation. The blues and jazz influence on his piano playing and "soulful" singing had always been strong. In the 1950s he was involved in the Sun scene with Sam Phillips at Memphis, and always seemed on the verge of great success; everyone from Sam Phillips to Bob Dylan predicted it for him. Moving to Nashville, Rich became known as a fine piano player, a blues-styled singer, and a writer of songs like "Lonely Weekends," "Sittin' and Thinkin'," and "Who Will the Next Fool Be?"

Sherrill produced Rich's hit of "Behind Closed Doors" in 1973, and the crossover sales began. The Sherrill treatment for Rich was typical of his method: a basic, simple country lament cushioned on elaborate orches-

tral arrangements, overdubbing, and background voices. It had worked earlier for singers like Jim Reeves, and it worked for Rich: He became a "country crooner," "the Silver Fox," a packaged, middle-of-the road commodity. It upset some of Rich's earlier fans, including his wife, who had enjoyed his funky-gospel-jazz-blues-rockabilly-unclassifiable style. It upset some country purists when Rich was named Entertainer of the Year in 1974—he was now too slick, too commercial. The same people were upset with him the next year, in 1975, when he set fire to the winner's envelope as he was announcing that year's CMA Awards winner—he was too gauche, not slick enough, a rebel. He seemed upset with the blandness of the Sherrill sound, and yet a prisoner of it: It made him the leading Nashville-based singer of the mid-seventies. He became a fixture at the Las Vegas Hilton and was one of the few country singers able to command as much in performance fees as the leading pop acts.

Sherrill had already perfected the middle-of-the-road formula he used with Rich some five or six years earlier when he, Sherrill, began successfully marketing the sound of Mississippi-born Tammy Wynette. Unlike Rich, who had already established a musical identity on which Sherrill had to impose a new image, Tammy Wynette was a product (some would say a victim) of Sherrill's packaging technique almost from the beginning of her career. Tammy had been turned down by four labels before Sherrill found her, signed her for Epic, and recorded "Apartment No. 9" in August of 1966. Her records immediately took off and quickly crossed over onto the pop charts. In 1967 she had one of country music's top five hits in "I Don't Wanna Play House," and the next year she had two of the top five in "Stand By Your Man" (which sold over two million copies and might well be the largest-selling single by any woman country singer) and "D-I-V-O-R-C-E." She has been voted the Top Female Vocalist by the CMA many times. Many of her hit songs were co-authored by Billy Sherrill.

The image Sherrill imposed on Tammy Wynette was one of a slightly masochistic *hausfrau*, a woman content with being a suffering, dominated, middle-class housewife. Such an image is nothing new to country music. It has been traditional in the

music for twenty years. The songs that sold millions for Tammy showed little or no consciousness of the sexual revolution; divorce was something to be dreaded and avoided at all costs —for the children's sake. You stood by your man, even if you had to endure the archaic southern double

Tammy Wynette. Photo by Marshall Fallwell, Jr.

standard of morality, and having a good man was much more important than any vague notion of self-fulfillment. Tammy accentuated this image of passivity by recording successful romantic duets with David Houston ("My Elusive Dreams") and later with George Jones, one of the "purest" male country singers. Tammy married George in the early 1970s, and Sherrill produced a series of George-and-Tammy duet albums that must rank among the best modern country duet recordings.

Even after the marriage broke up, Tammy continued to try to work with George. In spite of the fact (or maybe because of it) that Tammy's image, both in her music and in her personal life, ran counter to prevailing trends in feminism, she continued to be successful. Sherrill and Tammy argued that this image appealed specifically to a "target group" audience: the middle-class, middle-aged housewife who sympathized with the philosophy of "stand by your man."

It is doubtful if the message of Tammy's songs can by itself account for her popularity. Much of it stemmed from Tammy's own considerable abilities as a professional, adaptable singer; Sherrill said, "I can sing Tammy Wynette a song and she'll sing it right back to me." Such professionalism made it easier for Sherrill to impose the elaborate studio work that characterized his sound. It made it easier for him to cushion Tammy's voice with strings, with background vocals, and even with self-harmonization. Combine this with the fact that Tammy's voice is not that country-sounding—one critic

has said she sings in the style of Doris Day and Patti Page—and one can begin to see how simply the *sound* of Tammy Wynette, regardless of the message of the songs, had considerable appeal.

Image was a crucial factor in the career of one of Sherrill's later successes, Tanya Tucker. Where Charlie Rich and Tammy Wynette were both mature performers when they worked with Sherrill, Tanya Tucker began her career with him as a thirteen-year-old child prodigy in 1972. Born in Texas, Tanya spent her early life moving around to various towns in the West while her father tried to get both her and her sister, LaCosta, started on singing careers. After a couple of years struggling along trying to get auditions, doing demos, singing for amateur talent shows and doing a brief stint on Judy Lynn's show, Tanya's father finally got some home tapes to Sherrill. Sherrill was impressed with Tanya's voice and flew to Las Vegas, where he signed her on the spot, planning to record her as soon as the right song was found. He soon found it—Alex Harvey's "Delta Dawn." Within a month after signing Sherrill's contract, Tanya was recording the song for Columbia, backed by the full Sherrill studio treatment. The song was an immense hit, as usual on both country and pop charts, and by 1973 Tanya found herself on the "Opry," touring widely (sometimes with another young successful singer, Johnny Rodriguez), and being a nominee for two Grammy Awards, one for "Delta Dawn" and one for Female Country Singer of the Year. Tanya turned fifteen in 1973.

If Tanya has been "packaged" by Sherrill, it is not exactly clear which audience she was aimed at. Her youth obviously gave her a certain appeal to the teen-aged market, and *Rolling Stone* lavished a cover story on her, yet there is also evidence that she appeals in a Lolita-like way to older male country fans, especially in the West, where her tours were so successful. On tours she often dressed in skin-tight pants suits and used stage movements that owed more to Mick Jagger than to country tradition. Songs like "Would You Lay with Me in a Field of Stone?" had lyrics more suggestive than many sung by artists like Tammy Wynette, yet Tanya herself seemed oblivious to this element of sexuality; she said that the contrast between her mature sound (she has a big, husky voice) and her youthful appearance—the novelty of this contradiction—was largely responsible for her success. "When Billy Sherrill heard my demo tapes, he heard *my sound*," she once said. "Everybody says I sound older and look older than I really am, but I think being fourteen was really an advantage. People hear my records and then see me. It's hard for them to believe," Yet Sherrill himself emphasized another facet of the Tucker image—the quality of the songs: "You find a basic country station somewhere, and it'll put you to sleep.... That's why Tanya Tucker exploded. She had a unique voice and we did some blood-curdling songs. Somebody got killed in every record we did. I don't think anybody got killed in 'Would You Lay with Me,' but there was blood somewhere." Possibly because of this confusion about what Tanya's most appealing (and most marketable) quality was, Sherrill and she parted ways in 1974, before he had been able to establish her securely in either the pop or the country field. At the time, the notion that Tanya's future success would lie in this very fact—that she is not stereotyped into one category or another —seemed entirely credible.

Sherrill and the producers who emulated him showed that country hits could become crossover hits. Earlier in the game, Nashville had seen country hits become pop hits when rerecorded by pop artists, but Sherrill's recording style was able to embrace both markets with the same original record. His success implied a change in the economic philosophy that had governed the Nashville studios for years. This philosophy held that the average country album would sell a steady but rather limited number of copies—from fifteen to twenty thousand—to a well-defined country audience. One of the reasons behind the birth of the original Nashville sound was the holding down of studio costs; a large company, looking at the limited sales potential of a strictly country record, was reluctant to invest a lot of time, effort, and money in albums. Thus a technique was born whereby an artist went into a studio with five or six good musicians and hacked out an album. But Sherrill and his followers realized that to reach a pop audience, more care and expense would have to be given to production; he did this, and he showed that the larger market and sales of artists like Rich justified this added expense.

By expanding the definition of country music, Sherrill also made it possible for the crossover effect· to work the other way, from pop to country. The new Nashville sound acclimated listeners to the fuller, lusher arrangements of country songs, and thus they became more receptive to pop music recorded in this vein. Thus the early 1970s saw a number of "interlopers" in the country scene, artists who were established pop singers moving—some deliberately, some unwittingly—into the music. Names like Anne Murray, John Denver, Olivia Newton-John, and Emmylou Harris began crowding onto the country charts, jostling Tammy Wynette and George Jones, Loretta Lynn and Conway Twitty.

The case of Canadian singer Anne Murray, who in 1970 found her record "Snowbird" topping the country charts, was typical. She had made no effort to promote the song as a country tune, or herself as a country singer. "I had no idea it was a country tune," she recalled later. None of the background of the song was in any real sense connected to the traditional country music establishment. Murray had first heard the song performed by its author, Gene MacLellan, on a Canadian television show, and had recorded it for a small Canadian company. Murray herself came from a background of classical piano and Italian arias, and was only marginally involved in the Canadian country music scene; before this she had had little interest in country music. "I thought country music was just a bunch of people hangin' onto their noses and singing!" she said. Even

when she got a break with a major American record producer, it was with the California-based Capitol Records, and in the 1972 Country Music Who's Who she was described as a "Canadian singer." Yet during all this time "Snowbird" was selling over a million copies, both in the United States and Canada, and many of them were being sold as country singles. The record might have been shipped to the stores as a pop product, but it was received as country and was adopted by the country audience now accustomed to the slick sounds of Sherrill and Glen Campbell.

In the early 1970s a number of records were to follow this pattern. Anne Murray herself accepted her new role with grace, and by the time her star was installed in the walkway in front of the Country Music Hall of Fame, she was appearing with Glen Campbell on television and consciously striving for country hits. In 1974, "He Still Thinks I Care" was an even bigger country hit than "Snowbird."

A different sort of crossover pattern was exemplified by another major pop singer of the 1970s, John Denver. Denver got most of his initial national exposure at the tail end of the folk revival of the 1960s. Born in New Mexico, Denver learned to play both standard and twelve-string guitar (a staple of the folk singer) as a teen-ager, and like others of his generation he listened a lot to early Elvis before he got involved in the folk movement. Peter, Paul, and Mary recorded one of Denver's songs, "Leaving on a Jet Plane," and it became a gold record in 1969. Denver himself became famous after replacing Chad

Mitchell in the Mitchell Trio, with whom he performed from 1965 to 1969; the Mitchell Trio was one of the slicker folk acts of the time, an act whose style often verged on pop, and these lessons were not lost on Denver. He went out on his own in 1969 and began producing a couple of albums a year for Victor. These albums were mostly full of original but folklike melodies, and in 1971 one song, "Take Me Home, Country Roads," broke through in both the pop and the country fields. From here on, most of Denver's albums reached gold-record status; however, Denver made no overt attempt to market his product as country music. He did **not** work out of Nashville, he seldom recorded in Nashville, he did not make even token appearances at the "Opry"; his television appearances were always on mainstream shows. Yet in spite of this, his records were gaining airplay on country stations, and the CMA was nominating him for awards. In 1975 Denver's song "Back Home Again" was the top-selling country song of the year, and *Billboard* placed two of his albums in their list of the top-ten country albums; *Back Home Again* was pro-

John Denver.

nounced "best country album" of the year. By now the assimilation process was complete: Denver was country.

Actually, this acceptance of Denver as a country artist was not all that painful. Denver, after all, was about the only survivor from the urban folk revival to make a successful transition into country music. The virtues that the folk movement taught Denver served him well in his new milieu; he at least saw the need to maintain an image of simplicity, even in his well-crafted and carefully planned studio albums. Denver's songs, and the image he presented at concerts, were built around a new sort of bucolic romanticism. "Thank God I'm a country boy," he preached in one song; others dealt with the glories of Denver's adopted home state, Colorado, and with the kind of natural "Rocky Mountain high" that appealed to the youth culture of the 1970s. The tendency to romanticize rural life, of course, had long been present in country music, from the early Vernon Dalhart-Carson-Robison paeans of the 1920s, like "My Blue Ridge Mountain Home," but Denver's came at a time when many country performers who had actually lived through such rural backgrounds were trying to deromanticize it; Dolly Parton, who came from an impoverished community in eastern Tennessee, was singing "In the Good Old Days When Times Were Bad." However, much of Denver's audience was no longer from the farm or the mountains; they were second- or third-generation urbanites. When they went to see a Denver concert, they saw nothing ironic in his use of one of the most

expensive and sophisticated light shows to illustrate his song of simple, basic, homespun pleasures. The fact that this new sort of RCA/Victor romanticism could work so successfully not only with the youth audience, but with the country audience as well, showed that the old notion of the country audience as an identifiable ethnic or geographic entity was finally and completely obsolete.

By 1975, the crossover effect was becoming so common that nobody could treat it as an aberration, an exception to the rule. Country artists were crossing into pop, and pop artists were crossing into country, and the editors of trade publications like *Billboard*, who had to attempt to continue to categorize the music and musicians, were puzzling over the impact of the transition. Some members of the Nashville establishment professed that the crossover effect, working either way, was bad, and would destroy the purity of the music, but Billy Sherrill commented that he never knew of a country singer who "kicked in the doors of KHJ [a large top-forty station in Los Angeles] and said, 'Quit playing my record.'"

The Nashville establishment was having far more trouble in accepting the new pop interlopers into the country field. By 1975 country radio stations were willing to play heretofore pop artists like John Denver, B. J. Thomas, Linda Ronstadt, Olivia Newton-John, Mac Davis, Elvis, the Eagles, the Ozark Mountain Daredevils, Paul McCartney, Gordon Lightfoot, the Amazing Rhythm Aces, and the Pointer Sisters. Out of the top ten *Billboard* country music chart-winner albums for 1975, six were by former pop artists. The extent to which pop had invaded country was matched only by the speed of the invasion. Nashville's Music Row, which prides itself on spotting and anticipating trends, was caught off guard by these lightning developments of the seventies. In 1972, for instance, *Record World* published a massive directory called Country Music Who's Who, designed to reflect country's established stars, its new stars, and its behind-the-scenes people. For its time, it was a sound, reliable guide to the state of the music, but if you compare it with the top ten country albums of 1975, just three years later, you find that six of the top ten country albums are by artists not even mentioned in the 1972 Who's Who. Even more startling is the fact that not one of the singers of the top five country singles in 1975 is listed in the 1972 Who's Who. Nashville suddenly found itself playing a new kind of ball game, with vague and confusing rules.

An instinctive response to this kind of culture shock is to reject the new and to reaffirm the old. The older Nashville community felt it had to shore up the dikes, to preserve the well-defined purity of its music. This response crystallized in the form of the "Olivia Newton-John controversy" in 1973, a brief but traumatic episode that left more than a few emotional scars on the people involved and that brought into public view the confusion wrought by the pop invasion.

Olivia Newton-John was a young Australian singer who in 1973 and early 1974 began to record pop-ori-

Olivia Newton-John.

ented material in England. She sang in a strong, clear young voice, and though she had had little exposure to country music, her producers often backed her with a steel guitar and dubbed vocal harmonies; the results were records that sounded a lot like the later efforts of folk-pop singer Joan Baez. Furthermore, one of her first successful records was an attractive arrangement of "Banks of the Ohio," a native American ballad that had been recorded dozens of times by all sorts of country singers and that had been a staple in the urban folk revival of the 1960s. Perhaps because of the song, as well as the sound, Olivia's producers found that when they tried to get her records air play in the United States, they more often than not got it on country stations. When Olivia began touring in the United States in early 1974, she, like Anne Murray, was surprised to find that she was typed as a country singer, and objected, in a mild way, to the label. She told an interviewer: "Since I'm accepted as a country singer, I can do just about anything. So I'm lucky. I think I'm accepted by the country people, but I don't think people think of me strictly as country. Not now, anyway."

The gulf between Olivia and the traditional country singers soon became apparent to the public. When she was invited to do a guest shot on the "Opry," she didn't seem to be suitably impressed with the honor, and she embarrassed everybody by announcing, "I thought the 'Opry' was on Sunday night." A while later Roy Acuff, on a national telecast, referred to her as "Oliver Newton John." Probably no malice was intended in either of these comments—they were honest mistakes that reflected the vast difference between the new and the traditional country—but the friction was made more obvious a few months later when Olivia reportedly said she would refuse to work any more country concerts with artists like Porter Wagoner and Tammy Wynette. Nashville singers saw in this a tacit admission that Olivia had used country radio to establish herself, and was now trying to turn her back on her benefactor.

Things were at this stage in October 1974 when the CMA held its annual awards show, broadcast nationwide from downtown Nashville. At the time, Olivia Newton-John had two albums (*If You Love Me Let Me Know* and *Let Me Be There*) in *Billboard*'s best-seller list; the former was the top country album in October, and the latter had been on the charts for most of the year. *Billboard* had rated her the No. 4 country artist (behind Charlie Rich, Conway Twitty, and Loretta Lynn) in album sales. Her popularity was undeniable, and partly for this reason the CMA voted her Female Vocalist of the Year over a number of other singers who had been established for years in the country field. By design or by chance, Olivia was not even present for the award, accepting her laurels *in absentia*. The traditionalists were enraged, and lost no time in expressing their displeasure.

A few weeks after the national CMA Awards telecast, a group of about fifty Nashville singers met at the Nashville home of George Jones and Tammy Wynette. Ostensibly, the group banded together to protest the relatively few entertainers on the Country Music Association's Board of Directors, but in fact they were protesting the increasing acceptance of the pop singers into the country community. Bill Anderson, a spokesman for the group, called the Newton-John award "the straw that broke the camel's back." There was, in fact, some support for this idea in the CMA; one Board member said, "I don't feel it's right that the country music industry should prostitute itself just for the sake of one hour on national television." A week later the singers voted to unite into a new organization, the Association of Country Entertainers (ACE); unlike the CMA, which allowed anyone who made his or her living in the music business into its ranks, the ACE was to be restricted to country performers. The group named a "screening committee' to determine the country credentials of prospective ACE members, and the committee formed a Who's Who of old Nashville: Dolly Parton, Hank Snow, Johnny Paycheck, George Morgan, Tammy Wynette, and Jimmy C. Newman. Even "King of Country Music" Roy Acuff endorsed the group. Critics pointed out that many of the founders of the ACE were former pop or rock singers who had made a rather complete transition into country, and that earlier country giants like Jimmie Rodgers and Bob Wills had incorporated pop elements into their music, but Johnny Paycheck argued that the music content was only part of the issue: "Our chief complaint is that if an artist gets a crossover record that is played on both country and pop stations, that artist has an unfair advantage in the CMA Awards." Another ACE member, Billy Walker, was more candid about the group's purpose: at a Nashville press conference he explained that many members were concerned that "ouside influences" and the attempts to take country music to a wider audience would dilute country music "until it no longer exists." He continued, "We are mainly people who made country music what it is today, trying to protect our business because we see it flaking off in thousands of directions. We're trying to keep it at home."

So finally the confusion and the re-sentiments were out in the open, and the music's identity crisis was front-page news across the country. It's too soon to evaluate completely what effect ACE will have on the music, though country music history is full of artificial attempts to change musical trends, nearly all of them unsuccessful. By the late 1970s the ACE had had little practical effect on the industry; some of the ACE members were named to the CMA's Board of Directors, but the ACE itself was significant mainly as a gesture.

For better or worse, the battle lines between pop and country were being drawn—and drawn down the middle of Nashville's Music Row. On one side were the ACE people. On the other were three groups. First, there were the established Nashville producers who had helped put Nashville on the map and who now wanted to see it move more into pop: people like Buddy Killen of Tree International, Bob Beckham of Combine Music, Don Grant, Bergen White, Allen Reynolds, and of course Billy Sherrill. Then there were the inter-lopers, producers attracted to Nashville with the express intent of producing pop records at the city's superb studios. As early as the 1940s big-band leader Woody Herman cut sides in the old Ryman Auditorium, but in the 1960s and 1970s the list of pop acts recording in Nashville had grown astronomically: Simon and Garfunkel, Johnny and Edgar Winter, Neil Young, Wilson Pickett, Carol Channing, Connie Francis, Grand Funk Railroad, B. B. King, Perry Como, Bob Dylan, Tom Jones—the list goes on. These new producers, such as

Buzz Cason, whose Creative Workshop was attracting the best pop acts of the 1970s, complained only that people in New York or Los Angeles were too quick to label any record cut in Nashville as "country." Bob Montgomery, who produced top-forty hits for Bobby Goldsboro, admitted that on occasion he did not want to publicize the fact that some of his records were done in Nashville—"because as soon as I said it, people would say, 'That's a good country record.'" The Nashville pop producers had problems of their own, and in 1976 they talked of forming into a Pop Music Association to parallel the activities of the Country Music Association.

But it was the third group that gave the country traditionalists the most cause for concern: This was the anti-Nashville, anti-Billy Sherrill, anti-John Denver group of long-haired roughnecks known as the outlaws, a group that did not invade the music from "outside" but that grew with the music and effected the 1970s' most telling revolution—from the inside.

The "outlaw" rebellion—to use the word favored by the popular press of the day—seemed to revolve around three individuals: Kris Kristofferson, Willie Nelson, and Waylon Jennings. Since each of these made his move to "break out" of Nashville in the three-year period from 1969 to 1972, it's hard to say with any certainty who influenced whom the most, and who made the first move. All three, as well as many other younger writers and singers, were mutual and contemporaneous influences on each other. Mickey Newberry once compared the

Nashville artist colony of the late 1960s to that of Paris in the 1920s— a hyperbole perhaps, but an indication of the creative energy present among the younger writers and singers there. Given a new generation of talented and innovative musicians and composers, it was perhaps inevitable that some of them would want to expand the forms of their music, to experiment with new ideas and new directions. On the other hand, the Nashville establishment felt that *they* had just developed the formula that would, for the first time, make the music a totally respectable facet of mainstream pop, and they were reluctant to give up their new found security. The two philosophies had to clash. But many of the outlaws were not interested in revolutionizing the music they all loved; many saw themselves as royalists attempting to wrest the older, more traditional musical forms out of the hands of the Music Row popularizers. Dave Hickey, one of the first writers to chronicle this tension, described the outlaw rebels as "just about the only folks in Nashville who will walk into a room where there's a guitar and a *Wall Street Journal* and pick up the guitar."

Kristofferson came from a background that was in some ways radically different from that of the typical country singer. He was born in the South—in Brownsville, Texas—but he grew up as an Army brat moving around the country with his family. As a teen-ager, Kristofferson found himself listening to the only kind of energized music available to him in the prerock early 1950s: the lonesome white blues of Hank Williams. But Kristofferson soon found himself moving into more traditional forms of culture: In college he majored in creative writing, and he won several prizes in a short-story competition conducted by the *Atlantic Monthly*, then the country's leading literary magazine. Kristofferson, however, also played a lot of football in college, and he was good enough in Golden Gloves boxing to make *Sports Illustrated*. This combination of good grades, straight-arrow character, and athletic skills made him a natural candidate for a prestigious Rhodes scholarship, and the early 1960s found him at Oxford University studying the difficult, mystical poetry of William Blake. But something happened, and Kristofferson dropped out, began calling himself Kris Carson, and began writing country songs. He made *Time* magazine, but that was about it; soon he had joined the Army and was leading a country band of enlisted men around bases in Germany. The Army didn't quite know what to make of him—a good ROTC boy gone sour—and finally sent him back to the States with an assignment to teach English at West Point. He made it as far as Nashville, and resigned his commission.

This was 1966; Buck Owens and Jack Greene and Glen Campbell were riding high, and country music was still pretty pure. Kristofferson, who for some years had been responding to the honesty and simplicity of the "pure" music, set out to become a songwriter: He wrote songs, sung them on demo tapes, and made the rounds of the Nashville publishers.

In between times he married, started a family, and held a variety of jobs to keep himself together—everything from bartender to janitor at Johnny Cash's studio. During one particularly bad time, he took a job in the Gulf of Mexico flying helicopters out to oil rigs. Whatever people think of his *macho* image, he came by it honestly.

His songs were selling, and were being recorded by major Nashville singers. Dave Dudley recorded an early effort called "Vietnam Blues," and Roy Drusky did "Jody and the Kid"; other efforts were recorded by Faron Young, Jerry Lee Lewis, Bobby Bare, and Ray Stevens. Many of these early efforts were just good, typical country songs, distinguished mainly because they were well-crafted examples of a well-defined genre. Soon, though, Kristofferson was hanging out with some of Music Row's Young Turks, young experimental songwriters who were trying to expand the horizons of the music. These were people like Chris Gantry, Mickey Newberry, Tony Joe White, Donnie Fritts—people who were anticipating the ethic of what would become redneck rock, people who did marijuana *and* Lone Star beer, wore long hair *and* cowboy boots. Kristofferson summed up the group's contradiction when he said, "We weren't commercial. That was a dirty word, because we weren't." Kristofferson paid tribute to his circle in his well-known song "The Pilgrim—Chapter 33:" "He's a poet (he's a picker)/He's a prophet (he's a pusher)." He dedicated the song to many of the new Nashville writers, as well as to veteran folk singer Jack

Elliot, a buddy of Woody Guthrie's, and to Jerry Jeff Walker.

By the end of the 1960s some of his new songs were beginning to click. In early 1969 Bob Dylan had released his *Nashville Skyline* album, a collection of new Dylan songs that had been recorded on Nashville's Music Row with some of Nashville's best and most traditional sidemen. Many of Dylan's folk-protest fans were horrified at his apparent turn to country music; Dylan seemed to go out of his way to embrace it. He recorded a whole session of old country standards with Johnny Cash (only a few were ever released, though), and even overrode Columbia Records' objections to his putting the word "Nashville" in the title of the new album. The songs in *Nashville Skyline* were highly personal lyrics, nothing of protest in them, and with none of the arcane references of the long, dense songs of the mid-1960s Dylan. (They were country enough that some Nashvilles singers picked them up.) Dylan told interviewers at the time: "These are the type of songs that I always felt like writing when I've been alone to do so." His earlier songs were written in a "New York atmosphere," part of the self-conscious folk movement, but the new Nashville music had "a good spirit."

For many of the young composers in Kristofferson's circle, Dylan's endorsement of Nashville music justified their own faith in the music as a serious medium. And for many of the older Music Row publishers, the success of *Nashville Skyline* (it sold over a million copies, and one of the cuts, "Lay, Lady, Lay" became a single hit)

showed them the potential of the "new" country song in the youth market—a market to which traditional country had little appeal. The success of Dylan in Nashville certainly made it easier for Kristofferson's new songs, which, though country in form, reflected the culture of a younger generation. It also caused the executives of Music Row to look with a new respect on the songwriter in general; writers were no longer faceless hacks sitting around a table grinding out a song. They became poets, sensitive individuals who were about as important as the singers themselves.

A few months after *Nashville Skyline*, Kristofferson got "Me and Bobby McGee" recorded by Roger Miller. "Me and Bobby McGee," with its story of counterculture New West rambling, was not exactly a typical country song; it was one of the first of Kristofferson's "new" songs to get wide recognition. Folk-singer Gordon Lightfoot picked it up, and then in 1971 Janis Joplin, who had recorded the piece at her last session before she died, made it a big pop success; it was Kristofferson's first "crossover" hit. But before this even, Kristofferson had interested Johnny Cash in some of his songs while he was working as a janitor at Cash's studios. By 1970 Cash's friendship with Dylan and his carefully nourished "reformed outlaw" image had made him a sort of a mentor to the young new breed of Nashville songwriters. He sang a Kristofferson song on his television show that summer, recorded "Sunday Morning Coming Down," and even wrote a poem to Kris as the liner notes for Kristofferson's first album. All of this helped "Sunday Morning Coming Down" win the 1970 CMA award for Song of the Year. Kristofferson showed up to accept the award wearing shoulder-length hair and a scuffed suede suit; he seemed confused, stood with his back to the audience, and finally mumbled a few words of thanks. Emcee Tennessee Ernie Ford was visibly shaken, and the older Nashville crowd, standing around in their tuxedos and basking in their hard-won respectability, were outraged at this "gesture" appearing on the nationally televised show. They were even more puzzled when they confronted the fact that Kristofferson's song that won was not a drug song or a protest song, but just a good old-fashioned beer-drinking lonely song—if perhaps a bit lonelier and more alienated than most. The next year, Sammi Smith had one of the top country hits with another Kristofferson song, "Help Me Make It Through the Night." Music Row, as always, accepted success, and thus Kristofferson gradually gained a form of acceptance.

The country music fan magazines portrayed the CMA incident as a major traumatic event in country music's development. Certainly it signaled to the national audience that changes were occurring in Nashville, but it wasn't all that traumatic. Kristofferson's "new" music still had a lot in common with established country tradition. His own albums, produced with crack Nashville session men, used standard instrumentation and arrangements; his songs were, musically speaking, not at all daring, but crafted from simple, archetypal country melodies and chord patterns. Kristofferson never failed to acknowledge his respect for Hank Williams, and his first publisher found his early songs so reminiscent of Williams' that she had to warn Kristofferson about it. Even after the CMA incident Kristofferson continued to have his songs recorded primarily by country artists: Jerry Lee Lewis, Faron Young, Ray Price, Bobby Bare, Ray Stevens. And Kristofferson found himself embracing a large part of the value system of the Nashville scene. He attended a fundamentalist service at the church of the Reverend Jimmy Snow (the son of Hank Snow), got saved, and wrote "Why Me (Lord)?," which soon became a staple of modern gospel groups. Even after Kristofferson left Nashville, he still felt his mode was unchanged: "This is country music," he said backstage at one of his late 1974 concerts.

What then was it about the Kristofferson experience that was so revolutionary, so influential? Some people feel the lyrics of his songs, though simple and uncomplicated, contained reflections of the new values of the new generation. Kristofferson's protagonists often find themselves alienated not because somebody done them wrong, but simply because of the way life is.

Many country songs talk about freedom in one way or another, but Kristofferson's talked about it in a very open and self-conscious way: "Freedom's just another word for nothing left to lose." On the liner notes to his second album Kristofferson wrote of his songs: "Call these echoes of the goings-up and the coming-downs, walking pneumonia and run-of-the-mill madness, colored with guilt, pride, and a vague sense of despair." His songs also discussed sex in a frank, but in an easy and open way: "Help Me Make It Through the Night" is direct, but at the same time tender and serious. Some commentators on the music scene, such as historian Bill Malone, feel that if Kristofferson "has really contributed anything new to country music, it is the theme of sexuality openly discussed and endorsed without shame."

Yet all this is to see Kristofferson's influence stemming only from his music, and affecting only other music. His own albums sold fairly well, and his songs recorded by others sold well, but not all that well. Much of the effect Kristofferson had on the music came from the man, from Kristofferson the personality, the performing self. For one thing, a lot of his female admirers were attracted to him simply because of his rugged good looks. A close friend once described Kristofferson as "pretty," an unusual adjective for the world of country music. Country singers have, until fairly recently, hardly been characterized as handsome or pretty or good-looking; "Grand Ole Opry" faces might be distinctive (such as Porter Wagoner) or rugged (such as Johnny Cash) or intense (such as Hank Williams), but not especially handsome. Kristofferson's rather blatant sex appeal helped establish him as a leading Hollywood actor; by the mid-1970s he was appearing customarily in one or two films a year, and was the only male country singer to

grace the pages of *Playboy's* "Sex Stars of the 1970s."

To other people Kristofferson was influential simply through his lifestyle and individuality. He showed other young Nashville writers that it was possible to function as an *auteur* in Music City, that one could maintain integrity and still have commercial success. In one sense, he raised country song-writing from a vocational skill to a highly self-conscious art—for better or for worse. One of the Nashville writers who learned from Kristofferson's example was Willie Nelson. In later years, Nelson recalled: "He's got to be recognized as one of the first to really break open both fields [country and pop] without following what Nashville put down as the rules of the game. Kris made his own rules, did it his own way. That's why I admire and respect Kris. . . . It takes a lot of nerve and guts to do what people like Kristofferson have done."

Kristofferson's individuality extended far beyond his long hair and scruffy suits; he was an implausible mix of creativity and domesticity—in his own words, "a walking contradiction." He continues to be: By the late 1970s he had made a half-dozen films with people ranging from counter-culture figures like Dennis Hopper and Bob Dylan to slick establishment stars like Barbra Streisand. He got saved at the Reverend Snow's revival, did an album called *Jesus Was a Capricorn*, and then did nude scenes with Sarah Miles in a widely publicized movie.

By the mid-1970s Kristofferson had

left Nashville for the West Coast, married pop singer Rita Coolidge, and was considering his acting as important as his musical career. To what extent his future career may fall within the scope of country music is an open question, but his impact to date has been undeniable.

One of the members of the Nashville establishment who had been watching Kristofferson with more than passing interest was songwriter and singer Willie Nelson. If 1971 was Kristofferson's big year, with both pop and country hits, it was one of Willie Nelson's worst. He hadn't had a decent hit record for a couple of years, and he was finding that his membership in the Music Row club was not really satisfying him. His personal life was coming unstuck; in 1971 he divorced his third wife and managed to crack up four automobiles. The year ended with Willie getting a phone call at a downtown Christmas party: Better get out here, your house is burning down. "When I got there, it was in flames, and there were firemen everywhere," he recalled. "So I ran in and got my stash bag and ran out. I had a pound of good Columbian in there, and I knew I was gonna need it to get high." Willie took his stash, left the burned-out house, and moved to a dude ranch near Bandera, Texas. Though he didn't know it at the time, but the fire was to be a major turning point both in his career and in the direction of modern country music.

You can find Willie Nelson's name in the older histories of country music, but you have to look hard. In many ways his story was typical of the Nashville composer-singer who "made it" in the world of the 1960s: He was the composer of a few of the hundreds of songs that made the charts in those years and the singer of even fewer. Born in 1933 in Abbott, Texas, Nelson learned guitar from his grandfather, and was writing "poems and melodies" by the time he was six. In high school he organized a band (it included his sister Bobbi, who still plays in his outfit today) and grew up in the rough-and-tumble, mixed-up Southwestern musical scene of the late 1940s. From the first Willie accepted Texas music with enthusiasm; when he was only thirteen he somehow managed to book Bob Wills and the Texas Playboys into a dance at Whitney, Texas. Like most Texas musicians, Nelson knew Wills, and in 1960, when Nelson started out on his career, the king of western swing gave him a ringing endorsement: "I have had the pleasure of being an entertainer for nearly thirty-five years. During this time I've seen a lot of new talent appear on the music scene, but hardly ever have I seen the likes of Willie Nelson." Wills couldn't have known it at the time, but his testimonial was to become prophecy.

For ten years Nelson paid his dues. Dropping out of Baylor University in 1952, he began a career as a country disc jockey in Texas and points west like Oregon and Washington; for a time he taught guitar in Houston, and occasionally resorted to trades like door-to-door salesmanship. All this time he was trying to write country songs, and occasionally producing fine ones like "Family Bible," which he sold for fifty dollars. In 1959 he moved to Nashville to write songs for Pamper Music, owned by fellow Texan and honky-tonk pioneer Ray Price. Within a couple of years, Nelson found himself with a No. 1 hit when Patsy Cline recorded "Crazy" in 1961. (The song was revived in 1976 by Linda Ronstadt and became a hit again.) That same year a young Ralph Emery made the charts with a recording of Nelson's "Hello Fool," and Faron Young did even better with "Hello Walls." Recording executives thought they saw something promising in Willie's own singing, and Liberty Records gave him a performance contract. His first session was held in Hollywood, not Nashville, and though it contained thirteen good Nelson songs and the piano playing of a young Leon Russell, the album broke no sales records. A couple of Nelson singles on Liberty—"Touch Me" and "Willingly" (with Shirley Collins)—made the charts, however, and he found himself able to get personal appearances in the West. He was especially well liked in Las Vegas. He continued to write good songs: In 1962 Faron Young recorded "Three Days" successfully. By the mid-1960s Nelson was appearing on the "Opry" and had landed a contract with Victor; in 1967–68 he had a string of single hits for that label: "Blackjack County Chain," "The Party's Over," "Johnny One-time," "One in a Row," "Little Things," and "Bring Me Sunshine." But most of his money and fame still came from the songs he composed for other people to sing—people like Ray Price, songs like "Night Life." As the country waded through Vietnam, Willie wrote his well-crafted songs, played golf, toured with "Opry" regulars, and collected his checks from BMI. He built a house on a four-hundred-acre farm in the hills north of Nashville where he had run-ins with neighbor Ray Price's fighting roosters and named two of his pigs Lester and Earl, the Foggy Mountain Hogs.

It was a typical career up until that winter night in 1971—but if you look a little closer, you can see a few signs of the events to come. Along with writers like Mel Tillis, Wayne Walker, Merle Kilgore, and Justin Tubb, Willie comprised the second generation of writers in the honky-tonk tradition, writers who were skillfully using the forms and idioms of that tradition to create hard, tough, almost existential statements of human relationships. When Kristofferson's songs started hitting Nashville, Nelson felt an instinctive relationship: His own songs said much the same thing as Kris's did, if less directly. Nelson's own records of his songs more often took on a Spartan simplicity unusual for the time: His sharp voice was often backed only by bass, drums, and steel guitar. But the big change coming over Willie was that of lifestyle; he began to hang out with the new writers like Kristofferson, Mickey Newberry, Billy Joe Shaver, and Waylon Jennings. What Nelson saw in them was, as we have seen, nothing less than artists who were bent on retaining control of their product. Then he looked at his own situation with the corporate monolith of RCA/Victor. "I couldn't get anybody on the executive end of it interested in promoting me as an artist," he recalled. "There was a lack of communication and a lack of knowledge of what the people wanted." His producer, Chet Atkins, was sympathetic, but Willie felt that Chet's own hands were tied. "It was like a huge machine. 'We'll have to talk to New York.'" But Nelson also came up against the Nashville formula. "The people I had been involved with had done things their way for years and years and had been successful. They didn't want to change their way of thinking and I didn't want to change mine. I had definite ideas—things I wanted to carry out . . . and according to the regimented bureaucracy, I wasn't doing it right." Nelson had been bucking the system in mild ways before 1971—getting hairy, smoking pot—but the burning of his house was the event that helped him make the decisive split. When he left for Texas, he was thirty-nine.

Texas music had always been a part of Nelson's career. For years he had been associated with giants of southwestern music like Bob Wills, Ray Price, and Ernest Tubb (with whom Willie played for a time). Long before Texas style had become fashionable, Willie had recorded live albums in Texas and had even recorded an album called *Texas in My Soul*, which included such jingoistic bits as "Remember the Alamo" and the theme song from *Lyndon Johnson's Texas*. Thus it was not surprising that Nelson's first "liberated" album, cut the year after leaving Nashville, should be full of Texas songs and Texas musicians. *Shotgun Willie,* recorded in New York City for Atlantic, featured sidemen like Waylon Jennings, Doug Sahm (fresh from a successful album with Bob Dylan), ex-Wills fiddler Johnny Gimble, and ex-Ray Price steel guitarist Jimmy Day; the songs include a couple of Bob Wills standards, as well as newer fare by Nelson and Leon Russell. When Nelson later explained that "what Texas represents to me is where I relax," he was trying to make clear that for him, Texas was part of no public-relations image.

Nor was his break from Nashville and traditional country music all that drastic. In 1972 he began playing concerts in Texas with established country artists like Acuff, Tex Ritter, Roger Miller, Buck Owens, and Earl Scruggs. On July 4, 1972, he held his first festival at Dripping Springs—an event that was billed as the largest country music festival ever. Around sixty thousand people attended, but this was a lower figure than the promoters had hoped for. The event was more important as a symbol that a new generation of singers and writers had arrived on the scene, for Kristofferson performed, as did Waylon Jennings, Billy Joe Shaver, and Tom T. Hall: the cream of the new breed. But there was also Charlie Rich, fresh from his successes with slick Billy Sherrill; there was also old Nashville, Acuff and Monroe and Tex Ritter. This first festival, at least, suggested that Nelson wanted to build bridges between the different, polarized schools of the music; he said of his first concert at Dripping Springs, "It was the first time anyone had seen all types of people together listening to country music. It was actually the first time the hippie and the redneck had gotten together." After the 1972 festival, the Austin paper ran a front-page picture of Willie, country rocker Leon Russell, and University of Texas football coach Darrell Royal; it was "the best thing to come out of Dripping Springs. . . . In my mind it brought it all together."

The Dripping Springs festival became annual events after 1972, each festival becoming bigger and even more eclectic. By 1976 the likes of Monroe and Acuff had been replaced by the Pointer Sisters, and the festivals were acquiring the reputation of the Newport festival of outlaw music. They were also becoming mismanaged, brain-frying, counterculture extravaganzas. Disturbed by the turn they were taking, Nelson announced that the 1976 festival would be the last. By this time Willie had become the guru to hordes of young southern fans who insisted on wearing T-shirts saying, "Matthew, Mark, Luke, and Willie." In 1975 his Columbia album *Red Headed Stranger* became a best seller, breaking over not into mainstream pop but rather the rock charts. The album was produced by Nelson with a lean, sparse sound that made Columbia want to overdub it with strings; Nelson insisted on doing it his way, and he won out. A single from the album, "Blue Eyes Crying in the Rain" (an old Roy Acuff tune from 1945), sung by Willie with just acoustic guitar backup, became a surprise hit.

However, if any one album was responsible for introducing Willie and

his philosophy to the mainstream audience, that album was *Wanted: The Outlaws!*, released in 1976 by Victor. The album was conceived as a sort of sampler of "Nashville rebel" music, and included songs by Waylon Jennings; his wife, Jessi Colter; and Tompall Glaser in addition to Willie; much of the material had been released earlier, but not in this context. The album contained a number of hit singles, including Willie and Waylon's "Good-hearted Woman," Waylon's "Honky Tonk Heroes," and Jessi and Waylon's "Suspicious Minds." The style of the music was lean and spare, reminiscent of the tight Texas roadhouse bands. (Tompall even included his version of Jimmie Rodgers' classic "T for Texas.") The album sold amazingly well, and by the end of the year had been certified as a platinum album—a record that didn't sell merely a million dollars' worth (the traditional "gold" record album), but literally a million copies. *Wanted: The Outlaws!* was apparently the first strictly country album to attain this level of sales, and a milestone if for no other reason than that. As important as the music was the image the album presented of its artists: that of the outlaw. While the early use of the word "outlaw" to describe the music probably came from Jennings' successful 1972 song and album entitled *Ladies Love Outlaws*, the 1976 album made the identification more specific, both through its graphics and its liner notes. The cover design for the album was a mockup of an old western wanted poser, and the design was to be used often on later posters for concerts. In the liner notes, *Rolling stone* writer Chet Flippo emphasized the split between the Nelson-Jennings crowd and the Nashville scene: "They didn't wear Nudie suits and their music didn't conform to the country norm of songs of divorce and alcohol and life's other little miseries." The liner notes concluded by asserting that this music was "not country." The album may not have been the 1970s' Nashville music, but it certainly was solidly in the country tradition and style. Nelson's next two albums after *Wanted: The Outlaws!* were collections of country gospel tunes (such as "The Unclouded Day" and "There Is a Fountain") and a tribute to Lefty Frizzell, a quintessential country singer if ever there was one. But through the *Outlaws* album and its vast success, the image of the Nelson movement became fixed in the public's mind as a sort of dialectical revolt. Outlaws they were, proud, independent, western, rambling men who put individuality before social convention.

The image of the outlaw was nothing new to country music. From the folk ballads about Cole Younger in the nineteenth century to the popular gunfighter ballads of Marty Robbins, songs sympathetic to outlaws have always been popular. Even the image of the country entertainer as outlaw is not new: In the 1920s recorded skits portrayed people like Fiddlin' John Carson and the members of the Skillet Lickers as rough-and-tumble moonshiners who were always getting locked up. But as the music sought respectability in the 1930s and 1940s, singers consciously sought to upgrade their image; as we have seen, the sing-ing cowboys were a big step in this direction, and they were always the good guys. Hank Williams was an outlaw of sorts—if we count his drinking—and while this might have helped his popularity in some ways with the fans, the management of the "Opry" saw it only as a threat to their image. But by the mid-1960s, however, it became obvious that the outlaw image could become an asset rather than a liability. Johnny Cash played a significant role in this change.

During the 1960s Cash himself went through a bad period when he missed a lot of shows, popped a lot of pills, drank a lot, and was arrested on minor charges several times. He began to do albums that focused on western badmen and Indian rights; he broke with Nashville tradition and began to create "concept" albums, albums that were seen as a synergetic whole rather than as a collection of individual tracks, and he became one of the first big country artists to quit the "Opry." In these respects, Cash was a musical rebel. By the late 1960s his interest in prisons and prison reform and his apparent willingness to play up his own checkered past had given him the role of an outlaw in his personal life. He did a very successful live album at Folsom Prison in California, and followed it up with another one recorded live at San Quentin. He helped Glen Shirley, a former prisoner, get started in a career. Cash's national television show, begun in 1968, took some of the edge off his outlaw image; he began to emerge now more as a reformed outlaw, saved by the love of a good woman (June Carter) and a solid faith. Younger musicians in the 1970s were a little startled to find that when they went into Cash's studio to record they were allowed neither to smoke nor drink, but they continued to recognize Cash as an innovator who had defined a more realistic and humanistic mode for the country musician to work in.

Less overt and less postured than Cash in his use of the outlaw image was Merle Haggard. Unlike Cash, Haggard had actually spent a couple of years in San Quentin, and in many

Merle Haggard. Courtesy CBS.

ways was more of an outlaw. Yet he never openly sought to exploit this experience in his career; he refused to emulate Cash and record a prison album. He used the experience in some of his hit songs, like "Mama Tried" and "I Take a Lot of Pride in What I Am," and he never ducked questions about it; his audience of working-class Americans were obviously aware of Haggard's background, his "toughness," and by the late 1960s younger people were finding Haggard appealing as well. Arlo Guthrie began singing "Okie from Muskogee." By the dawn of the 1970s Haggard had confirmed the dictum that the country singer no longer had to have the pious lifestyle of a Roy Acuff or a Bill Anderson.

The success of the outlaw image had other implications as well. Kristofferson and Nelson and Jennings had shown that the personality of the artist was becoming as important as his songs or singing talents or ability to use the Nashville pipeline. The singer could now function as a sort of culture hero. In the old days, all the personality of a singer that could come across to much of his audience was what was on the old 78 record label. There were no fan magazines, no television close-ups, no major festivals—no way for a fan to get to know much about his favorite artist except through his music. By the 1970s, the country singer had all manner of access to media: colorful album covers, extensive media exposure, films, festivals, magazine and newspaper coverage. Singers who were singers and nothing more were facing a dilemma not unlike the old silent-film actors who were suddenly confronted with the change to sound. The spotlight was much, much brighter, and it was on you almost all the time. For better or for worse, the public-relations agent was finding work in country music.

Since the late 1950s, image had been a part of rock music, and the youth market accepted the concept of the performing self as a natural dimension of the music scene. Furthermore, from the time of Elvis and Chuck Berry up through the Beatles and the Rolling Stones and on into the acid rock of the early 1970s, rock musicians had utilized, in various forms, an outlaw image with shades of drugs, sex, and revolution. Thus by the 1970s, the youth market had found that country music could offer them the same terms as rock: strong personalities willing to buck the system, whether it be Nashville or the Bank of America. If Billy Sherrill had figured out a way to make country hits cross over into mainstream pop, Kristofferson, Nelson, and Jennings found a way to get country to cross over into rock. If Sherrill went after the middle-aged housewife in Topeka, the outlaws went after her teen-aged sons, and after the "young adults" in the eighteen-to-thirty age bracket, the bracket whose rapacious buying power makes sales-oriented demographers drool. And the outlaws were rewarded in ways traditional Nashville never was: platinum albums, films, national media coverage, ninety-thousand-plus festival attendance.

By the mid-1970s, outlaw music— "progressive country" is a milder term —had attracted a widely diverse group of practitioners and a broad-based and eclectic audience. Next to Willie Nelson, the most influential member of the group was Waylon Jennings. Born in Texas in 1937, Jennings, like Nelson, grew up listening to the sounds of Texas' most famous musical sons, Bob Wills and Ernest Tubb. Early in life, Waylon saw music as a way to escape from poverty; he recalls, "It's kind of like they say sports is with black dudes. It's a way to get up and away from something that's bad. I'll tell you what it is: Either music or pull cotton for the rest of your life. . . ." Jennings' first musical experience, though, came not with a country band, but with the now-legendary rockabilly band headed by fellow Texan Buddy Holly. After Holly's death, Jennings worked for a few years as a disc jockey in Texas, then played clubs around the Phoenix area. It was the Kennedy era, and the folk-music boom was under way. Jennings moved with ease into the "folk" (that is, northeastern coffeehouse) mode, and among his first records were versions of Dylan's "Don't Think Twice" and Ian and Sylvia's "Four Strong Winds." Even after he came to Nashville in 1965 and signed an RCA/Victor contract, Jennings continued to attract attention as a folk-styled performer. His first RCA album was called *Folk-Country*, even though it was a rather typical product of the Nashville sound, replete with Anita Kerr singers; the only real "folk" material on the album was old-time minstrel Dick Burnett's "Man of Constant Sorrow." Jennings continued to write songs, though, like "Julie," that were long, balladlike songs somewhat in the folk vein.

Waylon Jennings and Jessi Colter.

Jennings continued to work successfully in Nashville, as a session man (playing a distinctive style of guitar), as a songwriter, and as a performer. For RCA/Victor and Chet Atkins he was a good, steady album seller, and he began grinding them out every six months; between 1966 and 1973 he released two dozen albums. But even within the confines of Nashville success Jennings showed from the first a fondness for the eclectic, the different. Like Kristofferson, his strong personality led him into films; he played the lead and wrote the music for a 1966 American International pot-boiler called *Nashville Rebel*, a film that enhanced his image as a proto-outlaw. In 1970 he worked on the music to the Mick Jagger film *Ned Kelly*, and he recorded duets with the Rolling Stones' leader and with Kristofferson. Jennings was caught up in the Nashville song-writing renaissance of the late 1960s and was one of the first to record some of the new-sounding songs of Kristofferson, Mickey Newberry, and Shel Silverstein. Soon Jennings was expanding even beyond this into the pop/rock field, recording Jagger's "Honky Tonk Women," Chuck Berry's "Brown-eyed, Handsome Man," Simon and Garfunkel's "Bridge over Troubled Water," and Jimmy Webb's "MacArthur Park." This latter song won him a Grammy in 1969. It also helped his songs cross over more and more into pop charts. But none of this should obscure the fact that, prior to 1972, many of Waylon's songs were solidly in the traditional country vein—hits like "Love of the Common People," "I've Got You," "Walk on Out of My Mind," and "Don't Let the Sun Set on You in Tulsa."

Willie and Waylon had been friends from Waylon's Phoenix days: Willie, in fact, had advised Waylon not to follow him to Nashville. During the 1960s both men saw themselves as blood brothers waging a common fight against the formula music philosophy, and when Willie broke out in 1972, the lesson wasn't lost on Waylon. After Waylon saw Willie get out of his RCA/Victor contract and gain the right to control the production and marketing of his own records, Waylon followed suit; he went over the heads of the Nashville branch of Victor, went directly to the New York offices. Pointing to a picture of Willie hanging on the wall of the New York office, Waylon reportedly said, "You've already made a mistake with that man, Hoss. Don't make the same mistake again." They didn't, and Waylon soon had a new contract that gave him the same kind of freedom Willie had. Waylon also hired a veteran New York manager named Neil Reshem, an aggressive (some would say cutthroat) businessman to protect his interests against the monolithic corporations. "It's like

having a mad dog on a leash," Waylon said of Reshem, but Reshem's business instincts helped make the outlaw rebellion possible. (Willie soon signed Reshem to manage his interests as well.)

Two symbols of this new freedom became evident to Jennings in 1973. One was the spectacular success of the Dripping Springs festival that year. Witnesses reported that Waylon's eyes nearly popped out of his head when he saw the number of people in the audience at the festival, where he had joined Kris Kristofferson, Charlie Rich, Rita Coolidge, and others in performing free for the man Waylon called "the Pied Piper of Music," Willie Nelson. Though he was now convinced that his music, like Willie's, could attract hippies, rednecks, and middle-of-the-roaders, he did not follow in Willie's footsteps and move to Austin. He continued to live and work in Nashville—but by late 1973 he was in total production control of his own recordings and was working almost exclusively at the studio of Tompall Glaser, himself a leading figure in the outlaw movement.

Tompall had begun his career in Nashville as leader of the Glaser Brothers, whose harmony singing established them as a "hot" Nashville act in the early 1960s. Tompall ran into a Nashville rut, however: Trying to push "new"-style country songs by the likes of John Hartford, he foundered on the conservatism of the 1960s generation of music-business leaders. His response was to go out on his own. Using the proceeds from a successful song-publishing business, he built a modern recording studio and presided over it, making the studio available for the kind of extremely expensive, time-consuming approach to recording that could do justice to the outlaws' musical ambitions. Tompall also had a lot to do with the business end of the outlaw movement; he was one of the first Nashville artists to face down the recording companies and grab control of his own (and others') product. For many years, in fact, the commonly perceived Waylon/Willie duo was in fact a trio; Tompall stood behind them both with his studio and his savvy. He and Waylon shared office space for three of Waylon's most significant years, then quarreled and went their separate ways—Waylon into a more pop, rock 'n' roll-oriented organization, and Tompall back into his studio with yet another twist for the Nashville scheme of things, a "hillbilly blues band" featuring Tompall and two stellar ex-members of Bobby "Blue" Bland's band, guitarist Mel Brown and drummer Charles Polk.

During his stay at Tompall's, Waylon also connected with another luminary of the outlaw cadre, Jack "Cowboy" Clement, who produced

Tompall Glaser watching an engineer. Photo by Leonard Kamsler.

Waylon's *Dreaming My Dreams* album. Clement, who began his career as Sam Phillips' assistant at Sun Records and went on to produce such figures as Jerry Lee Lewis and Johnny Cash, had been in Nashville for ten years by the time he worked with Waylon. His string of "legitimate" country successes—the discovery and production of Charley Pride, endless other production credits, and a string of hits as a songwriter ("Miller's Cave," "Guess Things Happen That Way," "Ballad of a Teen-age Queen," and many others)—compensated for his manner and general approach, which Nashville at the time thought to be quite bizarre. Clement would, perhaps, have been more comfortable producing at the Old Vic than in the Nashville of the 1960s, but nevertheless he stuck to his guns, building a string of studios and encouraging protégés into his determinedly high-quality school of country-record production. By the mid-1970s Clement, having blown most of his assets on an ill-advised movie project (itself an indication of where he might be headed in the future), launched a career as a singer. He left his mark behind him, though. His insistence on a classic combination of melody and beat and his accompanying philosophy of "organic" recording set the trend for the outlaws, while his protégés (notably producer Allen Reynolds) carried his lessons into mainstream country music. During the formation of the outlaw movement, Clement and Tompall Glaser provided both studio expertise and shelter to the singing stars and other personnel of the outlaw cadre.

With the involvement of Tompall (and, for a while, Clement), Waylon was able to take the time to produce records with the care and effort he felt they deserved, and then turn the finished tapes over to RCA/Victor when he was satisfied with them. Albums like *This Time, Ramblin' Man,* and *Dreaming My Dreams* resulted from this new arrangement. Waylon was just as willing to use "noncountry" instruments on his records as was Billy Sherrill, but for different reasons: Sherrill's motives were rooted in marketing considerations, whereas Waylon was out for aesthetic effect. "If a beat compliments a song, then use it," he said. "If a kazoo compliments that song, then we got just as much right to use that as anyone else —or horns, or anything. But don't use them just to make it where it will get played in certain areas."

During the early years of the outlaw movement, Nelson and Jennings were often looked on as coleaders, or as coconspirators. Both had shared many common experiences, from Texas dirt-farm beginnings to Nashville success; both liked well-crafted country songs in the classic honky-tonk mold. Yet the two men were different: Willie was more up front, the organizer, the socializer, the crowd lover who would do four-hour sets when other people would do thirty minutes. Waylon was moody, introverted, hard to know. It was Willie who showed up on television in 1976 when he and Waylon swept the CMA Awards, both losing Entertainer of the Year honors only because votes were split between them. They have a mutual respect for each other's musical abilities, and, more important, each other's integrity. Jennings has told reporters: "We have been called crazy and wild and everything, but if they look at us, they know we're men. We stand up for what we believe in, and I think that is something people respect."

Waylon Jennings was also responsible for producing, in 1975, a song that became something of an anthem for the Austin scene: "Bob Wills Is Still the King." Besides being a tribute to Wills, the song makes explicit the difference between the Nashville and the Austin scenes; The "Opry" in Nashville is still "the home of country music," but "when you cross that old Red River, Hoss, it just don't mean a thing." This difference was further emphasized by the revival of interest in Wills' music that began in the early 1970s. It wasn't that Wills' music had ever fallen into any serious eclipse with traditional country music fans; in fact, Wills himself was still recording in Nashville until his incapacitating stroke in 1969. But in 1970 a number of things happened to popularize Wills' music with young new audiences who didn't remember him from the dance halls of Texas and Oklahoma, and with people who were not fully into country music. First, Merle Haggard recorded an album in tribute to Wills using some of the old members of his band, and Haggard's popularity assured that the music would receive a wide hearing. Among the indirect by-products of this album was a well-documented and well-produced set of historic Wills material that made his original great recordings available once again. Wills' last recordings were brought out in 1974 (shortly before his death)

in a deluxed boxed set and promoted through the pages of magazines like *Rolling Stone*. A full-length biography of Wills appeared, and the former sidemen who had helped define western swing were sought out and honored. Johnny Gimble, a former Wills fiddler, was named Instrumentalist of the Year by the CMA in 1976.

Soon a full-fledged western swing revival was taking its place next to Jennings and Nelson as part of the Austin scene. The first "revival" band to achieve national prominence, and to appeal mainly to a young audience, was Asleep at the Wheel, which surfaced in 1973. Formed around Chris O'Connell, Ray Benson, and Leroy Preston, the band came into Texas from Berkeley and soon attracted a following that wanted to hear "Take Me Back to Tulsa," "Cherokee Boogie," and the band's original songs in the older modes such as "Don't Ask Me Why I'm Going to Texas." Floyd Tillman, one of the old-time honky-tonk western performers who appeared with Asleep at the Wheel, summed up their style: "They're like the old bands, but with a difference: They play take-off solos. That's more like rock. Still I love 'em or I wouldn't play with 'em. They've moved the music back in the dance hall where it belongs." This last statement is important, for it emphasizes the fact that much of the Austin, Texas, swing is flourishing in the same setting occupied by the original western swing: the roadhouses, the bars, the honky-tonks, and the dance halls of the Texas plains. At a time when much Nashville music has taken more and more to the concert form, the informal beer-drinking and pot-smoking atmosphere of the roadhouse seemed quite a cultural contrast to the formal sterility of the new "Grand Ole Opry" House.

Even more faithful to the western-swing tradition was Alvin Crow and the Pleasant Valley Boys. Until 1975 Crow had primarily a local reputation, playing with many older Wills veterans like fiddler Jesse Ashlock at funky Austin dance halls like the Broken Spoke. Crow, a classically trained musician originally from Oklahoma, was one of the most aggressive spokesmen for the new Texas music (as opposed to the Nashville music). "Nashville's not interested in me. I won't fit into their hit machine. . . . I have the same ideas, along with everybody else in this town. None fit into the Nashville pattern." Austin soon saw a number of other local bands playing versions of western swing: Freida and the Firedogs, Marcia Ball and the Misery Brothers, and the freaky country act called Kinky Friedman and his Texas Jewboys, a band that specializes in numbers like "Asshole from El Paso" and "Get Your Biscuits in the Oven and Your Buns in the Bed." (Friedman is in fact an Austin native, even though by the mid-1970s he was seldom appearing there.)

Other bands were attracted to Austin much as groups were once attracted to Nashville: to energize themselves from the musical excitement there. Some merged western swing with rock. A California band, Commander Cody and the Lost Planet Airmen, enjoyed modest success as they combined country, swing, and 1950s rock;

they became extremely popular during their stay at the Armadillo World Headquarters in Austin. (The Armadillo became Austin's version of Fillmore West in the early 1970s, and was a center for much of the counterculture music of the town.) The Lost Planet Airmen broke up in 1976, but that same year saw the rise of ZZ Top, a three-piece Texas band that pushes Texas music even farther in the direction of rock. Spawned in Texas beer joints, the band made little claim to be a country band, but they didn't let anybody forget they were a Texas band. Their concert stage consisted of a three-dimensional, panoramic map of Texas, and they customarily shared the stage with two specially trained vultures, a longhorn steer, a buffalo, and four (count 'em) rattlesnakes. Yet in 1976 their concert tour drew more people than any other rock band had drawn in a single year.

Other aspects of the Austin scene involved musical styles quite distinct from western swing, and many of these styles resist easy categorization. As we have seen, outlaw ideology was not so much a musical one as a personal one: It involved a healthy sense of tradition, a certain pride in redneck culture, and an obsession with individual freedom. The scene could include, for instance, figures who got their start in the urban folk revival, or what was left of it in the late 1960s, people like Jerry Jeff Walker and Michael Murphey. Walker was a New Yorker who wrote a very successful song called "Mr. Bojangles," about an old minstrel; it was widely recorded, and Richard Nixon once said it was his all-time favorite. For the next few years Walker bummed around the country before finally settling in Austin, where he has acquired a stature next only to Willie Nelson's as a leader of the young poet-singers clustered in the town. Michael Murphey, for his part, popularized the term "cosmic cowboy," a catchword that soon caught on in attempts to describe the part-hippie, part-redneck values of the Austin crowd. Then there was Doug Sahm, leader of a late 1960s rock group called the Sir Douglas Quintet, who derived his unique style from his serious roots in black, Cajun, and Tex-Mex music. By the early seventies Sahm was singing "Faded Love" with Bob Dylan and moving into progressive country. There was Billy Joe Shaver, an old Kristofferson buddy from Nashville, and Delbert McClinton, a Fort Worth native who mixed rhythm-and-blues with honky-tonk music and like Sahm had genuine musical roots in the Southwest. And then there was David Alan Coe, perhaps the most self-conscious of the new breed (one of his songs was entitled "Willie, Waylon, and Me"), a singer who was so caught up in the outlaw image that he put himself in the awkward position of insisting that his prison record was worse than his warden said it was.

To go with the new alternative country music, Texas soon developed its own media: local television, radio, and films (including one effort entitled *Outlaw Blues*), as well as publications like *Pickin' Up the Tempo*, *Texas Monthly*, and the nationally distributed *Country Rambler*. The rock magazine *Rolling Stone* often printed material by one of its lead writers on the Austin scene, Chet Flippo. National magazines made much of the challenge Austin was posing to Nashville, but the very devotion to freedom that attracted so many of the progressive artists to Austin in the first place prevented the Austin scene from becoming a close-knit musical culture like Nashville.

Texas was by no means the only residence center for country music ouside of Nashville. As Nashville gained increasing acceptance by a northern audience, a number of singers moved to reaffirm their southern roots. For some time in the late 1960s, after the bitter taste of the civil-rights struggle had faded, a sort of redneck chic had been developing in middle-class America. For the Northerner, this led to a more open acceptance of country music in general; for the Southerner, it led to a new pride in southern folk culture and in southern identity. The election of Jimmy Carter as President in 1976 accelerated this trend even more. In addition to the Texas style, three other southern trends were very visible in the mid-1970s: the expansion of bluegrass, the "Atlanta sound," and what some chose to call "southern rock." These trends to some extent overlapped, and by no stretch of the imagination could the last two be considered "pure" country music. But country music was a part of all three developments, and all three movements caused repercussions that were felt in Nashville and throughout pop music.

By the 1970s bluegrass had emerged as a flourishing subgenre of country music. Yet there were a number of striking differences between it and mainstream country music. In contrast to the increasing professionalization of the country music world, the bluegrass scene included many semiprofessionals who worked at the music part-time. While bluegrass shared much of the same audience with country music, increasing numbers of bluegrass fans were scornful of the "commercialized" Nashville sound. For many of these fans, bluegrass was becoming a participatory experience, almost a lifestyle, that embraced outdoor festivals, a veneration of old instruments, and a love of amateur picking. Country music, on the other hand, was becoming more and more of a passive spectator sport. Furthermore, bluegrass found its audience without going through the normal Nashville channels of records and radio airplay. There were a few big bluegrass hits coming out of Nashville (such as the Osborne Brothers' "Rocky Top" in 1971), and the "Opry" maintained a short but illustrious roster of bluegrass acts, such as Bill Monroe, Lester Flatt, Jim and Jesse, and the Osbornes. But Nashville was really not all that sympathetic to bluegrass, and mostly contented itself by staging a token "early bird" bluegrass concert at the annual Fan Fair.

Yet the end of the seventies saw more bluegrass bands than at any time in the thirty-year history of the genre. Many recorded on small independent labels and heard their records occasionally played on local stations that set aside three to four hours a week for special bluegrass shows. But the main medium for bluegrass was a phenomenon known as the "bluegrass festival" or "bluegrass convention," and nearly everybody who played bluegrass spent at least some summer months playing at one. The first of these was staged near Roanoke, Virginia, in 1965 by a man named Carlton Haney. Haney had been a manager and promoter for the team of Reno and Smiley, and he sensed that there was a vast, if disparate, audience for bluegrass that would drive hundreds of miles to see their favorite bluegrass stars in one series of concerts. The festival was held out of doors, in an informal, simple, back-to nature setting. People arrived in campers and vans, set up tents, unfolded aluminum lawn chairs, and unpacked their own instruments. In between formal concerts, stars like Bill Monroe, the Stanley Brothers, and Mac Wiseman mingled easily with the fans and conducted informal workshops on picking techniques. The area was dotted with impromptu jam sessions and picking sessions, so much so that some scheduled performers missed their sets onstage. Bright-eyed fans were walking around saying, "I just played back of Ralph Stanley," or "Bill Monroe let me hold his mandolin." Sunday morning brought an old-fashioned hymn-singing, and on Sunday afternoon there was a nostalgic "history of bluegrass" program. Everyone left with a good, satisfied feeling full of praise for Haney's bright idea.

The idea of the festival spread, and soon bluegrass, which had gained most of its commercial exposure in the smoky bars of Detroit or Cincinnati or Baltimore, found a new home on makeshift stages set up in reformed cow pastures. Festivals were set up throughout the United States and Canada, and within a few years Bill Monroe, who established one of the major festivals at Bean Blossom, Indiana, was able to announce from his stage that the festival included people from every state in the union— including Hawaii and Alaska. Not all the festivals attracted the immense crowds that flocked to rock festivals like Woodstock, but the bluegrass festivals made up in frequency what they lacked in individual size. By the

Lester Flatt.

mid-1970s, every summer weekend brought news of five or six major festivals in different parts of the country, and bluegrass fans could, with a little hard driving spend most of their summer weekends camped out under a portable PA system blaring forth the sounds of a five-string banjo. The endless string of festivals also provided steady work for the many new bands that emerged as bluegrass sought to expand its audience.

The bluegrass audience, which had formerly been virtually identical with the traditional country music audience, now attracted many people who had little or only passing interest in other forms of country music. Bluegrass was attracting a broad, ecumenical band of listeners as early as 1959, when the Newport Folk Festival invited Earl Scruggs and the Stanley Brothers to appear. Soon other bands, such as the Osborne Brothers, were playing concerts at colleges in the North and the Midwest, and bluegrass found itself caught up in the intense fervor of the "folk revival." The music of Flatt and Scruggs reached vast popular audiences when it was used for the theme music to the hit television show "The Beverly Hillbillies" in the early 1960s, and later as the background music for the award-winning movie *Bonnie and Clyde* in 1967. Another major film success of the midseventies, *Deliverance*, made a national pop hit out of an old bluegrass standard called "Dueling Banjos." The simple, unamplified, down-home sound of bluegrass also formed a musical counterpart to the ecologically oriented, back-to-basics lifestyle of the seventies, and the music began showing up in all sorts of films and commercials. The music soon attracted an intellectual audience, an audience who found the dazzling, complex instrumental techniques of bluegrass more satisfying than the predictable sameness of most country music; not a few echoed the critic who openly compared Flatt and Scruggs' LP *Foggy Mountain Banjo* to jazz. A number of young musicians, some from quite sophisticated backgrounds, began to form up new bluegrass bands and to develop new styles. In the mid-1960s one such new musician, Amherst graduate Bill Keith, joined Bill Monroe's venerable band and proceeded to revolutionize banjo styles with his "chromatic" melodic style. Some old-timers scoffed at this and developments like it—they called Keith's style "Yankee picking"—but Monroe and others like him knew that bluegrass could not possibly survive by appealing only to its original southern audience. Many of the "good ole boys" in Durham and Roanoke and Chattanooga who had cheered Flatt and Scruggs in the 1950s were now listening to "ole Waylon" and Merle Haggard and Roy Clark. It was the college kids in Boston and the young professionals in California and Washington, D.C., who were buying the reissues of the old music from the 1940s and who were listening to the new bands that were developing ideas like those of Keith's.

Washington, D.C., in fact, became a center for the new styles of bluegrass. The group most responsible for this was The Country Gentlemen, formed in 1957 around tenor-mando-

lin player John Duffey, banjoist Eddie Adcock, and singer-guitarist Charlie Waller. Waller was from Louisiana; Duffey was the son of a Metropolitan Opera singer. Both had been exposed to the heady mixture of urban and rural bluegrass that had come to characterize the Washington scene in the 1950s. The Washington-Baltimore area was an ideal melting pot, where young northern musicians from the folk-revival movement could brush shoulders with the more traditional southern musicians who were eking out a living playing in the working-class bars of the area. The Country Gentlemen combined the best of these two worlds; they performed superb versions of old bluegrass standards such as "Red Rockin' Chair" and "Poor Ellen Smith," but they would just as often bring out jazz tunes like "Bye-bye Blues," Harry Belafonte's calypso hit "Banana Boat Song," or Shel Silverstein's parodies. Duffey's trained voice did not have the rural twang of so many bluegrass tenors, and the group's harmony was slick and sophisticated. In Eddie Adcock they found a banjo player who was willing to experiment with a bewildering variety of jazzy styles. It all worked. The Country Gentlemen appealed to all kinds of audiences, and in the 1960s they probably played more colleges and coffeehouses than any other bluegrass band. The Gentlemen did a lot to popularize bluegrass—more, probably, than any other band except Flatt and Scruggs.

Other young musicians followed the lead of Duffey, Waller, and Adcock into a more progressive, eclectic brand of bluegrass that was soon be-

Earl Scruggs.

ing called "newgrass." Actually an experimental trend had been set in the early 1970s by one of the founders of traditional bluegrass, Earl Scruggs. When he split from Lester Flatt in 1969, Scruggs formed a band with his two sons and began playing a type of music that was one part bluegrass, one part country, and one part rock. Scruggs soon outgrew (some would say turned his back on) his traditional audience, and on a famous television special was seen trading licks with everyone from Bob Dylan to a Moog synthesizer. At about the same time, the Nashville-based Osborne Brothers plugged in their banjo and mandolin and began crafting new three-part vocal harmonies derived from the sound of the main symbol of the Nashville sound, the pedal-steel guitar. But the real axis of the newgrass style was the Washington-Baltimore area; other area musicians like Bill Emerson and Cliff Waldron (who recorded one of the first newgrass standards, "Fox on the Run") flourished, and independent area companies like Rebel documented the new sounds. Eddie Adcock soon formed a new band called II Generation, while Duffey formed a new group called The Seldom Scene. Many newgrassers celebrated their new freedom and, like some members of the outlaw movement, felt a certain scorn toward Nashville. Eddie Adcock said "Nashville can only control their country music. It can't control any other kind of music. Bluegrass is one of these other kinds of music that Nashville can't control."

Newgrass music was characterized, on the surface, by shaggy hair, informal dress (gone were the classic white hats of Monroe's generation), and lots of laid-back jokes about how good the grass was. The music itself included an expansion of the standard bluegrass instrumentation to include, on occasion, drums, chromatic banjo styles, a penchant for long, jazzlike instrumental solos, and an eclectic repertory often borrowed from rock. Back in the 1960s, for instance, even Jim and Jesse, "Opry" regulars, had cut an album of Chuck Berry songs. The 1970s saw groups like the Louisville-based Newgrass Revival touring with rock star Leon Russell, and fiddler Vassar Clements appearing with ex-Allman Brothers guitarist Dicky Betts. Adcock's II Generation band recorded newgrass versions of songs popularized originally by groups like the Turtles and Bread, and Duffey's Seldom Scene won a Song of the Year award in 1974 with their version of "Rider," a piece popularized by the Grateful Dead. (Linda Ronstadt also appeared as a guest on one Seldom Scene LP.) Other newgrassers found jazz; young fiddlers found themselves listening a lot to Stephane Grappelli and Joe Venuti, swing-era veterans from the 1930s. An album called *Hillbilly Jazz*, produced on an independent label out of Chicago, became a surprise best seller; it featured the likes of David Bromberg and Vassar Clements playing swing-era standards like "C Jam Blues" and "Cherokee." Clements, who had once

fiddled for Bill Monroe, became the most popular fiddler of the generation, and his bluesy, angular style influenced thousands. An old-timey band from North Carolina called The Red Clay Ramblers added an electric piano and a trumpet ("the bluegrass three," as they introduced it) and expanded their repertoire to include everything from "Keep the Home Fires Burning" to Bill Boyd's "Wah Hoo." The David Grisham Quintet and Michael Melford moved even more toward jazz, and soon found that some bluegrass fan magazines wouldn't even review their records. But many of the young musicians echoed the sentiments of John Duffey, who described The Seldom Scene in these words: "We are a somewhat contemporary band who uses the term 'bluegrass' more as a method than a means. We use the instrumentation that is generally associated with bluegrass music, and just play anything we choose to. . . . This type of music is classified by instrumentation, not especially by song or vocal arrangements." There is much truth in Duffey's statement: A lot of young casual listeners applied the term "bluegrass" indiscriminately to any kind of music played with unamplified string instruments, whether it was honest-to-God bluegrass, western swing, old-time music, folk music, or whatever.

This trend was certainly exemplified by the success of guitarist-singer Doc Watson, one of the most influential individual performers of the 1970s. Doc (his real name is Arthel) came from a tiny mountain hamlet called Deep Gap, North Carolina, and came from a family that was a folklorist's dream: They sang old English ballads, droned archaic fiddle tunes, and picked all manner of rags and blues. In fact, folklorists from the Smithsonian Institution first discovered Doc and brought him to all kinds of folk festivals in the 1960s. Yet Doc's music was certainly not "folk" in the narrow sense; before being discovered by the folk audience, Doc had made his living playing all kinds of music, from straight-out country to rockabilly. He was a consummate stylist and technician; he admitted in 1975, "I'd define my music, or my style, as a conglomeration of a lot of things that I've listened to, plus a few notions of my own." His albums soon began to include original guitar instrumentals as well as traditional pieces, classic western swing as well as contemporary country. At festivals, acres of fans chanted for him to perform "Black Mountain Rag" or "Brown's Ferry Blues." More than anyone else, Doc made the guitar the trendy instrument of the late 1970s. Once confined to the role of little more than a rhythm instrument in classic bluegrass, the guitar now emerged as a solo instrument. Clarence White, a brilliant flat-top stylist who was featured on a classic album called *Appalachian Swing*, inspired a lot of younger musicians in this direction before his untimely death in 1973. One of these younger musicians was Tony Rice, perhaps the hottest soloist in newgrass in 1978, who played with the David Gresham Quintet on the West Coast. Others, and ones who learned more directly from Watson, included Norman Blake, an Ala-

bama guitarist who took his eclectic music seriously, demanded respect and attention from his audience, and on occasion walked out of club dates when the audience got too noisy. A third major young guitarist was Dan Crary, from Kansas, who began with the Bluegrass Alliance before leaving for a solo career. All three played what would have to basically be described as traditional music, but all three played it with what the old-time jazzmen used to call "hot licks."

Thus the famous split between Flatt and Scruggs became symbolic of an entire generation. Flatt, doggedly sticking to purist modes formed in the 1940s, continued to play to his traditional audiences in the South and steadily sell his 35,000–40,000 copies per record. Scruggs, experimenting with his music, played to college groups and youth markets across the country, his albums becoming fewer but more painstakingly crafted. No longer were the "good ole boys" upset at seeing long, shaggy hair at their bluegrass festivals, and a lot of people doted on how bluegrass music brought together the rednecks and the hippies. But by the end of the decade, the newgrass movement was affecting even this, and some festivals were pointedly advertised as "newgrass." And, to be sure, not all young groups were experimental; two of the hottest bands of 1977, J. D. Crowe and the New South, and Boone Creek, were basically traditional, and were composed mainly of musicians from the South. To complicate matters still further, the era saw a strong revival of young bands playing deliberately in the archaic, pre-bluegrass style of the 1920s string bands like the Skillet Lickers. The New Lost City Ramblers, featuring brilliant folklorist/performer Mike Seeger, began to copy arrangements off of old 78s as early as the 1960s. The 1970s bluegrass festivals were full of bands like The Highwoods String Band, from upstate New York, who specialized in old twin fiddle numbers; the Hotmud Family, from southern Ohio, who were equally at home doing Uncle Dave Macon or Stanley Brothers bluegrass; and the Red Clay Ramblers, from North Carolina, who even composed new tunes in old-time molds. Of course, to the typical fan, all these acts were simply "bluegrass," and by 1978, bluegrass, once the most easily defined of musical genres, was experiencing a perplexing but intriguing identity crisis. The only thing certain was that it was alive and growing.

The "Atlanta sound" was a heady mixture of black and white music, of rock, gospel, country, and soul. Far more than in Nashville, these different musical forms coalesced in Atlanta, and country artists in Atlanta were generally exposed to a much broader spectrum of music. Atlanta had been the center of country recording in the 1920s and had continued to function as a regional center for major companies up through the 1940s. Many of these early recordings were made in temporary studios set up in places like the Kimball House Hotel and the old Fox Theater, site of the famous premiere of *Gone with the Wind*.

Some blues had been recorded in Atlanta in the 1920s and 1930s, but Victor's A&R pioneer Ralph Peer complained that the blues musicians in Atlanta were not at all of the caliber he expected. But by the late 1940s the city was developing a healthy rhythm-and-blues culture; Piano Red recorded some of his important boogie woogie there, and Little Richard forged a music that was to make him a pioneer in rock. The 1960s saw Atlanta develop important soul-music groups like the phenominally successful Gladys Knight and the Pips. Paralleling the growth of rock and blues was the rise in gospel music, both

Doc Watson.

black and white. Atlanta was the scene, in 1946, of the first "All-night Singing," and was home base for major gospel artists like Hovie Lister and the Statesmen and Lee Roy Abernathy. In the 1950s and 1960s modern country singers like Brenda Lee and Ray Stevens hailed from Atlanta. These various traditions formed the background for the development in the early seventies of country-oriented rock bands like the Allman Brothers, the Marshall Tucker Band, Wet Willie, and Lynyrd Skynyrd.

The nerve center for much southern rock was actually not Atlanta, but nearby Macon, the center for the Capricorn record label complex. Like Sam Phillips' Sun label of some twenty years earlier, Phil Walden's Capricorn company achieved national success by working apart from the established recording centers and by experimenting with an unstable fusion of southern blues, rock, and country. It was Walden who, during the late 1960s, helped Duane and Greg Allman form what was to become the first of the southern rock bands. The Allman Brothers' band soon included Dicky Betts as a second lead guitarist, and experimented with the use of two drummers. Country was only a part of the background and repertory of the band; equally important was the Allmans' grounding in soul and rhythm-and-blues (Duane had played often behind Aretha Franklin), and Dicky Betts' serious interest in jazz (he was fascinated with Django Reinhart). But Duane Allman's innovative slide-guitar stylings were attractive to all manner of would-be country fans, and soon the teen-aged sons and daughters of old Hank Williams fans were flocking to the Allman concerts across the South. In many ways the band was a living symbol of the New South: It was integrated, into drugs, into electronics, and creating art that was original and yet based on the ingrained traditions of the region's two most distinctive subgroups, the working-class whites and the blacks. Even when Duane Allman died tragically in 1971 and when other members of the band fought long and painful drug battles, the band continued to produce million-selling records; albums like *Eat a Peach* were packaged in ways that deliberately played on the group's geographical base. Though the band dissolved in 1976—"self-destructed" would be a more accurate term—it defined a genre and established a path that others were soon to follow.

In 1973 the Allman Brothers' band performed a memorable concert in Nashville that did much to impress the power of the new music on the Nashville community. On that same show was a group from North Carolina, the Marshall Tucker Band. One of the members of the Tucker band later recalled: "Hell, we'd never seen so many people together in one place. . . . Thought it was a revival or somethin'." Formed around the Caldwell brothers, Toy and Tommy, and George McCorkle (there is no Marshall Tucker in the group—he was a blind piano tuner the boys knew from their youth), the Spartanburg, North Carolina, band found themselves inheriting the mantle of the Allman Brothers' band. As with most southern rock bands, Marshall Tucker built its career not on media promotion, but on personal appearances: over three hundred dates in one year. Marshall Tucker managed three gold records and several hit singles in the mid-1970s, but they were more at home in a southern football-stadium concert than in a studio or a television station. Like the Allmans, they worked out of the Capricorn studios in Macon when they recorded, and like the Allmans they stressed their own roots. George McCorkle, the group's rhythm guitar player, said: "You start playing your roots, whether it's country or blues or whatever." But unlike the Allmans, Marshall Tucker's roots were far more countrified: All the members are products of a culture that supported the honky-tonk music of the 1950s, Hank Williams music. It is thus perhaps significant that after Tucker's records began crossing from the rock onto the country charts, "pure" country singers like Hank Williams, Jr., and Waylon Jennings recorded their songs. The group maintained close ties with the Texas "outlaws" and experimented with what they called "heavy bluegrass." By 1977 the group was attracting a wide enough audience to be asked to play at the Carter Inaugural celebrations and to make joint appearances with Emmylou Harris. At times the Tucker band seemed more interested in presenting the image of a country band than in actually playing like one, but such disparities helped expand the definition of country music.

Even more country than the Tucker band was the Charlie Daniels band: Here there was little difference between image and performing style.

Daniels himself came on as a romping, stomping Mike Fink mountain of a man who liked southern cooking, southern drinking, southern girls, and southern music. One of the most colorful characters in modern country music, Daniels exhibited some of the gusto, boisterousness, and sheer love of the music that typified many of the pioneer country singers like Uncle Dave Macon. The music his band played was much like Daniels himself: It was raw, energetic, and undisciplined (concert numbers often stretched out to ten or fifteen minutes), and it was based on roots even deeper than the Hank Williams-honky-tonk tradition that informed Marshall Tucker. Daniels went back to the wild, free-wheeling string bands of the 1920s and 1930s and pulled out his fiddle, banjo, and slide guitar to modernize such staples as "Orange Blossom Special," "Fire in the Mountain," "Foggy Mountain Breakdown," and "Mountain Dew," and to write newer songs in these older modes. Though he was closely associated with the Capricorn-Macon complex, Daniels got his musical education as a Nashville sideman (a ten-year course), and he chose to make Tennessee the geographical image for his music. Starting in 1974, Daniels staged a series of annual "Volunteer Jams" (Tennessee politicians call their home the Volunteer State) in the Nashville area—long, marathon concerts that included jamming by most of the notable southern rock stars as well as Texas brethren like Willie Nelson, Jefferson Airplane alumnus Papa John Creech, bluegrass comedienne Roni Stoneman, and Nashville types like Tanya Tucker.

At the end of the concerts the assembled musicians often waded through "Tennessee Waltz," and few concerts got by without Daniels singing the less formal anthem, "The South's Gonna Do It Again." Unlike many southern rock bands, the shaggy Daniels crew succeeded in playing successfully before both young crowds and "Grand Ole Opry" audiences.

Some observers in the mid-1970s noted that in many cases there was little stylistic or musical difference between southern rock and just plain rock, and that the music of the Allmans, Tucker, Daniels, and company was little more than recharged basic rock. But southern rock had some distinctive stylistic elements, such as the use of a twin-guitar lead, an affinity for sets of fast, sharp guitar phrases and glissandos, and lyrics full of references to outlaws, geography, and a sort of runty *machismo*.

The development of those bands did signal a break from the domination of rock by East and West Coast groups. The almost aggressive pride that the bands took in being southern, and their obvious appeal to a regional audience, followed the classic developmental pattern of country music. Because of this, these bands were destined to have some sort of effect on country music, regardless of what they played. The exact nature of that effect has yet to be determined. "We're no advance army of what's to come," Charlie Daniels said. "Call us outcasts, but, basically, we are just musicians." This rejection of labels and schools is, paradoxically, one of the strongest links among southern

rock, the Texas outlaws, and Billy Sherrill's Nashville.

The style-geography equation breaks down totally when we turn to yet another facet of modern country music, the California scene. California in the 1960s had been the scene of two important developments: the rise of the Buck Owens empire in Bakersfield, and the flowering of country-flavored pop groups like the Flying Burrito Brothers. By the late 1970s both of these movements appeared to have reached a plateau: Bakersfield found much of its character being absorbed by the Texas outlaws, and the country-tinged rock groups found themselves eclipsed by southern rock and the emergence of individual stars like Linda Ronstadt and Emmylou Harris. Part of the problem lay in the fact that California had always been more of a technological center for country music than any sort of genuine ethnic or cultural center. The important singers who have worked out of California were, like so many other Californians, migrants to the state: Buck Owens came from Texas, Glen Campbell from Arkansas, Merle Haggard from Oklahoma. It's hard to find anything strikingly characteristic about "California country" music. In earlier days, one could point to a certain type of slick, Hollywood-cowboy sound (represented by people like the Sons of the Pioneers or Judy Lynn) as a distinctive California style, but in the 1970s the only thing that really characterized many California country artists was the fact that they recorded for the West Coast's giant Capitol Records. The lack of genuine roots had some immediate advantages for the packagers of the music, and it facilitated the merging of country and other styles prevalent on the Coast, but in the long run, it had its effect. Jerry Inman, the highly respected leader of the club band at the Hollywood Palomino Club, reflected this when he said, "It's hard to find good country pickers on the Coast who really want to work—who take the business as a business." By 1977 the two major West Coast record companies, Capitol and Warner Brothers, had shifted their country recording to Nashville, and even this technological identity was being shaken.

Whether or not they had any mutual musical bonds, Buck Owens, Merle Haggard, and Glen Campbell each continued to make considerable impact as individuals on the music as a whole. Owens continued to place albums on the country charts and developed into an ingratiating television personality through his weekly appearances on the syndicated "Hee Haw" show. He also continued to run his Bakersfield complex and to lightly refer to Nashville (where he had to return regularly to tape "Hee Haw") as "Bakersfield East." Like many other singers in the 1970s, he made brave noises about preserving the purity of the music; in 1965, he ran an ad in the trade papers that he called his "Pledge to Country Music": "I shall sing no song that is not a country song. . . ." But like other singers of the time, he experimented in adapting country styles to pop material, such as "Bridge over Troubled Water." His own songs crossed over into pop regularly, from the time the Beatles covered "Act Naturally" to Emmylou Harris's hit of "Together Again." Still, Owens is one of the many singers who have maintained extremely successful careers by staying within the general confines of solid, mainstream, noninnovative country. His career doesn't get him on the cover of *Time* or written up in *Rolling Stone,* but it quietly touches millions of fans in meaningful but unspectacular ways.

Campbell too touched millions, but with a much higher profile. In the late 1960s he began a popular national television show, and he continued to be one of the most visible singers; he was far more handsome and clean-cut than most country singers, and his pleasant tenor voice was relatively free from any regional accent or nasal twang. From his earliest hits ("By the Time I Get to Phoenix," "Gentle on My Mind," "Galveston," "Wichita Lineman") to his more recent ones ("Rhinestone Cowboy"), Campbell always used lush, popular arrangements. He was hardly an innovator in the music, and thus seldom receives the press attention lavished on his more dramatic contemporaries.

If Campbell came off looking like the slick professional, Merle Haggard in the 1970s continued to develop his music as an increasingly personal exploration of his heritage and his values. If a Glen Campbell type of song featured sweeping generalizations and broad metaphors, Haggard continued to chronicle, in simple and unromantic gestures, the gritty day-to-day reality of working-class America. Songs like "If We Can Make It Through December" were not really "protest" songs, but they did reflect a stoicism that is probably much more prevalent in working-class life than the effusiveness of Campbell's songs. Haggard also increasingly returned to the music of his rural Oklahoma background, the songs of Jimmie Rodgers and the music of Bob Wills. A 1976 album, for instance, showed a photograph of Haggard looking at a lonely, rundown rural farmhouse. Far more the artist than the *auteur*, Haggard in his music continued to have an intensity and honesty about it that transcended any genre of the music.

Mainstream country singers from California during this time were skilled practitioners of their craft, but they did little to really change the direction of the music or to add anything to it. They did, however, have an immediate and far-ranging impact on the young rock musicians based on the Coast. By the end of the 1960s Los Angeles had become the rock center of the country, and for this reason alone the area was bound to have at least a peripheral effect on country music: Los Angeles rock, after all, affected all areas of American pop music.

A number of rock bands had absorbed some country elements, and by the 1970s this country-rock tradition was feeding its product back into country. From the tradition that included the Byrds, the Flying Burrito Brothers, Steven Stills and the New Riders of the Purple Sage came two singers who were to figure considerably in the new country music of the late 1970s: Linda Ronstadt and Emmylou Harris.

Linda Ronstadt's road to country was the more roundabout of the two. She came to California from a well-to-do German-Mexican family in Arizona, and by 1967 had joined a pop-folk group called the Stone Poneys, who recorded for Capitol and who featured Linda's voice on their one hit, "Different Drum." The group broke up almost as soon as the record hit, and Linda found herself trying to work as a solo singer in the maelstrom of Los Angeles musical styles. She began to do solo albums for Capitol, albums that were full of dress-up folk songs and toned-down (popularized) country songs. For her first four albums in the early 1970s she was regarded, in the words of *Rolling Stone*, as "no more than a barefoot, braless, pleasant-sounding country singer." But the country influence on her at this time had filtered through the California folk-rock bands; she had had little direct connection with hard-core country, and few of her own records had reached the traditional country audience. This was to change with her 1974 album success. *Heart Like a Wheel*, which quickly reached the top of the pop charts. This album peaked at the time of the first big crossover surge, and Ronstadt found herself with a country audience as well. Some of her biggest single hits in the next three years were accomplished reworkings of older country standards: "When Will I Be Loved?" (from the Everly Brothers), "I Can't Help It (If I'm Still in Love with You)" (from Hank

Linda Ronstadt. Photo by Nicole Clark.

Williams), and "Crazy" (from Patsy Cline). By this time Ronstadt's influence on the country community was becoming much more pronounced; her success with "When Will I Be Loved?" helped make it the most performed BMI country song for 1975.

Linda Ronstadt's music resists categorization, in part because she is one of the young performers who have grown up in a musical world in which crossover and crosspollination are the rules rather than the exceptions. She feels no guilt or hesitancy about appropriating material from any genre, be it country, rock, reggae, Tex-Mex, folk, jazz, or soul. This is because the key to her success may lie in the fact that, unlike many performers today who stress original material, Linda is a supremely skilled interpreter of songs. Though she has resisted it, her youth and good looks have made her a country music sex symbol, a sort of female counterpart to Kristofferson. Although she is very much a product of rock-generation values—she is casual about both drugs and sex—she seems remarkably open and even vulnerable as a performer. There is no distance between her and her songs. Her style is intensely lyrical and intensely personal, what *Time* called in 1977 "torchy rock." With her there is little of the pop singer's customary detachment of personality from song. This is why Linda Rondstadt so desperately seeks out good material: She looks on her song as a function of her personality, not as some sort of product. "I'd take three giant steps toward an early death if I could find one good song," she once said.

This symbiosis between song and personality may seem rather unusual in pop or rock of the 1970s, but it is quite common in country music, and this is probably why Linda has been drawn increasingly to country material. Traditionally, however, this symbiosis was the domain of male singers: Hank Williams, Kristofferson, Willie Nelson. The great women singers of country music had always sung realistically about life, but the older singers had been products of a southern morality that frustrated their identifying too closely with the lyrics of the songs. No woman singer had really committed herself to a performance as did, for example, the great blues singers like Bessie Smith and Billie Holiday. Linda Ronstadt was able to make such a commitment, and to make it at precisely the right moment in music development.

Some of Ronstadt's most successful records contained some fine harmony singing by a young lady named Emmylou Harris. Like Linda, Emmylou had gotten her training in the urban folk revival of the 1960s, but unlike Linda, Emmylou had early developed clear affinities with classic country music. She met Gram Parsons, the brilliant guitarist for the Flying Burrito Brothers, in 1971 and went West with him to help him produce his two influential solo albums. "Gram introduced me to a vein of music I call the High Lonesome," she recalls, "the beautiful heartbreak harmony duets you hear in songs by the young Everly Brothers, Charlie and Ira Louvin, Felice and Boudleaux Bryant." The music to which she and Parsons were responding had virtually been extinct in regular country music circles since the late 1950s, though it survived in some bluegrass bands. The "High Lonesome" had grown out of the melancholy purity of the great brother acts of the 1930s (like the Blue Sky Boys and the Delmore Brothers) and represented one of the music's most unique characteristics. Emmylou and Parsons were beginning to explore and popularize this music in refreshing new ways when he died suddenly in 1974.

Shattered by his death, Emmylou eventually forced herself to carry on the tradition by herself, and in 1974 she used some of Parsons' former sidemen to help her make a solo album, *Pieces of the Sky*. The album was as poised, delicate, and personal as any by Linda Ronstadt. Emmylou had the same kind of high, pure voice that Linda did—quite distinctive from the husky alto range employed by most country women singers. But Emmylou also had another advantage: She was herself an accomplished composer. Her autobiographical "Boulder to Birmingham" (she had once worked in a club in Birmingham) was one of the highlights of *Pieces of the Sky*; it was nestled there among the other songs by Billy Sherrill, The Louvin Brothers, Dolly Parton, and Merle Haggard. Her Louvin Brothers song, "If I Could Only Win Your Love," became a hit single, and soon Emmylou was working with Bob Dylan and James Taylor and singing duets with the surviving Louvin brother.

The fact that both Linda Ronstadt and Emmylou Harris came, in a sense, out of the California scene was probably less important than another quality they shared: Both were young, articulate, independent, highly talented women who were being accepted on their own terms by a huge popular audience. This is not surprising in view of the way the creative impetus in pop music for the 1970s had been mainly carried forth by singers like Carole King, Carly Simon, and Helen Reddy, but the success of Ronstadt and Harris with a country audience suggested that the heavy *machismo* that had dominated both the music and its fans for years was finally giving way. Loretta Lynn, for instance, without making any pop concessions in her music, became a national heroine for millions of women who were finding that it was possible to take a new pride and a new strength from their roles and their lives.

In the fall of 1976, Linda Ronstadt and Emmylou Harris were asked to be guests on the new syndicated television show "Dolly," starring Dolly Parton. Both responded with enthusiasm, and what resulted was an important and symbolic meeting of minds between the newer pop country and the more traditional Nashville country. They all swapped songs, listened to each other's tapes, and did trio harmonies on "Silver Threads and Golden Needles" and "Bury Me Beneath the Willow" for the television cameras. Both Linda and Emmylou looked on Dolly as some sort of prime mover for their type of music, and were unabashedly impressed. Linda later recalled: "I've never met anybody so free of neurosis as that person. . . . She taught me that you don't have to sacrifice your femininity in order to have equal status." Yet, ironically, it was only shortly before this that Dolly Parton was beginning to find her own musical identity. And the story of her struggle to do this forms an important chapter in the story of modern country music. It is a story that brings us back to our original point of departure, Nashville, and the effects the various revolutions were having there.

The first part of Dolly Parton's career reads like the archetypal country music Nashville success story. She came from a rural dirt-poor family in the hills of Sevier County, Tennessee, just a few miles from where English folk-song collectors had found surviving English ballads as late as the 1920s. "My mama had twelve kids when she was thirty-five years old," Dolly recalls. The family all had grounding in the old-time gospel music sung at the local Church of God, a grass-roots Tennessee church that used "Great Speckled Bird" as one of its anthems. As a child of seven, Dolly

Emmylou Harris.

Dolly Parton. Photo by Marshall Fallwell, Jr.

had modified an old mandolin with guitar strings and was composing her own songs. In the way that black kids were later to use athletics as a means to escape from the ghetto, many poverty-stricken rural whites in the South sought to use musical talent to get out of the hills. "Music was a freedom," Dolly noted, but "none of our people had ventured out of the mountains with it." Dolly was different, and as a teen-ager in high school she was singing on the famous bluegrass show run in Knoxville by groceryman Cas Walker. She was well received, and the day after she got out of high school in 1964 she took the bus to Nashville. With the help of an uncle, she was able to establish herself as a singer and song-writer, and she had a

modest success with a song called "Dumb Blonde." (The symbolism of this initial image was to haunt Dolly for years.) In 1967 she was asked to join the popular Missouri singer Porter Wagoner, a classic straight country singer who had wagon wheels on his jackets and hawked a good old Tennessee patent medicine called Cardui. For seven years she was a feature of Porter's shows, and a singing partner for innumerable duets with him.

Dolly gained a following with Wagoner, but it was a following that was as attracted as much to her Playmate-sized figure as to her original songs or her vocal style. By 1974 Dolly could look around her at the changes in the music, and see that it was possible to find an audience that would be more willing to accept her on her own terms: the audience Waylon Jennings and Willie Nelson had found, the new demographic pattern that took country music more as art than ritual. But she could not reach this audience as part of Wagoner's troupe, and in 1974 she broke from Porter and went out on her own. At the time she said that the move would "just mean more people are aware of what I can do—my writing." She was right, and by 1975 and 1976 she was attracting nationwide attention, winning all kinds of industry awards, and producing some of the most distinctive hit songs of the decade. The CMA voted her the Top Female Country Singer for both 1975 and 1976, and her appearance at the 1976 Grammy Awards show drew a riotous ovation. Dozens of singers—including her forthright admirers Linda Ronstadt and Emmylou Harris—recorded her songs; she made appearances on the "Tonight" show; the New York *Times* reviewed her songs and lauded them as "full of a poetic imagery both true to life and evocatively expressed." And in late 1975 she became the first female country entertainer to have a nationally syndicated television show—the highest-budgeted show ever to be syndicated from Nashville, and one that soon garnered over 130 markets, many of them in northern cities.

Yet Dolly remained very much a country singer, and very much a Nashville singer. While other singers dressed in blue jeans or sweatshirts, she continued to appear in tight, flashy, sequined outfits topped off with a towering blond wig. "Part of the magic of me, I think, is that I look totally one way—an overall artificial look—but I *am* totally another. . . . My appearance has become just a gimmick. It goes back to having nothing as a child." (Such explanations also go a long way toward explaining why so many poor working-class fans respond so well to seeing their favorite stars decked out in Nudie suits and fancy boots.) Her songs continued to reflect the images and values of the rural eastern Tennessee hills, and in some cases they even echoed the tune patterns of the old-time music of the 1930s and 1940s. Her first successful hit as a single artist was a rendering of "Muleskinner Blues," a workhorse going back to Jimmie Rodgers days, and her original "Tennessee Mountain Home" could easily have fit into the Carter Family repertoire. "My Daddy Was an Old-time Preacher Man" is full of personal references, and "Coat of Many Colors" and "In the Good Old Days (When Times Were Bad)" both grew out of her family's experiences. "In the Good Old Days" captures brilliantly the ambivalent nostalgia of so many southern singers who grew up in poverty and are unable to completely romanticize it. Nor did Dolly romanticize love: "Jolene," "Bargain Store," and "Love is Like a Butterfly" dealt with the country theme of rematching and unpairing from a distinctly feminine perspective. "Jolene" is an especially intriguing example of the sociology of sexual politics. And in many of Dolly's songs is the age-old association of the mountain life with innocence and the city life with wickedness. Given all this, it shouldn't have surprised anyone when Dolly began hammering away at a five-string banjo on the 1976 CMA Awards show.

Some of Dolly's new audience doubtless responded to her refreshing feminine-but-not-feminist perspective; others continued to respond to her tight pants suits and Mae West glossiness, and still others, introduced to real country music through pop artists in the early 1970s, responded to her strong ties with the music's conventional aspects. But a great many more simply responded to her unique singing style and to her voice. It's a voice that has been described, on one hand, as that of a young mountain girl: "My voice is so small and high-pitched and sounded like a kid," she says. On the other hand, it has a haunting timbre that reminds one of stylists like Eartha Kitt.

Nashville first didn't know what to do with Dolly's voice; nobody thought it was a typical country voice. Her first record company made her do rockabilly songs, and Victor's Chet Atkins was at first hesitant to record her voice. "My voice was real different—not that it's good, because a lot of people just cannot *stand* to hear me sing. Anybody with a real different voice, a lot of people don't like to hear them sing, but people who do like them usually like them especially well." In 1973 Dolly developed nodes on her vocal chords, and by 1976 these were curtailing her singing activities somewhat. But she was also finding that with her national success, she didn't have to push herself as hard as she had when she was doing nothing but one-nighters. By the end of 1976, she was able to understand some of her new popularity: "My music is beginning to grow. I, the person, am country, and my music is country, but still, it's got a universal sound. It's just Dolly Parton's music. There is no way to classify it."

Dolly Parton's national success is symptomatic of a truism of the music in 1977: The center still holds. In spite of all the changes in country music seen by the 1970s—the rise of the new slick Nashville sound, the rise of the Texas outlaws, the emergence of southern rock, the rebirth of bluegrass, and the popularity of pop-country singers—there still were at the decade's end a large number of standard country singers who were relatively unaffected by these developments. There was still a very potent and active core of singers who did not attract the feature-story writers from *Time* and *People*, who did not see their albums go platinum, who were not patronized on Grammy Awards shows, but who quietly continued to appeal to large numbers of traditional country fans in traditional ways. Such a core would have to include singers like George Jones, Mel Tillis, Webb Pierce, Ray Price, Sonny James, Freddie Hart, Jean Shepard, Bill Anderson, Roy Drusky, Jack Greene, Conway Twitty, Jeanne Pruett, and others. And in spite of inroads made by some of the newer-styled singers, albums by these older singers continued to fill the best-seller charts year after year. Collectively speaking, there were probably more overall album sales of "classic" country music than newer or more hybrid music.

Certainly there has been little change in the message content of the best-selling country songs: During the ten years from 1966 to 1976 over half the top country singles dealt with various forms of unhappy love, usually either dealing with cheating, loneliness, or betrayal (for example, Conway Twitty's "Hello Darlin'," or his "How Much More Can She Stand?" or Sonny James' "Empty Arms"). But conventional notions of happy love were also celebrated in these songs, as were songs about middle-class lifestyles. All of these themes have been endemic to country music since the 1940s, and the fact that they are still the stuff from which top hits are made suggests that the new morality of the 1970s, as well as the new schools of country music, have apparently made little impact on the message content of the music. By the mid-1970s a few top hits were making more explicit references to physical love, but this was the only sign of any real new direction. The introspective individualism that marked some of the best songs of Kristofferson, Nelson, and Jennings was not visible in the top ten; nor was the geographical and historical celebration of the southern rock groups. Much of the real business of country music was still being carried out by the cadre of "centrists" mentioned above. And in spite of the new media access for country music, much of the business was still being done through the classic channels of radio airplay, bus touring to one-night stands, state fairs, and concerts, and occasional club dates. For many mainstream country singers, in short, both the medium and the message were still about the same as they had been before the age

of Opryland, Billy Sherrill, Willie Nelson, and all the rest.

A singer who came to typify much of the best of the modern mainstream country singers was George Jones. Jones' early career as a Texas honky-tonk singer has already been touched on: Suffice it to say that, like Dolly Parton, Jones came from a rural working-class southern fundamentalist background and that he came by his music honestly. He broke into Nashville in 1956 by singing "Why, Baby, Why?" (a song that's gone on to become a honky-tonk standard) and had the first big peak in his career in 1962–63, when he won all sorts of awards from *Billboard*, *Cashbox*, and the CMA. "She Still Thinks I Care" was the top country record of 1962. But by 1964 Buck Owens had replaced Jones as the leading honky-tonk singer, and Jones went into sort of a holding pattern in which he toured widely (especially on the West Coast), recorded an uneven series of albums, and dropped off and on the "Grand Ole Opry."

By 1969, on the heels of the Dylan-Cash-Nashville chic movement among the young, Jones found that some of his hard country records were getting airplay on pop stations and that he was being discovered by college students who found him, in the words of journalist Paul Hemphill, "quaint." It was at this time that Jones married Tammy Wynette and began working with her producer, Billy Sherrill, on his own records. Sherrill would occasionally saddle Jones with strings and background choirs, but he couldn't take the distinctive eastern Texas twang out of George's voice, and even in slick, cream-puff arrangements he sounded like a hard, hungry country singer. Sherrill hit two separate winning streaks with Jones albums, a first one with George alone and then a second series with George and Tammy doing duets. George continued to produce masterpieces like "The Grand Tour" and "I Just Don't Give a Damn" and "Ragged but Right," but he ran into drinking problems and in 1975 this led to the breakup of his marriage with Tammy Wynette.

Jones has always been known as a "singer's singer" in country music, and he has been listed as the favorite of such notables as Buck Owens, Charley Pride, Waylon Jennings, Connie Smith, Conway Twitty, and even Emmylou Harris. Not only does Jones have a fine voice, but also he has an incredible mastery and control over it, and he had adapted it perfectly to the basic country instruments of the steel guitar and fiddle. Bill Malone, the nation's leading authority on country music, has described Jones' voice this way: "Sometimes dropping into a low register, then sweeping into a high wail, often enunciating his words with rounded, open-throated precision, but occasionally moaning them through clenched teeth and with the classic pinched-throat delivery of the southern rural singer, Jones demonstrates why many people consider him the greatest country singer of all time." Jones has also always been a staunch defender of hard country music; he was one of the prime movers of ACE, the Nashville organization devoted to maintaining the purity of the music in the face of the pop invasion. In 1975 he

reopened his nightclub in downtown Nashville, Possum Holler, because he felt there was really no place in Nashville (aside from the "Opry") where a person could hear real country music. Possum Holler was to be a "place for the ones that love the kind of music I love—pure country music." This meant a club that would book the likes of Melba Montgomery, Porter Wagoner, Bobby Bare, and even Waylon Jennings—and, of course, George Jones.

Jones has been one of the most versatile and prolific recording artists in the music's history. Nobody knows for sure just how many albums he has cut in the past twenty years, but estimates range all the way from 80 to over 160. George himself can no longer keep track of them all, but given the number of his albums that have been reissued and repackaged and rearranged, the 160 figure may not be too far off. None of his albums, of course, have attained the platinum status of the Jennings-Nelson efforts, but the sheer number of them means that he has had an impact at least as great as Jennings-Nelson, if not as dramatic or colorful. Most of his albums have been pretty much straight-ahead country: "You're always going to hear a fiddle on a George Jones record," he has said. Fans like to remember certain classic performances: "Don't Stop the Music," "Just One More," "Window Up Above," "She Still Thinks I Care," "White Lightning," "If My Heart Had Windows," "A Girl I Used to Know," "I'll Share This World with You," and "Walk Through This World with Me." But Jones' influence cannot be measured by one monster hit or two: Like many hard-country singers, his impact is felt through his consistency and his ability to maintain a steady, predictable profile in the music. While the occasional country "protest" song or "new morality" song gets a lot of publicity and attention from outside the country community, it is the tried and proven classic love songs of Jones and those like him that continue to make the charts year after year.

By 1977 Jones seemed on the threshold of yet another peak in his career. His hit album *Alone Again* was cut with the basic five-piece country band he had used in the 1960s, and it was rated as one of the top albums of the year by the very northern *Village Voice*. Jones himself was voted Country Artist of the Year in a poll by the prestigious rock magazine *Rolling Stone*. His records were being heard on juke boxes across the country, North and South, rural and urban. Jones had done this without really compromising his music, without slicking it up, without adding new content, and without adding a beat to it. Was he benefiting from the groundwork of the pop-country singers who had introduced a large segment of America to the notion of country? Was he reaching an audience that, like the folk-revival audience of the 1960s, had tired of the imitation and was now wanting the real thing? Or had country music itself become so diffuse and complex that even Jones, with his hard-country approach, was now regarded as only a representative of a subgenre of the music, like bluegrass, honky-tonk, Sherrill-style, south-

ern rock, or whatever? Had the music become nationalized and broadened enough to appeal to a mass audience, or had America become southernized and willing to embrace a philosophy of grass-roots populist nostalgia that included country music? Whatever the answer, it seems oddly significant that by 1977, after almost ten years of revolutionary change and disruption and reaction, two of the hottest figures in country music were Dolly Parton and George Jones, both charter members of the classic country music establishment.

By 1977 country music had completed five decades of growth as a professional entertainment medium and as a definable facet of American

George Jones. Photo by Charlyn Zlotnik.

popular culture. The stature it has achieved can partly be measured by the increased attention paid it by the public at large: Never before has there been so much prodding and poking and documenting of the music, so much writing about it, so much explaining of it. Some have seen the music as a sort of Rosetta stone on which can be deciphered the values and fears and hopes of the great, inarticulate silent majority. People who have never listened to the music before are now enjoying it, explaining that the modern sounds of the outlaws or Emmylou Harris represent a sudden maturation of the music that has rendered it meaningful to an urban middle-class society. Others who have listened before are "coming out." But in spite of this it is well to remember that country music is still not all *that* popular; compared to the sale of rock and pop artists, country artists are having sales that are only mildly impressive. In 1976 a first album by a new rock group called Boston easily sold a million copies, a fact that raised few eyebrows; but when *Wanted: The Outlaws!* topped a million, it was a major event. Harsh economic realities remind us that country music still has a way to go before completely replacing pop or rock.

The triumph of country music may, in fact, be in the end a process of osmosis and transformation rather than one of displacement. The crossover phenomenon is obviously here to stay, and it will be flowing in both directions, regardless of the activities of ACE or the efforts of the people who make up *Billboard*'s weekly best-seller charts. After all, the whole question of what is or what is not country is partly a result of record-company structure and the merchandising need to classify and pigeonhole. The idea of a "crossover" may tell us less about the music than about the inflexibility of the classification system. The music itself has always been more a hybrid thing than its apologists have wanted to admit; far from being a continuation of a pure folk tradition, country music has been influenced to some extent by every major development in pop music in this century. Pop-music divisions themselves were more often than not merchandising devices, and thus the music itself was often defined through implicit class distinctions: easy listening was for the middle class, blues was for the blacks, jazz was for the urban intelligentsia, and country was for the working-class white. As long as society believed in these class distinctions, the music divisions held, but the social revolutions of the 1960s erased most of these distinctions in the minds of the young, and anyone could feel free to appropriate any music. Furthermore, the centralization of the mass media erased the old geographical distinctions that once convincingly defined country music as a southern regional music. So by the 1970s, both of the traditional labels for country music— "southern" and "working class"— were being rendered obsolete by the changes in society.

Looking around at the different styles and forms that all sail under the banner of "country music," one might surmise that the character of the music is hopelessly confused. How would a total stranger to our culture, one not familiar with the history and styles of country music, be able to listen to the music played at Nashville's Fan Fair or the CMA Awards show and come away with a definition of the music derived from their shared common traits? Yet much of the diversity is an illusion of sorts, a type of can't-see-the-forest-for-the-trees phenomenon generated by much of the recent self-conscious interest in defining and explaining the music. Twenty-five years ago these different musics were all confidently labeled simply "country music." It was all a big seamless whole. The different labels that sprung up in the 1970s were partly attempts to allow the audience to specialize, and doubtless each of these subgenres will continue to find its audience, but as we have seen with a look at the song lyrics of the past ten years, the different subgenres really have many themes in common, in spite of their different stylistic window dressings.

The minute one sets up schools of music and assigns artists to them today, the artists themselves begin crisscrossing these imaginary boundaries like cattle on an open range. And this brings us to another salient characteristic of the music that will probably have a lot to say about determining its future: The country artists are starting to take more control over their product. The big trend in the Nashville music in 1977 was toward independent production whereby the singers would simply bring their completed tapes, done the way they wanted to do them, to the record company.

Most singers see their music as a living, organic process that has little to do with categories or genres. "I look at it like, 'It's good,' and I don't care whether it's pop, rock, jazz, or country," said Glen Campbell. Before the 1970s, only a proven superstar could get away with this; now increasing numbers of younger performers are doing it. In the end, the companies may have to adjust their structures to the music, instead of vice versa.

The two categories we set up at the beginning of this chapter, the smooth and the hairy, may in the end turn out to be less a valid musical distinction than a social one. Where will the creative power of the music rest; with the artist or with his merchandiser? The lonely figure of Fiddlin' John Carson scraping out "The Old Hen Cackled and the Rooster's Going to Crow" in front of carnivals and on courthouse steps had no merchandiser, nothing at all to come between him and his audience. Yet country music would have remained at the level of the local courthouse steps or county fair if it had not been commercialized. Commercialization, after all, is the one quality that separates country music from folk music, and gives it its unique blend of nobility and hucksterism. This is why the history of the music has been a history of the singers and pickers, and a history of the shuckers and gunners. The music will change and will grow, just as it always has, and it will continue to move a great many people who have rather little in common except the universal emotions of pity and fear, love and hate, and the strength to endure.

About the Authors

PATRICK CARR, once a professional musician himself, is the former editor of *Country Music* magazine. He has contributed to countless national music magazines, including *Rolling Stone*, *New Times*, the *Village Voice*, *Crawdaddy*, and *Guitar Player*, and has served in various editorial capacities with these and other similar publications. Presently at work on *Guitar*, a definitive book of interviews with the world's greatest guitar players, he is a recognized authority on contemporary music.

DOUGLAS B. GREEN is the author of *Country Roots* and *The Illustrated Encyclopedia of Country Music* (one of three co-authors) as well as the editor of the Country Music Foundation Press in Nashville, Tennessee. A prolific writer, Green is a regular contributor to *Country Music* magazine, *Pickin'*, *Billboard*, *Bluegrass Unlimited*, *Country Song Roundup*, and other music magazines.

WILLIAM IVEY is the executive director of the Country Music Foundation and contributor to numerous books on the subject, including *The Stars of Country Music*. He is also the former editor of the *Journal of Country Music*.

BOB PINSON heads the Acquisitions Department for the Country Music Foundation in Nashville and is best known for his extensive discographies, including the comprehensive Bob Wills discography in Wills' biography, *For the Last Time*. In addition, Pinson is a regular contributor to numerous music magazines.

NICK TOSCHES is a former rock critic and author of the controversial book *Country!* He is a regular contributor to such magazines as *Rolling Stone*, *Penthouse*, *Esquire*, *Playboy*, *Gig*, *Country Music*, and others.

ROGER WILLIAMS is the author of the critically acclaimed *Sing a Sad Song*, the biography of Hank Williams, Sr.

CHARLES K. WOLFE is a professor of English at Middle Tennessee State University. He is the author of *The Grand Ole Opry: The Early Years, 1925–35* and *Tennessee Strings* and is a regular contributor to *Old-time Music* magazine, *Pickin'* magazine, *Country Music* magazine, and co-editor of the *Tennessee Folklore Society* quarterly. He is presently at work on a book about white gospel music.

J. R. YOUNG is a regular contributor to numerous magazines, including *Rolling Stone* and *Country Music*.